DALIT THEOLOGY, BOUNDARY CROSSINGS AND LIBERATION IN INDIA

DALIT THEOLOGY, BOUNDARY CROSSINGS AND LIBERATION IN INDIA

A Biblical and Postcolonial Study

Jobymon Skaria

I.B. TAURIS
LONDON • NEW YORK • OXFORD • NEW DELHI • SYDNEY

I.B. TAURIS
Bloomsbury Publishing Plc
50 Bedford Square, London, WC1B 3DP, UK
1385 Broadway, New York, NY 10018, USA
29 Earlsfort Terrace, Dublin 2, Ireland

BLOOMSBURY, I.B. TAURIS and the I.B. Tauris logo are trademarks of
Bloomsbury Publishing Plc

First published in Great Britain 2023
Paperback edition published 2024

Copyright © Jobymon Skaria, 2023

Jobymon Skaria has asserted his right under the Copyright, Designs and Patents Act, 1988,
to be identified as Author of this work.

Series design by Adriana Brioso
Cover image: *Togetherness*, 2010, by Ajiyan George. Courtesy of the Artist

All rights reserved. No part of this publication may be reproduced or transmitted in
any form or by any means, electronic or mechanical, including photocopying,
recording, or any information storage or retrieval system, without prior permission in
writing from the publishers.

Bloomsbury Publishing Plc does not have any control over, or responsibility for, any
third-party websites referred to or in this book. All internet addresses given in this
book were correct at the time of going to press. The author and publisher regret any
inconvenience caused if addresses have changed or sites have ceased to exist, but can
accept no responsibility for any such changes.

A catalogue record for this book is available from the British Library.

A catalog record for this book is available from the Library of Congress.

ISBN: HB: 978-0-7556-4235-9
PB: 978-0-7556-4239-7
ePDF: 978-0-7556-4236-6
eBook: 978-0-7556-4237-3

Typeset by Newgen KnowledgeWorks Pvt. Ltd., Chennai, India

To find out more about our authors and books visit www.bloomsbury.com
and sign up for our newsletters.

CONTENTS

Acknowledgements — vii

Chapter 1
DALIT THEOLOGY: APPROACH, CHALLENGES AND QUESTIONS — 1

Chapter 2
GENEALOGY OF DALIT THEOLOGY SEEN THROUGH DALITS' CRIES FOR DIGNITY — 17

Chapter 3
GENEALOGY OF DALIT THEOLOGY SEEN THROUGH LIBERATION THEOLOGIES — 31

Chapter 4
QUESTIONING DALIT THEOLOGY THROUGH DALITS' FORGOTTEN VOICES — 43

Chapter 5
DECENTRING DALIT THEOLOGY THROUGH DALITS' FORGOTTEN VOICES — 65

Chapter 6
SITUATING ABRAHAM'S POSTCOLONIAL CROSSINGS AS A PARTNER IN DIALOGUE — 77

Chapter 7
EXPLORING ABRAHAM'S CROSSINGS TO EGYPT AND GERAR — 89

Chapter 8
REIMAGINING DALIT THEOLOGY THROUGH DALITS' FORGOTTEN VOICES — 109

Chapter 9
AUTHOR'S NOTE: DALIT THEOLOGY, DISSOLVING DALIT-SYRIAN CHRISTIAN BOUNDARIES AND LIBERATION IN INDIA — 129

Notes — 141
Bibliography — 187
Index — 221

ACKNOWLEDGEMENTS

Preparing this book was not an easy task, and this book would not have been possible without the input and encouragement of my professors and mentors, family and friends. Academically, I am grateful beyond measure to my PhD supervisors Dr Peter Admirand and Dr Brad Anderson, who have sacrificially helped me in developing this manuscript. I owe a debt of gratitude to their time, energy, attention to detail and expertise. Similarly, I am grateful to Dr Peniel Rajkumar, Dr Anderson Jeremiah, Dr Jayakiran Sebastian, Dr Jonathan Kearney and Dr M. P. Joseph for their guidance, understanding, and valuable and constructive suggestions, which enriched this book substantially.

So too, several mentors, colleagues and friends have read, commented upon or decisively helped me to shape significant aspects of this book, such as Dr Brendan McConvery, Dr Adai Jacob Cor Episcopa, Fr Shibu Cherian, Fr Biju Mathew Parekkattil and Dr Aji George.

Likewise, I am beyond grateful for the prayerful support and encouragement of my spiritual fathers, such as His Beatitude Baselios Thomas I Catholicose, Dr Matthews Mor Ivanios Metropolitan, Matthews Mor Aphrem Metropolitan, Dr Gheevarghese Mor Coorilos Metropolitan and Dr Anthimos Matthews Metropolitan.

Similarly, on the personal front, I am incredibly grateful to my parents, P. T. Skaria and Sosamma Skaria, and my brother, Jibimon Skaria. The unstinting emotional and mental support of Jomi John, my wife, was priceless, and the boundless love from my precious children, Aaron, Basil, Jewel and Chris, was uplifting. Thank you for your patience and sacrifice, as I often invested the time that belonged to you to complete this book.

Finally, I am grateful and thankful to Dr Sophie Rudland and Yasmin Garcha, Commissioning Editors at I.B. Tauris, an imprint of Bloomsbury Academic and the whole team at Bloomsbury Academic, for their unfailing kindness and patience, despite delays.

Chapter 1

DALIT THEOLOGY: APPROACH, CHALLENGES AND QUESTIONS

Introduction

Dr B. R. Ambedkar (1891–1956) was an Indian scholar, politician and icon of Dalits' resistance. On 25 November 1949, in his concluding speech to the Indian Constituent Assembly, Ambedkar highlighted his anxieties over the caste hesitations, which can perpetuate Dalits' humiliation and sociopolitical exclusion in post-independent India:

> On January 26, 1950, we are going to enter into a life of contradictions. In politics, we have equality, and in social and economic life, we have inequalities. In politics, we will be recognising the principles of one man, one vote and one vote, one value. In our social and economic life, we shall, by reason of our social and economic structure, continue to deny the principle of one man, one value.[1]

Ambedkar's apprehensions, which demand a proper balance between Dalits' political status and social status, are still relevant. Dalits continue to suffer because of unresolved caste hesitations, despite various attempts to ameliorate Dalits' situation. *Hindustan Times*, for example, reported recently that the dominant caste villagers allegedly shot dead a seventeen-year-old Dalit boy who entered a village temple.[2]

As an Indian Christian from the St Thomas/Syrian Christian tradition,[3] born and raised in Kerala, I have been aware of caste contradictions and Dalits' epistemological dilemma from my childhood. Nevertheless, a Bachelor of Divinity at Malankara Syrian Orthodox Theological Seminary introduced me to the caste system's recalcitrance. Mathews Mor Aphrem Metropolitan also explained to me the mechanisms of the caste system and dominant caste Christians' selective historical and theological amnesia about casteism. He informed me that Dalits were called asuras in Hindu religious texts. Mor Aphrem's comments haunted me because Mahabali, the great mythic king of Kerala, was believed to be an asura king. Such a connection, I noted, radically reframes the identity of the people from Kerala as a community ruled by a Dalit king. Further, Mor Aphrem explained various caste discriminations in the churches. For example, he told me that a dominant caste priest stopped a Dalit Christian from reading during Mass, asking who had allowed a Dalit to read in the church. Such instances provoked me to learn more about the caste questions and their lingering impacts upon Dalit brothers and sisters.

The caste questions

In India's unique social contexts, the caste is an implicit yet submerged stratification system. As an ideology and practice, it is also an institutionalized inequality, which is embedded in Indian psyches.[4] Therefore, the caste system is diabolic. It is marked by hereditary membership, occupations and endogamy. The caste system sanctions differential treatment to people based upon the doctrine of purity and pollution, assuming that some human beings are inferior to others because of birth. The caste system classifies the people into four hierarchically ranked varnas – the Brahmans (priestly class), the Kshatriyas (warrior class), the Vaishyas (merchant class) and the Shudras (servile class).

The term 'caste', however, is not Indian though it is now widely used in Indian languages. Nor is it originally an English word. It derives from the Portuguese and Spanish word *casta*.[5] The etymology of *casta* is often disputed. The dominant view claims that the word is derived from *castus*, a Latin expression which means 'pure', 'unpolluted' or 'chaste'.[6] A competing tradition suggests that *casta* originated from the Gothic word *kasts*, which implies 'a group of animals' or 'a brood of hatchlings'.[7] A dominant section in the Iberian Peninsula, therefore, used *casta* as a term for 'species of plants and animals'. For them, *casta* signified pure or true strains and breeds.[8]

Casta acquired a new meaning with the Spanish and Portuguese colonial expansionism. The Spanish and Portuguese used *casta* to categorize the conquered peoples into corporate groups – Spanish, Indian and Black, each with associated rights, privileges and obligations in post-conquest South America.[9] They applied *casta* to mixed European and Amerindian descent. In such contexts, *casta*, with some exceptions as clarified by Laura A. Lewis,[10] referred to various mixed races like Mestizo (Spanish and Indian parentage), Mulatto (Spanish and Black ancestry), Castizo (Spanish and Mestizo descent) and Morisco (Spanish and Metatto parentage).[11] Consequently, *casta* designations became an umbrella term to designate the mixed descent in Iberian colonies.[12] One's location in the *casta* ladder defined one's access to education and other community resources.[13] The *casta* designations became part of the local vernacular in the Iberian colonies, where the people with the least amount of Iberian blood began to be treated the worst in society, paying higher taxes to the government and more money to the church.[14]

The situation in the Indian subcontinent, however, was different. *Casta* did not mean mixed race in India. The Portuguese used *casta* as 'an ambiguous term for the community'[15] to describe the social groupings that existed already in India, known as varna.[16] The English borrowed *casta* and changed it into caste, though they had some English equivalents like people, race and tribe.[17] They incorporated caste into their legal documents and census reports.[18] British Indian courts decreed separate rules of succession, adoption and marriage for various castes and imposed restrictions on commensality between castes. Over the years, the term 'caste' proliferated and became synonymous with the varna system.[19]

The Indian caste system (varna)

The exact origin of *Varna*, now known as the caste system, remains obscure. There are two competing views about the possible beginnings of the caste system. The dominant view interprets it as a set of practices that characterize Indian social organization, which may be recognized and analysed from historical, precolonial, colonial and postcolonial periods.[20] This view understands caste as one of the oldest surviving hierarchical segregations of society. Such a position draws on divine origin theory, race theory, occupational theory and evolutionary theory to explain the caste system's emergence. The competing view suggests that the British officials, missionaries and orientalists transformed caste from an existing sacred order into a rigid social structure.[21] Nevertheless, the caste system is a fundamental source of exclusion, which divides Indian society into four classes, with Brahmans at the top, Kshatriyas, Vaisyas and Sudras at the bottom. The caste divisions, however, are not homogenous categories since they are further divided into subgroups called *jatis*.[22] A fifth category, traditionally imagined as untouchables, who assertively call themselves Dalits now, fall outside the caste system.

Dalits were believed to have originated outside the physical structure of the divine. This creation myth implies that Dalits are ontologically separate and distinct from the divine and restricts Dalits from making any claims of being part of the Hindu community and establishes Brahmanic supremacy.[23] Some Hindu philosophers used this myth to marginalize Dalits. For example, the dominant Hindu philosophy considers the Dalit body as an untouchable 'self-enclosed body, which is denied of transcendence'.[24] Such denials are crucial, and they condition Dalits' fate significantly. *Manusmriti*, the law book of Hinduism, prescribes Dalits' behavioural pattern as follows:[25]

> The dwellings of 'Fierce' Untouchables and 'Dog-cookers' should be outside the village; they must use discarded bowls, and dogs and donkeys should be their wealth. Their clothing should be the clothes of the dead, and their food should be in broken dishes; their ornaments should be made of black iron, and they should wander constantly. A man who carries out his duties should not seek contact with them; they should do business with one another and marry those who are like them. Their food, dependent upon others, should be given to them in a broken dish, and they should not walk about in villages and cities at night.[26]

Such sanctioned delegation of roles and body dispensation establishes a difference, enacts inferiorization and seeks to keep Dalits 'apart socially along with denying their human and civil rights'.[27] So too, they resulted in structural inequalities and pushed Dalits to the margins of society, forcing them to live a life in ghettoes and engaging in the most demeaning and stigmatized occupations. Such practices, as will be seen, continue even today.

Situating Dalits in the caste system

The caste system is an existential reality, and it affects most of the unconscious assumptions of the Indian psyche, irrespective of caste orientations. However, Dalits are the worst victims of the caste system and thus remain economically weak, politically powerless and socially marginalized.[28] The caste system also relegates the Dalit as an 'untouchable' and irredeemable body.[29] Yashpal Jogdand, who researches the phenomenology of humiliation in Dalits' contexts, highlights Dalits' situation further.

> Even animals like dogs, cows, and buffalos could drink water from the common resource without fear. Despite being human, Dalits were incapable even to touch the water. The dehumanising message of this custom clearly indicated that Dalits are worse off than four-legged animals.[30]

Such denials restrict Dalits' life considerably and consign them to the margins of society. Sagar Shejwal, a 24-year-old Dalit student, was brutally assaulted and killed in Shirdi in 2015, allegedly over his mobile phone playing the ringtone venerating Dr Ambedkar.[31] Dr M. Mariraj, a Dalit, attempted suicide because of casteist abuse while pursuing a postgraduate degree at Ahmedabad's B. J. Medical College.[32] Similarly, an eight-year-old boy belonging to a scheduled caste in Maharashtra was stripped naked and forced to sit on hot, burning tiles at noon for entering a temple space. The attacker allegedly first ruffled the child up and then pushed him onto a heated flooring. The burning tiles have left grave burn injuries on the child's buttocks and back.[33] Likewise, in April 2019, a group of eight dominant caste men killed a 21-year-old Dalit man for sitting on a chair and eating in front of them at a wedding party.[34]

Such experiences have wounded Dalits' psyches and tempt Dalits to view themselves as an inferior race born only to serve. Dalit autobiographies further explain how the caste system demeans Dalits and restricts their access to opportunities, skills and resources from an insider's (emic) perspective. As my awareness of the Dalits' situation emerges mostly from an outsider's (etic) perspective, I will analyse Dalit autobiographies, which will complement my etic view and place this book in its proper context.

Dalits' trauma narrated in Dalit autobiographies

Autobiographies recount events that the narrator has personally experienced, bringing personal accounts to the public domain. Therefore, I expect some reservations against appropriating autobiographies as possible statements of historical truths. However, Dalit autobiographies, as Surekha Nelavala clarifies, are more than individual discourses. Dalits who did not find proper representation in dominant caste discourses embraced autobiographies to recount an alternative view of history.[35] Such autobiographies narrate Dalits' everyday experiences, which can offer essential insights if we navigate carefully through the text and its representations. Hence, we must read them as subjective experiences and trauma narratives by victims since they narrate Dalits' trauma, resistance and protest.

Bama's *Karukku*, translated from Tamil, is one of the first non-Marathi Dalit autobiographies available in English. Bama belongs to an untouchable family converted into the Catholic Church. She became a nun after resigning from her job as a teacher. However, she was shocked to note caste discriminations in the convents. Bama published *Karukku* in 1992. 'Karukku' means palmyra leaves, which have serrated ends on both sides, like double-edged swords. This metaphor indicates Dalits' sufferings in inter-Dalit and intra-Dalit interactions. As the title implies, *Karukku* illustrates some double-edged discriminations against Dalits. Bama uses a series of metaphors, like a bird with broken wings and a fish returned to the water, to explain her exit from the convent.[36] Who might have hurt the bird? Who might have taken the fish out of the water? *Karukku* indicates that the church wounded her and took her out of the water. However, Bama does not blame the church as the only oppressor:

> In this society, if you are born into a low caste, you are forced to live a life of humiliation and degradation until your death. Even after death, caste difference does not disappear. Wherever you look, however much you study, whatever you take up, discrimination stalks us in every nook and corner and drives us into a frenzy.[37]

Thus, the caste accompanies Dalits from birth to death. *The Policy of Dalit Empowerment in the Catholic Church in India*, published in 2016, notes that a crime is committed against a Dalit every eighteen minutes.[38] The harassment of a Dalit professor in the Indian Institute of Technology shows how the caste system operated in 2018.[39] Unfortunately, the caste hesitations have permeated the Indian churches also. For example, the Jesuits' Madurai province, after surveying 9,000 respondents, found that Dalit Christians suffer discriminations in the Catholic Church.[40] Cardinal Oswald Gracias, the Archbishop of Bombay, while participating in the National Council of Dalit Christians' annual gathering, which took place in March 2017, acknowledged the same.[41] So too, the Tamil Nadu Untouchability Eradication Front conducted a public hearing on 16 March 2017 on the atrocities against Dalit Christians in the Sivagangai Diocese of the Catholic Church and reported that discrimination against Dalits and caste practices are rampant within the church.[42]

Situating the Dalits in the Indian Christian churches

As noted, the caste system crippled Dalits, who suffered systemic human rights violations. Similarly, Dalits have unequal access to services and employment opportunities. Dalits challenge the caste hegemony in many ways, including conversion to well-established religions. They embraced Christianity in large numbers as part of such manoeuvres. However, conversion did not help Dalits significantly, and they remain as outsiders in Indian Christian churches, suffering multiple discriminations in inter-denominational and intra-denominational relations.

Dalits' sufferings began right from the time of their conversion. There was a written convention in the Catholic Church that no untouchable should be ordained to priesthood except under extraordinary situations.[43] The church also introduced the law to limit the ministry to Brahmins in 1613.[44] Dalit converts were forced to reject their cultural and religious practices before baptism in some denominations.[45] Christian denominations only began to denounce such discriminations in the past few decades. The Catholic Bishops' Conference, for example, stated in 1982 that caste discrimination should not have a place in the church.[46] So too, Pope John Paul II declared:

> Any semblance of a caste-based prejudice in relations between Christians is a countersign to authentic human solidarity, a threat to genuine spirituality and a serious hindrance to the Church's mission of evangelisation. Therefore, customs and traditions that perpetuate or reinforce caste division should be sensitively reformed so that they may become an expression of solidarity of the whole Christian community.[47]

I appreciate similar initiatives. However, it is inexcusable that the caste system remains active within the churches and the power of the dominant-caste Christians sideline Dalit Christians. In her 2009 book, Monica Jyotsna Melanchthon observed that only 4 per cent of the parishes are entrusted to Dalit priests. There are no Dalits among the thirteen Catholic Bishops of Tamil Nadu. The case is the same with the vicars general and rectors of seminaries and directors of social assistance centres.[48] Likewise, *Thadam Thedi*, a report on Dalit Christians' status, attests that Dalit Christians have not been given any prominent positions in church administration.[49]

The situation has improved recently. For example, Pope Francis has selected Archbishop Anthony Poola of Hyderabad as the first ever Cardinal in history from a Dalit background.[50] Similarly, Marampudi Joji, a Dalit priest, was installed as an Archbishop in the Catholic Church in April 2000.[51] Tamil Nadu followed Andhra Pradesh and got two bishops consecrated.[52] According to the Policy of Dalit Empowerment, released by the Catholic Bishops Conference on 8 December 2016, there are twelve Dalit bishops in the church in India.[53] Similarly, the leaders and officials of the Church of South India, the largest protestant denomination in India, were always elected from dominant caste Christians. Such practices have changed demographically. However, the Dalits' plight has not improved substantially even though half of the bishops in the Church of South India are Dalits since the new bishops represent the affluent urban Dalit communities significantly.[54]

The caste system is alive among Syrian Christians as well. Mathias Mundadan, P. N. Kunjanpillai and Ninan Koshy have noted that the Syrian Christians identify themselves with the dominant caste Hindus.[55] Such instances influenced the Syrian

Christians' social praxis, and they tended to mimic the dominant caste attitude to Dalits. Dalits from many parts of Kerala, for example, embraced Syrian Christians due to the missionary work of Mor Gregorios Chathuruthil (1848–1902), a Syrian Christian bishop.[56] Syrian Christians, however, objected Dalit converts worshipping with them.[57] P. P. Varkey and K. V. Mammen clarify:

> In many parishes, it was unthinkable standing along with *parayas* and *pulayas* inside the Church. In some places superiority of Syrian Christians was due to their Brahmin tradition. To them if an *Ezhava* woman touched a well, water would become unclean.[58]

It is to be noted, however, that present-day Syrian Christians seldom express their casteist views blatantly. But that does not mean that today's Syrian Christians are less casteist. It only means that their casteism is concealed or unconscious. Susan Visvanathan, a professor at Jawaharlal Nehru University, notes, more recently, caste contradictions among Syrian Christians like prohibiting low castes from entering their houses.[59] So too, a cousin of my friend was expelled from her house for marrying a Dalit Christian. Moreover, almost all matrimonial advertisements by Syrian Christians establish their caste preferences in matchmaking. The recent honour killing in Kerala also highlights how dangerous the marriage between Dalit Christians and Syrian Christians would be.[60] Geevarghese Mor Coorilos, a Syrian Christian bishop, has also noted the dominant caste tendencies among Syrian Christians.[61] Hence the Syrian Christians' response to casteism has been minimal.

Thus, Dalit Christians tended to suffer in various Christian denominations because of caste hesitations. So too, Dalit Christians had reservations against the moral crisis in the Indian Christian theology, the dominant mode of Indian theological imagination, which neglected Dalits' presence in the churches and used Hindu philosophical terms and Vedantic categories such as *Advaita* and *Vishishtadvaita* excessively. Likewise, the founders of Dalit theology were disappointed with the lingering impact of the Indian Christian theology's dominant caste legacy, which perpetuated the casteist society's ethics of status quo. Such an inculturation, which resulted in compromises and conciliatory incorporation of discriminatory power structures, they feared, is not a cultural accident but a product of a theological blindness to the Dalits' sufferings. From such contexts, the pioneers of Dalit theology argued that God is not caste-blind in a casteist society and accused the Indian Christian academics of being deaf, dumb and blind to Dalits' sufferings.[62] Scholars like Massey call this phenomenon Sanskritic captivity.[63] Dalit theology emerged from such contexts as a school of Indian contextual thinking from Dalits' outlook to reassert Dalits' space amidst India's dominant caste theological discourses.

The genealogy and development of Dalit theology (1980–2020)

Nirmal, Massey, Prabhakar, Azariah, Wilson, Devasahayam and Balasundaram are often designated as the pioneers of Dalit theology.[64] They believed that the Indian

Christian theology failed to embrace Dalits and denounced it for being too abstract, far removed from Dalits' existential realities and demanded a change in the Indian theological agenda.[65] Their call began to influence Indian theological enquiries by the 1980s. Dalit theology emerged as an academically informed enterprise from that background, revisiting the Bible from Dalits' perspectives, based upon Dalits' immanent experiences and their significance for theologizing in Dalits' contexts.[66]

The movement from philosophical explanations to Dalits' experience was bold, provocative and radical, and Dalit theology has already established itself as one of the significant contributions of Indian theological explorations. Dalits' pathos, caste-based oppression, God as a suffering God and Jesus as a Dalit are essential theoretical premises of Dalit theology.

Development of Dalit theology

James Massey considers Nirmal's paper 'Towards a Sudra Theology', presented at the United Theological College, as the inauguration of Dalit theology.[67] Nirmal's article challenged the then-dominant Brahmanical preferences in the Indian Christian theology and advised Dalit academics to develop a theological response to the renewed self-consciousness among the Dalits. Nirmal, often recognized as Dalit theology's predecessor, did not use the word Dalit in this paper. Nevertheless, Nirmal's paper functioned as a catalyst, providing a solid foundation for Dalit theology. Scholars like Clarke and Rajkumar rightly understand Nirmal's essay as a watershed event and a clarion call that demanded Dalit Christians to give up their theological passivity.[68]

Kothappalli Wilson's book *The Twice Alienated* was another ground-breaking publication. Wilson highlighted that Indian Christian theology impacted Dalit Christians negatively and called for a shift from transcendental and otherworldly concerns to the Dalits' immanent sufferings.[69] Wilson used the term 'Dalit' in his book. *The Twice Alienated*, however, was more a critique of Indian Christian theology than the presentation of a Dalit alternative, and it marked a transition from Indian Christian theology to Dalit theology.[70]

M. Azariah brought the term 'Dalit theology' to an international forum in 1984. The emergence of organizations like the Christian Dalit Liberation Movement and Dalit Liberation Education Trust also triggered the gradual development of Dalit theology.[71] Three successive seminars at Guntur (1986) and Chennai (1987 and 1988) further assisted Dalit academics in assessing Dalit theology's outlook. The conference in Guntur explored the concept, content and direction for Dalit theology.[72] 'Towards a Dalit Theology' was the theme for the meetings held in Chennai. The publication of the papers presented in these conferences bookmarked the beginning of serious theologizing by the Dalit academics.[73] Nirmal, in his article, clarified that the aim of Dalit theology is not only securing rights and privileges but also the realization of 'full humanness or conversely our full divinity, the ideal of the imago Dei in us'.[74] Such publications and seminars helped to affirm the vision of Dalit theology.

Development of Dalit theology in the 1990s

Emerging Dalit Theology, edited by Xavier Irudayaraj, opened the Dalit theological explorations in the 1990s.[75] This book is one of the essential publications in Dalit theology, which orients a reader towards much of the core principles of Dalit theology. Nirmal, in his essay in this volume, compares Dalits' embracing Christianity with the exodus experience.[76] *A Reader in Dalit Theology* and *Heuristic Explorations* followed Irudayaraj's publication.[77] Paratt describes *A Reader in Dalit Theology* as 'an invaluable sourcebook'.[78] *A Reader in Dalit Theology* and *Heuristic Explorations* mark the transition from experimental approaches to articulating a more robust conception of what Dalit theology is.[79]

Massey's book *Towards a Dalit Hermeneutics* is another milestone in the 1990s. Massey advises the Dalits to reconstruct their identity and assert their agency in redressing the Dalit situation.[80] Two edited works (*Indigenous Peoples: Dalits, Dalit Issues in Today's Theological Debate* and *Frontiers of Dalit Theology*) were also published during this period.[81] *Indigenous People* included articles from Nirmal,[82] Prabhakar,[83] Abraham Ayrookuzhiel[84] and Massey.[85] Nirmal, in his article, clarifies that Jesus encountered rejection and death as Dalits' prototype.[86] Prabhakar defined Dalit theology as a political theology demanding social praxis and transformation of the oppressive structures.[87] *Frontiers of Dalit Theology* highlights that the Dalits are deprived of human dignity enjoyed by non-Dalits.[88]

The scholarly discussions during the 1990s concentrated on the role of Dalit theology and its sources. Dalit academics also began to focus on Dalits' religio-cultural resources. The church's engagement in Dalits' assertions, the critique of the Indian Christian theology and the centrality of Dalits' experiences in theologizing in India were some critical issues during this period. Some Dalit academics, however, had already suggested a few modifications to these proposals based upon the changed circumstances of the twenty-first century.

Development of Dalit theology in the 2000s

Frontiers in Dalit Hermeneutics,[89] *Breaking Theoretical Grounds for Dalit Studies*,[90] *Dalit–Tribal Theological Interface*,[91] *Dalit Empowerment*[92] and *Re-imagining Dalit Theology: Postmodern Readings*[93] are essential publications in the 2000s. A hermeneutical consciousness and a demand for methodological clarification emerged strongly during this period. Scholars like Massey and Charles Singaram, for example, invited scholarly attention in developing a clear-cut methodology for Dalit theology.[94] The most critical event during this period, however, is an international conference held in Kolkata in 2008. The conference, after identifying the urgency to reposition Dalit theology amidst the changed circumstances in the twenty-first century, scrutinized how various ecclesial communities approached Dalits' realities with creativity, commitment and imagination. It suggested that Dalit theology needs to revisit some of its theoretical premises to become a theology of life in the twenty-first century.

This seminar was a significant milestone and a game changer. The presentations were published in 2010, titled *Dalit Theology in the Twenty-First Century: Discordant Voices, Discerning Pathways*. The book tracks the development of Dalit theology from the 1980s and revisits Nirmal's methodological formulations, Massey's historical reconstructions, Devasahayam's biblical interpretations, Prabhakar's Christological reflections, Ayrookuzhiel's appropriation of Dalits' religio-cultural foundations, Webster's construction of Dalit Christian histories and Appavoo's reclamation of Dalit folklore and liturgy against the changed circumstances in the twenty-first century.[95]

Emerging trends in Dalit theology

Dalit Theology in the Twenty-First Century inspired some Dalit academics who questioned some proposals of Dalit theology, believing that such interrogations would make Dalit theology more relevant to the Dalits. Such scholars, while accepting the radicalism of Dalit theology, critically revisit Dalit theology from its inception. Rajkumar's book *Dalit Theology and Dalit Liberation*, Jeremiah's book *Community and Worldview among Paraiyars of South India*, Y. T. Vinayaraj's book *Dalit Theology after Continental Philosophy*, Boopalan's book *Memory, Grief, and Agency: A Political Theological Account of Wrongs and Rites* and Joshua Samuel's book *Untouchable Bodies, Resistance, and Liberation: A Comparative Theology of Divine Possessions* emerged from this context. Such publications advanced Dalit theology by noting continuity and negotiation in Dalits' contexts, clarifying the necessity for appreciating Dalits' resistance and Dalits' agency, and utilizing European theological models in redressing Dalits' situation.

Continuity and negotiation in Dalit contexts

The Dalit academics' dominant outlook, with some exceptions like Abraham Ayrookuzhiel and Sathianathan Clarke, included that the Dalits forsake their cultural and religious belongings entirely. Such a perspective began to be challenged after 2010 when emerging Dalit academics acknowledged religious and cultural continuity and negotiation in Dalits' contexts. Jeremiah, for example, based upon his fieldwork among the Dalits in Thulasigramam, a village situated 120 kilometres west of Chennai, notes the process of religious and cultural continuity and negotiation among the Dalits.[96] Following similar routes, Joshua Samuel warns against overlooking Dalits' cultural and religious foundations.

> Self-righteous, Christian-centric attitudes of Dalit theologians that claim the gospel of Jesus Christ as the only means of liberation while simultaneously juxtaposing the Dalit religious values (now within Hinduism) as completely evil have had, I am afraid, reverse effects on the Christian Dalit communities by alienating them from the rest of the community.[97]

Besides alienating the Dalits, neglecting Dalits' culture, as Samuel, Vinayaraj and Rajkumar suggest, can shorten the history of Dalit liberation, limit the resources of Dalit theology and relegate the Dalits as memory-less/past-less/history-less people and can disempower Dalit theology significantly.[98] Further, such misappropriations can restrict the Dalits from celebrating the legacy of their responses to historical Dalit sufferings registered in their resources. Samuel's proposal that multiple religious belonging could become an essential tool for the Dalits to reconnect with their past can help Dalit theology reclaim Dalits' agency envisioned in Dalit contexts.[99]

Appreciating Dalits' resistance and agency

A dominant section of Dalit academics depended significantly on the pain and pathos of the Dalits.[100] *Dalit Theology in the Twenty-First Century* challenged such theoretical premises, and consequently, some scholars, while acknowledging the particularity of pathos, note that Dalit contexts involve more than just pathos. Deenabandhu Manchala, for instance, reviews the excessive focus on suffering, pain and pathos and suggests a way forward by focusing not only on pathos but also on Dalits' resistance and agency in overcoming their afflictions:

> There is an urge to expand the horizons of Dalit theology in order to include allies, to expand its ambit and relevance to wider realities, to affirm their identity of protest against an oppressive social system, and to move beyond a victim mindset. Therefore, it is not suffering, Dalit pathos alone but also their experience of struggle to overcome suffering and their determination to risk themselves for the sake of liberation and justice that now needs to be considered as the subject matter of theological reflection.[101]

Rajkumar also noted that the Dalit Christological formulations developed through pathos could operate only 'as a palliative inuring the Dalits to their existing suffering through marginalization and make the Dalits masochistic in their attitude towards suffering'.[102] This book follows similar paths and seeks to move beyond pathos without minimizing the extent of real, felt suffering and concentrates on Dalit resistances, whose active memory, as Boopalan rightly highlights throughout his book, can promote Dalits' agency.[103]

Appreciating European models and proposals

Dalit academics depended excessively on the theoretical and hermeneutical premises of Latin American and African American theologies. Such scholars, with very few exceptions, overlooked the philosophical and sociological contributions of the European scholars substantially. However, a new trend, which dialogues with European scholars, began to emerge among the Dalit academics. Jeremiah's article 'Dalit Christians in India: Reflections from the "Broken Middle"' seems to be one example. Jeremiah initiates a dialogue with the sociopolitical concept of Gillian Rosemary Rose, a British scholar, and suggests how the proposals of Rose can advance Dalit theology.[104] Jeremiah's article in *Dalit Theology in the Twenty-First Century* accelerated this trend and further clarified how and why he suggests such an interdisciplinary interaction:

> With the exception of a few works, we can tentatively conclude that Dalit theology in general, and Christology in particular, display a certain shallowness and apathy in terms of resourcing and adapting interdisciplinary approaches to learning from the vast strides made in biblical research, practical theology, and socio-anthropological studies rendering it ineffective and stagnated.[105]

From such perspectives, Jeremiah revisits the Dalit Christological discourse based upon the proposals of John Dominic Crossan, an Irish American scholar. Appropriating Crossan's observations on the Historical Jesus of the Greco-Roman history, as 'an artisan and a member of the exploited community', Jeremiah explains that Dalits' claim to ownership of their lands resonates with Jesus' own time of class-ridden society.[106] Following a similar course, Y. T. Vinayaraj, based upon the traditions of postcolonial theory and continental philosophers such as Gilles Deleuze, Giorgio Agamben, Catherine Malabou and Jean-Luc Nancy, suggests how continental philosophies can advance Dalit theology.[107]

Scholars like Jeremiah and Vinayaraj, who demand sensitivity to interdisciplinary approaches, prepare those who engage in Dalit theology in exploring the resources in other theological and sociological traditions. Following their undertakings, I will use recent developments in postcolonial biblical studies in this book.

Situating this book

This book seeks to collaborate with the dissenting voices that emerged after 2010 and questions the dominant outlook among Dalit theologians, which, I suggest, have tended to overlook continuity and negotiation in Dalits' contexts, despite some cautious warnings. Abraham Ayrookuzhiel, a Syrian Christian scholar like me, for example, had alerted the Dalit theologians to Dalits' counter-caste worldview and alternate moral visions, for theologizing in Dalits' contexts. Ayrookuzhiel's pioneering proposals, though taken up by several writers, Dalits and others, influenced neither Dalit theology nor Syrian Christian social praxis substantially.

From such backgrounds, this book revisits the proposals of the pioneers of Dalit theology through Dalits' forgotten voices. Such an interrogation does not discredit the founders or their lived experiences. Instead, this book acknowledges that the pioneers of Dalit theology also shaped their proposals out of their lived experiences. The Latin American and African American influences, this book suggests, created an imbalance in Dalit theology, which is evident in some proposals of the pioneers. This book, without denying the credibility and contributions of the pioneers, will critically evaluate their recommendations and will suggest that a hermeneutic of return to Dalits' resources, as suggested by the scholars like Ayrookuzhiel, can advance Dalit theology and offer new perspectives for Syrian Christian social praxis.

Decentring Dalit theology through Dalits' forgotten voices

As will be clarified, Dalit theology, though it emerged out of Dalits' immanent experiences, owes much to Latin American and African American theologies.[108] Those contextual theologies helped Dalit academics to propose Dalit theology in radical discontinuity with Indian Christian theology. This methodological and ideological indebtedness, this book suggests, injected biblical messages from Latin American and African American contexts extensively into Dalits' religio-cultural world, promoted Christian identity and imposed their biblical worldview into Dalits' contexts. Such an imposition often overlooked Dalits' religio-cultural resources, displaced Dalits' traditions to the periphery of Dalit theology, degraded Dalits' religio-cultural world as a dark world to be conquered and suppressed Dalits' liberative voices. It also estranged Dalit theology's theoretical and methodological framework from Dalits' counter-formulations and alternative moral visions substantially. Such unintended outcomes are alarming since Dalits' culture, as Devasahayam cautions, is vital to Dalits, and it forms Dalits as a community developing their collective consciousness and memory.[109]

The extensive use of biblical messages and worldviews designed in Latin American and African American contexts upon Dalit contexts necessitates further interrogation by turning to and giving voice to the suppressed voices in the Dalits' culture. Such a listening to Dalits' liberative voices and learning from them, as Ayrookuzhiel demanded, would be rewarding to Dalit theology. Perhaps, analysing how African American theologians responded to the comparable situation would assist in reclaiming suppressed voices. Victor Anderson summarizes similar attempts of African American theologians:

> Some black church theologians questioned whether black theology could be a theology of the black churches if it disentangled itself from the creeds, confessions, and liturgical practices of the traditional churches. Others asked in what sense black theology could be black if its theological method was derived from white European theologians, such as Karl Barth and Paul Tillich, and European philosophers, such as Albert Camus and Jean-Paul Sartre. Still, others wondered how black theology could be relevant to a culture of black radicalism and revolution and remain theologically and morally Christian.[110]

Appropriating similar African American attempts could be relevant in Dalits' contexts also. For instance, a discussion on whether Dalit theology could be a theology of the Dalits if it is disconnected from Dalits' counter-ontology and the epistemology of resistance is worth pursuing. However, such a unilateral attempt might undermine Dalits' exodus from Hinduism to Christianity. Similarly, questioning Latin American and African American baggage upon the Dalit hermeneutics would help Dalit theology redefine its methodological approaches. However, such discussions, I contend, should lead to the third approach, which combines Dalits' counter-caste Hindu Vedic worldview with Christian messages. Similarly, Devasahayam suggests that the gospel and culture are to be related in a theologizing endeavour and indicates a tension between gospel and culture, which affirms the liberative elements in Dalits' culture and rejects the demonic elements in Dalits' culture.[111]

I have some reservations against Devasahayam's master–slave perspective. It is a colonial view from above. It relegates Dalits' culture and implies a top-down intervention, which neglects the beneficiaries' role in identifying and solving the difficulties and could be disruptive to Dalits' culture. What I prefer is a constructive dialogue that anticipates the participants' willingness to be modified and updated. K. Renato Lings, for instance, notes an often-neglected aspect in biblical hermeneutics and argues that the picture of the Canaanites presented in the Bible could be political and inaccurate.[112] From a similar perspective, Pablo Richard, while addressing the Latin American situation from a bottom-up hermeneutic, reminds us that the Bible must participate in the dialogue between the Bible and culture with humility since the indigenous people have lived thousands of years without the Bible. Likewise, there is a profound and significant revelation of god in the indigenous cultures, and, therefore, evangelization, if it wishes to be liberative, Pablo suggests, must begin by listening, discerning and interpreting the revelation of god in indigenous religion and culture.[113]

Jawanza Eric Clark, in a similar but African American context, clarifies that 'exploring the rich theological and philosophical legacy of indigenous African religious systems and affirming their legitimacy and priority for black Christian theological construction, discourse and practice' can help African American theology to overcome its estrangement from Black contexts.[114] The same is true with Dalit theology. A hermeneutic of return to Dalits' resources and dialogues between the Bible and the values submerged in Dalits' resources, I hope, will help Dalit theology overcome its alienation from Dalits' contexts. However, what I propose is not borrowing certain externals of culture such as dress, diet and gestures in worship but embracing values submerged in Dalits' resources.[115] Such a conscious blending, I think, honours the revelatory value of Dalits' culture and the Christian message. It seeks not to conquer one or the other but to complement each other through creative tensions. Such listening and learning would be radical for Dalit theology. It would empower Dalit theology to be an authentic theology of the Dalits by analysing how the Dalit Christian worldview goes through negotiation and continuity.

From such contexts, I will analyse the dominant paradigms of Dalit theology through Dalits' forgotten voices. Such an exploration might show that Dalit hermeneutics overlook Dalits' liberative voices significantly, and Dalits' contexts demand a biblical paradigm that respects Dalit cultural resources. From such contexts, I will suggest Abraham's crossings to Egypt (12.10-20) and Gerar (20.1-18), read through the postcolonial optic, as a dialogue partner to advance Dalit theology through Dalits' forgotten voices. Such an undertaking weaves together an intertextual dialogue between Dalits' counter-caste assertions and counter-colonial assertions in Abraham's crossings, suggesting that these dialogue partners can offer an alternate path for Dalit theology and Syrian Christian social praxis.

The road ahead

This book has nine chapters. Chapter 1 is an introductory chapter. Chapters 2 and 3 trace the background and emergence of Dalit theology. Chapter 2, which examines Dalit theology's genealogy through Dalits' cries for dignity, begins with an engaging narrative from the autobiography of Omprakash Valmiki, a prominent Dalit writer and poet. The chapter uncovers how untouchability conditions Dalits' lives. It interrogates how Dalits' assertions in the 1970s, the insensitivity of the Indian Christian theology to the violence against the Dalits and the churches' failure in accommodating the Dalit converts convinced the founders of Dalit theology of the urgency to liberate Dalits. From such a background, Chapter 3, which interrogates the genealogy of Dalit theology through the Liberation theologies, discusses how the conceptual examples of Latin American Liberation theology and African American theology helped the founders in proposing Dalit theology in radical discontinuity with Indian Christian theology.

Chapter 4, which questions Dalit Theology through Dalits' Forgotten Voices, builds upon the observations of Chapters 2 and 3 and contrasts the hermeneutical examples of Dalit theology with some essential aspects of Dalits' contexts communicated through Dalits' religious, cultural and literary assertions. The chapter concludes that the Dalit hermeneutics, unfortunately, constructed the biblical paradigms developed in Latin American and African American contexts as the dominant self. Such an instance, I suggest, alienated Dalit theology from the liberative voices in Dalits' counter-assertions expressed through the dissenting Dalit voices and anti-caste philosophers such as Chokhamela, Karmamela, Ravidas, Kabir, Nandanar and Narayana Guru.

Chapter 5, 'Decentring Dalit Theology through Dalits' Forgotten Voices', depending on Chapter 4, suggests that Dalits' worldview, pathos and ethos require a hermeneutical switch to complement Dalit theology. This chapter further proposes the Second Temple community's counter-colonial assertions expressed through Abraham's crossings to Egypt and Gerar as a partner in dialogue to complement Dalits' counter-formulations. Such an intertextual reading can offer fresh perspectives for Dalit theology to promote Dalits' dignity and Dalit–non-Dalit dialogues and appreciations.

Chapters 6 and 7 explain Abraham's relevance for Dalits and how his crossings to Egypt and Gerar can advance Dalit theology in the Indian pluralistic contexts. Chapter 6, 'Situating Abraham's Postcolonial Crossings as a Dialogue Partner', after dealing with an engaging incident between Pope John Paul II and the representatives of the Peruvian indigenous communities, affirms the legitimacy of analysing Abraham's encounters against Persian contexts. It suggests how a postcolonial reading of Abraham's cross-cultural journeys can support Dalit theology. Chapter 7, 'Exploring Abraham's Crossings to Egypt and Gerar', evaluates Abraham's expeditions to Egypt and Gerar as attempts to subvert the ethnocentric policies of the Persian governors of Yehud by suggesting God as a liberator and the source of reconciliation between the oppressor and the oppressed, seeing morality and piety beyond Yehud and Sarah as a participant in God's mission.

Chapter 8, 'Reimagining Dalit Theology Through Dalits' Forgotten Voices', suggests that an intertextual reading of the counter-assertions of the Second Temple community narrated through Abraham's crossings and Dalits' counter-caste assertions can help Dalit theology develop and mature as a source of liberation and reconciliation by reimagining the agency of God, reorienting inter-Dalit and intra-Dalit solidarity and redefining the role of Dalit women.

Chapter 9, which is an authorial note, suggests how my crossings to Dalits' contexts benefited me, advanced my cross-cultural competence and convinced me (as an upper-caste, Indian-born, Syrian Christian priest) that Dalits' contexts have immense potential to teach and purify Syrian Christians and advance some proposals for embracing Dalits.

Each chapter of this book offers a different piece regarding how Dalit theology emerged, how Dalit theology can benefit from a hermeneutical switch and how Abraham's crossings would reconnect Dalit theology with Dalits' contexts. Read as a whole, the representation verifies the thesis that an intertextual reading between Dalits' counter-formulations expressed through the subversive voices and the Second Temple community's assertions narrated through Abraham's postcolonial crossings will offer rich possibilities for both Dalits and Syrian Christians. Such an analysis, while suggesting a way forward for Dalit theology out of its alienation from Dalit contexts, would be rewarding to Syrian Christians also.

Chapter 2

GENEALOGY OF DALIT THEOLOGY SEEN THROUGH DALITS' CRIES FOR DIGNITY

Introduction

Omprakash Valmiki was a prominent Dalit writer who lived in Uttar Pradesh in India.[1] *Joothan*, his autobiography, describes his experiences as untouchable in the 1950s. The term 'joothan' denotes the food scraps left on a plate, doomed to the litter or animals. Highlighting his life as a *Joothan*, Valmiki narrates about a Brahmin family from Maharashtra who became very close to him, thinking that Valmiki was a Brahmin. They allowed Valmiki to visit them frequently. Savita, the daughter of the family, had even fallen in love with him. A lengthy but enlightening exchange between Valmiki and Savita uncovers how untouchability impairs Dalits and informs the ironic turn in their relationship after Valmiki discloses his caste.

Then I asked her, 'What do you think of me?'
'Aai and Baba praise you. They say you are very different from their preconceptions about U.P. people,' Savita cooed.
'I had asked for your opinion.'
'I like you.' She leaned on my arm.
I pushed her away and asked, 'Ok ... would you like me even if I were an S.C.?'
'How can you be an S.C.?' she laughed.
'Why not, what if I am?' I had insisted.
'You are a Brahmin,' she said with conviction.
'Who told you that?'
'Baba.'
'He is wrong. I am an S.C.' I put all my energy into those words. I felt that a fire had lit inside me.
'Why do you say such things?' She said angrily.
'I am telling you the truth. I won't lie to you. I never claimed that I am a Brahmin.'
She stared at me, totally shocked. She still thought I was joking with her.
I said plainly as I could that I was born in a Chuhra family of U.P.
Savita appeared grave. Her eyes were filled with tears, and she said tearfully, 'You are lying, right?'

'No, Savi ... it is the truth ... you ought to know this.' I had convinced her. She started to cry, as though my being an S.C. was a crime. She sobbed for a long time. Suddenly the distance between us had increased.[2]

Valmiki's encounter reveals some practices and prejudices based on purity and pollution. Savita, for instance, refers to Professor Kamble scornfully because of his Dalit origin. Her parents offered Kamble tea in a cup exclusively reserved for Dalits. However, Savita and her family treated Valmiki courteously since they did not know his caste. Savita's response to Valmiki's disclosure is also striking. As Valmiki notes, Savita started to cry as though he being a Dalit is a crime. This incident communicates the taboos a Dalit may face in daily life. The dominant caste people considered Dalits as polluting agents and did not allow them to access public places such as temples and schools. They often disparage Dalits and hate the Dalits' presence and approach. From such contexts, Dalit theologians began to read the Bible from Dalits' immanent perspectives.

Dalits' fragility and early beginnings of Dalit theology

Dalits' situation, as noted, is close to destitution and dehumanization. Society attributes some derogatory names to Dalits. Hindu scriptures call them *Panchamas* (the fifth caste). They were also designated as *Avarnas* (without caste) since they did not fit into the varna system. The British administration named them depressed classes in 1919. Later in 1931, the Indian Census Commission designated them as exterior castes. The imperial administration called them scheduled castes in 1935. Breaking away from this humiliating history, Gandhiji renamed Dalits as Harijans since he believed that Dalits were dear to god because of their deplorable situation.[3]

Gandhiji struggled to popularize his title 'Harijan', hoping that this would elevate Dalits' social standing. Dalits, however, were not convinced by Gandhiji's attempts since the word 'Harijan', approaching from Dalits' perspectives, had an iniquitous connotation. It can indicate the devadasi system (temple prostitution), in which the devadasis' children were called Harijans.[4] Calling Dalits as Harijan, therefore, can relegate Dalits (knowingly or unknowingly) as illegitimate children. Likewise, Dalit academics like Ambedkar believed that the title 'Harijan' would not change Dalits' situation substantially.[5] Gopal Guru also disapproves of Gandhiji's title since Dalit, as interpreted by the Hindu Vedic worldview, is a materialist category disconnected from god.[6] The Dalits also found 'Harijan' a paternalistic and condescending term, insufficient for their liberation since it includes a top-down intervention from dominant castes.[7] Besides these drawbacks, Dalit researchers interpret Gandhiji's title as an attempt to spiritualize a social problem.[8] Hence, Dalits disapproved of the Gandhian Harijan ideology. Whatever be the case, these titles highlight the social, economic, cultural and political discrimination against Dalits.

Despite the titles the society has attributed to the former untouchables, they prefer to be called Dalits, a defiant and a self-attributed name. Nevertheless, Dalits are neither homogenous nor without internal hierarchies. There are different categories, and each of them may have diverging necessities and objectives. In the present contexts, Dalit communicates the resistance and resilience against the history of oppression, discrimination and violence. It also expresses Dalits' anger, dissent, anti-caste sentiments and political consciousness.[9] There are some scholarly disagreements on who devised this title. The dominant view claims that Jyotiba Phule coined the term 'Dalits'.[10] The competing thesis proposes that Ambedkar invented this term.[11] Scholars also trace the etymology of Dalit to both Sanskrit and Hebrew. Scholars like Clarke maintain that Dalit means 'crushed' in Sanskrit and explore its significance in Dalits' contexts.[12] Similarly, depending upon the nuances of the Hebrew word *dal*, which means physical weakness (Gen. 41.19) and pathetic social or economic situation (Exod. 30.15, Lev. 14.21, Ruth 3.10), some scholars explain Dalits' deplorable condition.[13] All these meanings, I suggest, have implications for Dalits.

As the etymology communicates, Dalits have been the most degraded and exploited in society. The social, political and economic subjugation reduced them to a state of an ox bearing the yoke of oppression with sheepish timidity. A total of 90,925 crimes against them were reported from 1995 to 1997.[14] Similarly, 47,064 crimes against Dalits were registered in 2014.[15] Amnesty International reports 40,000 crimes against Dalits in 2016.[16] The suicide of Rohit Vemula, a Dalit research scholar at Hyderabad University, due to discrimination by the dominant caste establishment is another instance.[17] A recent BBC report about a Dalit farmer killed by dominant caste men for riding a horse is another example.[18] Likewise, *The Times of India* reports on 29 April 2018 an assault on Sitaram Valmiki, a Dalit farmer, in Uttar Pradesh.[19] According to the *International Business Times*, the dominant caste men forced Valmiki to drink urine.[20]

Such incidents show that Dalits suffer enormously, and Dalit theology seeks to destabilize the dominant caste tendencies in Indian Christian theology. It revisits Indian theology from Dalits' perspectives and their immanent suffering that has been depleting, impoverishing and disempowering.[21] It functions as Dalits' advocacy theology to redress Dalits' 'pollution, poverty and powerlessness'.[22] The call for Dalit theology as theology from below, however, developed not out of nothing. Ely Aaronson, Karl Mannheim, Saturnino M. Borras, Christian Smith, Abdelrahman and Tore Bjorgo had already explained that social and political change emerges out of a long process of mobilization and networking.[23] Their proposal is right with Dalit theology also.[24] Therefore, analysing the historical and theological contexts is necessary to place Dalit theology in its context. This chapter will interrogate the historical contexts, and the next chapter will analyse the theological foundations.

From silence to assertions: Historical foundations of Dalit theology

The pioneers of Dalit theology were discontent with Indian Christian theology and advanced Dalit theology in radical discontinuity with the Indian Christian theology, combining theological reflection with theo-political action.[25] Their reservations against Indian Christian theology developed out of various long-term social and cultural advances. An awareness of that development can clarify the outlook and impetus of Dalit theology. Prabhakar, for example, specifies some causes and conditions that motivated Dalit academics and enlists the Dalit liberation movement as one of the primary inspirations behind Dalit theology. The Dalit liberation movement, Prabhakar claims, informed Dalit academics about the hegemonic espousal of dominant caste interests upon Indian Christian theology. Violence against Dalits and the churches' failure in embracing Dalit Christians also annoyed Dalit theologians.[26] They proposed Dalit theology as a theological alternative to complement Dalit movements.

The intimate bond between Dalit theology and the Dalit movement has confused some scholars who claim that Dalit theology is only a minor variant within a broader Dalit movement.[27] This proposal seems to be an oversimplification. Wilfred, however, has clarified that Dalit theology and the Dalit movement cooperate as two interconnected but independent movements.[28] Dalit theology has received some of its tools of analysis from Dalit movements. Nevertheless, it operates on Christian principles, while Dalit movements are secular mobilizations.[29] Hence, Dalit theology and Dalit movements are two separate engagements, even though there are many links.

Dalit liberation movement

The Dalit movement is political and cultural mobilizations to support Dalits' identity affirmations. It counters the sociocultural hegemony of the dominant caste Hindus.[30] The Dalit movement responds to the failures of the Indian political parties, who adopted a top-down approach to Dalits' predicaments.[31] Such interventions, being perceptions from above, constructed 'clients' of bureaucratic provisions or 'targets' of social work interventions. Further, they limited the recipients' participation, and the beneficiaries had minimal roles in identifying problems and proposing solutions. The policymakers, therefore, incorrectly identified glitches and resolutions based on their ideas. Such instances made policymakers-beneficiaries' cooperation unequal, placing the former at the centre of society and marginalized the latter to the periphery.

The same happened in Dalits' contexts also. Indian political parties promised loans and proper implementation of the reservations to Dalits. Such top-down endeavours often were not adequately administered, which infuriated Dalits who expressed their agitations through a plethora of booklets, newspapers and magazines.[32] Explorations in other parts of the world, like the African American struggle for dignity and freedom, influenced Dalits.[33] Modern education, industrialization, the democratic process and the communication revolution also helped them. Drawing inspiration from the above, the Dalit Panther Movement, the Dalit Sangharsh Samiti, the Bahujan Samaj Party, the Dravida Movement, the Scheduled Caste Federation and the Indian Dalit Federation emerged to mobilize Dalits.[34] There are more than five thousand Dalit liberation groups in India.

Nevertheless, there is no consensus about when the Dalit movement formally began, though some scholars claim that the Dalit movement originated in the mid-nineteenth century.[35]

Appraising all of them is beyond this chapter's scope, and I will only evaluate movements that might have contributed to Dalit theology significantly. Andrew Wyatt maintains that the Dalit Panthers popularized the term 'Dalit' in the 1970s. This phrase's broader use helped develop Dalit consciousness, which promoted a growing interest in Dalits' identity among Dalit Christians and inaugurated an innovative approach to theology.[36] Scholars consider Nirmal's lecture 'Towards a Shudra Theology' in April 1981 as the dawn of Dalit theology. This book, therefore, will only analyse the movements originating between these two events. Such a limitation does not mean that Dalit movements emerged at this time. Instead, a review of such assertions, I hope, can clarify the outlook of Dalit theology.

Dalit Panther movement The Dalit Panther movement emerged in Maharashtra as agitation from the margins. Atrocities by the dominant castes, the failure of the Republican Party and the Naxalbari insurrection fuelled the emergence of this movement.[37] Panthers held their first meeting on 9 July 1972 in Bombay (now Mumbai).[38] The Black Panthers inspired the Dalit Panthers.[39] They called themselves Dalit Panthers because they were supposed to fight for the rights of Dalits like the Black Panthers. They promoted the term 'Dalit'. They defined Dalit identity and self-respect through this title and criticized the caste as an evil that reduces them to a state of 'being no people'.[40]

Unfortunately, the Panthers movement did not last long because of factional disputes. However, we cannot underestimate the Panthers' contributions. They helped to unite Dalits, particularly Dalit youths and students, stimulating 'a new sense of Dalit identity, pride and protest against their oppressed condition'.[41] They united Dalits under one organization and helped Dalits to establish an overarching collective identity as Dalits.[42] Panthers' activities, as Azariah rightly acknowledges, facilitated Dalit Christian academics to comprehend the potential for a theology that highlights Dalits' immanent sorrows.[43] Dalit Sangharsh Samiti, which originated in Karnataka, is another catalyst for the formation of Dalit theology.

Dalit Sangharsh Samiti The Dalit Sangharsh Samiti has been the most significant Dalit mass movement in Karnataka. It is an 'umbrella' association of different Dalit groups, which mobilized Dalits in Karnataka. It is related to the Dalit Panthers movement. Their association, however, is not organizational but is ideological. The Panthers' activities inspired the founders of the Dalit Sangharsh Samiti.[44] Its slogan is 'Reject Caste, Reject Religion and Give Life to Your Humanity'. A speech delivered in 1974 by Basavalingappa, an untouchable and minister in the Congress Government of Karnataka, inspired this movement.

The *bhusa* (cattle fodder) event triggered the formation of Dalit Sangharsh Samiti. Basavalingappa, a minister in Karnataka and a spokesperson of Dalits in Karnataka in the 1970s, was the *bhusa* event's chief architect. The social teachings of Ambedkar influenced him.[45] While attending a function at Mysore organized by Dr Ambedkar Vichara Vedike and the Backward Class Students Forum of the University of Mysore (19 November 1973), Basavalingappa emphasized the dominant caste hegemony in Kannada literature and categorically labelled Kannada literature as *bhusa* that had nothing for Dalits.[46]

The 'allegation' of Basavalingappa caused a major political crisis. Prof. D. Javaregowda, then Vice Chancellor of the University of Mysore, and opposition party leader H. D. Devegowda criticized him. Rashtrakavi Kuvempu, Dr U. R. Ananthamurthy and former Chief Minister J. H. Patel, on the other hand, supported Basavalingappa. Basavalingappa's comments generated widespread and violent protests, and he was forced to resign.[47] The progressive thinkers rallied and organized a conference of Dalit writers, poets and artisans. This gathering paved the way for Dalit Sangharsh Samiti, which functioned as a forum to 'educate, organise and lead the Dalits in their agitation against their oppressors and the exploitative system'.[48] It became one of the strongest and enduring Dalit movements in India.[49] Dalit Sangharsh Samiti opened branches in many villages in Karnataka. Its members composed new revolutionary songs and mobilized and instructed Dalits. Through these branches and literature, Dalit Sangharsh Samiti generated intellectual and social awakening among Dalits.[50]

Dalit Sangharsh Samiti challenged dominant caste hegemony upon Dalits, their mindset and culture and provided a new orientation for Dalits. It played a significant role in Dalits' conscientization in Karnataka.[51] Though it succeeded at the initial stages, like its predecessor in Maharashtra, Dalit Sangharsh Samiti failed to realize its goals entirely since it split over leadership. However, it helped Dalits significantly and operated as Dalits' umbrella organization in Karnataka. This movement criticized mainstream Kannada literature as a dominant caste hegemony and demanded that Dalits' experiences become a subject matter for literary expressions. Such proposals, I suggest, share the basic presuppositions of Dalit theology. Thus, Dalit Sangharsh Samiti seems to be one of the forerunners of Dalit theology. The same is correct with Dalit literature.

Dalit literature movement

The Dalit Panther movement and Dalit Sangharsh Samiti motivated many writers and journalists from a Dalit background who alerted Dalits to the atrocities against them through their publications.[52] Such writers and journalists noted that traditional Indian literature overlooked Dalits' problems, culture and outlook.[53] For instance, Dalits often regard Ambedkar as one of their icons. He fought for Dalits' political rights and affirmative action favouring Dalits in education and government employment.[54] However, mainstream literature and historical discourse in India often overlooked Ambedkar's attempts to liberate Dalits and highlight Ambedkar mainly as the author of the Indian Constitution alone. Therefore, Arundhati Roy, the Booker Prize winner, claims that history has been unkind to Ambedkar.[55] The Dalit literature challenges similar neglects to Dalits and their cause. It encapsulates Dalits' pain, humiliation and poverty and narrates the world differently from Dalits' outlook. Its main objective is Dalits' emancipation.[56]

Dalit literature and mainstream literature

As noted, Dalit literature has been the most potent literary expression of Dalits' daily struggle for human dignity. As a counter-discourse from the margins, Dalit literature challenges conventional literary theories and the dominant caste ideologies submerged in them, blaming the mainstream authors for ignoring Dalits.[57] It also argues that Dalits' sufferings should be an essential source for literature.[58] However, Dalit literature is not a naming and shaming movement. Instead, it seeks the liberation of all humanity and acknowledges the greatness of human beings. It functions as an agency to destabilize the caste system.[59] Dalit literature has its limitations as well. Bharti, an Indian Dalit writer, explains that Dalit literature is the literary undertaking of Dalits alone. Non-Dalit writers have often challenged this aspect. Bharti clarifies that there is no restriction to write Dalits' problems. However, Dalit literature is the work of Dalits only since they have experienced Dalits' issues.[60] This explanation seems tricky. Nonetheless, this book intends to respect Dalits' rights to write their experiences.

Widespread interest in Dalit literature increased considerably in the 1960s. Shankarrao Kharatt, Baburao Bagul and Bandhu Madhav were prominent Dalit writers in Maharashtra.[61] They warned society, both within and beyond the Indian subcontinent, about Dalits' sufferings. They presupposed that traditional Marathi literature is superficial and distorted, alleging that Marathi literature was dominant caste oriented, which failed miserably to narrate Dalits' sufferings. Mistry, for instance, describes an event during the 1970s when the dominant caste people punished three Dalits for participating in an election campaign. They hanged the victims naked by their ankles from a Banyan tree and flogged them throughout the day. The collaborators also urinated on their victims' inverted faces and stuffed burning coal into their mouths. Their cries were heard through the village until their lips and tongues melted away. The dominant caste men displayed the dead bodies in the village square.[62]

Sadly, traditional Marathi literature failed to narrate the dark side of Dalit life as described by Mistry. Why did it happen? M. N. Wankhade and Valmiki had already hinted that a dominant caste Marathi writer's understanding could be limited since such a writer had not experienced Dalits' suffering in its fullness.[63] *Kanyadan* (Marriage), a Marathi drama written in 1983, clarifies their argument further.[64] Vijay Tendulkar narrates an inter-caste marriage between Arun Athawale, a Dalit man, and Jyoti Devlalikar, a Brahmin woman. Tendulkar depicts Arun as a wife-beater, drunkard, manipulator and blackmailer. Arun's alcoholism and his rude behaviour quickly worsen into physical violence after marriage. Notwithstanding this suffering, Jyoti remains with her husband. Many Dalit writers accuse this drama of circulating Dalits' distorted image. Ania Loomba, to quote one of them, reviews *Kanyadan*:

> Shanta Gokhale points out that Tendulkar offered various arguments in defence of his portrayal of Arun, arguing that 'in giving as much space as was required to delve into Nath's character, there simply wasn't sufficient space to devote

nuancing Athavale's character.' At one point he admitted that he didn't know more than a couple of Dalits personally. That was nearer to the truth. Then the Dalit argument was why write about something you don't know? To which Tendulkar replied by saying a writer needn't personally know the people and places he writes about. The Dalit argument seemed to suggest to him that only Dalits could write about Dalits because only they knew themselves. This was a solipsistic argument that couldn't hold water. But this was not what the Dalits meant. There are ways and ways of knowing people. Tendulkar had never met *Sakharam Binder* or anyone like him. But in imagining him into being, Tendulkar managed to create a full-blooded character with shades of grey. So clearly, Arun Athavale was not accorded that kind of personal interest by the writer.[65]

Sadly, mainstream literature, most often, depicts Dalits' distorted image. Kumar, a well-known Marathi poet and literary critic, acknowledges that traditional literature narrates Dalits' distorted image.[66] Trivedi, similarly, clarifies that mainstream Marathi authors use metaphysical, philosophical, symbolic and imaginative language, depicting their characters' physical beauty and heroic qualities. Hence, Trivedi argues, their language is complex and far from reality. They describe a god–man relationship or a man–nature relationship in a poetic way. Dalit writers, Trivedi explains, express their experiences more realistically. Their language and images come from their experiences. Hence, mainstream literature presents a romantic way of life, while Dalit literature represents the realistic way of Dalits' life.[67]

The principal themes of Dalit literature are the hopes and aspirations of Dalits, 'untouchability' and the exploitation of Dalit women by upper-caste men. Waman Nimbalkar, for instance, expresses the shame generated by caste hierarchy:

When I knew nothing, I knew
My caste was despised (low, despicable?)
The Patil had kicked my father,
Cursed my mother.
They did not even raise their heads
But I felt this 'caste' in my heart
When I climbed the step to school
Then too I knew my caste was low
I used to sit outside, the others inside.
My skin would suddenly shiver with little thorns,
My eyes could not hold back the tears.
Our lips must smile when they cursed.
How is caste? Where is it?
It isn't seen, so does it live inside the body?
All the questions float like smoke.
And the wick of thought is sputtering.
But when I knew nothing, then I knew
My caste was low.[68]

This song is an assault on the hierarchy of the caste system. It highlights that the Dalits' psyche internalizes the shame of being a Dalit, which follows Dalits wherever they go and disempowers them from resisting any abuses. Daya Pawar, another Dalit writer from Maharashtra, critiqued the upper caste hegemony that divides Indian society:

> One day someone dug up a twentieth-century city
> And, ends with this observation.
> Here's an interesting inscription:
> 'This water tap is open to all castes and religions'
> What could it have meant:
> That this society was divided?
> That some were high while others were low?
> Well, all right, then this city deserved burying
> Why did they call it the machine age?
> Seems like the Stone Age in the twentieth century.[69]

Pawar describes the Dalits' miserable life, recounting that the Dalits continued to be oppressed and discriminated against in villages irrespective of material progress. Pawar also mocks at the economical and mechanical developments of the twentieth century and suggests that the developments that disregard the Dalits have failed to break the barriers of the caste system. Hence, the poem criticizes caste supremacy and the development models that ignore the sufferings of Dalits. Another poem expresses Dalits' insecurities further.

> Oh cloud, do not leave rain here too
> Our streets too are a part of this country
> Do not let anyone cover a shroud on the memories of the past
> Having got up now and then, they are frightening us
> In our country, we are victimised by your colonial invasion
> We remained refugees, and you the citizens
> We too have asked for entry into the hearts of the temple but
> Not only to the gods, to the human beings too distant we became
> Rented houses also have rejected us
> Choultries too have honoured us by throwing out
> Let the tap water flow onto the drainage
> It would be an offence if we collect it in our hands
> When spat upon the cheek, we showed another cheek
> But, we show cyclone in the silence blasted now![70]

This poem highlights Dalits' circumstances, which relegate them as refugees in their country. This poem, however, does not idealize Dalits' sufferings or their silence. Instead, it compares Dalits' silence with a cyclone's power, a large-scale air mass that could be highly disruptive. Hence, Dalit literature, which challenges the caste system, is an inseparable part of the Dalits' protest movement.[71]

Dalit literature also protests the inequalities attached to the established system.[72] However, it is not a literature of vengeance. As Arvind Nirmal clarifies, it is 'an instrument of social change'.[73] Moreover, Dalit literature communicates the hopes and ambitions of Dalits about a reformed society and imparts a counter-ideology that contests caste and its implications.

As explained, Dalit literature has challenged the Brahminic hegemony in Indian literature. Dalit literature and Dalit theology have many parallels, such as criticizing mainstream literature for its disregard for Dalits' suffering and the focus on 'this world'. Thus, Dalit literature has engineered Dalit theology considerably. However, it is not the case of Dalit literature alone. As noted, the Dalit Panther movement, Dalit Sangharsh Samiti and Dalit literature have also inspired Dalit theology. Nirmal has already acknowledged this idea. He clarifies that his encounter with the Dalit Panthers and the Dalit literature motivated his theological task. As Nirmal implies, Dalit theology, as it is known today, would have been a Shudra theology or Harijan theology if he had not encountered the Dalit Panther movement and the Dalit literature movement.[74] Nirmal's interaction with Dalit movements convinced him of the urgency to propose Dalit theology.

Like Dalit movements that challenge caste and its influence upon traditional Indian literature, Dalit theology questions the dominant caste hegemony upon Indian Christian theology. Moreover, following the Dalit movement's proposals, Dalit theology affirms the centrality of Dalits and their experiences for doing theology in India. Therefore, Dalit theology can be explained as a theological appropriation of Dalit movements. However, some other contextual factors also motivated the founders of Dalit theology. Growing violence against Dalits and the failure of the Indian Christian theology to respond to such instances also provoked Dalit academics to search for a theological alternative for Indian Christian theology.

Growing violence against Dalits in the 1970s

The dominant caste people have been mistreating Dalits for many centuries. Dalits have been discriminated against, denied access to land, routinely battered and killed on an ongoing basis. Hostility against Dalits took many other forms like the forced consumption of human excreta and urine; denial of access to amenities such as drinking water, public ponds, roads, bus stops, markets; denial of civil rights; physical harm and social and economic boycotts. Outrages against them surfaced as a significant issue in the 1970s.[75]

The dominant caste tactics against Dalits changed considerably in the 1970s. They began to target Dalits as a group, even if only an individual transgressed caste boundaries. Violence against Dalits occurred not because of their collective wrongdoing but only because of their collective identity. A Dalit man named Baleshar, for instance, cultivated wheat on the land the government had allotted to him in Meerut. The dominant castes were not happy with Baleshar and killed him. The crowds were not satisfied. They attacked Dalit women in Meerut to terrorize them and deprived 92,000 Dalits of their assigned property because of Baleshar. Another Dalit man was killed in China Ogirala in the Krishna district in July 1977. The dominant caste men invaded the village, tore off the sarees and blouses of Dalit women, and brutally killed many Dalits.[76] In Belchi, Dalits were dragged out of their huts, shot dead in cold blood, and burnt. Mass rape and loot occurred in Jamatara also, where the raiders raped six Dalit women and tortured them by burning their thighs and breasts.[77] As seen, Dalits suffered brutal attacks, including massacres and rapes in many parts of India.

Dalits faced similar discriminations within Indian Christian churches also. Parratt, for example, argues that Dalit Christians are twice alienated. The church and the society discriminate against them.[78] Massey claims that Dalits suffer threefold discrimination from society, the government and fellow Christians.[79] Robinson and Kujur note that Dalit Christians suffer from Indian government, the caste Hindus, dominant caste Christians and the Dalit Christians' subgroups.[80] Unfortunately, Indian Christian theology failed to respond to Dalits' sufferings.

The Indian Christian theology and the Dalits' fragility

Dalits' discrimination within and beyond the Indian Christian churches is a well-documented fact. The majority of the Indian Christian theologians, though they had empathy for the poor and the needy, ignored Dalits' contextual sufferings. They interpreted Dalits' predicaments through a philanthropic lens, overlooking the ontic problems associated with Dalits' lived experiences significantly. Sebastian Kappen, for instance, published *Jesus and Freedom*, *Jesus and the Cultural Revolution* and *Liberation Theology and Marxism*.[81] Following the same course, Mar Osthathios suggests the possibilities of God's universal saving potential.[82] Dalit academics denounced such interpretations and alleged that Indian Christian theology ignored the Dalits' sufferings. They began to ask why and how it is possible for the Indian Christian theologians to do theology without taking seriously the history and ongoing reality of Dalits' suffering. Nirmal, for example, clarifies:

> It was in the seventies that Indian theologians began to take questions of socio-economic justice more seriously. The Indian theological scene thus changed considerably, I felt that liberation *motifs* in India were of a different nature, the Indian situation was different and that we had to search for liberation *motifs* that were authentically Indian.[83]

Perdue and Irudayaraj also noted that Indian Christian theologians discounted the brutal attacks against Dalits and their continuing sufferings within Indian Christian churches.[84] Similarly, the church also failed to include the Dalits, and Dalit theology emerged as a counter-discourse to churches' failure to accommodate them.

Dalits' mass conversions to Christianity: Search for liberation

Individual religious conversion has been an ongoing phenomenon in India because of the multireligious setting. Dalits' conversions to other religious traditions, however, took place as massive group movements.[85] Conversion to well-established religions was their primary strategy for freedom, acceptance and legitimacy. Dalits converted to Buddhism, Islam, Christianity, Sikhism and other religions at various times. However, there is little evidence of Dalits' conversion to Christianity until the arrival of the Western missionaries.

Tens of thousands of Dalits joined Christianity when they heard missionaries preaching freedom and human dignity. The Paraiyars from India's south-eastern tip (1535–7) and Mukkuvars from India's southwestern parts (1544) joined Christianity after responding to Portuguese missionaries.[86] Paraiyans in Salem, Coimbatore and Erode converted to Christianity through the London Missionary Society.[87] Similarly, Pulayans in Kerala, Tigalas in Karnataka, Malas and Madigas in Andhra Pradesh, Chamars in Madhya Pradesh and Bihar, Churhas from Punjab, Vankars from Gujarat and Mahars from Maharashtra embraced Christianity.[88]

Churches' failure in accommodating converts Dalits believed that conversion would improve their social status.[89] However, Dalits' situation did not improve substantially after conversion. Paulson Pulikottil, for example, narrates an event that confirms the point. Charles Mead, a missionary of the London Missionary Society, married an educated woman from the Paraya caste in 1850. Mead's fellow evangelists opposed the marriage because of his wife' lower caste origin. They feared that the wedding would damage their mission in Travancore. Mead was forced to leave the London Missionary Society.[90] Mead's incident does not necessarily mean that the missionaries came to India with caste reservations. Instead, it suggests that they were concerned about hurting the sentiments of dominant caste Hindus. They might have worried that this marriage would hinder dominant caste Hindus from converting to Christianity.[91] Their hesitation, however, helped the survival of the caste system.

Robert de Nobili (1577–1656) represents another instance of this accommodative approach. He established a Catholic mission centre in Madurai in 1606, modelling himself as a dominant caste Hindu sage. Nobili followed dominant caste mannerisms and distanced himself from dominated caste Hindus.[92] He believed that conversion to Christianity does not force one to denounce their caste, nobility or usages. The Protestant missionaries also followed a programme of accommodation. They permitted the converts to retain their caste identity and accepted caste distinctions within their congregations.[93] Such techniques helped the survival of the caste system in the Indian churches. Nevertheless, I do not intend to overstate the missionary factor either. The dominant caste converts had formed the Caste Christian Associations in some parishes. They resisted the missionaries' attempts to enforce social interaction between the Dalit and the dominant caste converts, arguing that the missionaries have no rights to interfere with caste observances.[94] Because of such oppositions, most missionaries left the caste system untouched.

Similarly, the Catholic missionaries did not view caste as a religious institution. They approached it as a system of social stratification and chose to work within this system.[95] The Protestant missionaries also permitted their converts to retain their caste practices.[96] The case, as will be explained in Chapter 9, was similar in the Syrian Christian churches also. Hence, caste continued to control the churches because of the missionaries' attitudes and the dominant caste converts. It is evident from the Dalit Christians' report to the Simon Commission (1929). It states that they remain what they were before they became Christian untouchables.[97] Their self-designation does not necessarily disown Christian spirituality. It expresses their discontent with the presence of caste within the church. The exploitations of Dalits continued even after Indian independence. Thus, hierarchical thinking is deeply rooted in Indian society, and it has infiltrated the church as well. Consequently, the Dalits live as an oppressed majority within the churches.[98] The failure of the church is a grave mistake, and the church must repent. James Theophilus Appavoo voices a similar demand:

> You make us your flock of sheep,
> but they cut us up and make biriyani. (rice and lamb dish)
> They fry us like a side dish and recklessly eat us.
> Oh, father, you are the only true shepherd.[99]

Such failures in the 1980s alarmed the Dalits and, as will be further clarified in the next chapter, prompted them to search for theological answers to redress the Dalit situation.

Conclusion

The present chapter evaluated historical contexts, and the lived experiences behind Dalit theology's emergence as a counter-discourse to the dominant caste hegemony in the Indian Christian churches. As noted, Dalit theology did not develop overnight out of a vacuum. Instead, Dalit theology emerged out of historical necessities. Dalits have been living the life of a *Joothan*, suffering multiple discriminations socially, economically, culturally and politically. Some of them thought that the conversion would free them from caste oppression and joined Christian churches. However, the conversion failed the Dalits since it did not change their social status substantially. The Dalits continued to live as an oppressed majority at the periphery of the churches.

Secular mobilizations, which emerged from the subcontinent's margins, like the Dalit Panther movement, Dalit Sangharsh Samiti and the Dalit literature movement, highlighted Dalits' precarious situation and promoted Dalit consciousness. They inspired the Dalit Christian academics to evaluate Dalits' status within and beyond the boundaries of the Indian Christian churches. The churches' failure to facilitate the Dalits, assuring their freedom and the insensitivity of Indian Christian theology to the Dalit concerns, infuriated the Dalit academics and convinced them of the need to offer a theological alternative to complement secular movements to redress Dalits' situation. They searched for new avenues to solve their religious and cultural struggles. As will be explained in the next chapter, they found Latin American liberation and African American liberation theologies as their dialogue partners.

Chapter 3

GENEALOGY OF DALIT THEOLOGY SEEN THROUGH LIBERATION THEOLOGIES

Introduction

Badri Narayan recounts the story of Ekalavya, a tale from *The Mahabharata*, an ancient Indian epic.[1] According to this story, Dronacharya was a Brahmin archery tutor and the instructor of Pandavas and Kauravas.[2] Dronacharya refused to accept Ekalavya as his student because of Ekalavya's Dalit origin. Ekalavya went back to the forest and practised archery before a statue of Dronacharya. When Dronacharya learnt that Ekalavya had become a highly skilled warrior, he asked Ekalavya for his right thumb as *gurudakshina*.[3] Ekalavya, without hesitation, chopped off his thumb for Dronacharya. There have been some attempts to idolize Ekalavya. Shashikant Hingnekar, a Dalit poet, however, identifies caste influence in this episode and denounces Ekalavya.

> Oh Ekalavya,
> If you had kept your thumb,
> history would have happened somewhat differently,
> But you gave your thumb,
> and history also became theirs.
> Ekalavya, since that day they have not even given you a glance.
> Forgive me, Ekalavya, I won't be fooled now by their sweet words.
> My thumb will never be broken.[4]

Researchers like Arun Prabha Mukherjee, however, uncover favouritism in Ekalavya's episode and denounce Hingnekar, suggesting that Dronacharya feared that Ekalavya would surpass Arjuna, his much-loved student.[5] There is some truth in their claim. However, their suggestions overlook the dynamics of the caste system in this story. Dronacharya declined to accept Ekalavya not because of his preference for Arjuna, but because of his caste reservations. Similarly, scholars like Uma Chakraborty interpret this story as an upper-caste conspiracy to wipe out the Dalits.[6] Whatever be the case, the life of Ekalavya narrates the systematic oppression of the Dalits who dared to challenge the caste system.

The plight of the Dalits like Ekalavya is not a memory narrated in Indian classical literature alone. Dalits remain the most oppressed community in the present also. Ram Niwas Jatav, a Dalit farmer from Uttar Pradesh, for example, was murdered, and his wife and daughter were critically injured by dominant caste villagers in April 2018.[7] Similar incidents are noted globally and nationally. Zeid Ra'ad Al Hussein, UN High Commissioner for Human Rights, for instance, in his annual report and oral update on 7 March 2018 to the United Nations Human Rights Council, noted that he is disturbed by the discrimination and violence against Dalits.[8] Similarly, Dr Manmohan Singh, former Prime Minister of India, while delivering the first S. B. Rangnekar Memorial Lecture at Punjab University, in Chandigarh, on 11 April 2018, lamented that atrocities against Dalits are increasing steadily.[9] Hence, Dalits continue to be the worst victims of the caste system. Indian churches and Indian Christian theology tended to neglect them. Dalit theology, as clarified, emerged from that historical and social contexts, responding to Dalits' exclusion in Indian society, church life and theological discourse. It addresses Dalits' longing for a new heaven and a new earth, and as will be clarified, owes much to the family of liberation theologies. The proposals of liberation theologians were a strong point of departure for the Dalit academics. They developed the conceptual and hermeneutical frameworks based on Latin American and African American liberation theologies.[10]

Nevertheless, Dalit theology is not a carbon copy of liberation theologies. Indeed, the Indian context has played a significant role in formulating Dalit theology. The founders developed Dalit theology as a theological alternative to complement Dalit movements. Dalit theology disapproves of the philosophical and Vedantic influence upon Indian Christian theology and establishes that theology in India should not be relegated to abstract enterprises.[11] It demands people and praxis-oriented theology in India.[12] From such perspectives, Dalit theology seeks to find out what the Bible says about Dalits' liberation. The present chapter examines how the concepts of the liberation theologies motivated Dalit academics, who were discontented with the failures of the Indian Christian churches and the Indian Christian theology.

Indian Christian theology

Christianity has an oral tradition in India, which extends to 52 CE. According to this tradition, St Thomas, the Apostle, brought Christianity to India. However, Christianity did not develop as an Indian phenomenon because of Western missionary influences. Keshab Chandra Sen (1838–84), for example, criticized the 'foreign' nature of Christ and accused the missionaries of bringing a 'Western Christ' to India.[13] So too, Kappen, Wilson and Pieris note that the Christ of theology and popular devotion in India bears the marks of His origin in the West.[14] Similarly, John Mansford Prior observes:

> Whatever the nuances, however great the social contributions of the mission Churches in the past, however, heroic sacrifices of cross-cultural missionaries over the centuries, the fact remains in stark clarity: the Latin Churches of Asia are a

foreign presence. They are alien in the official dress of their rituals (despite use of the mother tongue); alien in their formation of cultic and community leaders in foreign thought patterns in seminaries whose professors are foreign-educated; alien in its large, often rich, institutions among people who are generally poor; above all alien in that Christians have had to uproot themselves from their own cultural identity in order to claim a 'hybrid' Christian one.[15]

Such reservations inspired some scholars, who began to explain Christian principles using Indian categories of thought. They wanted to represent Christianity intelligibly and commendably to Hindus. Keshab Chandra Sen, for instance, suggested that the Trinity could be expounded based on the Hindu concept of Brahman as *sat-cit-ananda*.[16] Hence, Indian Christian theology seeks to present Jesus in an inculturated and indigenized manner using Hindu philosophical systems.[17] Nevertheless, Indian Christian theology is more than drawing parallels between Christianity and Hinduism. It restates theological propositions pertinent in India and initiates a dialogue between Christ and Indians.

Brahmabandhav Upadhyay (1861–1907), Vengal Chakkarai (1880–1958), Pandipeddi Chenchiah (1886–1959) and A. J. Appasamy (1891–1975) were prominent figures in its early phase. They attempted to reinterpret Bible relevantly to the Indian contexts, using Hindu philosophical expressions. Brahmabandhav, for instance, did not renounce Hinduism after his baptism.[18] He wanted to live as a Catholic without ceasing to be a Hindu by culture. Rabindranath Tagore (1861–1941), the first non-European Nobel laureate in literature, described Brahmabandhav as 'a Roman Catholic ascetic yet a Vedantin'.[19] Brahmabandhav sought to win over Hindu philosophy to the service of Christianity and followed Hinduism as his set of social obligations but Christianity as his way of salvation and religious life.[20] Brahmabandhav used the teachings of Sankara extensively.[21]

Scholars like Chakkarai, Chenchiah and Appasamy followed similar routes. Thus, Indian Christian theology attempted to liberate Indian Christianity from Western influence. However, Dalit theologians have some reservations against it. They rightly argue that the Indian Christian theology failed to include Dalits' immanent experiences and their contextual concerns.[22] Dalit academics also found Indian Christian theology as an articulation of philosophical and theological constructs.[23]

Dalit critique of Indian Christian theology

Indian Christian theologians mostly come from elite backgrounds. They used Hindu categories to explain the Christian faith. Appasamy, for instance, elucidates Jesus' claim that 'I and the Father are one' (John 10.30). He worried that Jesus' assertion can mislead some Hindus to interpret it based on the Advaitic assertion that 'I am Brahman'.[24] Appasamy ruled out the dualistic reading and suggested (using Ramanuja's *Vishishtadvaita*) that the oneness between Jesus and His Father was moral.[25] It is a union of love and work. It is not an identity in their essential nature.

We can, therefore, say that 'I and the Father are one' did not refer to any oneness or identity in the real nature of God and Jesus. The relation between God and Jesus was a personal one. God was his Father and Jesus was His Son. He loved his Father; he realised his entire dependence on Him.[26]

Thus, for scholars like Appasamy, Jesus' claim implies that Jesus was utterly submissive to the Father's will, loving what the Father loved and carrying out the Father's intentions. Dalit theologians disapproved of such interpretations, based on sophisticated Sanskritic vocabularies since they feared that the philosophical readings could alienate the Dalits and strengthen the caste communities' interests. They believed that Sanskritic obsession reduced Indian Christian theology to an academic discipline and an intellectual activity which failed to include Dalits' immanent experiences.[27] From such backgrounds, Dalit academics turned to contextual theologies. Latin American theology was their first dialogue partner, which provided them with the hermeneutical principles and ideological background.

Latin American liberation theology

Liberation theology is a Christian response to the Latin American situation, which emerged in the 1960s. Liberation theology responds to the unjust situation of the Latin Americans, who have been living with starvation wages, unemployment, lack of adequate housing and labour unrest.[28] Further, liberation theology counters some failures of the Catholic Church. The collaboration between the church and the corrupt political regimes, for example, provoked many believers and clergy. They felt that traditional theology and its conciliar-dogmatic definitions were inadequate to address the Latin American situation.[29] They began to associate with secular and political ideologies to redress their social standing, which resulted in the political and ecclesiastical division.[30] Theologians like Father Ernesto Cardenal and Miguel d'Escoto became ministers in Daniel Ortega's revolutionary government.[31] It needs to be emphasized, though, that the teachings of Vatican II (1962–5) deeply inspired liberation theology.[32] Gutiérrez clarifies:

> Liberation theology (which is an expression of the right of the poor to think out their own faith) has not been an automatic result of this situation and the changes it has undergone. It represents rather an attempt to accept the invitation of Pope John XXIII and the Second Vatican Council and interpret this sign of the times by reflecting on it critically in the light of God's word.[33]

David G. Timberman also claims that Latin American theology is the continuation of the Vatican Council.[34] Similarly, Latin American theology is theology for Latin Americans by the Latin Americans, which emerged out of religious, political and social necessities.[35] Latin American theology interprets the Bible through the eyes of the victims in Latin America.[36] It is a movement of the lost and the least, which approaches poverty and other social misappropriations as a manifestation of structural sin, emphasizes social praxis over dogma and envisions a restructuring of Latin American society.[37]

As Mario I. Aguilar clarifies, Latin American theology evolved through a rereading of theological paradigms associated with traditional dogmatic statements.[38] Base communities, small groups of Christians, perhaps fifteen to thirty people, who get together about once a week, played a significant role in developing liberation theology.[39] Lay members interpreted the Bible according to their local situations in such gatherings.[40] Through similar initiatives, liberation theology works from the bottom-up to empower Latin Americans to affirm their cultural and religious identity.[41] It explains mundane realities from the underside of history and challenges domination and suppression, imperialism and colonialism, undernourishment and shortage, power and powerlessness, frustration and despair.[42] Its insights come from small communities of the poorest and least literate men and women in Latin America.[43]

Latin American liberation theology guided Dalit academics. Indeed, scholars like Mukti Barton have already suggested that Dalit theology shares the Latin American critique of Western theology.[44] This book will now explain some possible points of conceptual contacts between them. Such a study hopes to place Dalit theology in its ideal setting.

Critique of traditional theology

Latin American academics were discontent with traditional Western theology. They found traditional theology as an ideology for the bourgeois, securing freedom as individual and ahistorical.[45] From such backgrounds, liberation theology demands a substantial commitment to historical transformation in theological interpretations.[46] Latin American theology also includes a hermeneutical switch from Western theology to a theology of the poor. Likewise, it affirms that scholastic endeavours should not begin from the head, and theologians should be in touch with human experiences.[47] Liberation theology reflects the experiences of ordinary believers.[48] It is a theology for and by the losers of the world.[49] Dalit theology, as clarified, shares Latin American theology's critique of Western theology. It critically revisits traditional Indian Christian theology from a Dalit outlook.

God as liberator

Traditional theology explains God's essence, nature, attributes and existence in philosophical terms.[50] It narrates God as the uncaused cause of all things which exists. Traditional theology affirms that God is the ultimate origin and sovereign governing principle of all that exists. It emphasizes God's sovereignty, placing God beyond whatever human beings can imagine.[51] Further, traditional theology suggests that God is one (Deut. 6.4-6; 1 Cor. 8.4-6), unique (Isa. 40.13-28), transcendent (Num. 23.19; Ps. 50.21), eternal, uncreated and changeless.[52] Latin American liberation theology challenges such philosophical and monarchical proposals and approaches God from the perspective of the poor, seeking to redefine the image of God popularized by dogmatic theology.[53]

Latin American theology also highlights that God sides with the poor.[54] From such contexts, Latin American theology depicts God as a liberator more than anything else. The Exodus narrative, which explains how God identifies with the dispossessed and aids them in their struggle against their oppressors, helped liberation theology develop such an image. Gutiérrez, for instance, remarks that the God of the Bible is liberating, a God who destroys myths and alienations. God intervenes in history to break down structures of injustice. He raises the prophets to point out the way of justice and mercy. Furthermore, God causes empires to fall and raises the oppressed.[55]

Dalit theology has appropriated the Exodus paradigm, which has incredible implications for Dalit theology. James Massey, for instance, notes that the Exodus event communicates God's solidarity with the oppressed, including the Dalits.[56] Dalit theology redefines God's initiative in liberating Israel as God's willingness to redeem the Dalits. It suggests that the God of the oppressed will liberate Dalits from all forms of dominance.[57]

Jesus as liberator

Christology, as developed by European Catholic missionaries, dominated Latin America for more than 470 years.[58] They concentrated on epistemological issues and stressed the 'divinity of Christ rather than his real and lived humanity'.[59] They highlighted an image of a suffering, dying Jesus, a helpless infant or Jesus as a divine monarch. Latin American theology challenges such Christological formulations and demands a hermeneutical switch since they do not help the suffering Latin Americans to overcome their present situations. Latin American theology suggests that the Christological formulas must attend to Latin American realities of life.[60] Sobrino, for instance, criticizes the Chalcedonian Christological affirmation for being too abstract and failing to resonate with people's experience of Jesus.[61]

What is innovative with Latin American Christology? Latin American Christology uses the same information about Jesus as classical Christology. However, it interprets traditions differently. Instead of spiritualizing biblical information, it interprets the Bible to suggest how Jesus can empower the poor in Latin America.[62] Similarly, Latin American theology projects Jesus as 'part of the ongoing dialogue between the oppressed and oppressors'.[63] From such perspectives, Latin American academics highlight Jesus as one amidst the rejected and the 'nobodies'.[64] They claim that the most suitable image of Jesus in Latin America is that of a liberator who saves the oppressed from slavery.[65] Jesus breaks down the obstacles that had limited human potential and empowered the disadvantaged. Further, he proclaimed God's preferential option for this sector of society and died as one of them because he clashed with the established structures of power.

Dalit theology developed this concept. For Dalit theologians, Jesus is more than a Liberator of Dalits. He is a God who became a Dalit. Dalit academics assert

Jesus' Dalitness as a principal key to understand Jesus' divine–human unity. Dalit theology uses Jesus' mixed ancestry, implied in the Matthean genealogy, as a clue to his Dalitness. Dalit theology also elaborates Jesus' association with impure sections of society like tax collectors, prostitutes and lepers. He also stood with the Samaritans, the Dalits of his time, who were the nobodies in his society. Hence, Jesus is a friend of the Dalits and suffered like the Dalits. K. P. Kuruvila, for example, notes that Jesus was the hungry one, the thirsty, the naked and the unwanted one in his society who had a shameful death like most of the Dalits.[66] After recognizing such similarities, Martien E. Brinkman suggests that Jesus became a Dalit:

> If God wants to be present in Jesus' earthly life, with the 'impure' family tree containing two prostitutes (Rahab and Tamar), four 'foreign' women (Rebecca, Rachel, Rahab and Ruth), someone who committed adultery (Bathsheba), a mother who had a child out of wedlock, a father belonging to the working class, whereas Jesus himself led a life filled with 'impure' contacts with Samaritans, adulterous women and tax collectors, he would all the more want to be present among the Dalits.[67]

As seen, Dalit theology, along with Latin American liberation theology, believes that Jesus is a Liberator. However, for Dalit theology, Jesus is not or an external empathetic supporter. He is a Dalit who fights for their rights together with them.

Preferential option for the poor

Latin American liberation theology functions as the authentic source for understanding Christian practice in Latin American political and economic assertions.[68] It affirms that God has a preferential option for the poor. Nevertheless, God's option, as Latin American academics understand, is not an abstract theological concept.[69] God's preferential option demands that theology must begin from below with the sufferings and distress of the insignificant.[70] God's option further invites the church and society to respond to the cry of the needy by changing the structures that enslave the poor and limit their potential.[71] Latin American interpretation of God's option is one of the most significant contributions of liberation theology.[72] However, God's option is not exclusive. Gustavo Gutiérrez clarifies:

> God's love is universal. At the same time, God clearly prefers the least, the abandoned, the insignificant person. The preference is a manifestation of the universality of God's love. There is no contradiction between universality and preference … One is not the negation of the other.[73]

As seen, Latin American liberation theology emphasizes God's option for the poor. Dalit theology develops it as suggesting God's preferential option to the Dalits. Dalit theologians like T. Victor, for instance, propose that God's preferential option suggests an option for the Dalits also.[74]

Dalit appropriation of Latin American theology

The emergence of Dalit theology owes much to Latin American theology. However, it is not a duplicate of liberation theology. Dalit theology appropriated the call for a contextual theology because of historical necessity. It adopted insights from liberation theology and applied them to Dalit contexts. However, there are many notable differences between Latin American and Indian contexts. Dictatorship and a predominantly Christian culture characterized the former, while the latter is democratic, multireligious and multicultural. Moreover, Dalit culture and spirituality, as will be explained in the next chapter, is radically different from the Latin American context. However, Latin American theology is not the only theological impetus behind Dalit theology. As will be clarified, African American theology has also impacted Dalit theology.

African American theology

The descendants of enslaved Africans proposed African American theology during the late 1960s and the 1970s.[75] It counters racial segregation and discrimination of more than 20 million African Americans.[76] African American theology promotes the African American struggle for a better world in the present.[77] Its roots go back to the early slave days, which dislocated millions of Africans.[78] While estimates vary, approximately 20 million Africans were transported to America.[79]

The slave trade was a horrific and brutal system. Women and men were chained together and kept dirty on the slave ships. Malnutrition and disease were part of the life of the enslaved people.[80] Slave women also faced rape and sexual abuse.[81] Their troubles did not end in the slave ships if they survived the journey. Their masters in their new world mistreated them and labelled them as infidels, pagans, heathenish, non-being, primitive, barbarians and without a soul and feelings.[82] The contempt, mistreatment and segregation resulted in the structured political alienation of enslaved Africans. Their descendants continued to be oppressed and encountered racial inequalities because of their skin colour. They have been the American outcasts par excellence like Native Americans.[83] They have been the permissible victims of American society. African American theology emerged from that historical context when some African American priests reinterpreted the Christian faith through the Black sufferings.[84]

African American theology applies the power of the Gospel to African Americans who live under white oppression.[85] It is also a religious counterpart of the secular movement called Black power.[86] Ultimately, African American theology responds to the suffering and alienation of African Americans. It is a radical response from the underside of American religious history.[87] It interprets the socio-historical experiences of the African Americans in light of the revelation of Jesus Christ. It attempts to reinterpret biblical texts in the context of human striving for African American emancipation. Therefore, many scholars describe it as 'people's theology', 'theology of the streets' and 'an earthly theology'.[88]

African American theology and Dalit theology have some points of contacts. African American theology focuses on the African Americans, while Dalit theology concentrates on the Dalits. Oppression and suffering characterize the status of the Dalits and the African Americans.[89] Shetty and Rashidi, therefore, call Dalits 'the Black Untouchables of India'.[90] Scholars like Schouten acknowledge the African American theology's influence upon Dalit theology.[91]

Black Panther movement and Dalit theology

The Black Panther movement was one of the most influential revolutionary organizations developed in America.[92] It emerged as African Americans' protest against their treacherous living conditions. Its followers perceived African American communities as colonies occupied by white police.[93] The Panthers aimed at empowering African Americans and attempted to liberate African Americans from white racist oppression. It influenced the Dalit Panther movement in Maharashtra.[94] The name 'Dalit Panther' movement also echoes the 'Black Panther' movement. Dalit Panthers' manifesto highlight the relationship with Black Panthers:

> Due to the hideous plot of American imperialism, the Third Dalit World, that is, oppressed nations, and Dalit people are suffering. Even in America, a handful of reactionary whites are exploiting blacks. To meet the force of reaction and remove this exploitation, the Black Panther movement grew. From the Black Panthers, Black Power emerged. The fire of the struggles has thrown out sparks into the country. We claim a close relationship with this struggle.[95]

Dalit Panthers, as seen, have influenced Dalit theology. The concept of a Dalit Christ seems to be another example of African American influence.

Black Christ and Dalit Christ

African American theology considers traditional American theology as a theology of the white oppressor, conditioned and distorted by white supremacy, which created a white Christ as a genuine picture of Jesus.[96] African American theology disowns such images and claims that Jesus, as seen in the biblical narratives, was not a romantic hero. He was involved in the sufferings of the destitute.[97] For them, 'Jesus was the non-white leader of a non-white people struggling for national liberation against the rule of a white nation, Rome'.[98] So too, Douglas claims that Jesus has black skin and features and is committed to the Black community's struggle.[99] Noting Jesus' preference for the oppressed, Cone had already explained Jesus' preference for the Black people in the *God of the Oppressed*. For him, Jesus Christ enters the world where the poor, the despised and the Black are, disclosing that he is with them, enduring their humiliation.[100] He explains:

> [Jesus] meets the blacks where they are and becomes one of them. We see him there with his black face and big black hands lounging on a street corner ... For

whites to find him with big lips and kinky hair is as offensive as it was for the Pharisees to find him partying with tax-collectors. But whether whites want to hear it or not, Christ is black, baby, with all the features which are so detestable to white society.[101]

Thus, for African American theology, Jesus is a companion of the oppressed. He fights against the entire structures of injustice that dehumanizes those who live on the brink of existence. This portrait has influenced Dalit theological undertakings. Dalit theology perceives Jesus as a Dalit because of his birth and vocation. Antony Kalliyath, for instance, acknowledges that 'Jesus had a Dalit birth, Dalit life, a Dalit death, and a Dalit burial'.[102] Similarly, Jesus works with Joseph, a carpenter. He had been employed as a manual labourer like the Dalits. Moreover, Jesus had identified himself with the outcasts of his day like lepers, tax collectors and Samaritans. He had touched the sick and the dead. Hence, Dalit theology proposes Jesus' Dalitness based on his birth and his identification with the voiceless community.[103]

Dalit theologians were likely influenced by African American theology to designate Jesus as a Dalit. Like African American theologians who assert the blackness of Jesus, Dalit theologians affirm Jesus' Dalitness because of his birth and identification with the poor of his day. Kuruvila, for example, had already identified African American influence behind 'Dalit Christ'. He substantiated his claim by noting that James Cone, in an interview with the Advisory Board of *Dalit International*, appreciated the Dalit appropriation of African American theology.[104]

Black experience and Dalit experience

African American theology counters white hegemony and accuses white Christianity of failing to address the African Americans' immanent experiences. Traditional American theology, African Americans rightly accuse, neglected the African American situation as illegitimate and inauthentic.[105] African American theology recommends that theology, which overlooks the African American experiences, is only an alienated and abstract discourse.[106] Cone clarifies:

> Theology [in America] is largely an intellectual game unrelated to the issues of life and death. It is impossible to respond creatively and prophetically to the life-situational problems of society without identifying with the problems of the disinherited and unwanted in society. Few American theologians have made that identification with poor blacks in America but have themselves contributed to the system which enslaves black people.[107]

Cone alleges that white theologians marginalized the Black experience.[108] However, Cone does not claim that such neglect is intentional. He clarifies that white theologians overlook the Black experience because they live in a racist society. The oppression of African Americans does not occupy a significant item on the agenda of white academics. From such a background, Cone questions the relevance of traditional American theology. He proposes that the theology developed for white oppressors cannot represent African Americans and, therefore, he demanded African Church leaders to create a theology relevant to their experience.[109] Cone suggests that American theology must include the African American situation, their tears and sorrows. There can be no theology relevant to African Americans, which disregards the Black experience. It must be the point of departure for theologizing in America.[110] Thus, African American theology presses the primacy of Black experience for theologizing in America.

As noted, Dalit theology has benefited from the Black experience. Dalit theology, as seen, is a theology articulated by the Dalits on behalf of Dalits.[111] It maintains that dominant caste converts produced Indian Christian theology. It believes that Indian Christian theology ignored the Dalit experience. Wilfred, K. V. Kuruvila, K. P. Kuruvila and Nirmal rightly affirm that Dalit experience is a primary source for theology in the Indian subcontinent.[112] It seems that African American theology's emphasis on African American experience has helped Dalit theologians to develop their insistence on Dalit experience. Like African American theologians who criticized white theologians and white theology, Dalit theologians condemn non-Dalits and Indian Christian theology.

Dalit appropriation of African American theology

Dalit theology, as seen, appropriated some conceptual examples of African American theology. It used them to articulate a theology for the Dalits. Dalit theology and African American theology, as clarified, developed out of the discontent towards Western Christianity and traditional theology in their non-Western contexts. The Black Panther movement influenced Dalit theology also. Furthermore, African American theology came into being in the 1960s. Dalit theology, on the other hand, was proposed only in the 1980s. The two intervening decades might have helped Dalit theologians to read African American theological insights.

As seen, the Dalit academics were discontent with Dalits' situation. Their association with Latin American and African American theologies provided them with new subjects and contexts for theologizing. They helped Dalit academics to affirm the legitimacy of doing theology based on Dalits' immanent experiences and empowered Dalit theologians to advocate the primacy of their experiences for their theological reflection. From such perspectives, they proposed Dalit theology in radical discontinuity with Indian Christian theology.

Conclusion

Dalit theology did not emerge overnight, and one single moment that constitutes the inauguration of Dalit theology does not exist. It is the product of multiple, long-term historical and theological developments. The period between 1970 and 1980 was a time of great revolutionary ferment for Dalit theology. During these formative years, a growing sensitivity to the political disregard for the problems of

Dalits, violence against Dalits, the formation of Dalit movements for promoting Dalit struggles against casteism and the Dalit literature movement to educate Dalits and the Church's failure in accommodating Dalit Christians informed Dalits of their deplorable situation. Further, those movements convinced the Dalits of the need to engage in the process of liberation from the caste system. This conviction evoked a sense of urgency to respond theologically to the caste system. Dalit consciousness further prompted Dalit theologians to search resources for their response. Moreover, contacts with Latin American liberation theology and African American theology further convinced Dalit academics that Indian Christian theology, with its Sanskritic obsession and dominant caste inclination, failed to recognize Dalits' pathos and the negative impact of the caste upon Dalits. It was striking for them that Dalits' horrid condition, their sorrows and their daily exclusion did not influence theological expressions in India substantially.

Such a dangerous situation convinced the first-generation Dalit theologians that there is 'a vacant space' to be explored for a theology that recognizes that Dalits are disenfranchised in Indian society. From this background, they proposed Dalit theology in radical discontinuity with Indian Christian theology. Dalit theology attempted to articulate principles that Indian Christian theology has underappreciated. This attempt has been innovative in the Indian theological scene. However, as will be argued in the next chapter, the relevance of such attempts needs to be established. The next chapter, therefore, will question Dalit theology through Dalits' forgotten voices and will propose that Dalit theology needs a hermeneutical switch and a paradigm that is more sensitive to Dalits' contexts.

Chapter 4

QUESTIONING DALIT THEOLOGY THROUGH DALITS' FORGOTTEN VOICES

Introduction

Bede Griffiths (1906–93) was a British Benedictine monk who lived in South India as a guru named Swami Dayananda. His book published in Brazil recounts his cross-religious encounters as a Western Christian with Indian spiritual and cultural resources:

> Besides being a Christian, I need to be Hindu, Buddhist, Jainist, Zoroastrian, Sikh, Muslim and Jew. Only in this way will I be able to know the truth and encounter the point of reconciliation of all religions. This is the revolution that has to happen in the mind of Western peoples. For centuries now, this has been cast aside.[1]

Building inspirations from his associations with outsiders in India's pluralistic contexts, Griffiths demands a similar initiative from Western Christians. He wanted them to open their doors for their religious others. Griffiths's call was crucial in Latin America in the 1990s since Latin America has been homogenous to a considerable extent because of the overwhelmingly Catholic population.[2] With some exceptions, like the Jewish community in Argentina, Latin America did not have significant and organized non-Christian religions.[3] Religious pluralism and ecumenism, therefore, had not been a priority there.[4]

Such contexts influenced liberation theologians, and they tended to neglect the diversity and the liberative potential of non-Christian traditions by implicitly promoting a theological camp mentality. Michelle A. Gonzalez, for instance, notes:

> Liberation theologies have historically ignored the substantial influence of non-Christian religions on Christianity, instead arguing for a biblically based liberationist message that is revealed in the concrete religious practices of marginalised communities. In addition to relying heavily on the Christian bible, some liberation theologians draw from the theology revealed in the popular religious practices of Christian communities, particularly in their understanding of Jesus and in Catholic circles, Mary.[5]

The same is true of African American theology also. Gonzalez, for example, argues that even though African American theologians speak of the Black Church and Black experience as though their research addresses the Black community entirely, what they mean is Christian (overwhelmingly Protestant) African American religious experience. They overlook the diversity of Black religion in the United States and ignore non-Christian religions.[6] Similarly, Delroy A. Reid-Salmon clarifies:

> African American theology neither considers the Caribbean Diasporan experience as an appropriate starting point for theological inquiry nor does it address the issues and concerns of the Caribbean Diaspora despite this phenomenological entity being in existence in America for just over a little more than one hundred years.[7]

The founders of Dalit theology, as argued, were influenced by Latin American and African American theologies, and they followed Latin American and African American conceptual backgrounds. So too, they adopted Latin American and African American hermeneutics significantly. They proposed the wandering Aramean (Deut. 26.5-9) and the suffering servant (Isa. 53.3-12) as Dalit theology's fundamental paradigms. Nirmal, for instance, discusses how the Deuteronomic creed can advance Dalit theology, which shows Latin American and African American influence upon his methodological framework. The Deuteronomic creed, for example, is a proclamation of the Exodus narrative, which is one of the primary motivations behind Latin American and African American theologies.[8] Using the Deuteronomic retelling of Israel's affliction and oppression, Nirmal narrates Dalits' movement from 'no people' to 'God's people'.[9] Nevertheless, Nirmal was not satisfied with the Deuteronomic creed. The historical Dalit consciousness, Nirmal clarifies, depicts greater and deeper pathos than the Deuteronomic creed since Dalits have been denied their basic humanity and the wandering Aramean's nomadic freedom for many centuries. Therefore, Nirmal suggests that Dalit theology's goal is the 'realisation of our full humanness or conversely, our full divinity, the ideal of the *imago Dei*, the Image of God in us'.[10] Similarly, Balasundaram explains:

> The goal of Dalit theology is the liberation of the Dalits and their empowerment, i.e., strengthening Dalits, providing comfort to them, the good news that God is with them in their struggle, that they are God's children and that they have their own God-given identity and that they are people with worth and dignity. That is, human dignity is more important than the question of economic emancipation.[11]

Scholars like Nirmal and Balasundaram often move from Dalit consciousness to a biblical paradigm without inquiring about Dalits' contexts sufficiently, which, as Boopalan notes, have incredible resources to subvert the caste, making fun of its cruel presuppositions and imagining ways of being and doing that envision a just world.[12] Nirmal, however, limits his discussion to the biblical contexts substantially, identifies features of the Deuteronomic creed, illuminates their implications and integrates them to Dalits' contexts. Similar attempts may have some advantages in predominantly Christian contexts like Latin America. However, such undertakings, which Christianize Dalits' worldview significantly, are problematic. Superimposing such hermeneutical examples, for example, can also overlook how Dalits' worldview and counter-formulations underpin the caste hegemony.[13] Likewise, Dalits' resources become objects, and biblical understandings are injected into them.[14] Such impositions can override Dalits' counter-formulations, marginalize Dalits' identity envisioned in Dalits' contexts, implant Christian identity developed in Latin American and African American contexts and impose a different worldview onto Dalits' historical-cultural world.[15] This superimposition may marginalize Dalits' subversive voices into the periphery of Dalit theology.[16] Similarly, as Jeremiah notes, it may reduce the possibility of Dalit Christians continuing their pre-Christian worldview.[17] Such a cross-cultural and cross-religious discontinuity in Dalit hermeneutics necessitates further interrogation.

Perhaps, the proposal of some African American theologians who suggest the hermeneutics of return to Black resources like African traditional religions, slave narratives and folklore to help African American theology overcome its alienation from Black contexts can reorient Dalit theology.[18] A reappreciation of Dalits' religio-cultural worldviews, similar to African American undertakings, will assist Dalit theology if we take Dalits' counter-ontology and the epistemology of resistance seriously. Abraham Ayrookuzhiel, as noted, cautioned against Dalits turning their backs entirely on their religious and cultural foundations and proposed that Dalit culture and religion are not vacant spaces. He reminded that Dalits' culture and religion have abundant resources to further Dalit theology by interrogating, challenging, rejecting and deconstructing the caste discourses and advised Dalit academics to explore the lived experiences narrated through the cultural and religious symbolism and their impacts upon the Dalits.[19]

Admittedly, Ayrookuzhiel's demand is a wake-up call for the Dalit academics to reclaim and explore the liberative voices in Dalits' worldview. So too, I acknowledge the implications of his proposals for Syrian Christian academics like me also. A crossing into Dalits' contexts can unpack Syrian Christians' caste prejudices, improve cross-cultural adaptability, develop an awareness of the surprises, confusions and, sometimes, tensions of the Dalit world and empower Syrian Christians to connect with the Dalit ethos profoundly. It is to be noted, however, that my attempt is not entirely new. Some Syrian Christians, such as Aleaz and Mor Coorilos, had already taken up Ayrookuzhiel's proposals. The Dalit academics have accepted them, though with some reservations. This book seeks to join such academics who share my social location in pursuing further dialogue within and between these traditions, making Dalit theology more relevant to Dalits' contexts and advancing Dalit–Syrian Christian dialogues.

However, I am not proposing any romantic nostalgia but a conscious attempt to rediscover and rehabilitate Dalits' religio-cultural values to promote a continuous dialogue between the Bible and Dalits' culture. In related but African contexts,

Luke Mbefo suggests that African American ancestors had their view of their world and their place within it. They had their lifestyle and religious upbringing. Further, they possessed a self-contained and independently developed cultural integrity. From such contexts, Mbefo demands to resurrect the culture of African ancestors to establish an authentic African American theology.[20] Mbefo's proposal is an urgent demand in Dalits' contexts also. Samuel, for instance, clarifies:

> Dalit communities have had their own distinct worship, theology and metaphysics throughout history. Ostracized from main society as untouchables and outcastes, (whenever that originated in history), they were pushed and forced to evolve their own religious practices. And scholars are strongly convinced that these religious faiths, no matter how illogical and irrational it might have appeared for the caste communities and the European colonizers, must have been and indeed continue to be meaningful and empowering for the Dalits.[21]

As will be further clarified, Dalits' culture and religion are essential locations to identify their assumptions, values, judgements and commitments underlying their understanding of reality; their ethical and ontological choices and their responses to the absolutist claims of the caste hegemony. Such culturally structured and sanctioned elements have incredible resources to challenge the caste discourses, reimagine the world and seek redress. Dalit theology should develop its theoretical premises along the lines of Dalit contexts. Nevertheless, this book does not suggest a unilateral borrowing of Dalit culture either. Instead, I propose a deliberate attempt to listen to Dalits' voices and learn from their resistance to socio-political humiliation, which will help Dalit theology develop and mature as an authentic Indian theology. From such backgrounds, this book will question the dominant paradigms of Dalit theology through Dalits' forgotten voices and anti-caste philosophers like Chokhamela, Karmamela, Ravidas, Kabir, Nandanar and Narayana Guru.

Revisiting the paradigms of Dalit theology

The wandering Aramean in the Deuteronomic creed and the suffering servant in Isaiah are two fundamental paradigms of Dalit theology. The Deuteronomic creed describes God as Dalits' God by invoking parallels between God's activities among the Jews and God's continuing mission among Dalits. Nirmal expounded the Deuteronomic account because he believed that it would help the Dalits to reflect upon their experiences. However, a reinterpretation of this creed is not without problems, and as will be argued, it has only limited potential in Dalits' contexts.

The Deuteronomic creed

The Deuteronomic creed is a confession of faith; the Israelites were obliged to profess while offering first fruits at the sanctuary. It recalls their past, their migration to Egypt, their sufferings in Egypt and their miraculous escape. Gerhard von Rad understood this creed as 'an ancient credo', confessing the most authentic core of Israel's faith.[22] Van Seters, however, noted that this creed overlooks the patriarchal sojourn in Canaan, which is evident in Genesis.[23] His proposal has influenced some scholars who claim that this passage was most likely to be a Deuteronomic composition from the post-exilic period.[24] Whatever be the composition history, the creed affirms that the Lord who revealed his name to Moses is the same Lord who had liberated Israel and led them into the Promised Land. Deuteronomic creed clarifies the Lord's identity, Israel's identity, Israel's sufferings and liberation.

Dalit theology takes Hebrew cultural and religious consciousness in the Deuteronomic creed as a model for its theological base. As Dalit theology interprets, this confessional formula combines Israel's identity and liberation and speaks to Dalits' experience and situation.[25] Nirmal, for example, suggests that God's actions in Israel's history can help Dalits understand their historical situation and celebrate their new existence as Christian Dalits. He emphasizes that the wandering Aramean becomes a mighty nation despite their modest beginnings. Nirmal finds inspiration from this upbringing that changed the fate of the wandering Aramean's descendants and suggests that the Dalits should be aware of the historical Dalit consciousness and the present Christian consciousness.[26] He expounds further that Dalit Christians are 'not just Dalits', but 'are Christian Dalits' and clarifies that Dalits' exodus from Hinduism to Christianity is a valuable experience.[27] He compares Dalit consciousness with the wandering Aramean's sufferings and highlights the redundancy of the creed in describing Dalit:

> When my Dalit ancestor walked the dusty roads of his village, the Sa Varnas tied a tree-branch around his waist so that he would not leave any unclean foot-prints and pollute the roads. The Sa Varnas tied an earthen pot around my [D]alit ancestor's neck to serve as a spittle. If ever my Dalit ancestor tried to learn Sanskrit or any sophisticated language, the oppressors gagged him permanently by pouring molten lead down his throat. My [D]alit mother and sisters were forbidden to wear any blouses, and the Sa Varnas feasted their eyes on their bare bosoms. The Sa Varnas denied my Dalit ancestor any access to public wells and reservoirs. They denied him the entry to their temples and places of worship. My Dalit consciousness, therefore, has an unparalleled depth of pathos and misery.[28]

Further, Nirmal suggests that the pathos, misery and Dalit consciousness should inform Dalit theology. His claim is profound and challenging. However, without elaborating the claim, Nirmal discusses how the Deuteronomic creed may further Dalit theology. He proposes that the creed informs that 'signs and wonders' are not enough for Dalit liberation and clarifies that Dalits need a 'mighty hand' and an 'outstretched arm'.[29] While offering a sound biblical model, such a methodological orientation overlooks the richness and wisdom of Dalits' heritage; how Dalits resisted caste hegemony and maintained an alternative worldview, counter-ontology, the epistemology of resistance; and their relevance to Dalits' liberation.

So too, this methodology elevates the biblical paradigms developed in Latin American and African American contexts as the dominant self. It relegates the subversive voices in Dalits' resources as the dominated self in Dalit theology. From such contexts, this chapter will evaluate Dalits' appropriation of the Deuteronomic creed and Isaiah's suffering servant against the counter-formulations; alternative moral visions and Dalits' liberation and reconciliation ethic and their proposals for orienting Dalits in ethical and ontological choices.

Deuteronomic creed and Dalits' contexts There have been some challenges to the Dalit appropriation of the Deuteronomic creed. Keith Hebden and Antony Thumma, for example, lament that Dalit theologians continue to explore the Deuteronomic creed and the Exodus background even after liberation theology has moved away from it.[30] Clarke and Rajkumar challenge it because of the creed's incompatibility with Dalits' backgrounds. Unlike Nirmal, Clarke and Rajkumar incorporate a journey through Dalits' worldviews, cultural symbols and religious practices before arriving at Dalit theology. They argue that Dalit culture and religion, though include Dalit pathos, have more to offer than just pathos.

Clarke, for instance, cautions that Dalit theology failed to take seriously the symbolism of pathos manifested in the Dalit religion and culture.[31] From this context, Clarke compares God's image submerged in the Exodus narrative with god's image in Dalits' thinking. He notes that the Deuteronomic picture of an omnipotent God who reconfigures the world with a 'mighty hand' and an 'outstretched arm' does not find a principal place in Dalits' religion. In Dalits' contexts, Clarke clarifies, the mighty acts of God, which deliver the oppressed, have either changed their aim or exhausted themselves. Therefore, Clarke demands Dalit scholars to revisit God's image suggested by Dalit theology against Dalits' contextual realities.[32] Rajkumar suggests that God's image in the Deuteronomic creed contradicts Dalits' contexts.[33] Dalits' deities in Tamil Nadu, for instance, are not masters. They are servants of master gods, and like their devotees, they serve the deities of the dominant castes. The temple authorities place them outside the temple wall.[34] Thus, God's image that emerges out of the creed seems incompatible with Dalits' contexts. Dalits' devotion to Pochamma will clarify this further.

Dalit worship of Pochamma Devi The Dalits of Andhra Pradesh worship Pochamma Devi.[35] She is supposed to take care of everyone in the village.[36] She is gender-neutral, class-neutral and caste-neutral in her dealings with human beings. The devotees can talk to Pochamma as they speak among themselves. They may call their goddess 'Mother'. The prayer to Pochamma seems like dialogue as they say, 'We have seeded the fields, now you must ensure that the crops grow well, one of our children is sick it is your bounden duty to cure her.' This dialogical nature indicates a close relationship between the deity and the worshippers.[37]

Pochamma understands all languages and dialects, and people can talk to her in their words. For example, a Brahmin can speak to Pochamma in Sanskrit, and an English person can pray to her in English. The spirituality that emerges around Pochamma, therefore, does not divide the people, nor does it create conditions of conflict. Dalit spirituality, as evidenced in the worship of Pochamma, does not make one person a friend and another an enemy. Also, there are no restrictions in the Pochamma temple. People can go to the temple irrespective of their religious orientations. So too, Pochamma does not specify what should be offered to her since offerings depend on the devotees' economic conditions. The rich may offer a sari and blouse, while the destitute can go to her without anything.[38] Similarly, Dalit deities do not exploit a section of the community.[39] They create a shared cultural ethic that would re-energize the whole community, projecting a stable social structure that respects every person. They promote an intimate relationship between the gods and worshippers.[40] Such a shared social ethic demands further research since the Deuteronomic creed has an unhealthy us/them opposition, which, as will be seen, is alien to Dalits' contexts and Dalits' forgotten voices.

Binary opposition and Dalits' forgotten voices The Deuteronomic creed and the underlying Exodus motif have a binary opposition between Israel and Egypt. Egypt is given a negative valence in the creed and demonstrates Egypt and Israel as two categories, structurally distinct and unbridgeable.[41] Appropriating such a model can create imbalances between Dalits and non-Dalits since they are mutually exclusive in this representation as falling along bipolar dimensions. Rajkumar and Samuel have already noted that theological articulations based on this bipolar methodology can be counterproductive and might result in othering, debasing and even criminalizing of the caste people and their cultures.[42] The present section seeks to listen to Dalits' forgotten voices to clarify how they approach binary opposition models. The following poem, written by Kapila, who lived in the Sangam Age, for instance, endorses an essential unity of humanity and oneness of God:[43]

> Do rain and the wind avoid
> some men among the rest
> Because their caste is low?
> When such men tread the earth
> Hast saw it quake with rage?
> Or, does the brilliant sun
> Refuse to them its rays?
> Oh, Brahmans has our God
> E'er bid the teeming fields
> Bring forth the fruit and flowers
> For men of caste alone?
> Or, made the forest green
> To gratify the eyes
> of none but Pariahs?
> Oh Brahmans, list to me!
> In all this blessed land
> There is but one great caste,
> One tribe and brotherhood
> One God doth dwell above,

And he hath made us one
In birth and frame and tongue.[44]

Kapila notes that the wind, rain, earth and sun do not discriminate because of caste preferences and concludes that there is only one caste, one tribe and brotherhood. The fields also bring fruits and flowers for the entire creation, without discrimination. Kapila further asks, 'When shall our race be one great brotherhood unbroken by the tyranny of caste?'[45] Hence, Kapila promotes universal brotherhood and the oneness of god. Such an understanding, which envisions universal fraternity and cross-cultural partnerships, communicates an essential aspect of Dalits' worldview and challenges the binary opposition implied in the Deuteronomic creed.

Indian pluralistic contexts also challenge the Dalits to work for their full humanization and that of the dominant castes since India is a cradle of world religions like Hinduism, Sikhism and Buddhism. Indian cultural diversity is well acknowledged. Linguistic and ethnic diversity is another issue. India has more than 1,652 languages, of which 47 are used in education as a medium, 87 in the press, 71 in radio, 13 in cinema and 13 in state-level administration, and large numbers of different regional, social and economic groups live together in India. Learning from outsiders and engaging with them are significant in such contexts. The binary opposition has limitations in promoting cross-cultural equality, and therefore, it needs to be resolved. Scholars like Rajkumar have also challenged the liberation potential of God's triumph in the Deuteronomic creed because such an image has only limited potential to enhance Dalits' emancipation.[46]

So too, Rajkumar rejects Nirmal's emphasis on Israel's liberation based on the critique of Robert Allen Warrior and challenges the Dalit appropriation of the Exodus motif since the Dalits identify neither with Egyptians nor Israelites but with Canaanites.[47] Rajkumar further concludes that the 'Deuteronomic paradigm would serve more the interests of the Aryan invaders than the Dalits' since Dalits were the original inhabitants.[48] Similarly, I have reservations against using the 'wandering Aramean' since the identity of the Aramean has confused some scholars.

The identity of the wandering Aramean Jacob was traditionally acknowledged as the wandering Aramean. A. D. H. Mayes, however, has challenged such proposals.[49] The Vulgate, for example, renders it as *Syrus persequebatur patrem meum* (A Syrian persecuted my father). The Septuagint, on the other hand, reads Συριαν απεβαλεν ὁ πατηρ μου (My father abandoned Syria). Jewish Rabbinic interpretation reads Deuteronomy 26.5 as 'An Aramean tried to destroy my father', which complicates the attempts to identify the wandering Aramean as Jacob.[50]

The Jewish interpretation is based on the ambiguity of *Arami oved avi*. *Oved* usually means perish or destroy. It can also mean lost or strayed (1 Samuel 9,3 and 20). This usage, however, is not widespread in the Pentateuch. Similarly, Genesis does not use *oved* to describe the wanderings of the ancestors.[51] Jewish interpreters read *oved* in the creed as a piel form and vocalize it as *ibed*.[52] It is not easy to neglect the validity of this vocalization since biblical texts were not vocalized at the time of early rabbinic literature. *Ibed* as a piel form means 'to destroy'.[53] Deuteronomy 26.5, according to this interpretation, is 'An Aramean tried to destroy my father'. The Aramean mentioned in this verse, Midrash and Haggadah explain, is Laban, the Syrian.[54] The Scripture uses Aramean only for Laban and Bethuel, Jacob's maternal uncle and grandfather (Gen. 25.20, 28.5, 31.20, 24).[55] Hence, 'My father', according to this interpretation, is not Jacob.[56] From such a context, Passover Haggadah instructs:

> Go and learn what Laban the Aramean attempted to do to our father, Jacob! Pharaoh decreed only against the males, but Laban attempted to uproot everything, as it is said, An Aramean destroyed my father. Then he went down to Egypt. (Deut. 26.5)

Thus, the wandering Aramean is not an ancestor to be venerated but an archenemy who tried to annihilate the Jews. The Targum tradition to Deuteronomy 26.5 also provides a similar interpretation.[57] R. Menahem Kasher explains why Midrash portrays Laban as a villain. For Kasher, Jacob would have married Rachel if Laban had not tricked him. Joseph, Jacob's son through Rachel, would have been the firstborn and Leah's children would not have been born to Jacob. Kasher assumes that there would not have been any siblings' rivalry between Leah's and Rachel's children. Thus, Joseph would not have ended up in Egypt, and Jacob's family would not have followed him. So, Laban initiated the oppression.[58] From such contexts, Deuteronomy 26.5 could remind some Jews about Laban, who tricked Jacob into marrying Leah before Rachel and trapped him into twenty years of servitude. Therefore, Laban was crueller than Pharaoh. This demonizing of Laban does not mean that Pharaoh is not cruel. Instead, it suggests that Laban initiated the sufferings under Pharaoh. Moreover, Laban attempted to kill Israel's male and female children, not only male children like the Pharaoh.[59]

Lawrence A. Hoffman, based on the ambiguity of the word *Arami*, which would have appeared consonantly as 'RMI' suggests an alternate understanding of the Aramean's identity. After the Romans' war, Hoffman postulates, Jews were reading *RMI* not as *Arami* but as *Romi*, a Roman.[60] The meaning which emerged out of this context, Hoffman explains, is that the Roman emperor who attempted to wipe out the Jews entirely is worse than the Pharaoh. In all these scenarios, *Arami* is a villain who plotted against Jews. How can Dalit theology that asserts Dalits' right to speak for them disregard how Jews interpret their Scripture and history? Thus, despite their popularity among Dalit theologians, the Deuteronomic creed reading through liberation lenses does not do enough justice to Dalit contexts.

The suffering servant and Dalit contexts (Isa. 53.3-12)

Suffering is one of the starting points of Dalit theology, and it rejects gods that endanger Dalits. For example, Dalit academics reject Rama, one of the popular gods, who had killed Shambuka, a Dalit, for undertaking a life of prayer and asceticism.⁶¹ From such contexts, Dalit Christians began to search for a god who shares their pathos. They analysed Jesus' person and work through the epistemological lens of Dalits' suffering and proposed the suffering servant as another paradigm of Dalit theology to complement the Deuteronomic creed.⁶²

However, the suffering servant is a recurring theme in liberation theologies. Thomas Hanks, for example, notes that the servant has striking similarities with the poor in Latin America.⁶³ Cone remarks that 'God in Christ became the suffering servant and thus took the humiliation and suffering of the oppressed'.⁶⁴ Dalit theology appropriated the servant song and claims Jesus shared the Dalitness of the Dalits of his time and elaborates Jesus' sufferings to the present, suggesting that Christ is Dalits' co-sufferer. Further, Jesus participates in Dalits' pathos, and Dalits continue Jesus' pathos-filled ministry. Rajkumar, for example, has pointed out that Dalit Christology and the issue of Dalitness are inseparably connected.⁶⁵ Dalit theology relates God's saving acts through Jesus with Dalits' dehumanized social existence. It affirms that the God revealed in Jesus is a Dalit God since he encountered rejection, mockery, contempt and death like the Dalits.⁶⁶ Dalit theology elaborates the presence of Tamar (Gen. 38.1-30) and Rahab (Josh. 2.1-21) in Jesus' genealogy as suggesting Jesus' intimate relation to the historical Dalits.⁶⁷ Similarly, it holds that the nuances of the word Dalit blend well with the passages describing the suffering servant (Isa. 53.3-12).⁶⁸ Nirmal suggests how Jesus identifies with Dalits' servanthood:

> God whom Jesus Christ revealed and about whom the prophets of the Old Testament spoke is a Dalit God. He is a servant God – a God who serves. Services to others have always been the privilege of Dalit communities in India. The passages from Manu Dharma Sastra say that the Shudra was created by the Self-existent (Svayambhu) to do servile work and that servitude is innate in him. Service is the Sva-dharma of the Shudra. Let us remember the fact that in Dalits we have peoples who are avarnas – those below the Sudras. Their servitude is even more pathetic than that of Shudras. Against this background, the amazing claim of a Christian Dalit Theology will be that the God of the Dalits, the self-existent, the Svayambhu does not create others to do servile work, but does servile work himself. Servitude is innate in the God of the Dalits. Servitude is the sva-dharma of the God; and since we the Indian Dalits are this God's people, service has been our lot and our privilege.⁶⁹

Moving forward from Nirmal, Samuel Rayan interprets Jesus' participation in Dalits' suffering based on Jesus' suffering and death outside the gates of Jerusalem. He uses Hebrews 13.11-13 as a paradigm for interpreting God's participation in Dalit suffering.⁷⁰

> The high priest carries the blood of animals into the Most Holy Place as a sin offering, but the bodies are burned outside the camp. And so Jesus also suffered outside the city gate to make the people holy through his own blood. Let us, then, go to him outside the camp, bearing the disgrace he bore.

This passage is relevant in traditional Indian contexts, where Dalits were forced to live in a separate place outside the villages. Analysing against this background, Rayan explains that Jesus' suffering outside the gates of Jerusalem immerses the Godhead in 'the Dalitness of the oppressed to rescue its victims and plant them in the realm of freedom, dignity and creative living'.[71] The invitation to share Jesus' humiliation shows that the content of discipleship is not in sharing Jesus' throne but in sharing his cup of suffering. Hebrews 13 invites believers to participate in Jesus' humiliation. This sharing, he explains, extends to the servants of our times, including the Dalits. Rayan's proposal does not intend to romanticize Dalitness. Instead, it seeks to empower them to assert equality and freedom. Further, Rayan's call to share Jesus' degradation implies a socio-cultural revolution that can liberate Dalits out of their sufferings.[72] Hence, Dalit theology promotes a God who reveals Godself through deliberate sharing of Dalits' pathos. Such a reimaging may help Dalits identify Jesus as one who has endured the same sufferings and rejection like them. Clarke clarifies:

> The deliberate reimagining of the Divine from being a killer-God to servant God valorizes Dalits and repositions their agency. Related to this reconstruction of a majestic and violent God into one who serves human society, there is also the resolve of Dalit theology to remove the distance and aloofness of God from the toiling people and bring the divine close to what was thought to be polluting locations. God becomes so identified with 'polluting' professions (that is, scavengers and the washerman, who epitomise polluting occupations, become images of the Divine in the world) that encountering God and embracing Dalits become synonymous.[73]

However, the Dalit appropriation of Isaiah 53 raises a few questions. For example, Jews do not recognize Jesus as the Messiah. Their understanding had not been Messianic.

The identity of the suffering servant Christians understood Isaiah 53 as a Christological prophecy. However, Jewish scholars assume that Isaiah's servant is not a Messianic figure.[74] They understand the servant as a symbol of the people of Israel.[75] Isaiah 52.13–53.12, for example, does not mention the term 'Messiah'. Advancing further, David A. deSilva explains that the servant represents either Israel's sufferings on behalf of the Gentiles or the plight of a remnant within Israel for the whole nation.[76] George A. F. Knight regards the servant as a personification of exilic Israel.[77] There are also alternate proposals. Mordecai Schreiber claims that Isaiah 53 is a biography of the prophet Jeremiah.[78] Christopher R. North identifies the servant as exiled Jehoiachin.[79] James L. Crenshaw, on the other hand, argues that the suffering servant could be either second Isaiah or King Josiah.[80] Von Rad maintains that the servant is a second Moses.[81] C. Begg suggests that the suffering servant is Zedekiah.[82] Ulrich Berges clarifies that the servant could be any prophet who suffers on behalf of Yahweh and proposes that the servant could be Job, Jeremiah, Ezekiel or David.[83]

Hence, traditional Jews and many scholars identify the servant as representing Israel or an individual, but not Jesus. Christians, however, interpret him as symbolizing Jesus. I contend that the Christian interpretation of the Jewish scripture must respect how Jews understand their scripture. Similarly, Christian interpretation must also abide by the differences in scholarly interpretation. From such contexts, Dalit theology can only agree with Jewish and scholarly interpretations while confessing that the claim is mainly the case of one Israelite in particular. Such openness, which recognizes the multiple scholarly interpretations, is not a threat but a reality to be respected. Similarly, uncritical acceptance of a pathos-filled identity has another risk. It may idealize suffering as a virtue.

The servant paradigm through Dalits' forgotten voices The Deuteronomic creed, as seen above, has an internal binary opposition and highlights Dalits' suffering as paramount. Such a position, as clarified, contrasts with Dalits' contexts and may hinder Dalits from developing intra-Dalit solidarity. So too, God's servant nature and God's identification with suffering can idealize suffering and reinforce Dalits' low self-esteem. The following poem by F. M. Shinde implies that idealizing suffering may persuade Dalits to endure pain and suffering without seeking justice in this world.

> Once you're used to it
> You never afterwards
> feel anything;
> your blood nevermore
> congeals
> nor flows
> for wet mud has been slapped
> over all your bones.
> Once you're used to it
> even the sorrow
> that visits you
> sometimes, in dreams,
> melts away, embarrassed.[84]

So too, Mary Daly clarifies:

> The qualities that Christianity idealises, especially for women, are also those of a victim: sacrificial love, passive acceptance of suffering, humility, meekness, etc. Since these are the qualities idealised in Jesus 'who died for our sins,' his functioning as a model reinforces the scapegoat syndrome for women.[85]

Though Daly is concerned with women's freedom, her proposal can be applied to contexts where virtues like sacrificial love, passive acceptance of suffering and humility are glorified. Similarly, passive acceptance of suffering may reinforce the scapegoat syndrome among Dalits. In a similar but foreign context of patriarchy,

Elisabeth Schüssler Fiorenza questions the potential of passive acceptance of injustice. She says:

> If one extols the silent and freely chosen suffering of Christ, who was 'obedient to death' (Philippians 2:8), as an example to be imitated by all those victimised by patriarchal oppression, particularly by those suffering from domestic and sexual abuse, one not only legitimates but also enables acts of violence against women and children.[86]

Likewise, Rajkumar believes that the suffering servant paradigm can reinforce Dalits' inferiority, rather than helping the Dalits to transcend their Dalitness, which, as Rajkumar understands, is not a virtue to be venerated, but the status to be transformed.[87] Hence, the emancipatory potential of Isaiah's servant needs to be established since they can idealize suffering.[88] Balasundaram also critiques Dalits' appropriation of the suffering servant:

> We may accept suffering to the extent that suffering helps to overcome the suffering inflicted on us by others. Thus, in preaching, projecting and emphasising the servant image, we need to be careful. This means that we should not romanticise the concept of suffering.[89]

As noted, promoting a pathos-filled identity might halt Dalits' liberation by idealizing present suffering. This study will now analyse how the Bhakti movement, the Kummi songs, Pottan Theyyam and Dalit reformers like Narayana Guru respond to Dalits' sufferings. Such a study might further clarify if Dalits ever accepted pathos like Isaiah's servant.

Idealizing suffering and Bhakti movement

The Bhakti movement was one of the earliest challenges to Brahminic dominance. It spread much of India from the twelfth century onwards and emphasized that there is only one god and the best way to please god is total submission to His will and chanting mantras.[90] Dnyaneshwar and Eknath, saint poets from dominant castes, were the chief architects of the movement. Dalits, who were excluded from the Hindu temples, were inspired by this message and joined the Bhakti movement. Such members included Mahar saints Chokhamela, Karmamela, Banka and Nirmala. Some of their poems, especially those composed by the Mahar caste's poets, challenge the inequalities and injustices that limited Dalits' life.[91] Some academics, however, do not approve of the Bhakti movement and maintain that it was not radical enough to challenge the caste structure. Narendra Jadhav argues:

> Even the most compassionate saint-poets tended to uphold the divisive caste system in the social realm. While the Bhakti movement raised awareness, it was not radical enough to challenge the social system in daily life.[92]

However, there is an alternative view that upheld the spirit of protest in the Bhakti tradition. George Oommen and Rajkumar, for instance, accept the Bhakti movement as a socio-religious protest movement.[93] Following their lead, I will analyse some Bhakti poems to identify the counter-assertions and alternative moral visions in the Dalits' worldview.

Idealizing suffering and Chokhamela

Chokhamela, who belonged to the Mahar caste, is one of the most celebrated lower caste saint-poets in the Bhakti tradition.[94] Mahars were the traditional inhabitants of Maharashtra.[95] They were one of the untouchable castes, and Chokhamela followed the duties of Mahars obediently. He did not dare to enter the temple even. So too, his wife Soyrabai was reluctant to feed a Brahmin.[96] However, a competing tradition claims that Lord Vitthal took Chokhamela by the hand and led him into the shrine in Pandharpur. A Brahmin priest overheard Chokhamela talking to the Lord and asked Chokhamela to go to the other side of the Chandrabhaga River. Chokhamela left the temple and worshipped from afar.[97] Lord Vitthal, however, came to Chokhamela and dined with him.

The tradition says that Chokhamela's wife spat some food on god, and a Brahmin heard Chokhamela talking to god about the accident. The Brahmin slapped Chokhamela on the mouth, who later found food scraps and a swollen cheek on the image of the Lord. The Brahmin repented and took Chokhamela to the temple.[98] Brahmin taking an untouchable by hand and god dining with him would have been revolutionary in the caste-ridden society. It would have served as Mahars' anti-caste counter-discourse. Most of Chokhamela's poems express his deep devotion and concern for Lord Vitthal.[99] However, there is a subversive voice in his *abhangs* that challenges the Lord for creating dominated castes. The following poem, for instance, asks:

> You made us low caste.
> Why don't you face that fact, Great Lord?
> Our whole life-left over food to eat.
> You should be ashamed of this.[100]

Hence, there is a dissenting voice in Chokhamela's poems that challenge the concept of purity and pollution.[101] Reclaiming them might uncover the spirit of protest among Mahars and their vision for their agency in redressing their deplorable situation.

Anti-caste discourses in Chokhamela

As noted, Chokhamela's poems have an anti-caste discourse in them. Concentrating on them could disclose Mahars' counter-assertions and their quest for liberation since literature, as Massey clarifies, 'is the mirror of a society in which it is born' and represents the people in a particular societal context.[102] Hence, Chokhamela's poems, including his challenges to purity and pollution, can offer clear insights into Mahars' counter-worldviews and alternative moral visions. The following poem is one such instance:

> The only impurity is in the five elements;
> the same impurity pervades the whole world.
> Then who is pure and who is impure?
> The cause of pollution is the creation of the body.
> In the beginning, at the end, there is nothing but pollution.
> No one knows anyone who was born pure.[103]

The poem implies that Chokhamela was troubled by his social location. Chokhamela's questions 'who is pure and who is impure?' are ontological and communicate Mahars' counter-assertions, projecting a casteless society, where everyone is equal. Chokhamela remarks that everyone is born out of impurity and there is no one beyond impurity. Such a position would have been radical in Chokhamela's historical context, and it implies the element of protest in Mahars' worldview. Chokhamela further critiques the essentials of Hinduism:

> The Vedas are polluted, the Shastras are polluted;
> the Puranas are full of pollution.
> The soul is polluted; the oversoul is polluted;
> the body is full of pollution, Brahma is polluted,
> Vishnu is polluted, Shankar is full of pollution
> Birth is polluted; death is polluted.
> Chokha says: there's pollution at the beginning and at the end.[104]

Chokhamela designates the Vedas, Shastras and Puranas, the primary sources of Hinduism, as polluted. There are four Vedas, namely Rig Veda, Yajur Veda, Sama Veda and Atharva Veda. The Shastras are the textbooks of Hinduism.[105] The Dharma Shastras, the Artha Shastras and Kama Shastras are the prominent ones.[106] Puranas are one of the primary sources for studying the development of Hinduism.[107] Hence, criticizing the Vedas, Puranas and Shastras as polluted can be seen as Chokhamela's challenge to Hinduism's fundamental premises. Chokhamela asserts further that the soul and oversoul are polluted. Oversoul or Brahma, according to Hinduism, is the essence of the universe, immaterial, uncreated, limitless and timeless.[108] Lord Vishnu, the Lord of preservation, is believed to be the transcendental Lord, who watches the universe and manifests in the world to restore righteousness.[109] Hence, Chokhamela's poem is an assault on Hinduism and further reveals Dalits' epistemology of resistance and the quest for liberation and empowerment. Some Mahars, therefore, consider Chokhamela as a symbol of their assertions and call themselves as Chokhamelas. Saint Karmamela, another Bhakti poet, also communicates Mahars' protest.

Idealizing suffering and Karmamela

Karmamela, Chokhamela's son, was a fourteenth-century poet. The following poem challenges the Lord for the 'impurity' of Dalits.

> You made us impure
> I don't know why Lord
> We've eaten leftovers all our life
> Doesn't that trouble you
> Our house is stocked with rice and yoghurt
> How do you refuse it?
> Choka's Karmamela asks
> why did you give me birth?[110]

Karmamela questions the Lord for being silent when Dalits continue to eat leftovers. His question 'why did you give birth?' is piercing and highlights god's role in creating Dalits as untouchables. Such a daring question is a cry for deliverance and highlights the Mahars' urge for liberation and empowerment. They were not passively accepting the dominant caste hegemony, as Isaiah's servant may suggest. The same is evident in the songs of Ravidas, another poet from the Bhakti tradition, known as an icon of Dalit consciousness.

Idealizing suffering and Ravidas

Ravidas was born near Varanasi to an untouchable family. He was a poet and a singer. He is one of the best-known untouchable saint-poets. Some Dalits still identify him as a model and call themselves Ravidasis.[111] He challenged the caste system and anyone who treated another person with disgust and disrespect. An episode often narrated from Ravidas's life clarifies his discontent with the caste hegemony. A Rajasthani princess wanted to honour Ravidas and arranged for a feast in his honour at her palace. The Brahmins objected and demanded that she should honour the caste stipulations and treat Brahmins first. The princess yielded to the Brahmins' demand. However, when the Brahmins sat down to eat, they found a miraculous manifestation of Ravidas in between every Brahmin. They were humbled and humiliated by Ravidas's magical power and invited him to the feast with them.[112] Such an instance, though its historicity needs to be established, would have challenged the Brahminic hegemony. One of his poems rebukes the Brahmins who tried to sideline him:

> Oh well-born of Benaras, I too am born well-known:
> My labour is with leather. But my heart can boast of the Lord.[113]

Ravidas asserts his dignity even though he belongs to the cobblers' family, suggesting that caste and occupation do not hinder one from devotion to the Lord. It is to be noted, however, that Ravidas abandoned neither his religion nor his occupation. Perhaps he considered every caste and occupation as equally dignified. He used Bhakti to challenge the caste system. Hence, Dalits were not accepting suffering like Isaiah's servant. Instead, they used their culture and spirituality as essential locations for constructing and communicating their discontent and their longing for liberation and empowerment. A Kummi song from Tamil Nadu folklore tradition also critiques the social structure.

Idealizing suffering in a Kummi song

Kummi is a folk dance famous in Kerala and Tamil Nadu, danced by women. The term *kummi* is derived from the word 'Kommai', which means to 'dance with clapping of hands'.[114] This folk dance is thought to have originated when there were no musical instruments. The essential themes in Kummi songs are related to the day-to-day life of Dalit villagers. One such Kummi song reads:

> A cartload of plantains
> Comes from the North
> Are we, women
> Destined only to cook them?
> A cartload of coconuts
> Comes from the south
> Are we, women
> Ill-fated just to cook them?[115]

This song narrates the insecurity and helplessness of women who lived under the patriarchy. However, the song does not indicate a sense of masochistic acceptance. Instead, it questions the practices that de-humanize women. The Pulaya version of the Pottan Theyyam further highlights how Dalits appropriated culture and spirituality as essential locations for countering the attempts to reduce them according to caste hierarchy.

Idealizing suffering in Pottan Theyyam

The Pulayas are one of the Dalit communities from Kerala. Theyyam is a popular ritual among them. Theyyam's characters were often heroes who lived among them or animals or trees. Chinnappulayan is the hero of Pottan Theyyam. The Pulaya community has worshipped Pottan Theyyam from ancient times. Pottan Theyyam narrates an event that occurred when Chinnappulayan, with a child in his arm, walking along a narrow path, comes across a Chovar, a dominant caste man.[116] This conversation reaches its climax when Chovar asks the Chinnappulayan to give way to a dominant caste man.[117] Chinnappulayan hesitated because he had his child on his arm and a pot of toddy on his head. The thorns on the other side of the road prevented him from giving way to the dominant caste traveller.[118] Theophilus Appavoo translates Pulayan's reaction.

> 'What is that called a Brahmin Women
> What is that called an Outcaste
> 'Is there any number marked
> On the skin, On the flesh?
> Or on the bones?'
> 'Is there any difference
> Between Brahmin women and Outcaste
> During sexual intercourse?'[119]

Chinnappulayan criticizes the social structure that legitimizes Dalits' suffering, asking why to quarrel over the caste because the same blood gushes out when the body is wounded.[120] Chinnappulayan's critiques are reasonable. He argues that the Pulayan and Chovar may have diverse ways of doing things, but they are both human beings, and they have the same red blood, and they eat the same rice. Pulayan reminds the Chovar that his community has been serving the dominant caste men by supplying them fruits, leaves and flowers.[121] Chinnappulayan claims further that the dominant caste people offer their deity from the tulsi planted by his community. Chinnappulayan highlights the hypocrisy that relegates a dominant caste person as untouchable and unapproachable but considers his labour as acceptable to the dominant caste gods. Chinnappulayan's philosophical approach to life and criticism against irrational religious practices were part of Dalits' life.[122] The Theyyam concludes with an appeal to the Chovar to let the Pulayan live in peace in Wayanadu.[123]

This study shows that Chinnappulayan was a Dalit humanist. His arguments were logical, sharp and convincing. They suggest the interconnection between god, body and earth. Many more movements, which highlight Dalits' counter-assertions against caste hegemony emerged in Kerala. They challenge any model that could promote passive acceptance of suffering. In 1859, the Shanars (Nadars) revolted for the right to cover the bosom of their women like dominant caste women.[124] Later in 1891, Dalits submitted a memorandum to the King of Travancore against systematic exclusion from higher grades of service.[125] Again in 1896, a mass memorandum signed by 13,176 Ezhavas was presented to the King of Travancore, demanding employment for their community in government services and admission for their children in state schools.[126] Such movements underline the spirit of protest and longing for liberation and empowerment in Dalits' worldview. The social critique of Sree Narayana Guru, a social reformer of Kerala from the Ezhava community, is also an essential episode in backward caste assertions.

Sree Narayana Guru: A Dalit social reformer

Ezhavas are one of the most significant backward caste communities in Kerala considered untouchables. They were subjected to various forms of untouchability, though not to the same extent as the Dalits. The dominant castes, for example, considered them untouchables and denied Ezhavas social, political and economic opportunities. So too, Ezhavas were not allowed to walk within a distance of twelve feet from the dominant castes. Similarly, the Ezhavas were not permitted to enter the temples until 1936. After considering the historical injustices done to the Ezhava community, scholars such as Ramesh P. Mohanty consider the Ezhava community as a Dalit group of Kerala, even though the Ezhavas are now classified not among the Scheduled Caste, which is a title exclusively reserved for Dalits, but among the Other Backward Classes by the Government of India.[127]

Sree Narayana Guru (1856–1928) was one of the most famous ascetics who emerged from the Ezhavas. He started his career as a traditional schoolmaster. He championed the cause of the downtrodden, including the Dalits, and initiated a paradigmatic reformist movement in Kerala. He believed that there is only one caste and all men belong to the same rank:

One Caste, One Religion, One God for man
One Womb, One Form, difference herein none.[128]

This sweeping statement declares that men and women belong to the same species and are only different manifestations of one god. The Brahmins and untouchables, Guru understood, are one in social content, which was a blow to the Rig Vedic creation narrative that disconnects Dalits from Brahma and disempowers them in India's caste-ridden society. From such contexts, Guru stipulated, 'Ask not, speak not, think not of caste.'[129] He asserted further that the caste–outcaste dichotomy is artificial:

Human nature is essentially one and fundamentally of one single sameness. The idea of dualism or plurality in the nature and race of man is a superimposition on reality by interested parties. Thus, the terms 'Pariah' and 'Brahmin' exist only in imagination. In the light of reason, they are bound to disappear.[130]

Narayana Guru further critiqued the caste system based on birth and claimed that birth was not a hindrance for Parasara or Vyasa in getting recognized as great sages and teachers.[131] Nataraja Guru, one of the famous disciples of Narayana Guru, explains that Guru wanted to inform the people that Parasara and Vyasa came from the much-abused and misunderstood Pariah community and not from the Brahmin stock. However, every Hindu family, irrespective of their caste orientation, celebrates them as ancestors. Nataraja Guru explores further and comments that this phenomenon challenges the very notion of the caste system. Nataraja Guru emphasizes the ultimate contradiction in adopting the Pariah on the first pedestal as a sage and concludes that 'all caste prejudices based on heredity, dynasty and blind tradition must be dispelled and the social atmosphere of the present ultimately and finally cleared of this significant caste-impediment'.[132]

Narayana Guru challenged the practice of not permitting Dalits to enter and worship in temples by installing a Siva idol at Aruvipuram near Trivandrum for the lower caste people in 1888. The inscription in that temple reads:

> This is the ideal house
> Where all live-in full fraternity
> Without distinction of caste or prejudice of creed.[133]

This revolt against Brahmin supremacy in religious and social practices showed that Dalits could not only make offerings to the deity but also consecrate the same god worshipped by dominant caste Hindus. Therefore, this event was challenged by Orthodox Hindus. Guru responded that 'I installed not a Brahmin Siva, but an Izhava Siva'.[134] Narayana Guru further instructed that money received as offerings should be utilized for the benefit of the poor.[135] The temple envisaged by Narayana Guru was not only spiritually enriching but also culturally and financially beneficial. Moorkoth Kumaran, a long-time associate of Guru, once commented that the 'temples as envisaged by Swami should be such as would enrich the people culturally and financially through their groves, libraries, lecture halls, educational institutions and industrial centres'.[136]

Guru's contribution is not limited to temple consecration and teaching. He started schools and libraries and admitted pupils irrespective of caste orientations. Speaking at a meeting in Cherai, he remarked in 1912:

> In our community, only a few have higher education. During the last few years, members of our community have turned their attention to education. This is indeed heartening. Education leads any community to higher standards and therefore if we are interested in the welfare of the community, we have to encourage it. The importance of Sanskrit education is declining gradually. The chief language now is English. Therefore, our attention has to turn towards English. Women also should be educated. They should not be left in the lurch. After education comes industry.[137]

Together with education, Guru was alert to the possibilities of industrialization. He felt that industrialization is the best option for improving social status and asked the rich to explore manufacturing and adapt to new machinery.[138]

These movements, including Chinnappulayan's protest and Guru's reformation, appropriated culture and spirituality as important locations for Dalits' resistance. Such assertions resisted every form of social exclusion and challenged the attempts to divide the society as friends and foes based upon purity and pollution. It is to be noted that scholars like Felix Wilfred have also noted similar instances among subaltern communities:

> The subalterns who are oppressed and marginalized have always sought in their religious experience and symbols an important means to counter the domination they suffer. In fact, revolutionary and subversive elements are built into their tradition. At particular historical junctures, the energies for the liberation of the subalterns from the dominant religious tradition and its ideological legitimation of power and control are released and set in motion. The subaltern religion goes even further to challenge the cultural, social, political and economic structures.[139]

Such instances, which narrate Dalits' agency, their counter-worldviews, their proposals for an alternative yet empowering moral vision and Dalits' willingness to risk their lives in fighting for their human rights, have overturned my cultural presuppositions. Also, they offer immense possibilities to undermine, challenge and change the dominant caste hegemony, ethics and worldview among Syrian Christians, which demands a self-reflexive analysis from Syrian Christian outlook. So too, they highlighted some limitations of the dominant paradigms of Dalit theology, which necessitates further interrogation and a hermeneutical switch in Dalit theology along the lines of Dalits' resistance and their counter-ontology to the dominant culture by suggesting a united society bridged through mutually enriching partnerships.

Conclusion

Dalit theology, as seen, is a people's theology. It was proposed out of Dalits' immanent experiences. However, Dalit theology's hermeneutical frameworks have tended to overlook Dalits' counter-caste assertions, which I suggest, estranged Dalit theology from Dalits' worldview, their counter-ontology and epistemology of resistance. From such backgrounds, the present chapter contrasted the hermeneutical examples of Dalit theology with some essential aspects of Dalits' religious, cultural and literary assertions.

Such an undertaking clarified that Dalit hermeneutics overlooks the liberative voices and alternate moral visions expressed through Dalits' dissenting voices and anti-caste philosophers such as Chokhamela, Karmamela, Ravidas, Kabir, Nandanar and Narayana Guru significantly. For example, as seen, the image of God suggested by the Deuteronomic creed and suffering servant paradigms disagrees with Dalits' contexts. So too, Dalits' worldview does not promote binary opposition, and Dalits were not accepting sufferings like Isaiah's servant. Some of them, who were compromised by the caste hegemony, as seen, challenged the caste system, which relegated their humanity and used their culture and spirituality as essential locations for constructing and communicating Dalits' counter-history, counter-ethics and counter-worldview. Such instances, which are evident in Dalits' religion, culture and history, are minimal in the dominant paradigms of Dalit theology. It necessitates further interrogation and a hermeneutical switch in Dalit theology to make Dalit theology more relevant to Dalits' contexts. The following chapter, depending on the conclusions of this chapter, interrogates Dalits' forgotten voices further to identify the possible directions of the hermeneutical switch and the ideal biblical dialogue partner.

Chapter 5

DECENTRING DALIT THEOLOGY THROUGH DALITS' FORGOTTEN VOICES

Introduction

Walt Harrington, an award-winning American journalist, is a white man married to a Black woman and father of two mixed-race children. One day, while in a dentist's surgery, Harrington overheard a casual racist joke. Harrington was disturbed by his own race's misunderstanding of the Blacks and their culture. Harrington decided to travel through 'America's parallel black world' to educate himself on America's racial conundrums. *Crossings: A White Man's Journey into Black America* narrates Harrington's 25,000-mile journey through Black America.[1]

The present research is a similar enterprise. Its seeds, as clarified, were planted in my classroom at the Malankara Syrian Orthodox Theological Seminary. Mor Aphrem's reflections, as indicated, also touched me, and I was humbled and humiliated by my misunderstanding of the Dalits' world. It further convinced me that I did not have significant awareness of the Dalits' contexts. Therefore, I began to read more about the caste system and its impacts upon the Dalits to educate myself. What I developed, unfortunately, was not a reflective knowledge well informed by an internal dialogue but only a passive awareness of the Dalits' contexts.

My encounters with Dalits' subversive voices, as will be clarified further, provided an opportunity for an internal dialogue, which advanced my cross-cultural competence, educated me about various mechanisms included in Dalits' encounters with and resistance against Hindu Vedic worldview and guided me through a process of active learning, unlearning and relearning. Further, these experiences have convinced me that Dalits' resistance expressed in cultural ways and historical events highlight Dalits' counter-ontology and epistemology of resistance. So too, as seen, there is a dialectical relationship between the dominant caste Hindu Vedic ontology and epistemology, which have been regulating most of the social interactions in the Indian subcontinent, and Dalits' attempts to develop a counter-hegemonic ontology and epistemology. Such instances and undercurrents, as noted, have played only a minimal role in the pathos-filled paradigms of Dalit theology and such paradigms, therefore, do not attend the liberative voices in Dalits' culture, their spirituality and their hope for a life with dignity. From such a background, this book proposes that Dalit theology needs to develop a paradigm that listens to and learns from Dalits' counter-hegemonic worldview, and my encounters with Dalits' subversive voices can add another constructive element to the diverse and vibrant field of Dalit theology.

As seen, the subversive voices are important spaces to identify Dalits' epistemology of resistance, counter-worldview and alternative moral visions. Such subjugated knowledges, which had gone unnoticed and unremarked in most cases, demand not only the liberation of Dalits but also reconciliation between Dalits and non-Dalits, aimed at peaceful co-existence as manifestations of every human being. From there, the present chapter proposes that Dalit theology requires a hermeneutical switch that is more sensitive to the epistemology of resistance embedded in the subversive voices in Dalits' contexts and an intertextual dialogue between Dalits' resistance to the caste hegemony and the resistance of the Second Temple community against the imperial ambitions of the Persian administration narrated through Abraham's crossings can advance Dalit theology. My proposal, however, does not include a one-way affair, from the Bible to the Dalits or the Dalits to the Bible. Instead, it acknowledges the Bible and Dalits' resources as two independent dialogue partners, working together to advance Dalit theology and Dalit–Syrian Christian dialogues.

Admittedly, the intertextual reading I am proposing is not entirely new to Dalit theology. Maria Arul Raja, for instance, has already undertaken an inter-textual study of biblical texts and the Dalit world when he juxtaposes two murdered warriors, the Markan Jesus and the South Indian legend Madurai Veeran,[2] who were later transformed into weapons by which the weak could fight their cause.[3] So too, Rajkumar's proposal for a Dalithos (Dalit ethos) reading of the Markan exorcism narrative (Mk 5.1-20) is another attempt in this direction. Though Rajkumar does not use the term 'intertextual reading', he appropriates the Markan narrative through some features of Dalits' ethos like pragmatism, the primacy of community and emancipatory demythologization. Such a conversation between the Dalit ethos and the biblical passage, as Rajkumar highlights, can assist the Dalit theology.[4] The intertextual reading I am proposing undertakes a similar task and offers proposals that may advance Dalit theology and Dalit–Syrian Christian dialogues.

Negotiations between Dalit theology and Dalits' worldview

Dalit theology addresses Dalits' sufferings. However, Dalit theology has tended to overlook the counter-caste assertions imagined in Dalits' forgotten voices and depended heavily on the biblical paradigms developed in Latin American and African American contexts for inspiration. Such attempts placed the biblical paradigms developed in alien contexts as the dominant self. They marginalized the liberative voices in Dalits' worldview – how Dalits' worldview comprehends the world, Dalits and non-Dalits and underpins the caste hegemony's absolutist claims to the periphery of Dalit theology. Therefore, I suggest an ongoing dialogue between the Bible and Dalits' counter-formulations to advance Dalit theology through Dalits' forgotten voices. As noted, Dalits' subversive voices aim neither at Dalits' isolated existence nor their dominion over the dominant castes. The poems of Kapila and Chokhamela, as seen, dream of a casteless society in communal solidarity. Narayana Guru projects the oneness of god and the oneness of humanity. The following section will further review the subversive voices in Pottan Theyyam, Kabir's poems, Ravidas's poems and the ballad on Nandanar, hoping such reviews might direct this book towards a biblical paradigm that listens to and learns from Dalits' counter-formulations and alternate moral visions.

Liberative voices in Pottan Theyyam

Pottan Theyyam, as noted, was a protesting voice from the dominated castes. The introductory prayer in Theyyam clarifies Dalits' social praxis imagined in their worldview:

> Let the village prosper, the world prosper,
> Let the state prosper, the city prosper
> Let this one Pandal and the Gate prosper
> Let house and pedestal prosper
> Let the hall of Ganapathy prosper
> Let the four bulls for Saraswathy prosper
> Let Ponnan and Poliyan, Manian and Manikandan prosper.[5]

The prayer, though it stems from the dominated castes, does not condemn dominant castes. The prayer uses the verb prosper seven times. However, it is not used in the narrow sense denoting Dalits' prosperity alone. Instead, it envisions the prosperity of the whole universe. The greetings to Saraswathy, for example, are significant. Saraswathy is the goddess of knowledge, music, art, wisdom and learning, venerated by dominant castes. Her name derives from two Sanskrit words, *Sara* and *swa*, which mean essence and self. Hence, Saraswathy is the essence of self. The four bulls of Saraswathy are her four hands, which implies the four aspects of human learning, namely mind, alertness, ego and intellect.[6] The radicalism in the wish 'Let the four bulls for Saraswathy prosper' will be apparent if we note that Hindu Vedic epistemology excluded Dalits from learning. *Manusmriti*, the law book of Hinduism, for instance, decrees that if a dominated caste person 'intentionally overhears the Veda chants, he shall have his ears filled with molten tin and dark red pigment'.[7] How radical would it be when a dominated caste community that has been systematically refrained from learning wishes prosperity for the goddess of wisdom, worshipped by their oppressors?

Such contestations, which highlight the essential features of Dalits' worldview and epistemology of resistance like their courage, openness and longing for a reconciled society, further clarifies that pathos and victimhood were not the only elements of Dalits' worldview. Instead, they are only two aspects, and Dalits had an alternative yet empowering moral vision, which ensured the human race's prosperity. A similar ethic is evident in Kabir's poems.

Liberative voices in Kabir's poems

Kabir is a revolutionary poet in Indian history. He was born in Varanasi into dominated caste weavers. Kabir remains as an embodiment of the dominated castes' protesting spirit amidst the Indian casteist discourses. The following poem demonstrates Kabir's commitment to human equality:

> Pandit, look in your heart for knowledge.
> Tell me where untouchability
> came from, since you believe in it.
> Mix red juice, white juice and air –
> a body bakes in a body.
> As soon as the eight lotuses
> are ready, it comes
> into the world. Then what's untouchable?
> Eighty-four hundred thousand vessels
> decay into dust, while the potter
> keeps slapping clay
> on the wheel, and with a touch
> cuts each one off.
> We eat by touching, we wash
> by touching, from a touch
> the world was born.
> So, who's untouched? Asks Kabir.
> Only he who has no taint of Maya.
> And
> It's all one skin and bone
> One piss and shit
> One blood, one meat
> From one drop, a universe.
> Who's Brahmin? Who's Shudra?[8]

Kabir presents the poem as a conversation between Kabir and a pandit.[9] Kabir's request to answer from the heart is nothing but an invitation to denounce Hindu scriptures and knowledge systems that communicate the dominant caste Vedic worldview, limiting Dalits' life and relegating Dalits' bodies. From such contexts, Kabir demonstrates the illusoriness of untouchability. He clarifies that all bodies are made from the same essential substances and notes that everything humans do is by touching. Such a daring remark is another instance from Dalits' worldview that challenges the Vedic epistemology and Rig Vedic creation narrative that relegates Dalits' body and denies transcendence to Dalits' body.

So too, Kabir uses the word *chutti*, which means touch, eight times. *Chutti* can also suggest 'defiled touch' and untouchability in common usage. Kabir employs all the possible meanings of *chutti* and suggests that everything is made in the same way from the same stuff.[10] Kabir establishes radical equality, not only of all people but also of all substances and interactions.[11] The questions who is Brahmin, who is Shudra and who is untouched also remind the overarching collective identity and interconnectedness of humanity. A similar openness to a shared cultural existence is evident in Ravidas also.

Liberative voices in Ravidas's poems

As noted, Ravidas challenged the social structure that de-humanizes the dominated castes. 'Adi Granth', a poem by Ravidas, challenges the caste system. The poem claims:

> A family that has a true follower of the Lord
> Is neither high caste nor low caste, lordly or poor.
> The world will know it by its fragrance.
> Priests or merchants, labourers or warriors,
> halfbreeds, outcastes, and those who tend cremation fires –
> their hearts are all the same.
> He who becomes pure through the love of the Lord
> exalts himself and his family as well.[12]

Ravidas challenges the caste system and argues that a person can transcend the caste system's limitations by following the Lord. He implies that the dominated castes and the dominant castes are all but the same, and the world would know a person who follows the Lord irrespective of his caste. Ravidas further preaches a religion of love that would unite the entire humanity. Hence, Ravidas's challenge did not aim at dominated castes' isolated existence or their dominion over the dominant castes but a union between dominated castes and the dominant castes. Such a shared cultural ethic, as noted, is crucial to Dalits' worldview, and it demands not only the liberation of dominated castes but also reconciliation between dominated castes and dominant castes. *The Ballad on Nandanar*, a Saivite saint from Tamil Nadu, also highlights that everyone receives god's grace irrespective of caste distinction.

Liberative voices in the ballad on Nandanar

The ballad on Nandanar is an elaborate story of Nandanar based on *Periyapuranam*, composed in the twelfth-century CE. Nandanar belonged to the Paraiya caste, categorized as untouchable in Tamil Nadu, India. He was a devotee of Siva. He wanted to enter the temple in Chidambaram to worship Siva. The ballad on Nandanar is a self-recollection. It asks:

> Will even the Paraiyan Nandanar receive *mukthi*?
> Four Vedas and Sastras do not say that low caste will not receive mukthi!
> Body which roasted and ate, crabs and snails
> Wants to have the vision of Siva, who dances
> Which is the path to be followed?
> Only the Lord Siva knows the path.
> The soul who does not long to go to Chidambaram is a sinner
> Now my soul is peaceless without seeing the Lord![13]

Nandanar examines his worthiness to attain mukti (salvation). Mukti, according to Hinduism, is the ultimate aim of spiritual life. Nandanar worries whether a Paraiyan can attain mukti. As Annie notes, Nandanar has internalized the caste system and did not question it in the beginning. However, he gradually dares to question it because his soul is restless without having a vision of Siva, and he questions the religious system because of his spiritual aspirations.[14] Nandanar finds that four Vedas and Sastras do not deny mukti to the dominated castes. Such a conviction is liberative, and it can empower dominated castes. There is also a transition from particularity to universalism in this poem. The poem starts with the suffering of Paraiyars. However, Nandanar transcends the caste structure and concludes that the soul which does not desire the Lord is the sinner. The soul is an inclusive term, not limited to a caste order. It can denote dominant castes and dominated castes. What Nandanar attempts, I think, was to unite the society through devotion to the Lord and to envision a society reconciled through the Lord.

Perhaps, drawing inspiration from Dalits' counter-formulations against dominant caste ontology, their counter-hegemonic worldview and the epistemology of resistance may help Dalit theology. Such voices, as seen from the noted examples, clarify that Dalits are not mere victims, and they have more to offer than just pathos. For example, as seen, Pottan Theyyam narrates the story of Dalits' resistance and remains as an active account of Dalits' recalcitrance, offering an alternative worldview that challenges the caste system. Kabir and Ravidas, as clarified, suggest radical equality of all people and substances, while Nandanar attempts to unite society through devotion to the Lord. They call for the liberation of Dalits and suggest a radical reconciliation between Dalits and non-Dalits. Listening to and learning from such orientations can advance Dalit theology.

In similar but African American contexts, Dwight N. Hopkins explains that the liberation of Black people as a stepping stone to their reconciliation with white people. The liberation of Blacks, Hopkins clarifies, should serve as an intermediate measure towards reconciliation.[15] Hopkins clarifies that reconciliation in African contexts means that Black freedom does not deny white humanity but meets whites on equal grounds.[16] My encounter with Dalits' contexts, as noted, convinced me that a similar demand is evident in Dalits' contexts. It challenges the Dalit researchers developing a biblical paradigm that respects Dalits' subversive manoeuvres and their assertions against unjust social structures.

Dalit theology through Dalits' resistance, liberation and reconciliation

As seen, there are multiple layers of thought, resistance, pathos, agency and social vision carefully crafted, often subversively, into Dalits' worldviews. Such undercurrents are significant directives which demand that Dalits' liberation and reconciliation between liberated Dalits and non-Dalits should be Dalit theology's twin goals. The reconciliation imagined in Dalits' worldview and epistemology of resistance, as will be clarified, is not an alternative to liberation or pursuing justice. So too, Dalits' reconciliation ethic does not mean compromise that distracts from true liberation or passive acceptance of suffering. What Dalits' context suggests is not a dichotomy or a hierarchical explication between liberation and reconciliation also, but a conscious blending between liberation and reconciliation, where Dalits liberated from caste oppression engage in mutual partnerships with non-Dalits, as two dignified communities.

Liberation and reconciliation ethic in Dalits' contexts

As noted, my encounters with the subversive voices have been liberating. As will be clarified further, they convince me that liberation and reconciliation are important aspects of Dalits' worldview. The conversation between Chinnappulayan and the taskmaster clarifies:

> We planted a plantain tree
> In the rubbish heap
> With the fruit thereof
> You make an offering to the god.
> Yes, we planted a Tulasi
> In the rubbish heap
> With the same Tulasi
> You make offerings to the god.
> Why then distinctions
> Between us?[17]

Chinnappulayan's arguments echo his longing for breaking the barriers and stereotypes between the dominated castes and dominant castes. However, Chinnappulayan is not merely ridiculing his opponent or suggesting an isolated Dalits' existence. Instead, Chinnappulayan, based on his reasoning, questions the legitimacy of caste distinctions. Pulayan's question 'Why then distinctions between us?' was not a threat or a compromise. Instead, it was an invitation to come together in peace and harmony, denouncing differences. Likewise, Chinnappulayan reminds some mutual partnerships that existed previously:

> We ploughed seven times
> With the yoke that is Ganapathy
> And plough-shaft that is Saraswathy
> We sowed the wetland Vayanadon,
> No seed is needed, no nurture needed
> The wetlands yield a good crop
> By itself.[18]

The poem denotes an agricultural society, where different people have different roles. The images of Ganapathy and Saraswathy, dominant caste deities, as the yoke and ploughshare were significant since they were essential tools in ancient agricultural societies. The symbolism of Ganapathy and Saraswathy working together with dominated castes suggests collaborations between deities of the dominant castes and the dominated caste people. Chinnappulayan narrates such associations' vitality and comments further that no seed was needed, and no nurture was needed. The wetlands, Pulayan clarifies, yield good crops by themselves. Such extraordinary results, when analysing against the social contexts of Pottan Theyyam, illustrate Dalits' visions of a liberated-reconciled society connected through mutually enriching partnerships. The following section explains how Dalits' forgotten voices can offer an alternate path for Dalit theology.

An alternate path for Dalit theology through Dalits' forgotten voices

The Dalits' worldview and epistemology of resistance, as seen through Dalits' subversive voices, include liberation and reconciliation in the fragile caste contexts. Reconciliation in Dalits' contexts is not an event. Instead, as seen, it is a process, which continuously renegotiates the space between the Dalits and non-Dalits. As a Christian, I have been aware of liberation and reconciliation from my childhood. However, my understandings overlooked the horizontal dimension of reconciliation significantly and emphasized the vertical dimension (God–human/ Jesus–Christian). My encounters with the liberation and reconciliation ethics along the horizontal axis in Dalits' assertions, which emphasize Dalits and non-Dalits like Syrian Christians as agents and messengers of liberation and reconciliation, were liberating.

Perhaps drawing imperatives from the thrust towards liberated-reconciled society, bridged through mutually enriching partnerships, embedded in Dalits' contexts, may reorient Dalit theology and Dalit–Syrian Christian partnerships. Partnerships have incredible potential to reconcile Dalits with non-Dalits, including Syrian Christians. James H. Olthuis, for instance, explains that associations can facilitate attunement of expression and recognition using the diverse needs of each people.[19] The aim of such relationships, Olthuis suggests, 'is not to eradicate, accommodate, suppress, or repress difference, but to allow contact with a difference to move, enhance, and change'.[20] This openness is vital in Dalits' contexts also. Dalits belong to various religious affiliations since India has an extraordinary heterogeneity.[21] In such contexts, mutual partnerships will help Dalits and the dominant castes to work together for a liberated-reconciled Church and society.

Nevertheless, I foresee some reservations about my proposal from Indian academics, who are sensitive to Dalits' concerns. For example, Reverend Fr Shibu Cherian, my professor at Malankara Syrian Orthodox Theological Seminary and Arvind Nirmal's student, expressed his reservations about the proposed cross-cultural partnerships.

> The cross-cultural relationship you propose is very difficult to achieve, and the dominant caste people won't accept such a collaboration. The dominant caste people are very rich and powerful. The Dalits, on the other hand, are weak, poor and downtrodden. How can there be a meaningful relationship between them? (Fr Shibu, personal communication)

Fr Shibu's concerns are valid, and they represent the dominant view among Dalit theologians. However, my crossings to Dalits' contexts through the subversive manoeuvres convince me that Dalits' subversive voices require an openness to diversities and envision a liberated-reconciled society bridged through mutually enriching collaborations. My crossings to Dalit contexts, which began in my seminary, influenced me significantly. The epistemology of resistance and protest among Dalits and their longing for a casteless society, I believe, has much to offer to Dalit theology and in developing Syrian Christian interactions.

From such contexts, this book proposes an intertextual dialogue between the Second Temple community's resistance to the Persian imperial ambitions and Dalits' resistance against caste hegemony. Such a move acknowledges the spirit of resistance and protest among Dalits expressed in cultural expressions and historical events and the protesting spirit among the Second Temple community, expressed through various narratives like Abraham's crossings to Egypt and Gerar. Such a conversation, it is hoped, can advance Dalit theology through Dalits' forgotten voices while challenging and enlightening Syrian Christians.

Abraham's postcolonial crossings as a dialogue partner

As seen, Dalits' culture and spirituality have been important locations for developing and transmitting Dalits' resistance and counter-ontology. The richness and wisdom embedded in such subjugated knowledge are incredible, and they offer clues to challenge and subvert the caste discourses. The liberation and reconciliation ethic in Dalits' resources do not divide the society but demand Dalits' liberation from the dominant castes and reconciliation between Dalits and dominant caste people. The epistemology of Dalits' resistance does not include attempts to reduce their oppressors according to Dalit categories. They envisioned a society that promotes liberation and reconciliation. Reconciliation in Dalits' contexts, however, is not a compromise but a conscious attempt towards a social order in great brotherhood. Such a spirituality and culture submerged in Dalits' subversive voices, as illustrated, necessitates further interrogation in developing a biblical paradigm that respects Dalits' assertions for a liberated-reconciled society, bridged through mutual partnerships. Such an approach can offer a constructive element within Dalits' contexts, with the possibility of bridging Dalits' liberative voices with Dalit theology.

From such backgrounds, this book will analyse how an intertextual dialogue between the counter-colonial hegemony in Abraham's crossings to Egypt (Gen. 12.10-20) and Gerar (Gen. 20) and Dalits' counter-caste assertions can offer fresh, dialogical perspectives. However, this does not mean that Abraham is without blemishes. There are some episodes in his life that narrate his indifference to the least and the lost. The moral and ethical issues in how he used Hagar, an innocent foreign maid, as a surrogate mother after yielding to Sarah's persuasion, for instance, is questionable (Gen. 16.1-4). His rejection of Hagar without any compelling reason narrates his moral weakness (Gen. 16.5-6). The near-sacrifice of Isaac is also perplexing (Gen. 22). Those blemishes, however, do not invalidate the vitality of his virtues, and Abraham's crossings, as will be seen, will help Indian Christian denominations to overcome the barriers in inter-Dalit and intra-Dalit relationships.

The image of God which emerges out of the Abraham narrative is more in line with God's image this book identified in the worship of Pochamma Devi. Abraham's dialogue with Yahweh (Gen. 19.30-38) and Yahweh's dining at Abraham's tent (Gen. 18.1-15), for example, narrate Yahweh's intimate relationship with Abraham. Yahweh's apparition before Pharaoh (Gen. 12.10-20) and Abimelech (Gen. 20.3), as will be explained later, show that Yahweh was available to all irrespective of their national and tribal associations. Similarly, Abraham's crossings, as will be clarified, highlight Yahweh as a liberator and an author of reconciliation, which would be liberating in Dalit contexts, recognizing how Dalits' subversive voices envision a liberated-reconciled society. Furthermore, like most Dalits, Abraham, narrated in the book of Genesis, was a landless man who had no burial ground for his wife. I will make my arguments further in the following chapter.

Conclusion

The present chapter analysed how Dalits' contexts can offer dialogical perspectives to Dalit theology. As seen, Dalit culture and spirituality demand a hermeneutical switch and a biblical paradigm that is more sensitive to Dalits' worldview, pathos, ethos, vision and discontent towards Brahminic hegemony and the concepts of purity and pollution. Chokhamela, Karmamela, Ravidas, Pottan Theyyam, Kummi song and Narayana Guru, as seen, communicate some essential aspects of Dalits' worldview like longing for unity, liberation, empowerment and reconciliation.

Such dissenting voices demand a biblical paradigm that suits the liberative voices in Dalits' contexts, empowering Dalits to break the caste system's barriers and provide a vision for a liberated-reconciled society in pluralistic contexts. Therefore, this book suggests an intertextual dialogue between the counter-colonial formulations in Abraham's crossings and the counter-Hindu Vedic hegemony in the subversive voices in Dalits' contexts to redress cross-cultural disconnects in Dalit theology. This proposal, however, needs further clarification, and therefore, Chapter 6 will suggest how and why Abraham's postcolonial crossings can be an essential paradigm for Dalit theology.

Chapter 6

SITUATING ABRAHAM'S POSTCOLONIAL CROSSINGS AS A PARTNER IN DIALOGUE

Introduction

During a visit to Peru, Pope John Paul II received an open letter from various Peruvian indigenous movements, which stated:

> John Paul II, we, Andean and American Indians, have decided to take advantage of your visit to return to you your Bible since in five centuries it has not given us love, peace or justice.
>
> Please, take back your Bible and give it back to our oppressors because they need its moral teachings more than we do. Ever since the arrival of Christopher Columbus, a culture, language, religion and values which belong to Europe have been imposed on Latin America by force.
>
> The Bible came to us as part of the imposed colonial transformation. It was an ideological weapon of this colonial assault. The Spanish sword which attacked and murdered the bodies of the Indians at night became the cross which attacked the Indian soul.[1]

What was their problem? Why did they propose to return the Bible? Indeed, the delegation was not questioning the Bible. They knew that the values of the Bible could transform their colonizers. Ultimately, they challenged how their colonizers interpreted the Bible to justify the post-Columbus (1492) settlements and mass killings of the native populations in Latin America.[2]

What has this to do with Dalit theology? The delegation was challenging the discursive and cultural formations of colonialism that had superimposed a European culture, language, religion and worldview upon Peruvian indigenous communities, which displaced indigenous culture and worldview to the margins. They also demanded a reading from the margins that promotes a more humane and cross-cultural hermeneutic, recognizing the brother and the neighbour in religious, cultural and ethnic Others. A similar discontent, as observed, was one of the reasons for the advent of Dalit theology. Dalit Christian academics, who were dissatisfied with caste hegemony, perceived that Indian Christian theology and the church did not address the caste system from Dalits' perspective but instead re-affirmed the dominant caste Christians' ideologies through various compromises. Therefore, Dalit researchers demanded a hermeneutical switch from Sanskritic obsession to Dalits' pathos that could transcend the caste hegemony in Indian Christian theology. However, their move had some limitations since Dalit theology followed the hermeneutical examples of liberation theologies developed in predominantly Christian contexts.

The methodological and conceptual dependence upon liberation theologies alienated Dalit theology from the alternative moral visions, the liberation and reconciliation ethic in the subversive manoeuvres in Dalits' worldview. This book, therefore, suggests a hermeneutical switch and a reading from the margins, which honours Dalits' counter-formulations and longing for a liberated-reconciled society, envisioned in Dalits' worldview to bridge the cross-cultural and cross-religious divides in Dalit theology. From such backgrounds, I argue that an intertextual reading of Dalits' counter-formulations and the Second Temple community's counter-assertions to the Persian Empire can advance Dalit theology through Dalits' forgotten voices. A postcolonial reading of the Abrahamic narrative, however, needs further clarification since there is a long gap between this narrative and the emergence of postcolonial theory. Therefore, the present chapter will clarify the basic premises of postcolonial criticism, hoping to establish the validity of the proposed reading, and how such a task can uncover the Second Temple community's resistance.

Postcolonial criticism

Postcolonial criticism is an intellectual response from the formerly colonized communities that emerged from their sufferings under colonialism's continuing effects.[3] It surveys various social and ideological mechanisms of the colonialists and interrogates how colonialism has reshaped the colonizer and the colonized.[4] Postcolonial studies were popularized after Edward Said's (1935–2003) critique of the Western representations of the East as depicted in his book *Orientalism*.[5] In this influential work, the Palestinian author argues that the colonial discourse constructs Europe as the dominant self at the centre and the colonized as the dominated self at the periphery. This reality and its continuing impact on subjugated cultures and peoples' perceptual frameworks are primary resources for postcolonial inquiry.[6]

Likewise, postcolonial reading attempts to ensure that the sufferings of the poor take primacy over the interests of the wealthy and highlights the resistance of the colonized towards the colonizing strategies of Britain, France and the United States.[7] This reading strategy searches textual indications for colonial ideologies and investigates how these texts approve or disapprove of the establishment.[8] Further, it examines various associations between the insider and outsider and societies and cultures, wrestling with identity and representation dilemmas.[9] Such an optic uncovers the underrepresented voices from the margins, unmasks colonial epistemological frameworks, decodes Eurocentric logics and interrogates stereotypical cultural representations.[10]

Postcolonial criticism, as noted, is a literary critique of Western imperialism. When aligned against British expansionism, it has been called the Commonwealth study also.[11] The Eurocentric view of postcolonial criticism can challenge my attempt to read the Abrahamic narrative through a postcolonial optic if postcolonialism is defined in historical terms, referring only to the societies liberated from European governance.[12] Can we explain the Abrahamic narrative using the tools developed for studying modern Empires?[13] What does the 'postcolonial' in 'postcolonial biblical criticism' mean? The Eurocentric and Anglocentric aspect of postcolonialism, however, is not an uncontested position. Timothy Brennan, for instance, clarifies that the Persians, Macedonians, Romans, Mongols, Mughals and Ottomans had great empires.[14] Ultimately, there were many ancient empires, and it is not reasonable to limit postcolonial studies to the modern era alone.

'Postcolonial' in postcolonial criticism

As noted, the postcolonial study is commonly understood methodologically and conceptually as either a Eurocentric or Anglocentric reading strategy. However, colonization is not a modern phenomenon alone. Instead, colonialism and deterritorialization have existed throughout history.[15] Sadly, postcolonial scholars have often overlooked ancient Empires' colonial strategies and limited the scope of their studies to European expansions.[16] Such a situation requires scholars to redress the mistake by attending to ancient kingdoms and their colonial manoeuvrings in Africa, Asia and the Americas.[17] Further, as John Marshall warns, the narrative of the birth of postcolonial analysis should not set the limit on the theory's application.[18] Thus, postcolonial studies do not exclusively mean Western empires only but include the ancient kingdoms and present ongoing injustices linked with colonial time.

Such openness to diverse possibilities reoriented biblical hermeneutics. Musa Dube, for instance, suggests that Israel's subjugation by the Babylonian, Persian, Syrian, Greek and Roman Empires was part of colonial expansionism.[19] Similarly, Sugirtharajah, after inquiring about the impacts of colonialism upon the composition of biblical narratives, claims that the military interests of Israel and the need to respond to the military demands of Egypt, Assyria, Persia and Rome shaped the biblical narratives.[20] Hence, biblical texts can be a resource for studying nationalism, ethnicity, deterritorialization, multiple identities and citizenship.[21] From such backgrounds, scholars analyse the Bible as a work of literature, noting that biblical authors lived under colonial strategies.

Postcolonial Biblical criticism

Postcolonial studies began to inspire biblical scholars in the 1990s.[22] It concentrates on rereading biblical texts against their colonial contexts by questioning the Bible's role in the imperial cause and the extent to which biblical narratives communicate colonial assumptions.²³ Such a reading provides the theoretical and conceptual framework within which the originating colonial contexts of the biblical writings can be studied.²⁴

There are two essential proposals in postcolonial biblical hermeneutics. One of them interrogates how the Bible has been interpreted to support or challenge the ideology, activities and institutions of colonialism.²⁵ Musa Dube, Kwok Pui-lan, Janet Wooten, Sarah Travis and Uriah Y. Kim, for example, argue that the Bible had authorized the subjugation of foreign nations and lands historically down to the present.²⁶ The Exodus–conquest account, among other biblical texts, has been used to legitimize the 'barbaric behaviour' of colonizers over the past 2,000 years. Such is not, however, the entire story. There are many instances of the formerly colonized people interpreting the Bible to challenge the legacy of colonialism, too.

The second approach evaluates how colonialism influenced the composition, editing and transmission of the Hebrew and Christian scriptures. This reading is a historical-critical enterprise that considers how empires' social and cultural environment work within the biblical compositions and evaluate the colonial contexts of the biblical narratives. Hence, biblical narratives, according to postcolonial biblical studies, are not neutral or disinterested objective or aesthetic discourses, but instead are narratives immensely influenced by the imperial contexts of their composition. So too, Carolyn J. Sharp and Dube clarify that Israel and Judah's scribes, whose national interests were compromised by either the threat of military subjugation or colonization by Assyria, Babylon or Persia, produced the Hebrew scriptures. Such narratives, therefore, could be impregnated with colonialist rhetoric and fantasies of the empire, reflecting the pressure experienced by Israel to endorse, resist or accommodate imperial powers.²⁷ Hence, a reading from the margins on the biblical texts' production can help reclaim many subversive voices. Without denying the validity of the former approach, I believe an unveiling of the colonizing techniques can make a postcolonial reading of Genesis 12.10-20 and Genesis 20 more relevant to the readers.

Thus, a postcolonial reading of Abraham's crossings will clarify how Genesis 12.10-20 and Genesis 20 have been interpreted to support or challenge colonialism and how the ancient world's colonialism shaped these narratives. However, I suggest that a postcolonial reading of its imperial contexts of composition, editing and transmission may be more illuminating to Dalits' background. Such a strategy will help us uncover the resistance to colonialism and alternative moral visions, skilfully embedded in these narratives.

Postcolonial reading of the Abraham narrative

Many postcolonial interpretations have already projected Abraham as a colonizer. Indeed, there are traits of a colonizer within Abraham.²⁸ What else can designate a person who was entrusted to go to an unknown territory to inherit it? Israel Kamudzandu, for example, named 'Abraham as a coloniser who believes he may rightly travel to, enter, kill, and possess resources and lands that belong to foreign nations'.²⁹ Similarly, Abraham's characterization, especially the promises to him, has been extensively used to support modern colonialism. As Obvious Vengeyi notes, some colonizers understood themselves as actualizing Abraham's promise (Gen. 12.1-3).³⁰ Therefore, peripheral and thematic interpretations may invalidate attempts to find anti-colonial elements in the Abrahamic narrative.

Such blemishes, however, do not comprehensively refute the vitality of the virtues in his life. Further, studying this narrative against its composition and transmission history might uncover the anti-colonial elements submerged in this narrative. Such undertakings will help us to place the Abrahamic narrative in its colonial context. My attempt to reread the narrative does not discredit other reading strategies. As a complex text, the Abrahamic narrative can be studied from various angles, depending on the interpreter's choices and convictions. My articles published elsewhere discuss the promises to Abraham against the bureaucratic policies of the Persian governors of Ezra and Nehemiah, while another one discusses how Genesis 19:30-38 subverts the concept of the Moabite and Ammonite Others popularized by the Persian Empire.³¹

Composition history of the Abraham narrative

Diachronic reading dominated Abrahamic studies at an earlier stage, which tended to underestimate Abrahamic narrative's historicity, interpreting Abraham as an invention of unconscious art.³² From such backgrounds, Julius Wellhausen claimed that a modern reader could not obtain any historical information on the patriarchs from these narratives since the historical context of the composition was most likely projected back into hoary antiquity.³³ Likewise, Gunkel considered the patriarchs as personified tribes instead of historical figures.³⁴ Later, archaeological discoveries shifted the focus and convinced scholars about the Abrahamic narrative's substantial historicity.³⁵ They suggested that the names and customs in this narrative reflect the second millennium BCE genuinely.³⁶

The scholars who analysed the language and rhetorical features of the Abrahamic narrative highlighted Ur of the Chaldeans (Gen. 11:28, 31, 15:7), Philistines (Gen. 21.34) and Abraham as Father of the Arabs (Gen. 25:1-5) as possible anachronistic references and challenged the proposals based upon archaeological discoveries.³⁷ T. L. Thompson (1974), for instance, showed that the attempts to locate the patriarchal age around the second millennium are without substance.³⁸ J. Van Seters (1975) carried the debate further and advocated that the names, customs and institutions in the Abrahamic narrative have their closest parallels in the Ancient Near Eastern societies of the first millennium. For him, the Abrahamic tradition reflects 'only a late date of composition'.³⁹

These new insights challenged some scholars to reread the Abrahamic narrative through the political, social and religious conflicts of Achaemenid Yehud. According to this trend, the Abrahamic narrative informs more about the time of its final editing, the Persian Yehud, than some pre-exilic 'past' as narrated peripherally in the text.⁴⁰ Further, this hypothesis suggests that the political and social conflicts of Persian Yehud are the clues for interpreting the Abrahamic narrative. A modern scholar, therefore, may not decipher significant historical data from the Abrahamic narrative as actual history.[41] This narrative, on the other hand, informs the ideologies of their editors who lived in Yehud. Hence, the Abrahamic narrative may not be a reliable source for reconstructing the historical period it seems to narrate.

However, we can identify the concerns of its authors (editors) by studying the function of the Abrahamic narrative against the historical reconstructions of the Persian period. Mario Liverani's *Israel's History and the History of Israel* is an attempt in this direction.[42] This book tries to separate the history of ancient Judah and Israel from the story in the biblical text that reflects later historical contexts and agendas. Liverani suggests that the returning Judean exiles rewrote the available traditions to create a temple city Jerusalem on a Babylonian model. This history, Liverani suggests, became the founding narrative of Israel.[43] This document attempted to normalize the social circumstances by reinterpreting paradigmatic situations from the past.[44] Similarly, Mark G. Brett, R. C. Heard and Naveen Rao suggest that Genesis is related to the Persian period's politics.[45] Following this lead, some scholars began to decode the Abrahamic narrative through Persian eyes.

Postcolonial contexts of the Abrahamic narrative

As indicated, some scholars interpret the Abrahamic narrative as a late composition. The references to Ur of the Chaldeans in Genesis 11.28, 31 and 15.7, such scholars claim, show that this narrative might be a late composition since Chaldeans did not appear on the historical scene until the ninth-century BCE.[46] The frequent references to Abraham in exilic and post-exilic writings (Isa. 41.8f, 51.2; Ezek. 33.24; Isa. 63.16) are further clues. Norman Whybray, for instance, notes that such references imply that the stories used by the editor of the Abrahamic narrative were implausible to be much earlier than the Babylonian Exile.[47]

Similarly, the geographical and historical references in this narrative call for a post-exilic composition.[48] Yahweh's command to Abraham to leave Mesopotamia and go to the land that Yahweh would show him might be an exilic composition when part of the Jewish population resided in Mesopotamia.[49] Moreover, Abraham migrating from the Ur of the Chaldeans to become a blessing for the nations would have appealed to exilic Judah.[50] Also, Abraham who observes the Torah and teaches all his sons to do the same comes, Ska observes, from a composition or a series of post-exilic re-readings.[51] Thus, emerging scholarly consensus claims that the Abrahamic narrative in its final form was penned in Babylon to exhort the Judean exiles that they are not in an alien land but their ancestors' land.[52]

Some interpreters, based on the post-exilic appeal of the Abrahamic narrative, interpret it against Persian policies.[53] Stavrakopoulou, for instance, proposes that the Abrahamic narrative is a Persian period manifesto, promoting a peaceful, cooperative relationship between returning members of the Golah community and the indigenous communities who remained in Jerusalem.[54] Thomas Römer suggests that Genesis 11.27-32 constructs Abraham as an identity marker for the Babylonian Golah community.[55] So too, Blenkinsopp, Dijkstra and Michael conclude that Abraham is a model for those who returned from Babylon.[56] Thus, the Abrahamic narrative is likely to be a product of the Persian Yehud. The rhetorical features also suggest this.

Rhetorical features and context of the Abraham narrative

The rhetorical features in the Abrahamic narrative also point to later editing. The universal blessing found in Genesis 12.1-3 is one indication since this theme does not appear again until Deutero-Isaiah. F. V. Winnett, for example, claims that an exilic and post-exilic context is the most natural background to explain Genesis 12.1-3.[57] Admittedly, there are some objections to such a claim. Ska, for instance, states that the text says nothing about a universal blessing; instead, it mentions the universal renown that Abraham will acquire. However, Ska also dates this text to the late post-exilic period.[58] Lot's separation from Abram (Gen. 13.7-12) is another instance.

Similarly, the affinity of Genesis 14 to Jewish stories in the Persian period is well known. Scholars like Westermann, Gunkel and Mark W. Bartusch suggest that Genesis 14 is a post-exilic composition.[59] Seters explains Genesis 15 as a post-exilic composition since it shares the worldview of Deutero-Isaiah.[60] Likewise, many scholars interpret Genesis 17 as a post-exilic document, which portrays the hopes and fears of the exilic period.[61] So too, Paul R. Williamson suggests that Genesis 18–21 is a post-exilic composition.[62] Hepner argues that Lot's departure from Sodom (19.1-29) might have been written for a post-exilic audience.[63] Scholars like Tracy Maria Lemos note that Genesis 24 may be a post-exilic document.[64] Thus, there are plenty of scholarly proposals that acknowledge the post-exilic appeal of the Abrahamic narrative. There are also frequent references to Abraham in the post-exilic texts.

References to Abraham in the Hebrew scripture

Abraham plays only an insignificant role outside the Pentateuch. Abraham is mentioned only twenty-four times, including Joshua 24.2-3; 1 Kings 18.36; 2 Kings 13.23; 1 Chronicles 1.27-28, 32, 34, 16.16, 29.18; 2 Chronicles 20.7, 30.6; Nehemiah 9.7; Psalm 47.10, 105.6, 9, 42; Isaiah 29.22, 41.8, 51.2, 63.16; Jeremiah 33.26; Ezekiel 33.24 and Micah 7.20 in the Hebrew scriptures.

Abraham in Joshua

Joshua 24 mentions Abraham retrospectively. The text establishes Israel's salvation history, starting with Terah and Abraham.[65] This document, as Römer understands, has some parallels with Nehemiah 9, which may indicate post-exilic dating.⁶⁶ Joshua 24 mentions Abraham as an exemplary person who comes from an idolatrous family. The narrator asks his readers to put away such Gods as Abraham did. The narrator's appraisal of Abraham in Joshua 24, especially when reading against Nehemiah 9, is vital. It is reasonable to assume that Joshua 24 might have functioned as a paradigm for the ethnocentric policies of the Achaemenid Yehud.

Further, as Römer and Granerod note, Joshua 24 combines the patriarchal narratives with the Exodus tradition.⁶⁷ Such a merging is another clue since Schmid had already suggested that the Patriarchal and the Exodus narratives existed as two independent traditions until the exilic period and a Priestly source combined them in the exilic period to form a single narrative. A post-Priestly redactor combined the P source with two non-priestly sources in the post-exilic period.⁶⁸ Joshua 24 was one of Schmid's important clues to advance this hypothesis.⁶⁹ Similarly, Seters, Mayes, Popovic, Römer and Macchi suggest that Joshua 24 is a post-exilic text.⁷⁰

Abraham in Kings

Scholars like Rodney A. Werline suggest that the books of Kings are post-exilic compositions.⁷¹ There are only very few references to Abraham in them (1 Kgs 18.36, 2 Kgs 13.23). Among them, 1 Kings 18.36 mentions the God of Abraham, Isaac and Israel. The tradition which Elijah invokes in 1 Kings 18.36, Roger Tomes clarifies, is that of the Patriarchs and reference to Yahweh as 'the God of Abraham, Isaac, and Israel' is rare and found only in the late post-exilic books (1 Chr. 29.18, 2 Chr. 30.6).⁷² After noting this affinity to post-exilic books, Jyrki Keinänen suggests that this terminology appears to be late.⁷³ Likewise, R. N. Whybray claims that 1 Kings 18.36 is highly unlikely to be a pre-exilic text.⁷⁴

The second passage, 2 Kings 13.23, refers to the covenants with Abraham, Isaac and Jacob. The Abrahamic covenant has an exilic and post-exilic implication. The promise of land and progeny (Gen. 15.18-20, 17.3-8) would console a nation that had lost its sovereignty and faced an uncertain future.⁷⁵ Thus, the references to Abraham in the Kings have post-exilic significance.

Abraham in Chronicles

The books of 1 and 2 Chronicles are often understood as post-exilic compositions.⁷⁶ They address the post-exilic community and assure them that God is still with them.⁷⁷ Abraham is mentioned frequently in them (1 Chr. 1.27-28, 32, 34, 16.16, 29.18 and 2 Chr. 20.7, 30.6). Thus, it seems that the figure of Abraham resurges in the post-exilic period.⁷⁸

Abraham in Prophetic literature

The ancestral traditions receive little attention in the literature of the pre-exilic prophets.⁷⁹ The pre-exilic prophets seldom refer to Abraham even though they address events like Sodom and Gomorrah (Hos. 11.8; Amos 4.11; Isa. 1.9; Zeph.

2.9) from the life of Abraham.⁸⁰ However, Abraham is frequently mentioned in exilic and post-exilic prophetic writings (Isa. 41.8f, 51.2; Ezek. 33.24; Isa 63.16).⁸¹

The exile is the first time Abraham is mentioned as a significant figure (Ezek. 33.24; Isa 41.8, 51.2).⁸² Abraham became a symbol of Yahweh's promise to the displaced people during this time.⁸³ Some scholars connect this exilic and post-exilic preference to the composition of the narrative and claim that the Abrahamic narrative can be dated to the post-exilic period.⁸⁴

The Abrahamic narrative's post-exilic appeal does not mean that there were no written or oral traditions behind it. Instead, I believe that the Abrahamic traditions existed before the Babylonian Exile. However, as will be seen, those traditions were carefully edited to address the needs of the post-exilic community. In my argument, how the post-exilic community rescripted the pre-exilic material for the theological and existential purposes of the postcolonial context, as will be suggested, can be a significant resource for Dalits to advance Dalit theology. As noted, Dalits have been living the life of a displaced community. The dominant caste people denied their fundamental human rights for many centuries in their home country. Therefore, the post-exilic community's historical and theological responses to their traumatic experiences could be a valuable resource for Dalits. They have been living the life of an exiled people in their land. This book will now study the Abrahamic narrative before the Exile to clarify the function of the postcolonial attempt of the Second Temple community.

Abrahamic Narrative before the Exile

Abrahamic traditions existed in some form before the Babylonian Exile.⁸⁵ Römer, based upon the reference to Abraham in Ezekiel 33.24, assumes that Abraham was a well-known figure for the exilic community and suggests that the Abrahamic traditions existed before the Babylonian Exile.⁸⁶ Such a claim does not include that there was an Abrahamic narrative as a single document before the Exile either. Instead, as Whybray clarifies, Abrahamic traditions had not been incorporated to form a record of Abraham and Sarah as we have it today before the Exile.⁸⁷ The exiled Judeans edited those traditions during and in response to Exile and diaspora.⁸⁸

From such contexts, scholars read the Abrahamic narrative against the post-exilic contexts.⁸⁹ Most of them understand Genesis as an anti-colonial text resisting the Persian Empire's socio-economic programme. Mark Brett and Moberly, for example, claim that the book of Genesis is a critique of Ezra and Nehemiah's ethnocentric policies.⁹⁰

There are alternative proposals as well. Roland Boer clarifies that Genesis' dominant position is like the one we find in Ezra and Nehemiah. Indeed, Boer does not disregard Genesis' dissenting voices. He designates the opposing voice as quieter and subversive, challenging the policies of Ezra and Nehemiah. This provocative voice, Boer clarifies, is from an editor who might have worked carefully through the material of Genesis to voice his anti-colonial sentiments, always seeking to avoid the heavy hand of the censors.⁹¹ After recognizing the clash of interests between colonial and anti-colonial elements, Yee and Brett claim that Genesis is the product of postcolonial hybridity.[92] The elites governing Yehud had a unique social location since they were Persian agents with Jewish ethnicity. They share the ethos of the colonizer and the colonized simultaneously. This postcolonial hybridity, Yee proposes, influenced the text. The text itself is a hybrid, codifying Israel's ancient stories and laws, which provided a sense of ethnic identity and advanced the Empire's interests.[93] The pro-colonial and anti-colonial elements are significant. However, a postcolonial reading of Abraham's encounters will be more illuminating since it will help us identify the resistance to colonial hegemony in these narratives. Similarly, Abraham has many striking resonances with Dalits' contexts.

Abraham and Dalits' contexts

Abraham has many parallels in his life with Dalits. God called Abraham out of his comfort zones, away from his language and the security of his father's house. Abraham, like Dalits, remained as a landless man, pressed by famine and nomadic life.[94] He lived as an alien in the land, which God had promised to his descendants. Abraham, like Dalits, acts as a 'helpless pawn in the clutches of ruthless landholders' (Gen. 23.1-4).[95] Hence, Abraham is reminiscent of a Dalit ancestor, narrated by Nirmal. Similarly, there is a clash of interests in Abraham. He shares the ethos of a colonizer and a colonized simultaneously. Dalits also share the same characteristics. They are oppressed by the dominant castes, and, unfortunately, some Dalits, as will be further explained, mistreat fellow Dalits.

Likewise, Abraham functioned as an identity marker for the Golah community, which shares much ethos with Dalits. Like the Golah community who lived away from their homeland, Dalits live as aliens in their homeland, oppressed by the dominant caste. Hence, Abraham, as an identity maker, could appeal to Dalits. Further, Joshua 24 depicts Abraham as an exemplary person from an idolatrous family. Such an image would inspire Dalits because of their pre-conversion religious orientations. Such contextual similarities invite scholarly interrogation, and this book will analyse Abraham's crossings as a postcolonial anticolonial literary construct. The delimitation to Abraham's crossings, however, does not imply that they are the only relevant resources for Dalit theology in the Abrahamic narrative.

Abraham narrative and Dalit theology: Further possibilities

As indicated, there are many instances in the Abrahamic narrative, which may further Dalit theology. Genesis 19.30-38, for example, is one such example. Of course, it is an infamous account. However, as Dube identifies, there are multiple similarities between Abraham and Genesis 19.30-38. For instance, Abraham and Lot are involved with two women who bear them children. Sarah and Lot's daughters are concerned with descendants, but Lot and Abraham remain silent. The daughters, like Sarah, plot and bring forth two sons. Lot, like Abraham, seems to be a victim of two women.[96] A careful reading of the literary structure of this narrative reveals the potential of this narrative further. J. A. Loader has suggested that Genesis 19.30-38 is part of a concentric structure:[97]

A 18:1-16 Three men visit Abraham
    B 18:17-33 Abraham's question about Sodom
        C 19:1-26 God's wrath over Sodom
            1-11 Two messengers visit Lot
            12-22 Rescue from Sodom
            23-26 Destruction of Sodom
    B' 19:27-29 Abraham witnesses the destruction
A' 19:30-38 Lot and his daughters

The outer layers of a concentric structure are essential, and they hold opposing ideas in tension with one another.[98] As the concentric structure shows, Genesis 18.1-16 and Genesis 19.30-38 are the outer layers, and they present opposing views in tension.[99] Genesis 18.1-16 is commonly understood as an instance of a formal annunciation delivered to Abraham and Sarah that guarantees the end of Sarah's barrenness.[100] If that is the case, Genesis 19.30-38 could well be a narrative about Abraham's relatives acquiring their offspring in a challenging situation. So too, the text clarifies that Lot's daughters acted not out of lust but of the desire to fulfil their womanly destiny and preserve their lineage.[101] There would have been no Moab, Ruth or David without the incest of Lot.[102] Therefore, the text designates Lot's daughters as proud 'royal ancestresses' because of the connection between Genesis 19.30-38 and the Davidic lineage.[103] Hence, there is no stigma attached to the mothers' action, and Genesis 19.30-38 treats Lot and his daughters as members of the family of promise.[104]

Such a reading can open avenues for appropriating Genesis 19.30-38 in Dalit theology, especially since Dalits have many matriarchal deities. Similarly, the suffering, rejection and divine intervention to save Hagar would be another resource for Dalit theology. There could be many more instances in Abraham's life which demand further research and appreciation from Dalit theologians. Let me clarify that my focus on Abraham's crossings does not discredit other incidents in his life. Instead, I wish to invite scholarly attention to the possibilities in the Abrahamic narrative for theologizing in Dalit contexts. The following chapters hint how Abraham's encounters may assist Dalit theology in actualizing a liberated-reconciled society and church, as envisioned in Dalits' contexts.

Conclusion

Traditions about Abraham are not an invention of the post-exilic period. They existed in some form before the Exile. However, the post-exilic community reinterpreted and reimagined their historical traditions therapeutically when the community encountered the Persian Empire's disruptive policies. Therefore, the Abrahamic narrative reflects the colonialist rhetoric and imperial ambitions of Persian Yehud. As a product of postcolonial hybridity, this narrative has both colonial and anti-colonial interests skilfully embedded in it. I will, however, concentrate on the subversive voices that challenge the colonial propaganda and will study the boundary crossings of Abraham as a post-exilic counter-metaphor amidst the ethnocentric programmes of Achaemenid Yehud. Such a study might uncover the elements of protest embedded in these narratives and offer some praxis-oriented guidelines to highlight the brother and the neighbour in the colonial, cultural and religious Other.

This book will follow the significance of these postcolonial tactics and will explore their implications for Dalits. As noted, caste influences Dalits and non-Dalits. They are unconsciously imprisoned by the sociological, religious and cultural boundaries defined by the caste system, deeply embedded in their psyche. The caste system also regulates many behavioural patterns, even though it is not always visible in postcolonial India. Therefore, as argued, Dalit theology needs a paradigm that breaks the walls which reinforce the sociological, religious and cultural boundaries set by the caste system and reconciles Dalits with non-Dalits. The cross-cultural, cross-religious and cross-ethnic encounters of Abraham have immense potential for facilitating cross-cultural exchanges and appropriation in this context. Also, it can promote liberating mutual partnerships in India's multicultural contexts. Furthermore, it will help Dalit theology build bridges across the gulf that separates Dalit Christians and Syrian Christians.

Admittedly, such an attempt is in line with the message of Jesus and the early church's praxis. The mission of Jesus is nothing but crossing borders and breaking through the walls of separation. Jesus crossed the boundaries to be available to the marginalized of his day. Similarly, the early church's story, as we know, is a story of crossing boundaries. Acts of the Apostles narrate the Gospel's movement from Jerusalem to the ends of the earth (1.8). Philip's encounter with an Ethiopian official (Acts 8.26-39) is another example. The vision of Peter (Acts 10.9-16) challenges the definition of boundaries. Thus, the mission of Jesus, the history of the early church and the cross-cultural encounters of Abraham invite us not into life within boundaries and distinctions and borders and differences but to celebrate unity in diversity. Hence, this book, as proposed in the previous chapters, will explore the boundary crossings of Abraham as a dialogical partner for Dalit theology. A similar undertaking was the real request of the Peruvian indigenous movement to John Paul II. It might help Dalit theologians to develop a theology that seeks piety in the religious and cultural Other.

Chapter 7
EXPLORING ABRAHAM'S CROSSINGS TO EGYPT AND GERAR

Introduction

Onam is the national festival of Kerala, India.[1] It is a harvest festival celebrated in August–September and recalls the defeat of Mahabali by Lord Vishnu. There is a dominant caste as well as a Kerala version of this festival. The dominant caste people celebrate it as the birth of Lord Vishnu, who had liberated Kerala from Mahabali. Kerala, with its compelling anti-caste assertions, does not accept this version and celebrates Onam annually to venerate Mahabali. Onam's theme song shows that Kerala's people challenged the dominant caste Hindu Vedic worldview that relegates Dalits' bodies as untouchable.

> Maveli nadu vaneedum kalam
> manusharellarum onnupole
> amodhathode vasikkum kalam
> apathangarkkumottillathanum
> kallavum illa chathiyumilla
> ellolamilla polivachanam
> kallapparayum cherunazhiyum
> kallatharangal mattonnumilla
> adhikal vyadhikalonnumilla
> balamaranangal kelppanilla[2]

This song projects Mahabali as a humanist and socialist and imagines an interconnected casteless society where every person has equal access to rights without any impediments. '*Manusharellarum onnupole*' means that the people were equal in all aspects of life, and there were no social, economic or caste barriers under Mahabali. '*Apathangarkkumottillathanum*' indicates that people were free from every form of harm. So too, the people were happy, and there was neither sickness nor anxiety among people. Hence, the song imagines a liberated-reconciled society under Mahabali. Surprisingly, such assertions and counter-formulations do not name or demonize either Vamana or the dominant castes. The poem indicates that Kerala's resistance to and protest against dominant caste hegemony was more than an act of exclusion and includes embracing the dominant caste men in an inter-connected world.

Nevertheless, longing for collective liberation and a casteless society connected through mutually enriching partnerships is not particular to Kerala alone. As seen by noted attempts in Dalits' spirituality and culture, Dalits' worldview and epistemology of resistance envision a casteless society linked through cross-cultural, cross-ethnic and cross-religious partnerships. Such openness is pertinent to bridge the gap between various castes in India's multicultural and multireligious contexts. Raymond Allen Morrow and Carlos Alberto Torres, though in foreign contexts, have already suggested that the oppressed cannot regain their humanity by merely repressing their oppressor.[3]

Such instances demand further interrogation since Dalit theology, as noted, overlooks Dalits' counter-hegemonic worldview, the epistemology of Dalits' resistance and Dalits' alternative yet empowering moral visions significantly. Therefore, this book suggested that Dalit theology needs a hermeneutical switch and listening to Dalits' subversive voices and learning from them would be liberative in Dalits' contexts. From such contexts, this book proposed that an intertextual reading between the Second Temple community's resistance to the Persian Empire narrated through Abraham's crossings and Dalits' assertions against Hindu Vedic worldview can empower Dalit theology and advance Dalit–Syrian Christian dialogues.

The present chapter will explain the communicative contexts of Abraham's crossings to Egypt and Gerar. As we know, Abraham's encounters with Egyptians and Philistines are part of the wife-sister/endangered ancestress narratives, which occur in Genesis 12.10-20, 20.1-18 and 26.1-11. These stories, which depict a patriarch (Abraham/Isaac) passing his wife off as his sister to avert a perceived danger, are typical stories with differing specifics.[4] Those similarities can signal historical or literary dependency.[5] Source critics, therefore, assign 12.10-20 and 26.1-18 to the Yahwist and 20.1-18 to the Elohist, considering these narratives as multiple versions of the same story.[6] On the other hand, form critics search their transmission history based on their similarities. Accordingly, they claim that Genesis 12.10-20 is the earliest episode.[7] However, there is an alternate proposal that argues that the Isaac version is the original one.[8]

The attempts to understand wife-sister narratives diachronically helped biblical scholars abundantly. However, as clarified, I will not analyse these stories' sources or transmission history. Such a reservation is not to underpin or challenge their composition history. These stories, as explained, might have an oral or literary history. Nevertheless, this research seeks to analyse the communicative contexts of the present version of these narratives as documents composed during Achaemenid Yehud. Scholars such as Roy B. Zuck, for instance, note that the biblical narratives have a communicative intent and the textual indications are part of a carefully crafted episode.[9] Building upon similar presuppositions, Meir Sternberg, Adele Berlin and Jeannine K. Brown alerted readers to the biblical narratives' communicative contexts.[10] Following such proposals, this book will analyse Abraham's crossings as communication between an anonymous author who lived in Achaemenid Yehud and his intended readers. Such an analysis might clarify how an intertextual reading between Abraham's itinerates and Dalits' subversive voices could redirect Dalit theology.

Communicative contexts of Abraham and Sarah crossing the Egyptian border

Genesis 12.10-20 begins with the report that there was a famine in Canaan and Abraham went down to Egypt. The Hebrew word יְהִי (*way-hi*) in 12.10 marks the beginning of a new narrative unit.[11] This unit ends with the narrator's notice that the Pharaoh let Abraham and Sarah go out of Egypt. There are some alternate proposals also. Sailhamer argues that the narrative continues to 13.4, where the story returns to the original point of departure.[12] However, Genesis 12.20 seems to be the boundary of this narrative. The episode has a meaning of its own in this pericope. Similarly, it is natural to view the journey out of Egypt as marking the conclusion because the episode has started with an inward journey. So too, the final verb in Genesis 12.20, 'sent away', does not mention Abraham. Genesis 13.1, on the other hand, reintroduces Abraham.[13] Thus, the voyage to Negev begins a new episode.[14]

A peripheral reading of Genesis 12.10-20 can suggest fear and distrust towards Egyptians. Abraham fears that the Egyptians would kill him to get his wife.[15] He imagines Egypt as alien in values (Gen. 12.11-13). Abraham's prejudice, as will be seen, distorts the truth and triggers poor judgements.[16] The fear and Abraham's reaction to this dilemma are the driving forces behind this narrative. However, it is not clear why Abraham thought that the Egyptians would kill him and take Sarah. Moreover, there are many inconsistencies with Abraham's fear. Abraham had not encountered Egyptians before, and Egypt was known as a land of plenty in Genesis.[17] The Joseph narrative presumes Egypt as a symbol of safety and provision (Gen. 42.1-5, 43.1, 47.4).

Nevertheless, the Abraham narrative portrays Egypt as the oppressed.[18] Sarah mistreats Hagar, an Egyptian maidservant, and urges Abraham to expel Hagar.[19] Similarly, Abraham is the oppressor in Genesis 12.10-20. Sarah, Pharaoh and his household are the victims of Abraham's deception.[20] Moreover, it is the Pharaoh who recognizes the status of the couple. Similarly, Pharaoh's question, 'What is this you have done to me?' is almost a repetition of the accusatory question that Yahweh asks Adam and Eve after their disobedience (Gen. 3.13).[21] However, Abraham perceives Egypt as a threat. The demonizing of Egypt, seen through the Second Temple context, is striking. Why the post-exilic community imparts a compromised image of Egypt is an essential question to follow.

Abraham's fear and postcolonial representation of Egypt

Abraham's fear and distrust, as noted, triggers Genesis 12.10-20. His value judgements based on this presupposition lead him to deception. Despite many positive attributes, Abraham's behaviour in this narrative raises many questions about his character, conduct and moral standing.[22] Clare Amos clarifies:

> Abram's next actions do not cover him with glory either. He is selfishly far more concerned with his own safety (they will kill me) than with protecting his wife

Sarai or preserving her dignity. Abram acknowledges that her life would never have been in danger: they will let you live. Sarai is treated merely as a chattel to be traded for Abram's own advantage.[23]

Similarly, scholars like Cheryl Exum and Shula Keshet, reading through a psychoanalytic literary approach, propose that Abraham's apprehension encodes unthinkable and unacknowledged sexual fantasies of Abraham.[24] They interpret Abraham's fear as a symptom of patriarchal hesitation of losing his wife as a sexual object and the desire to share the wife with another man.[25] This interpretation does not do justice to Abraham. Abraham, for instance, was not uneasy about travelling to Canaan with his wife (Gen. 12.1-3). He had not made similar plans while leaving Ur of the Chaldeans or Haran. However, an alternate proposal considers this story as part of a series of episodes from Abraham's life, who feared to encounter the 'Other' and responded with deceit and trickery.[26] However, there are also exceptions to this fear of meeting the 'Other'. Abraham was not afraid to encounter the Canaanites (ch. 12), mighty kings (ch. 14), Melchizedek (ch. 14) and three visitors (18.1-15). Hence, there might be something more fascinating about Abraham's fear, and uncovering them might help us place this narrative in context.

Abraham's crossings and anti-imperial worldview

Abraham's crossings to Egypt and Gerar, when studied through Achaemenid Yehud's political and religious contexts narrated in the books of Ezra and Nehemiah, seem to be an anti-imperial construct of an anonymous editor. Such an editor, I believe, attempted to reframe, reconstruct and subvert the fear of encountering the Egyptians included in the Persian colonial worldview propagated by the pro-Persian Achaemenid regime, represented by Ezra and Nehemiah. This claim might look like an exaggeration. However, I note that scholars often interpret Genesis 12.10-20 against the expulsion of wives recommended by Ezra and Nehemiah.[27]

Matt Waters and Rainer Albertz explain the exilic community's return through Persian military strategies. Cyrus might have been establishing a military base for his intended operations against Egypt.[28] The Persians were anxious that the Egyptians would become powerful and make alliances with Persia's enemies.[29] Persia's fear of Egyptian expansionism enhanced Judah's strategic value.[30] Consequently, Ezra was appointed as a Persian official in 458 BCE when Persia was fighting against Athens in Egypt.[31] Robert J. Littman, Franz V. Greifenhagen, Michael David Coogan and Samuel Eugene Balentine suggest that Ezra's selection was part of the imperial policy to strengthen Yehud as a military outpost for ongoing wars against Egypt and Greece.[32] Yehud's fortification might have been an attempt to counter an Egyptian attack.[33]

Ezra was a pro-Persian Jew who suspected Egyptians because of their rebellion against the Persians.[34] Ezra's reservation against Egyptians is a much-explained topic. Many scholars have already noted the anti-Egyptian policy in Ezra's divorce policy. For example, Ezra had commanded Israelite husbands to divorce and expel their

Egyptian wives and children (Ezra 10.3). Donald P. Moffat and Eve Levavi Feinstein remind us that Deuteronomy 23 excludes Egyptians and Edomites for three generations but allows their descendants to become members of the assembly of the Lord (*qĕhāl Yahweh*//יְהוָה קְהַל).[35] The precise meaning of the 'assembly of the Lord' is often debated.[36] Many commentators interpret it as a reference to intermarriage or physical entry into the tabernacle/temple. Whatever be the possibilities of interpretation, Deuteronomy 23 provided the Second Temple community with a theological basis for their endogamous perspectives. However, Deuteronomic prohibition includes both sexes, while Ezra challenges marriage with foreign women only.[37] Ezra's instruction to divorce Egyptian wives, therefore, is confusing.[38] It could have been a political conspiracy of the colonial regime, which he represents.

Ezra might have projected Egypt as a colonial Other to the Persian Empire. Ingeborg Mongstad-Kvammen, for example, clarifies that an imperial power requires 'the Other' as someone to subjugate and serve as the negative contrast to the colonial master.[39] Similarly, Wietske de Jong-Kumru, Shaun L. Gabbidon and Jane M. Jacobs contend that colonialism negatively portrays other cultures and peoples.[40] Thus, Achaemenid Yehud, under the Persian Empire, might have vilified, demonized, trivialized, exoticized, mystified and represented Egypt as vicious and seductive.[41] Such representations might have impacted the lives and identities of the Second Temple community considerably. This phenomenon has many parallels in modern colonial contexts as well. In similar but Indonesian contexts, Abidin Kusno explains that a national culture of fear was formed in postcolonial Indonesia.[42] This postcolonial apprehension, Kusno demonstrates, is not merely bewilderment against the state but a sense of fear regarding other groups with whom they live side by side.[43]

Egypt's imperial representation may have influenced Yehud's socio-political aspects.[44] Such traumatic experiences impacted the Second Temple community considerably and forced them to reshape their worldview according to the colonial agenda, internalizing an anti-Egyptian perspective. It divided the class layers sharply and deeply within Yehudites and strengthened hostility and intense opposition to an internal minority such as foreign wives, creating 'Outsiders' within Yehudites.[45] Thus, Ezra's anti-Egyptian approach forced a change in worldview and implanted a predominantly colonial worldview, which created Outsiders internally and externally. Many religious movements emerged in Yehud to counter this colonial hegemony and their reservations towards Ezra are evident in the Bible. Mary Douglas, for instance, suggests that Leviticus and Numbers respond to the exclusivist policy of Ezra.[46] Third Isaiah (Isa. 56-66) also criticizes the ethnocentric policies, while Ruth's book is another example of an inclusive voice of the post-exilic Yehud.[47] Abraham's crossings, which offer an alternative, yet empowering moral vision, could also be part of this movement.

Reimagining the Egyptian Other

As noted, Abraham acts according to the colonial worldview that imagined the 'Egyptian Outsider' as a vicious Other. As will be further explained, there appears to be a conflict between Abraham's worldview and the text, though there is no explicit comments from the narrator that disapproves of Abraham.[48] The text, for example, highlights Pharaoh's innocence through many textual indications.[49] Yahweh's presence in Egypt and His dialogue with an Outsider are essential themes in this direction. Yahweh's intervention to help Sarah is also remarkable. Such indications challenge Abraham's actions and his worldview indirectly. They question Abraham's taboos and narrate morality and piety among Egyptians. Such narrative strategies demand further research. What did it mean to the worldview of the Second Temple community? What are the narrators' viewpoints, communicated through Abraham's crossing? For my purposes, moreover, how will this interpretation help Dalit theology? Answering these questions will position this book to propose a cross-cultural theology in Dalits' contexts.

Outsider (Pharaoh) as a behavioural model

Genesis 12.10-20 emphasizes Pharaoh, the Outsider, as a better behavioural model than Abraham, the insider. The text accomplishes this task through many indications. The text clarifies that Abraham's fear has nothing to do with Egypt or Egyptians. As Orlinksy explains, הִקְרִיב לָבוֹא (*hiq-rîḇ lā-ḇō-w*) in Genesis 12.11 does not refer to a place but to time.[50] Genesis 12.11, therefore, informs that the couples were yet to arrive. So, Abraham planned the deception, not in Egypt, but when the couples were about to enter Egypt. Abraham's mendacity, therefore, is entirely predetermined, in no way prompted by the factors related to their life in Egypt.[51]

The text also highlights that Abraham's fear was unfounded. Abraham worries that Egyptians will kill him for their sexual gratification. Genesis 12.15-16, however, shows that Sarah was not abducted.[52] The text uses לָקַח (*laqach*) to denote Pharaoh's action (12.15). This verb usually translates to 'take', can also mean 'accept' or 'receive'.[53] It represents the formal taking of a wife and is distinguished from sexual intercourse (Gen. 20.2-4, 34.2; Deut. 22.13-14).[54] Mosaic law uses this term for a man getting married (Lev. 21.13).[55] Thus, Pharaoh was marrying Sarah.[56] He takes Sarah with full honour and gives Abraham rich gifts as bride price also (12.16).

The text emphasizes Pharaoh's innocence.[57] The monarch states that he would not have taken Sarah if he had known she was Abraham's wife (12.19). Pharaoh sounds genuinely shocked. He returns Sarah and lets the couple go even after discovering their trick. Pharaoh permits Abraham to keep all the gifts he had given him. Nothing in Genesis 12.10-20, therefore, implies that Abraham was in any way realistic in his fear.[58] The text favours Pharaoh, and noting the text's option for Pharaoh, many commentators have rightly observed that Pharaoh is a better behavioural model than Abraham.[59]

Another indication, the structure of this narrative, going a step further, depicts a close relationship between Abraham and Pharaoh. The structure is an internal arrangement and an essential aspect of the stories.[60] As noted, Abraham's encounter with the Egyptians starts in Genesis 12.10 and ends at 12.20. The synchronic approaches propose that this narrative has a concentric structure.[61] Gordon J. Wenham, for instance, offers a concentric structure:

A. Exposition: Entry (10)
    B. First Scene: Abram's Speech (10–13)
        C. Second Scene: The Ruse at Work (14–16)
    B1. Third Scene: Pharaoh's Speech (17–19)
A1. Conclusion: Exit (20)[62]

Genesis 12.14-16, the central element, is significant to interpret Abraham's crossings.[63] According to this passage, the Egyptians whom Abraham encountered were not the ones that he had anticipated. Abraham imagined that the Egyptians would kill him upon seeing Sarah (11-12). However, 12.14-16 does not depict any contacts between Pharaoh's officials and Abraham. They did not attempt to kill him. Nor did Pharaoh's officials try to take her by force.[64] Instead, they praised her beauty to Pharaoh. Pharaoh, as noted, took her as his wife and treated Abraham well for her sake. The verb הֵיטִיב (hēyṭiyḇ) used in 12.16 to denote how Pharaoh treated Abraham is the hyphal perfect third person masculine singular of יטב (yawtab). As W. L. Moran notes, יטב (yawtab) is very significant in interpreting this passage.[65] The Hebrew Scriptures usually use this verb to denote a covenantal relationship between God and Israel and between Israel and Kenites.[66] Thus, יטב (yawtab) in 12.16 indicates Pharaoh's intention to establish a close bond with Abraham. So too, Gerard Gertoux and J. Rosalie Hooge argue that Pharaoh wanted to develop an alliance with Abraham by marrying his sister.[67]

Hence, it is clear that Pharaoh was not after sexual gratification. Instead, he was trying to establish a close relationship with Abraham. Similarly, the text narrates morality and righteousness in Pharaoh and his subjects through many textual indications. Genesis 12.10-20, for example, presents Abraham as a man acting out of his self-interests and Pharaoh as a man with a divine commission. This narrative strategy undermines the Second Temple community's colonial worldview, highlighting how Abraham misreads the Egyptians and invites scholarly attention to Yahweh's injustice to Pharaoh. How can Yahweh plague an innocent Egyptian ruler? Why did Yahweh bless the liar? What is the point of view of the narrator here? Margaret Nutting Ralph also asks these questions.[68] However, because of some unknown reasons, she does not answer them.

Yahweh as liberator and author of reconciliation

The image of God narrated in Genesis 12.10-20 is very important. Yahweh, as will be clarified, is presented as an immanent destabilizing agent who liberates the endangered couple. However, Yahweh frees Sarah from Pharaoh's harem, not through mighty acts but by informing Pharaoh about Sarah's status. The Hebrew verb נגע (naga) used in 12.17 is significant to this reading. The term naga means 'touch'.[69] It denotes the state of ongoing contact between inanimate objects (1 Kgs 6.27, 2 Chron. 3.11f). It could also mean a simple connection with an inanimate object (2 Ks 13.21), a dead body (Isa. 6.7), glowing coal (Ezek. 17.10) or with an animal (Dan. 8.5). Further, *naga* denotes a physical contact with a person (2 Sam. 23.7; Job 6.7, Dan. 8.18, 10.10, 16, 18) or God's messenger (Judg. 6.21; 1 Kgs 19.5, 7).[70] Genesis 32.25 uses *naga* to denote the touch of the angel of the Lord upon Jacob's thigh. So, 12.17 could mean that Yahweh touched Pharaoh with His great touches (strokes).

Nevertheless, Genesis 12.10-20 does not explain what this great touch was. Generations of translators and commentators, however, have interpreted 12.17 as Yahweh plagued Pharaoh. Such reading questions the morality of Yahweh. Perhaps, analysing how the exilic and post-exilic texts use *naga* might offer another perspective. The exilic and post-exilic texts, for instance, use *naga* against the vision and commission of Isaiah and Jeremiah. Both prophets receive God's touch. Jeremiah 1.9, for example, reads, 'Then the Lord put forth His hand, and touched (*naga*) my mouth.' Yahweh is the subject of Jeremiah's call. Jeremiah 1.9 goes on to say that the Lord has put His words into Jeremiah's mouth. Similarly, Isaiah 6.6-7 reports:

> One of the seraphs flew to me, holding a live coal that had been taken from the altar with a pair of tongs. The seraph touched my mouth with it and said: 'Now that this has touched your lips, your guilt has departed, and your sin is blotted out'.

Thus, exilic and post-exilic texts use *naga* as a means of revelation and communication. The divine hand is the 'key' principle in the prophetic opening of the mouth and the resolution of the objection against the call in Isaiah and Jeremiah's prophetic call narratives.[71] So too, as Jonathan Macy notes, *naga* could also mean the life-giving touch that heals, comforts and strengthens.[72] Hence, the *naga* in Genesis 12.10-20 can suggest a dialogue, Yahweh's immanent presence, healing touch and conflict resolution (like Isaiah and Jeremiah). Indeed, Genesis 12.10-20 does not narrate a dialogue between Yahweh and Pharaoh. However, as *naga* implies, Yahweh probably informed Pharaoh about Sarah's status through this vision. Though the narrator does not explain, I think there was a dialogue between Yahweh and Pharaoh, as in Jeremiah and Isaiah's case.

Hence, the anonymous author who lived in Yehud used *naga* to indicate Yahweh's immanent presence and action in Egypt, Yahweh's dialogue with Pharaoh and Yahweh's magic touch that heals, comforts and empowers Pharaoh. Such a possibility is evident from Genesis 12.18-20. Pharaoh does not claim that plagues have afflicted him. Instead, Pharaoh was fully aware of Abraham's deception. For example, Pharaoh asks Abraham, 'What is this that thou hast done unto me? Why didst thou not tell that she was thy wife?' We do not know how Pharaoh knew that Sarah is Abraham's wife.[73] It seems that Yahweh had informed Pharaoh that Sarah is Abraham's wife. This appraisal bridges the gap in the narrative also. Once Yahweh told Pharaoh the truth, he called Abraham and questioned him. The interrogation did not last long since Pharaoh knew the truth, and Yahweh had already resolved the crisis with Yahweh's healing touch.

Hence, Pharaoh lets Abraham go out of Egypt with his wife and all that he had. Probably, 'all that he had' indicates a peaceful sending away, and there was no chasing like the Exodus narrative. Hence, Genesis 12.10-20 highlights that Yahweh is an immanent and active God, involved in this world as a liberator and an author of reconciliation. Such an image is significant to Dalit theology since Dalit contexts demand an immanent God and a liberated-reconciled society. Besides these thematic suggestions, the text narrates Sarah as an agent of God's liberation. It is especially relevant to Dalit women, who are socially ostracized by the caste and patriarchy.

Sarah: The marginal woman in Egypt

Many scholars believe that Sarah participated in cheating Pharaoh. Hermann Gunkel, for instance, believes that Genesis 12.10-20 glorifies Abraham's intelligence and Sarah's self-sacrifice.[74] Similarly, Claus Westermann, after elaborating the speech in 12.11-13, suggests that Abraham's deception is a joint venture of the couple.[75] Following Westermann, many scholars interpret Sarah's silence as agreement.[76] There are alternative proposals as well. S. P. Jeansonne, for instance, claims that Sarah's silence shows her powerlessness.[77] I have reservations against questioning Sarah's morality based on her silence since she is silent throughout the Abrahamic narrative.[78] Naomi Steinberg, from a feminist perspective, offers another interpretation.[79] She imagines that Abraham was trying to get rid of a barren wife to get another wife for himself, and Sarah could not resist because of her precarious position as a barren woman.[80] Thus Sarah was a powerless victim in Egypt. Similarly, Trible and William E. Phipps rightly note that Sarah is the object of her husband's calculation and Pharaoh's pleasure in this narrative.[81] She is a manhandled woman. She has no name at the place of betrayal.[82]

This discussion does not mean that Sarah has accepted her fate in Pharaoh's harem. There is an important clue that many commentators had left out in 12.17. Most translations read the final clause in 12.17 as 'on account of' or 'because of Sarai'.[83] Such translations drop the term דבר (*dabar*) at 12.17. The Hebrew word דבר (*dabar*) has a highly complicated meaning. The King James Version, for instance, translates *dabar* into seventy-five different words.[84] However, the usual translation is to speak, to tell and a word.[85] Thus the final clause in 12.17 could also mean because of the word of Sarah.[86] This reading suggests that Sarah did not accept Abraham's plan. Instead, she was communicating with Yahweh. Perhaps, Sarah's word to Yahweh might have been a plea for deliverance. Whatever be the case, Yahweh did not abandon her. He is her refuge. He intervenes to save the abandoned wife out of her troubled situation because of her word (12.17). After noting this fundamental reality, Irmtraud Fischer claims that Yahweh takes the abandoned spouse's side – not to return Abraham his wife, but to rescue the victim of Abraham's prejudices.[87] This divine initiative, which highlights Yahweh as an immanent and active God, as will be explained, has tremendous implications for Dalit theology.

As noted, the textual indications in Genesis 12.10-20 question the Second Temple community's dominant worldview that relegated internal and external Outsiders. The narrative condemns Abraham, who misreads Egyptians. The textual indications depict Yahweh's proximity to the Outsiders and highlight Yahweh as a liberator as well as a reconciling force. These techniques have a communicative intent and analysing them will clarify the function of Abraham's crossings.

The function of Abraham's journey to Egypt

Genesis 12.10-20 reinstates that Pharaoh was not the one that Abraham was anticipating. This story highlights Yahweh as a liberator and an author of reconciliation, Yahweh's immanent presence in Egypt and Pharaoh's intention to establish a relationship with Abraham. What did Abraham's crossing communicate to the intended readers in Achaemenid Yehud?

As noted, the Achaemenid Yehud vilified and demonized Egypt and Egyptians because of political reasons. Ezra's command to divorce and expel Egyptian wives created 'an Outsider' within Yehud and affected inter-Yehud and intra-Yehud relationships. Such colonial undertakings forced the Second Temple community to reformulate their dominant worldview according to the Persian agendas, which displaced a significant portion of the community to society's margins. Such Outsiders and their empathizers, who were critical of Ezra's pro-Persian worldview and its impacts upon Yehud, crafted Genesis 12.10-20 to undermine the colonial agenda. They challenged the imperial attempts to demonize the Egyptians by offering an alternative moral outlook, highlighting how Abraham's crossing to Egypt and Yahweh's immanent presence and activities to liberate the endangered couple subvert the Persian representation of Pharaoh and the Egyptians. Thus, Genesis 12.10-20 might have been an attempt to destabilize and undermine the colonial worldview and the postcolonial representation of Egypt and promote a counter-colonial worldview filled with liberation and reconciliation through cross-cultural undertakings.

This model is relevant in Dalits' contexts also. The dominant Hindu Vedic worldview dissociates Dalits from the divine and dehumanizes them. Further, the Indian caste system compartmentalizes different castes. Each caste has some prejudices against the other. There are also inter-Dalit as well as intra-Dalit misreadings. Such preoccupations are present within Indian Christian churches too, and Dalits' experience has not always been positive within Indian Christian churches. This historical and sociological hegemony, as noted, has tempted Dalit theologians to propose Dalit theology. Such attempts, as suggested, overlooked Dalits' counter-hegemonic worldview expressed through Dalits' subversive voices, which highlights the liberated-reconciled society, connected through mutual associations. Abraham's crossing journey offers a counter-colonial worldview, projecting liberation, reconciliation and cross-border relations envisioned by the anti-imperialists in Achaemenid Yehud. It will help Dalit theology revisit the concept of the Dalit/non-Dalit Other embedded within the

Dalits and the non-Dalits. The same insight is true with Abraham's encounter with Abimelech.

Communicative context of Abraham and Sarah crossing the Philistine border

Abraham's relocation to the Philistine's land is often understood as an alternate version of Genesis 12.10-20.[88] However, there are some differences between these two narratives in their present contexts. The former took place in Egypt, while Genesis 20 was in Gerar. Abraham encounters Pharaoh in 12.10-20. He meets Abimelech in this narrative. Abraham was fleeing from famine in Genesis 12.10-20. He was moving freely, without any compulsion in Genesis 20.[89] The text does not inform why Abraham goes to settle in Gerar. Also, the text does not explain why Abraham presents Sarah as his sister to Abimelech. Genesis 20 describes Abimelech's encounter with God in detail. Genesis 12.10-20 does not object to the possibility that Pharaoh had sex with Sarah. Genesis 20, on the other hand, clarifies that Abimelech had not touched her. Pharaoh rewards Abraham after taking Sarah. Instead, Abimelech gifts Abraham after discovering the deception.[90] Thus, these stories vary in their present literary context.

Moreover, the final editor found Genesis 12.10-20 and Genesis 20 as two episodes and included them without fear of narrative or historical contradiction.[91] So too, these narratives have their own life and meaning. Joel S. Baden, Kenneth A. Mathews and D. L. Petersen have already noted that these narratives might not necessarily be different versions of the same story.[92] Each incident can be an independent episode composed around the patriarch who lies about his wife to save himself.[93] Furthermore, as Clines clarifies, each narrative has its purpose.[94] Therefore, we will analyse Genesis 20 as a stand-alone narrative.

Genesis 20 begins with Abraham's journey towards Gerar, a Philistine city.[95] The change in place and new characters indicate a new narrative's beginning. The story ends at 20.18. We do not know what caused Abraham's movement. There was neither famine nor divine commission. Perhaps, it might be a voluntary movement.[96] However, Abraham avoids telling the Philistines that Sarah is his wife.[97] What might have prompted Abraham to hide such crucial information again? Perhaps, as he explains later, Abraham worried that there is no fear of God in Gerar (20.11). He thinks that the Philistines would endanger him to get his wife. The text, however, does not substantiate Abraham's prejudices. How did Abraham know that there is no fear of God among Philistines? As the tale stands now, Abraham had not had any conflicts with them so far.

There are many proposals on Abraham's fear of the Philistines. Abraham's unsupported position as a sojourner, Moberly believes, caused Abraham's anxieties.[98] This argument seems unconvincing. Indeed, the events started after the couple entered Gerar.[99] However, the text does not narrate any difficulty that challenged Abraham's life in Gerar. Furthermore, unlike Genesis 12.10-20, Abraham had no compelling reasons for his relocation. Why the editor narrates this cross-cultural journey remains puzzling. I will analyse Genesis 20 against the historical and political realities of Yehud, especially Nehemiah's hostility with the Philistines of Ashdod (Neh. 4.1, 13.23-24), to clarify such riddles.[100]

Abraham's fear and postcolonial representation of Philistines

Ashdod was one of the five Philistine cities that the Persians incorporated into their Empire.[101] Ashdod was a famous town in Philistia during Nehemiah's time.[102] The Babylonians had reassigned some parts of Judah to Ashdod to reduce Judean territory. This land remained with Ashdod during Nehemiah's time. Indeed, the book of Nehemiah does not use the label 'Philistine' either for Ashdod or independently.[103] However, as Eve Levavi Feinstein notes, the Philistines continued to live in Ashdod during Nehemiah's time.[104] Moreover, an association of Ashdod with various national/ethnic groups, as Benedikt Otzen suggests, shows that Ashdod represents more than a city in the book of Nehemiah.[105] Hence, Ashdod could mean Philistines in general or a significant portion of Philistines.[106] Similarly, Andrew Knowles and Paul Heger argue that the women of Ashdod imply Philistine women in general.[107] Thus, Ashdod continued as a Philistine city during Nehemiah's time and represented Philistines to a large extent.

As we know, the Philistines were the Jews' traditional enemy. However, the Deuteronomic stipulations do not include the Philistines with Ammonites and Moabites. Deuteronomy prohibits the Ammonites and Moabites from the Lord's assembly forever (Deut. 23.3-4). They are the only groups that are permanently excluded from Israel.[108] Deuteronomy does not provide any such prohibitions against the Philistines. Moreover, Ezra had not included the Ashdodite women in his marriage ban. Nehemiah, deviating from the Deuteronomic stipulations and Ezra's prohibition, linked Ashdod together with the Ammonites and Moabites for unknown reasons. After responding to this inconsistency, Rainer Albertz suggests that Nehemiah's ban had included Ashdod initially, and Ammon and Moab were added to the list at a later stage.[109]

What might have prompted Nehemiah to isolate Ashdod? Nehemiah's updating of the Deuteronomic ban might respond to the political and social life in Yehud. The book of Nehemiah narrates two events that alarmed him. The Philistines of Ashdod plotted together with Sanballat, Tobiah, the Arabs and the Ammonites to fight against Jerusalem (Neh. 4.7). The enemies surrounded the Jews from the east (Ashdod), the west (Ammon), the north (Sanballat of Samaria) and the south (Geshem the Arab).[110] This coalition started a campaign to discredit the Jews and incite violence or anger against them (4.7).[111] The text does not explain the details of their activities. Therefore, we do not know whether this took the form of infiltrating Jerusalem's citizenry, or agitating throughout the surrounding regions, or trying to discredit the Jews at the Persian court. Nehemiah, however, responds to their threat with prayer and a military watch (4.9). Perhaps, Nehemiah might have also initiated some counter-propaganda against his enemies. Such enterprises, as noted in Ezra's anti-Egyptian policy, is common in colonial contexts. Nehemiah might have projected the Ashdodites as a vicious Outsider. This historical and political reality is one of the crucial clues in interpreting Nehemiah's attempts to discredit the intermarriage between Jewish men and women from Ashdod (13.23).[112]

This discussion does not mean that Nehemiah had no other reasons to challenge the intermarriage with the women from Ashdod. Nehemiah, for instance, reminds that Jewish children born out of marriage with the women from Ashdod spoke the language of Ashdod (13.23-24). This reality alarmed Nehemiah. He fears that these unions will destroy the purity of the Jews and their faith.[113] Therefore, Nehemiah rebukes them and warns the Judahites against marrying the women of Ashdod (13.25-27). He imposes an oath based on Deuteronomy 7.3 (Nehemiah 13.25) that requires the Jews to avoid marriage with Outsiders, either for themselves or their children.[114]

There are competing proposals as well. Yee links the intermarriage ban in Nehemiah with socio-economic life.[115] Nehemiah fears that the Jews were in danger of losing their political existence and religious identity because of intermarriages with the women from Ashdod.[116] Such intermarriages might have alarmed Nehemiah against the possibility of foreign influence on Judah's internal affairs. Moreover, Nehemiah might have feared that the land could be transferred from the Jerusalem elite into Outsiders through marriage with foreign women. Furthermore, Yee notes that intermarriage with foreign women among the priestly class could lead to external influences on the Jerusalem Temple's affairs.[117] Thus, Nehemiah had many reasons to update the Deuteronomic stipulations to include the Philistines of Ashdod. Such programmes might have aimed at maintaining Jewish ethnic identity by precise and dogged boundary maintenance.[118] However, what might have caused Abraham's reservations needs to be clarified further.

Abraham's crossings to Gerar and anti-imperial worldview

Nehemiah had political, sociological and religious reasons for limiting contacts with the Philistines of Ashdod. Nehemiah's enterprise reinforced hostility between Judea and Ashdod.[119] Furthermore, it projected the Philistines of Ashdod as an Outsider. Likewise, such a ban interrupted the normative order by changing the nature of the social, political and economic relations, which were part of the social structure. It forced the Second Temple community to reframe their worldview significantly. Consequently, the institutions began to be informed by and built around the Persian hegemonic worldview's central ideas. This emerging worldview might have influenced the Second Temple community, their thinking patterns and how they perceive themselves and others. Mimicking the Persian colonial worldview resulted in many personal tragedies as well.[120] It might have split family bonds between husband and wife and father and children.[121]

Further, it seeded a culture of suspicion within and beyond Yehud. The economic and social prospects for divorced foreign women and their children must have been practically nil.[122] Thus, Nehemiah's anti-Ashdod policy disrupted the life in Achaemenid Yehud and created Outsiders in inter-Yehud and intra-Yehud relationships. The Outsiders in Yehud, who was critical of the Persian domination in Nehemiah's policies, challenged the colonial ontology and epistemology circulated under Nehemiah. I suggest that they crafted Genesis 20.1-18 subversively as a counter-colonial discourse to destabilize the Persian Empire. This narrative, therefore, was a response to the political and religious worldview of a dominant section of Achaemenid Yehud and functioned as a dissenting voice of the Outsiders. If so, what might have been the communicative intent of these Outsiders?

Reimagining the Philistine Other

Abraham worries that there is no fear of God in Gerar. The text, however, casts doubt on Abraham through many textual indications. The text, as will be seen, highlights that the Philistine Outsider is a better behavioural model than Abraham, the insider. Furthermore, the text implies God's presence among the Philistines as well as their fear of God. The text also shows that Yahweh intervenes to save Sarah, whom Abraham had abandoned for his safety. It is to be noted, however, that Abraham's migration was not a forced displacement. He opted to live in the Philistines' land because of some unknown reasons. In Gerar, as in Egypt, Abraham fails to foresee the effects of his action. So too, the story does not imply that Abimelech took Sarah forcefully after exploiting the sojourner's vulnerability. The text uses לָקַח (laqach) to denote his action. As explained, it most likely means that Abimelech was marrying Sarah. It is also probable that Abraham initiated the marriage by implying Sarah as a sister. Similarly, Abimelech might have wanted Abraham as an ally to increase his political power.[123]

This discussion does not claim that Abraham had no reservations against the Philistines. Admittedly, Abraham had reasons to worry. Those reasons, however, had nothing to do with his life in Gerar. Also, the text does not share Abraham's reservations. It narrates morality and righteousness in Abimelech and shows that Gerar was not a place where people kill husbands to get their wives.[124]

Outsider (Abimelech) as a behavioural model

Genesis 20 suggests that Abimelech is innocent, and there was fear of God in Gerar. First and foremost, God speaks only to Abimelech in this chapter.[125] Abraham acts without divine commission in this narrative. Abimelech designates Gerar as צַדִּיק-תַּהֲרֹג (tsaddiq Tahárog) in 20.4. Some translations read it as an innocent nation. However, it is apt to translate tsaddiq Tahárog as a righteous nation. Such a reading reminds Abraham's request to God not to punish the righteous ones with the wicked ones in Genesis 18.25. It is remarkable that Yahweh also acknowledges Abimelech's claim (20.6ff). God agrees with Abimelech's self-defence that he was 'pure in heart' when he took Sarah (20.5-6). The Hebrew word for 'pure' here is תם (*tom*).[126] This word is related to *Tamim*. Genesis 6.9 uses this term to describe Noah's integrity and perfection.

Thus, the text presents Abimelech as a man like Noah and clarifies that there were no compelling reasons for Abraham to assume that his life would have been in jeopardy had his real relationship with Sarah been made public. This narrative technique is innovative. It narrates that Outsiders may have greater integrity before God than insiders.[127] Moreover, this episode clarifies that revelation is possible to Outsiders.[128] Hence, together with Yahweh, the text informs readers that Abimelech and his servants were not the ones that Abraham had expected.[129] Moreover, Abimelech did not defend his right to Sarah when God confronted him.[130] His response suggests that he would not have married Sarah if he knew she was Abraham's wife.

Abimelech's willingness to be open and share the truth with his officials contrasts with Abraham and his subterfuge.[131] Abimelech was also quick to correct his fault (20.8).[132] He bestowed presents upon Abraham and Sarah. He permitted them to live wherever they wanted even after recognizing their fault (20.14-16).[133] Thus, the text shows that Abraham's assessment of Gerar had been wrong.[134] Further, it confirms that Abraham's prejudices might have been pure fiction. Hence, the Philistines' image in the Abraham narrative, as will be explained, is contrary to the Philistines we see in other parts of the Hebrew Scriptures.

We encounter Philistines in the books of Genesis, Judges, 1 Samuel and 2 Samuel and Nehemiah. We have detailed information about the group we find in Judges, 1 Samuel, 2 Samuel and Nehemiah from extra-Biblical sources. However, we have no information about the Philistines in the Abraham narrative (20.1-18, 21.32, 34 and 26.1). Moreover, the Philistines in Judges and beyond are bellicose, hostile and live under lords.[135] The Philistines in Genesis, on the other hand, are peace-loving and live under a king.[136] Many scholars explain this discrepancy as an anachronism penned at a later stage.[137]

Hamilton, however, believes that the editor would not have created the Philistines' image antithetical to the Philistines' stereotype if it is an anachronistic projection.[138] This argument is valid. However, it seems to limit the freedom of the final editor. The composer might have his intentions for such a presentation. Based on the analysis so far, I contend that one possibility is that this was an innovative attempt to reimagine the Philistines of Ashdod.

So too, the structure of Genesis 20, as will be seen, highlights how this narrative endeavours to reimagine the Philistines. As suggested, the structure of the narrative might help us clarify its communicative intent. Bruce K. Waltke proposes the following concentric structure for this narrative:

A. Abimelech takes Sarah into his Harem (20:1-2)
    B. God Sues against Abimelech (20:3-7)
        X. Abimelech and Officials become afraid (20:8)
    B'. Abimelech Sues against Abraham (20: 9-13)
A'. Abimelech compensates Abraham and Sarah, and Abraham prays for Abimelech[139]

Genesis 20.8 is the centre of the concentric structure. As noted, this verse is crucial to explain this narrative. Genesis 20.8 emphasizes how Abimelech and his officials responded to God's communication. The verb used here to describe their fear is ירא (*yir'ah* or *yare*). The semantic range of *yare* is quite broad. It ranges from a fear of animals, enemies, punishment, sickness and death to the fear of God.[140] This verb is found approximately 330 times throughout the Old Testament.[141] Its object is God in almost 80 per cent of such occurrences. It implies reverential awe when a person is in God's presence (Exo. 1.17; 1 Sam. 12.14, 18; 2 Sam. 6.9; 2 Kgs 17.28, 35-39; Pss. 33.8, 102.15; Jer. 5.22, 24; Jon. 1.16).[142] Thus the text points to the reverence of God among the Philistines of Gerar.

Furthermore, Genesis 20.8 had another function in Yehud under Nehemiah. The same word *yir'ah*, which is predominantly used to show the fear of God, is used to describe Nehemiah's fear of the Persian King Artaxerxes (Neh. 2.2). Could it be the comparison between Nehemiah's imperial association and Gerar's fear of God? Such a reading suggests that the text wishes to place Abimelech and Gerar above Nehemiah and the Jews. Yahweh's dialogue with Abimelech also supports this reading.

Yahweh as liberator and author of reconciliation

Unlike Genesis 12.10-20, Genesis 20 elaborates Yahweh's immanence and revelation to Abimelech, who is a non-Israelite king from an unchosen line, in detail.[143] So too, Genesis 20.3-8 presupposes that Abimelech is familiar with God.[144] There are no questions of uncertainty, such as 'Who are you?' from Abimelech.[145] Instead, he answers God with a reverential address. Abimelech's response also indicates his familiarity with God.[146] This encounter introduces an essential characteristic of God's liberation. God reveals Godself directly in a dream. Similarly, God listens to the foreign king's plea.[147]

Genesis 20 also highlights Yahweh as a liberator and depicts an extreme example of conflict resolution, which did not end in liberating Sarah, but culminates in reconciling the couple with Abimelech. Abimelech, for example, gave cattle and enslaved people to Abraham after returning Sarah and permitted Abraham and Sarah to live in Gerar. Abraham, in turn, prays for Abimelech. Such an instance of helping each other is an essential model for liberating the oppressed.[148] Yahweh's concern for Sarah is, again, another important theme.

Sarah: The marginal woman in Gerar

Genesis 20 places Sarah in Abimelech's harem. As noted, Abraham hides crucial information, and Abimelech takes Sarah. Sarah remains a voiceless character in this narrative also. However, there is a hint in Abimelech's defence to God that Sarah participated in carrying out Abraham's plan (20.5). Again, does it mean that Sarah was a wilful participant in Abraham's plot? The text does not say anything about it. Perhaps, she might have trusted Abraham's words that there is no fear of God in Gerar. However, Yahweh intervenes to save her before Abimelech approaches her (20.4). This incident shows Yahweh's concern for Sarah's dignity and well-being. This divine initiative, as will be explained, can have tangible implications for Dalit theology.

The function of Abraham's crossing to Philistia

Genesis 20 projects Yahweh as a liberator as well as the source of reconciliation. Further, the narrative reiterates that Abimelech is not the one that Abraham had suspected. He has morality and righteousness. According to the story, Abimelech was marrying Sarah without knowing that she is Abraham's wife. Moreover, Genesis 20 narrates the fear of God among the people of Gerar. What did Abraham's crossing journey communicate to the intended readers living in Achaemenid Yehud? And again, how will this model help Dalit theology?

As clarified, the Achaemenid Yehud under Nehemiah vilified the Philistines of Ashdod because of political, religious and economic reasons. Nehemiah's reservations to intermarriage with Ashdodite women could be another factor as well. Such preoccupations, as seen, forced the Second Temple community to alter its worldview significantly. The emerging worldview impacted the Second Temple community, and consequently, the members began to pattern their behaviours according to the colonial worldview, knowingly and unknowingly. It created 'an Outsider' within Yehud and affected inter-Yehud and intra-Yehud relationships. These Outsiders and their sympathizers composed Genesis 20 as a counter-colonial formation with a set of suggested societal practices, challenging and unmasking the attempts to demonize the Philistines by narrating a crossing journey. Such a crossing, as noted, depicts God as the source of liberation and reconciliation and shows that Abimelech and the Gerarites are not the ones that the Persian regime forecast. Thus, the crossing of Abraham functions as an inversion.

This understanding might have helped the Second Temple community reimagine, reinterpret and reframe the Philistines' image. Furthermore, this narrative highlights God as the source of liberation and reconciliation and God's preferential option for Sarah. Likewise, this tale projects dialogue as God's methodology. Such a model has tremendous potential to subvert Nehemiah's representation of the Philistines. It might have helped the Second Temple community to revisit their concept of the Philistines. Similarly, this story should have invited the community to promote dialogues within and beyond the borders of Yehud. Likewise, it should have helped them reflect on the fate of the internal minorities like the Ashdodite women. This model is relevant in Dalits' contexts also. The Indian caste system, as noted, is a system of segregation. It compartmentalizes different castes. Each caste has its prejudices against the other. Such preoccupations, as indicated, influence inter-Dalit and intra-Dalit contacts. Therefore, this approach might help Dalit theology reimagine the Dalit/non-Dalit Other concept embedded within the Dalit psyche. Such attempts to reimagine the

Other might promote inter-Dalit and intra-Dalit partnerships. Similarly, it will help the Dalits and non-Dalits to understand the sad fate of internal minorities like Dalit women.

Abraham's crossings and Dalit theology

The pro-Persian regimes of Ezra and Nehemiah, we have seen, dehumanized the Egyptian and the Philistine Outsiders because of political, religious and social reasons. Exclusivity became the mode of operation in Jerusalem.[149] Such attempts forced the Second Temple community to reformulate their worldview. The members began to conceptualize, produce and imagine individual and collective identities in an included/excluded space, creating many barriers within Achaemenid Yehud.[150] It made a polarization against a minority like Egyptian and Philistine women. Such practices created an Outsider within and beyond the boundaries of Achaemenid Yehud. They constructed the followers of Persian governors as a dominant group at the centre of Yehud and Egyptian and Philistine Outsiders at the periphery of Yehud. It halted inter-Yehud and intra-Yehud dialogues.

After analysing the representation of the Egyptians and Philistines in Genesis 12.10-20 and 20.1-18, this chapter suggested that Abraham's crossings have been the dissenting voices in Achaemenid Yehud, challenging the attempts to demonize and expel the internal and external Outsiders. This discussion does not intend to discredit the historicity of the traditions associated with Abraham's crossings to Egypt (12.10-20) and Gerar (20.1-18) either. Such traditions, as explained in the previous chapter, existed before the exile. However, the final editors who lived in Achaemenid Yehud reinterpreted, reframed and reconstructed the available traditions to express their discontent with the Persian regime's characterization of the Egyptians and the Philistines. Nevertheless, these narratives are more than a voice of dissent. They invited the intended readers to a crossing journey beyond the borders set by the political and religious authorities of the Achaemenid Yehud by narrating morality and righteousness among the Egyptians and the Philistines. Such a model might have promoted Egyptian and Philistine Outsiders' liberation; reconciliation between Jews and their religious, cultural and ethnic Outsiders; and inter-Yehud and intra-Yehud participation and dialogue.

The proposed paradigm is significant in Dalits' contexts since an invitation to a crossing journey, the liberation of the dominated castes and reconciliation between the dominant castes and the dominated castes are part of Dalits' culture and spirituality. However, as noted, Dalit theology has overlooked such inclusive voices submerged in Dalits' culture and spirituality significantly. From such backgrounds, this research proposes a resurrection of the submerged voices and an intertextual reading between the counter-assertions of the Second Temple community against the disruptive policies of the Persian Empire narrated through Abraham's crossings and the counter-formulations against the dominant Hindu Vedic worldview expressed through Dalits' subversive voices, to redirect Dalit theology in actualizing liberated-reconciled church and society, connected through partnerships.

Conclusion

This chapter has analysed Abraham's crossings to Egypt and Philistia as documents composed in Achaemenid Yehud. These narratives, as noted, seek to reimagine the Outsider by highlighting the God of Israel as the liberator of the oppressed and an author of reconciliation between the oppressor and oppressed, morality and purity among Yehud's colonial Others, and God's preferential option for Sarah, who functions as God's agent of liberation. Such undertakings have great potential in Dalits' contexts. For example, God, narrated in Abraham's crossings, does not participate in sufferings but liberates the endangered couple out of their mess through peaceful intervention. Such an aspect may reorient how Dalit theology approaches God's mission. Further, Abraham's crossings highlight God as a source of liberation and reconciliation, God's presence beyond the boundaries of the promised land and His dialogue with Outsiders. Yahweh informs Pharaoh and Abimelech that Sarah is Abraham's wife (12.17//20.3-7). The text narrates that Yahweh is the God of Dialogue who comes down to help the oppressed (12.17//20.3-7). The dialogues have great possibilities in India's multireligious context. The image of Yahweh as the God who settles the disputes with an Outsider through dialogue will guide Dalit theology in promoting inter-Dalit and intra-Dalit dialogues. The next chapter will clarify how these imperatives might help Dalit theology.

Similarly, Abraham's trips highlight morality and piety among Outsiders and Outsider as a behavioural model rather than an insider. Such imperatives can be liberative in Dalit contexts since the Dalits and the non-Dalits, as noted, imagine the Other to be alien in values.[151] The proposed paradigm would help the Dalits and non-Dalits to seek the best in their religious, cultural and caste Other. Such a radical re-orientation, as will be explained in the next chapter, can help Dalit theology overcome the caste–outcaste dichotomy and methodological exclusivism, promoting a liberated-reconciled society connected through mutual partnerships. Moreover, it will guard Dalit theological deliberations against the danger of absolutizing Dalit experiences, which, as Duncan B. Forrester cautions, can lead to poor theological reflection.[152] Furthermore, as will be explained, the proposed model will empower Dalit theology with a willingness and readiness to listen to the religious, cultural and ethnic Others as fellow human beings with dignity and learn from them.[153] Thus, my reading of Genesis 12.10-20 and 20.1-18 will help Dalit theology come out of its present alienation from Dalit culture and religion.

Sarah's trauma is also relevant in the Dalit context. Abraham neglects Sarah while Pharaoh and Abimelech abuse her (unknowingly).[154] She endures the sufferings and rejections silently. However, Sarah did not remain silent before Yahweh. She communicated her deplorable situation with Yahweh, and Yahweh intervenes to help her. She appears to be of particular concern to Yahweh.[155] This intervention is relevant in Dalit contexts. Indeed, Dalit theology is ideologically pro-women. Dalit spirituality has matriarchal deities as well. However, caste, class and gender have alienated Dalit women. Surekha

Nelavala, a Dalit feminist theologian, laments that Dalit theology 'has failed to debate and discuss the issues of Dalit women.'[156] Therefore, she calls for a Dalit feminist standpoint to examine the issues of Dalit women.[157] Thus, Yahweh's initiative in Genesis 12 and 20 might also inspire theological discussion on Dalit women's sufferings.

Chapter 8

REIMAGINING DALIT THEOLOGY THROUGH DALITS' FORGOTTEN VOICES

Introduction

The Ramayana is an Indian epic. It narrates the life of Rama, a dominant caste king. Valmiki, its author, is supposed to be a dominated caste man called Ratnakar. Some Dalit communities venerate him as their ancestor also.[1] Valmiki was a hunter and robber in his early life. The course of his life changed after his encounter with the sage Narada.[2] Narada convinced Ratnakar of his faults, and so Ratnakar became an ascetic. Ratnakar started chanting 'Rama' in the reverse order, as suggested by Narada. He kept on doing this without moving from his posture, and an anthill covered his whole body. Narada returned to Ratnakar after a long time and took Ratnakar out of the anthill. Narada renamed Ratnakar Valmiki, and he started living near the river Tamasa.[3]

The tradition behind the composition of the Ramayana narrates Valmiki's confrontation with a hunter. He saw a hunter's arrow killing a male bird while a pair of Krauncha birds (water birds) were mating. He became very dejected at the sorrow of the female bird. A few words came out of his mouth, spontaneously, beginning with *Ma Nishada* (No, oh, hunter, no).[4] There have been some attempts to glorify Valmiki's distress.[5] Ramesh Menon, for instance, recounts:

> Valmiki himself could not forget the morning. Again, and again he heard the rapturous song of the birds, the evil hum of the arrow, the cry of the male Krauncha and the soft sound of his small body striking the ground.[6]

Dalit scholars, however, tend not to acknowledge Valmiki. They challenge Valmiki for glorifying Rama, noting that Rama had committed a crime against Dalits since he had killed Shambuka, a Dalit, because Shambuka had defiled the caste system.[7] Daya Pawar, one of the prominent Dalit poets, questions Valmiki's morality:

> Oh Valmiki
> Should you sing the praises of Ramarajya
> Because you are the great poet of poets?
> Seeing the heron's wounded wing
> Your compassionate heart broke out in lament.

> You were born outside the village
> In a shunned neighbourhood
> where misery itself was born
> Never festooned with fruit or flower
> The dejected faces ... furrowed with care
> Is it true you never heard?
> Their lament as they cried for liberation?
> One Shambuk of your own blood
> Caught fire, rose in anger.
> Oh, the great poet,
> Singing the praises of Ramarajya,
> Even there, the icy cliff of humanity towered up!
> Oh, great poet,
>   How then should we call you a great poet?[8]

The poem decries Valmiki's indifference to his dominated caste neighbours. Pawar asks how a tender-hearted Valmiki, who lamented at the sight of a heron's wounded wing, could leave Dalits' anguished cries unnoticed. Pawar also wonders how a Dalit poet could praise Rama, who had killed a Dalit, and designates Valmiki as a traitor. Dalit theology, as noted, emerged to voice a theological response to similar assertions. It is also a product of many religious and secular movements, which inspired the Dalit academics, who revisited traditional Indian Christian theology from Dalits' immanent perspectives. They found that Indian Christian theology and Indian Christian churches overlooked Dalits' lived experiences. Chatterji, for example, clarifies:

> The perceptions that creep into and finally dominate theological education, ministerial training, and Church perspective are conducive to the maintenance of the status quo ... the official theology of the churches tends to be influenced by the ideology of these higher castes trained in the climate of indifference to the realities of the socio-cultural factors.[9]

From such backgrounds, Dalit theology emerged as Indian liberation theology. It was innovative. Dalit theology highlights the faults in Indian Christian theology and Indian Christian churches, interpreting scriptures through the Dalits' lived experiences. It transformed theological thinking and placed the Dalits at the centre of theology, providing praxis-oriented guidelines to the Dalits and empowering them to address their survival, liberation and development. However, there is much to explore, and there was an unforeseen danger in Dalit theology's appropriation of Latin American and African American theology's methodological principles.

Deconstructing Dalit theology

Liberation theology, as seen, is one of the significant Roman Catholic innovations. The Second Vatican Council and the Latin American Bishops' General Conference at Medellin inspired it.[10] It emerged in predominantly Christian cultures and amid the political tensions of Latin America.[11] Liberation theology has become an essential aspect of political life in many Latin American countries like Nicaragua, El Salvador and Haiti.[12] Liberation theology has had worldwide reverberations and influenced other contextual theologies like African American theology and Minjung theology that emerged in similar situations to demand radical structural changes. Consequently, it has inspired Dalit theology also.

This book, following recent attempts to reimagine Dalit theology according to Dalits' contexts and the changed circumstances of the twenty-first century, revisits the influence of Latin American and African American conceptual and methodological proposals upon some proposals of the pioneers of Dalit theology. The concepts of multiculturalism and religious pluralism, as seen, were not substantial concerns in Latin America in the 1970s. The Indian subcontinent, on the other hand, is multireligious and multicultural. It is a land of many religious traditions. Further, India has welcomed various religious traditions. Hindus, Buddhists, Jains, Muslims, Parsees and Sikhs live together with Christians in India. Christians are only a minority among other religions. Hence, Dalits live together with other faiths, cultures and races.

While adopting the methodological principles of Latin American and African American theologies, Dalit theology missed the contrasts noted above considerably and suggested how biblical paradigms and their derivatives, proposed in predominately Christian cultures in Latin American and African American contexts, could redress Dalits' situation. Such attempts, as argued, overlooked the contrasts in worldview presuppositions between Latin Americans and Dalits, Dalits' counter-hegemonic worldview and Dalits' alternative, yet empowering moral visions. It created an imbalance in Dalit theology and reduced Dalit traditions as objects and hermeneutical examples developed in alien contexts, and their derivatives were injected into Dalit theology. Such undertakings alienated Dalit theology from the liberative voices and the counter-hegemonic formulations in Dalits' contexts. So too, it constructed the biblical messages developed in Latin American and African American contexts as the dominant self at the centre and the subversive voices in Dalits' traditions as the dominated self at the margins of Dalit theology. Such a situation is alarming. This book seeks to redress this situation by analysing how a hermeneutic of return to Dalits' resources, like the proposal of Abraham Ayrookuzhiel, who advocates a return to Dalits' religious and cultural resources, can harmonize Dalit theology with Dalit contexts.

Reconstructing Dalit theology

This research, as clarified, seeks to suggest some guidelines to advance Dalit theology through Dalits' worldview, counter-assertions and counter-ontology. Such discussions highlighted that Dalits are culturally rich people with their views and values. Dalits' subversive voices, in particular, transmit their cultural and spiritual heritage. Their cultural heritage has an inalienable dignity and has incredible resources to advance Dalit theology. In similar contexts, Sharon Welch notes that liberation theology is an insurrection of subjugated knowledge.[13] Scholars like James Cone, Cornel West, Dwight N. Hopkins and Anthony B. Pinn, likewise designate Black culture as an embodiment of Black genius. For them, rhythmic singing, swaying, dancing, preaching, talking and walking are God-given resources for furthering African American theology.[14] The same is evident within Dalits' contexts as well. Dalits' contexts have abundant resources like a vibrant cultural heritage, a folk tradition of tales, songs and performing arts, a fantastic variety of practices in their daily life, craftsmanship and a highly developed world of gods, goddesses and devils.[15]

Hence, Dalits' religious and cultural contexts are not vacant spaces. Dalits' folk literature, performing arts and spiritual traditions have resources to counter the caste system.[16] Dalits' cultural legacy is an epithet of Dalits' intellectual gifts. They are essential locations to identify Dalits' resistance to the dominant Hindu Vedic worldview and communicate the crucial aspects of Dalits' counter-hegemonic worldview, which can remodel authentic living in the Indian subcontinent. This claim, as clarified, seeks to endorse neither a romantic sentimentality nor an uncritical acceptance of the sources. Instead, this book assumes that a critical rereading of Dalits' contexts and the counter-assertions in them are vital for theologizing in Dalits' contexts.

Such an attempt demands Dalit theology develop its theoretical premises along with Dalits' epistemology of resistance. Therefore, this book assessed the compatibility of Dalit theology's paradigms against Dalits' counter-hegemonic worldview and alternate yet challenging moral visions. This enterprise uncovered some limitations of the methodological proposals of Dalit theology. From such contexts, I suggested that a biblical paradigm, respecting Dalits' counter-assertions and their visions for collective liberation, is essential to reorient Dalit theology. From such contexts, I indicated that an intertextual reading between Dalits' counter-assertions and the Second Temple community's counter-formulations would advance Dalit theology as a source of liberation and reconciliation for Dalits and non-Dalits.

Revisiting the paradigms of Dalit theology

As seen, the founders of Dalit theology followed the conceptual and hermeneutical examples developed by Latin American and African American theologies, which alienated Dalit theology from Dalits' assertions and worldview. For example, Dalits' assertions, as noted, acknowledge the presence of the caste system. They narrate the vulnerability of the Dalits and their sufferings also. However, they do not divide the members of the society based on the injustices done to Dalits. Instead, they envision a liberated-reconciled society connected through mutual partnerships. Praveen Gadhvi, one of the Dalit poets, also reflects the same concern:

Let us say farewell to arms,
Hold a round-table conference.

No country have we,
No field to plough, no home to stay.
From the age of Aryavart till today,
Not a blade of grass have you left for us.
Yet we are prepared to forget everything.
Are you ready to pull down walls you've built?
Like sugar in the milk are we willing to merge.
Would you endure if your Draupadi
Garlands are Galiya in Swayamvar?
Come, let us take turns in disposing the dead cattle.
Do you agree?
Let us say farewell to arms,
Plough the country's rich soil together,
Will you give us our share of the harvest?[17]

Gadhvi proposes to give up weapons. He suggests a round-table conference between the dominated castes and the dominant castes. Round-table conferences are significant in India. There were a series of round-table talks between British Parliament members and Indians held in London in three sessions between 1930 and 1932. Those meetings discussed various outlooks on the constitutional and political future of India. Here, Gadhvi is proposing similar enterprises between dominated castes and dominant castes. His proposal for conversation is pertinent to Dalits' epistemology of resistance. It envisions a greater union between Dalits and non-Dalits. The Dalits, he says, are willing to merge with dominant castes like sugar in the milk. Gadhvi's invitation alludes to a narrative of the Parsees. When they landed in India, the local Hindu king sent them a full glass of milk, indicating that the town was packed. The Parsee leader added some sugar to the glass and returned it, suggesting that the Parsees could mix among the Hindus. This metaphor means communal integration, liberation and reconciliation in which an individual or group changes society by melting into it, flavouring it with their essence.

Gadhvi's use of the Parsee narrative is significant to Dalits' vision for collective liberation and resistance. It recommends an ultimate union (liberation and reconciliation) between Dalits and non-Dalits. Further, Gadhvi invites the dominant castes to a cross-cultural journey beyond the walls of separation that they had built. He suggests some joint ventures like ploughing the country's fields and disposing of the dead cattle. The caste system reserves such menial jobs for Dalits. Thus, Gadhvi invites dominant castes to a partnership in undertaking the menial jobs reserved for Dalits. Similarly, Chandrabahen Shrimali, another Dalit poet, highlights the potential of loving Dalits.

With a sincere heart
And without expectation,
When man will love man
The hell will no more be in sight,

The paradise will just be at a stone's throw away.
But the paradise will turn into heaven
If man remembers That there is a man called Dalit
Waiting to be loved.[18]

Shrimali's concepts of heaven, hell and paradise are not otherworldly. They are praxiological, immanent and intimately related to Dalits' troubles. For example, Shrimali advises the benefits of loving Dalits in the present. He suggests that the mutual love between Dalits and non-Dalits can offer them avenues to work together for collective liberation. He designates such an existence as heaven. Perhaps, Shrimali suggests a liberated-reconciled casteless society connected through mutual partnerships as envisioned in Dalits' worldview and epistemology of resistance. So too, Shrimali highlights an initiative to remodel intra-Dalit relations and demands a crossing journey that advances partnerships. Such partnerships have incredible potential to liberate Dalits. It can challenge the barriers that reinforce the sociological, religious and cultural boundaries of the caste system. Mutually enriching corporations can nurture contacts with a difference to move, enhance and change. This openness will help the Dalits and non-Dalits to work together. Abraham's cross-cultural journeys, which transcend the limitations of the Second Temple ideology, as demonstrated, are significant in this scenario.

Abraham's crossings as a paradigm

Abraham's crossings, as noted, were postcolonial counter-metaphors amidst the ethnocentric policies of the Persian Empire. They were part of the subversive voices in Genesis, which are essential locations to identify the Second Temple community's counter-assertions against imperial propaganda. The traditions behind those narratives might have existed before the exile. The postexilic community, however, edited them to respond to their existential realities. Such counter-assertions expressed in Abraham's postcolonial crossings, as explained, are harmonious with Dalits' counter-formulations. Hence, they have great potential for facilitating cross-cultural exchanges and appropriation in Dalits' contexts. From such backgrounds, this book suggests an intertextual reading of the Second Temple community's counter-assertions and Dalits' counter-hegemonic assertions to advance Dalit theology. Such undertakings can offer praxis-oriented guidelines to realize a liberated-reconciled church and society, bridged through mutual partnerships. A poem published by the Dalit Panthers suggested a similar enterprise:

We can love each other,
if you can shed your orthodox skin.
come and touch, we will make a new world –
where there won't be any
dust, dirt, poverty, injustice, oppression.[19]

Dalit Panthers request the dominant castes to embrace Dalits to form a new world of partnerships. Such a crossing, Panthers envision, will realize a world without any inequalities, connected through collaborations. A similar journey will help Indian Christian churches move beyond sociological, cultural and geographical limitations in search of collective liberation. This model will assist the Dalits and Syrian Christians focus not on the prejudices against each other but on breaking barriers, crossing boundaries and bridging differences. Abraham's crossings, which question the preoccupations with Egypt and Gerar, are ontological in such contexts. They highlight God as a liberator and an author of reconciliation and narrate morality and piety beyond Yehud. Such a paradigm, like the Dalit Panthers' proposal, will help Dalit theology promote a crossing across the gulf that separates Dalit Christians and non-Dalit Christians.

Such an attempt is in line with the messages of Jesus, who often crossed the borders to undertake his mission. This research, however, concentrates on Abraham's crossings since much work has already been done on how Jesus' mission can advance Dalit theology. There are also some reservations against Christological paradigms in Indian pluralistic contexts.[20] K. C. Abraham, Stanley J. Samartha and John Mohan Razu claim that Indian contexts require liberative ecumenism, which affirms God's work without relying entirely on Christological formulations.[21] Such remodelling, as Felix Wilfred clarifies, is radical indeed:

> Reducing other religions (without attempting to enter into the world of their experience) into our theological categories and condemning them (without giving them an opportunity to explain themselves) would be an *epistemological naïveté and an ethical impropriety*. Our cognitive efforts should be such that they respect the self-understanding of these religions and cultures. By forcing other religions into our mould, we would, apart from missing what is valuable in them, fail, more basically, in fidelity to truth.[22]

Thus, Dalits' counter-hegemonic worldview, moral visions and Indian religious pluralism require developing an openness to diversities. Abraham's sojourns can help Dalit theology advance exposure to diversities, which, as clarified, will reconnect Dalit theology with Dalits' contexts.

Abraham's crossings and Dalit theology

Abraham's crossings, as noted, offer counter-colonial rhetoric, reconstructing the Second Temple community's outsiders, whom the Persian Empire had maligned because of political, religious and sociological reasons. The Persian governors introduced a divorce policy to accomplish their imperial goals. It disturbed social harmony and forced the community to reshape its worldview. The final editor who lived in Yehud revised pre-exilic traditions about Abraham to subvert the outsiders' concept constructed by the Persian administration. This new narrative offers a counter-colonial discourse, which acknowledges God as a source of liberation and reconciliation, outsiders as behavioural models, morality and purity among outsiders and God's preferential option for Sarah. These imperatives, as will be explained, can reconnect Dalit theology with Dalits' counter-hegemonic worldview by advancing God's agency in initiating the process of liberation and reconciliation and Dalits' agency in actualizing a liberated-reconciled society, connected through mutual partnerships with outsiders, as envisioned in Dalit contexts.

Reimagining God's image in Dalit theology

Dalit theology affirms God as Dalits' liberator who redesigns the world with mighty hands. Some Dalit scholars, however, are discontented with this image since such an image does not have a principal space in Dalits' contexts. They also fear that venerating God's participation in Dalits' suffering may not help Dalits' emancipation significantly. From such contexts, I will explain how God's image in Abraham's crossings can offer an alternative proposal. Abraham's crossings, for example, narrate the God as a source of liberation and reconciliation, who inaugurates the process of liberation and reconciliation immanently not through mighty hands, but peacefully by informing the emperors that Sarah is Abraham's wife (12.17//20.3-7) and through a process of dialogue and negotiation. Such initiatives will help Dalit theology reimagine God's participation in Dalits' suffering, God's presence in alien territories, God's agency in liberating Dalits and reconciling them with outsiders, as envisioned in Dalit contexts.

God's participation in Dalit suffering

Dalit theology affirms Jesus' association with the 'Dalits' of his time, Jesus' participation in their sufferings, and emphasizes Jesus as Dalits' prototype. Such undertakings, as seen, may idealize suffering. God's image in Abraham's crossings would help Dalit theology revisit its concept of God's response to the Dalit suffering. As seen, God is not a suffering God in Abraham's crossings, and God, though aware of the endangered matriarch's grief, does not share her suffering. God, as narrated in Abraham's crossings, is not a mighty warrior also. Instead, God intervenes and convinces the monarchs to liberate Sarah through dialogues and negotiations. Such an immanantization can empower Dalit theology to break the caste system's barriers without idealizing Dalits' sufferings by emphasizing God's agency in liberating the endangered couple. So too, God in Abraham's crossings is not dichotomous but was available to the insiders and outsiders, like Pochamma Devi.

God's immanent presence in alien territories and Dalit theology

Abraham's crossings depict God's activities in Egypt and Gerar. They use languages similar to prophetic commissions with foreign monarchs. God's presence in foreign lands and association with outsiders suggest that God exists independently of human beliefs. The same God who is active in Israel is active all over the world. God is working within varying cultures, worldviews and individuals. Isaiah and Jeremiah also highlight God's sovereignty over the earth. God chooses non-Jewish leaders like Nebuchadnezzar (Jer. 27.6) and Cyrus (Isa. 45.1). Such projections are vital in caste contexts, and they can break caste enclosure by challenging exclusive claims. Further, they can empower Dalit theology to move beyond sociological, cultural and geographic boundaries, searching morality and piety among outsiders.

Perhaps, the proposal of John Hick will help us clarify our claim. Hick designates a similar transition as a 'Copernican revolution', adopting this term from astronomy. It suggests a shift from the belief that the earth is the centre of the universe to the proper understanding that the sun is at the centre of the solar system.[23] Hick's argument also involves a shift from the traditional belief that Christianity is at the centre of theological formulations. He advocates that God should be at the centre and all religions, including Christianity, should revolve around God.[24] Such an orientation demands Christianity to drop some of its historical claims of offering the best way to salvation, recommending that pluralism is part of the divine plan. Also, it necessitates a positive assessment of outsiders, acknowledging God's activities among outsiders. This platform is relevant to Dalit contexts, and Abraham's crossings will empower Dalit theology to celebrate God's presence and morality and piety among religious, cultural and ethnic outsiders.

Further, Hick's proposal demands a movement from Christocentrism to theocentrism. While Christocentricism has some advantages in predominantly Christian cultures like Latin American and African American contexts, it has some limitations in pluralistic contexts like the Indian subcontinent since religious pluralism demands an openness to diversity. The same is true in Dalit contexts also, since Dalits cut across various religious faiths. Note, however, that I have some reservations against such absolute claims. J. Peter Schneller, one of the proponents of such a transition, for instance, suggests that Jesus' mediation is non-constitutive and non-normative to achieve salvation.[25] I acknowledge Jesus' mediation as normative and constitutive for Christians. However, I believe that emphasizing Jesus' role should not deter Dalit Christians from openness to diversities. In such contexts, God's image in Abraham's crossings can complement Christological formulations in developing exposure to diversity by redefining God's agency in liberating Dalits and reconciling them with non-Dalits.

God as a source of liberation and reconciliation

Abraham's crossings highlight God as a liberator and a source of reconciliation. Such an emphasis is ontological in Dalit contexts, which, as seen, demand a liberated-reconciled society. As noted, Yahweh liberates Sarah and reconciles the couple with Pharaoh and Abimelech. Liberation, as narrated, was not the end of the journey but an intermediate step before reconciliation. So too, reconciliation was not a compromise but a possibility to accept each other as persons with dignity. Abraham and Sarah did not lose any of their privileges or possessions after liberation but were treated with dignity. Such an orientation can empower

Dalit theology to reimagine itself as a source of liberation and reconciliation, which are essential to Dalit contexts. As suggested in Dalit contexts, the reconciliation is not a sacrifice but a courageous attempt to advance mutually enriching partnerships.

Abraham's crossings also envision God as responding to the words of the oppressed and initiating a process of liberation and reconciliation immanently without participating in their sufferings. Further, God acts peacefully through dialogues. God's activities in alien territories and dialogue with outsiders demand greater sensitivity to outsiders and necessitate inter-Dalit and intra-Dalit dialogues. Such an image can break the caste system's barriers, promote cross-cultural crossings and bridge the gap between various castes and sub-castes. Similarly, Abraham's crossings highlight morality and piety among Yehud's outsiders and suggest that the outsiders were not the persons Abraham was anticipating. Such perspectives can help Dalit theology to empower the Dalits and the non-Dalits to develop mutually enriching partnerships.

Inter-Dalit and intra-Dalit partnerships

The caste system categorizes the Hindus into four groups. As explained, it is one of the central symbols in India. It has far-reaching implications. It regulates social interactions and political alignments and restricts inter-Dalit and intra-Dalit associations. It also dehumanizes Dalits considering even their shadow as contaminating. It deliberates them as ritually impure and disconnects Dalits from the divine. Unfortunately, the caste system has intruded into the churches and distorts the balance of power in some parishes. The Dalits and the non-Dalits, as seen, function as two factions in the Indian churches, as explained in the introduction. The following section describes how Abraham's crossings can reimagine this messy reality.

Caste in Indian Christian churches

The conversion, as observed, did not improve the social situation of the Dalits considerably. They remain as an oppressed majority. They do not have full rights in some parishes and do not get their feet washed on Maundy Thursday. The dominant caste Christians also do not allow decorated cars through the streets of Dalit Christians during parish festivals. There are only a few Dalit priests. The dominant caste Christians do not welcome Dalit priests to serve communion or perform marriage rites. The Dalits are underrepresented in the parish councils, pastoral councils and social service societies. There are also separate seating arrangements for the Dalits in some parishes, and some Parishes conduct liturgical services separately.

Such exclusions, unfortunately, do not end with death. For example, some parishes have different graveyards for the Dalits.[26] The dominant caste Christians do not permit the Dalits' dead bodies into the church for funeral masses. Such mistreatments reduce the Dalits as passive members in the parishes. Hence, caste dictates the exclusion of the Dalits in the Christian denominations. In short, caste is institutionalized in Indian Christian churches, and the Dalits remain as the outcastes in them. Note, however, that the Dalits are not entirely free from the influence of the caste system, and it dictates inter-Dalit relations, which complicates the situation further.

Caste system in inter-Dalit relations

The notions of purity and pollution have penetrated Dalits' psyches, and Dalits are not a homogenous category. They are divided into hundreds of sub-castes.[27] There are separate endogamous groups among them, who do not intermarry, not because of their preference for their spouses but because of their caste prejudices. The worst victims of this internal stratification among Dalits are Dalit women. Caste and patriarchy continue to influence the lives of Dalit women negatively. They are placed at the absolute bottom of the caste hierarchy. A recent study by a faculty member at the Central University of Karnataka among Dalit families in Puducherry shows that Dalit women are prone to multiple forms of discrimination in inter-Dalit and intra-Dalit relations. All the respondents had undergone minor and major forms of violence regularly in their family. Fifty-six per cent had experienced marital rape more than once, 30 per cent had faced forced sexual relations, 73 per cent had verbal abuse from their husband and their in-laws, and 53 per cent experienced sexual harassment and were bullied by Dalit and upper caste members in their villages.[28]

Also, Dalits replicate the concept of purity and pollution among themselves. Dalits in Hirapur village, for example, observe purity and impurity among themselves.[29] The ongoing tension between the Malas and the Madigas is another instance.[30] This messy reality, along with intra-Dalit stratification, remains one of the significant issues and invites further interrogation and a crossing beyond one's religious, cultural and ethnic limitations to reconnect these disconnects by promoting inter-Dalit and intra-Dalit partnerships.

Dalit theology and mutual partnerships

Dalit theology is an advocacy theology for the Dalits. It challenges the injustices against them. However, as clarified, Dalit theology has an unhealthy binary opposition model. It names and shames the dominant caste Christians for the caste's presence in the Indian churches, arguing that the dominant caste people cannot understand Dalits' sufferings. Some Dalit theologians have already expressed reservations against such exclusive claims. The Dalits and non-Dalit Christians' polarization as insiders and outsiders within Indian Christian churches is inadequate for Dalit liberation. Such hermeneutics contradicts Dalits' worldview and disempowers Dalit theology considerably in Indian pluralistic contexts.

My proposal, however, does not seek to discredit the particularity of the Dalit suffering. This research, as clarified, is aware of the Dalits and their sorrows. They have been suffering for many centuries. However, the attempts to emphasize Dalits' suffering as the principal element in Dalits' contexts disregard Dalits' counter-ontology and epistemology of resistance. They also overlook the heterogeneous composition of the Christian churches in India. Further, it may hinder the Dalits from developing local and global partnerships with other suffering communities. Similarly, a wounded psyche is not a Dalit problem alone. It is a dominant caste issue as well. The concept of untouchability exists among the dominant caste Christians, which controls their attitudes and manipulates them to imagine Dalit Christians as an inferior other.[31]

Therefore, Dalit Christians and non-Dalit Christians need liberation and reconciliation to promote a liberated-reconciled church connected through mutually enriching partnerships. Paulo Freire, in a similar but foreign context, cautions against the binary opposition model. Reversing the roles of oppressor and oppressed, Freire warns, will not help liberation. Instead, the oppressed should try to restore the humanity of the oppressor as well as the oppressed.[32] Such an enterprise, Freire expected, will liberate the oppressed as well as the oppressor.[33] In a similar but African context, Ezigbo notes that God does not identify with the poor any more than He identifies with the rich. God does not criticize the rich any less than He blames the poor. Similarly, the rich and the poor can be oppressors. For example, the rich people, who exploit the poor, who use their wealth to perpetuate injustice and who refuse to use their resources to help the least and the lost, are oppressors. Similarly, poor people who steal, kill and engage in some appalling acts to improve their conditions are also oppressors. From such a context, Ezigbo clarifies that theology must define sin to include all peoples – the poor and the rich, white and Black, the oppressors and the oppressed.[34] Dalits' worldview and epistemology of resistance warrant a similar openness.

Nevertheless, as seen, openness is needed not only in intra-Dalit relations alone. Some Dalits, as seen, oppress their fellow Dalits, and internal stratification prevents Dalits from joining together to fight for their common interests.[35] Unfortunately, Dalit theology has disregarded the internal stratification substantially. Dalit theologians like Nelavala, Rajkumar and Melanchthon have already critiqued this neglect. They want Dalit theology to address the internal stratification seriously.[36] The Second Temple community's strategies to subvert the colonial representation of outsiders, as will be seen, can advance inter-Dalit and intra-Dalit associations.

Reimagining intra-Dalit and inter-Dalit partnerships

Abraham's encounters contest the Persian administration. Persian officials had demonized Egyptians and Philistines because of colonial interests. It compelled the community to reformulate their worldview, which disrupted everyday life in Yehud eventually and created outsiders within and beyond Yehud, halting inter-Yehud and intra-Yehud contacts. Abraham's trips challenged such colonial tactics by providing a counter-colonial worldview and ontology, highlighting the couple and the monarchs as representing two legitimate sides, morality and piety among the outsiders, an outsider as a behavioural model, monarchs listening to Yahweh and Abraham, God's dialogues with the emperors and liberation and reconciliation through God's interventions. Such initiatives can empower Dalit theology to foster inter-Dalit and intra-Dalit contacts.

The Dalits and the non-Dalits, it is to be noted, observe their counterparts to be alien in values. So too, both sides have sceptics who indicate some barriers that may hinder interactions. The Second Temple community's assertions to subvert the colonial worldview can inform Dalit theology on promoting inter-Dalit and intra-Dalit partnerships. It would help Dalit theology empower the Dalits and the dominant caste Christians to develop mutual understanding and endorse respect, sympathy and appreciation towards outsiders. Such undertakings, I think, can help Dalit theology to encourage an enterprise similar to the Peace Village founded in Neve Shalom.

Neve Shalom is a shared Israeli–Palestinian village situated some thirty kilometres west of Jerusalem.[37] Bruno Hussar (1911–96), a Dominican friar, founded it in a demilitarized zone in 1972. It promotes peaceful reconciliation between Jews, Muslims and Christians and facilitates an intercultural understanding between them. Children in Neve Shalom celebrate each other's holidays and make friendships, irrespective of ethnic differences.[38] Neve Shalom offers an alternative model for living based on co-operation and equality.[39] Ellie Wiesel, a Nobel Peace laureate, acknowledged it as follows: 'When Jews and Arabs get together, live together – they create their own miracle; Neve Shalom/Wahat al-Salam is such a miracle.'[40] It has inspired many similar movements. Bishop Paride Taban, for instance, created Kuron village in Kauto county of South Sudan in 2004.[41] It is a model for warring tribes to live together in peace.[42] It offers the possibility of living beyond tribalism. Abraham's crossings can empower the Dalits and non-Dalit Christians to promote a shared existence connected through partnerships, similar to Neve Shalom and Kuron village.

Redefining inter-Dalit and intra-Dalit encounters

Abraham and the rulers, seen from their perspectives, represent two legitimate sides. Abraham had some reasons to doubt the integrity of the kings. The monarchs had justifications for taking Sarah also. Such a situation, as noted, requires a shift in focus from categories like Abraham, Sarah, Pharaoh and Abimelech to an understanding of the internal processes, which generate categories, and this research found postcolonial tactics against the Persian colonial worldview working subversively in these narratives. From similar but Middle Eastern perspectives, Marc Gopin, John Valk, Halis Albayrak and Mualla Selçuk undertook a similar task. They clarified that right and wrong are culturally and socially constructed concepts.[43] Likewise, Hick has suggested that different religious traditions are alternative paths.[44]

A similar approach will help Dalit theology break the caste barriers by concentrating on the categorization processes functioning in the Indian churches. Perhaps, the proposal of Thomas J. Fararo and Kenji Kosaka, though in a different context, will further clarify the situation. They note that the categories are 'the panoply of images or representations of actors within a stratified space.'[45] Such reappraisals will help Dalit theology revisit its dominant view that the Dalits and the non-Dalits represent two unbridgeable categories by noting how such representations emerge from the stratification processes. It will reorient Dalit theology to discover the categorization processes as the subject and the categories like the Dalits and the non-Dalits as the products of these processes. Such a perspective will help Dalit theology promote a shared responsibility of Dalit Christians and non-Dalit Christians in overcoming the caste questions through listening and learning, as narrated in Abraham's crossings.

Listening, healing and reconciliation

Abraham's crossings highlight that the kings listened to God's communication, which inaugurated a process of liberation and reconciliation. Pharaoh seems impatient in his dealings with Abraham after the plot was uncovered. However, he lets Abraham leave without any harm. Abimelech starts a lengthy conversation and allows Abraham to explain his situation. God's initiatives and the monarch's responses to them can inspire Dalit theology to empower the Dalits and the non-Dalits to be active listeners.

Active listening will help the Dalits and the non-Dalits identify the context, process or experience that puzzles Indian Christians through deliberate and careful listening. Listening, as Yael Petretti acknowledges from the perspective of the Israeli–Palestinian conflict, has healing potential also.[46] Listening to other people's convictions can eliminate bias and lead to an empathic condition that transcends most of the differences.[47] For example, as clarified, I was ignorant of the Dalit situation to a great extent. However, my education and encounters with the subversive voices helped me understand Dalits' worldview, which improved my cross-cultural adaptability and made me reflect on my theological context and assumptions. Hence, listening can help the Dalits and the non-Dalits to understand each other and heal their wounds by participating in God's call for reconciliation. So too, the dialogue as a path to knowing each other and resolving conflicts, as narrated in Abraham's crossings, can help Dalit theology advance the process of reconciliation.

Dialogue: An opportunity to know each other

Abraham's trips recount God's conflict resolutions through dialogue, which ends not in liberating Sarah but in reconciling the couple with the monarchs. As the narratives recount, the emperors did not know Sarah's marital status, and God informs them of her status through constructive dialogues. They also narrate how Abimelech uses dialogue as a tool to understand unrevealed facts about the couple.

Such instances will help Dalit theology reimagine the Dalits and the non-Dalits as potential knowers who understand some truths and are ignorant of others.[48]

The central question in this undertaking is 'What can the Dalits/non-Dalits learn from their counterparts?' Perhaps, Felix Wilfred's proposal for an ongoing inter-Dalit and intra-Dalit dialogue is pertinent in this context.[49] It can lead the Dalits towards mutual understanding and enrichment and can promote justice, peace and harmony in society and church. Similarly, the inter-Dalit and intra-Dalit dialogues are more than an exchange of ideas. It redresses inequalities and promotes inter-group and intra-group relations. The partnership is God's will and purpose for God's people. Abraham's crossings can empower Dalits and non-Dalits to partake in the essence of God's mission. Likewise, the Second Temple community's attempt to rescript ancient traditions to undermine the colonial worldview is another catalyst for promoting inter-Dalit and intra-Dalit partnerships.

Rescripting traditions to enhance partnerships

An anonymous editor, as seen, rescripted pre-existing Abrahamic traditions to challenge the Persian ethnocentric policies. Their model can revitalize inter-Dalit and intra-Dalit understandings and partnerships. A conscious and radical retelling of ancient narratives might help the Dalits and the dominant castes to seek more avenues of co-existence. Such an adventure does not imply agreement to all proposals and narratives. It does not underestimate the sufferings of a particular group or participant as well. On the other hand, it can provide a framework within which acceptance can take place. It helps to analyse individual narratives and their traditional interpretations as stories compromised by theological, cultural, ethnic and religious positions.

In a similar but Vietnamese context, Laurel B. Kennedy and Mary Rose Williams note how the Vietnamese tourism industry rescripted its image in Western popular consciousness to counter the overwhelmingly negative picture of the Vietnam War. It narrated Vietnam as a nation of picturesque and quiet rural villages, growing beyond the wounds of conflict and a nation proliferating towards modernity and industrialization.[50] Such a reinterpretation evoked the days before the troubles began. It softened the memories and mood of the international community, which revitalized the tourism industry in Vietnam.[51]

The model of the Second Temple community and the Vietnamese tourism can reorient the Dalit academics. As we know, the Dalits and the non-Dalits have many narratives. Such narratives have been formed from different historical experiences. Some of them could be mutually exclusive as well. However, a conscious retelling of such stories can promote inter-Dalit and intra-Dalit partnerships. The *Manusmriti* (the law book of Manu), for instance, indicates that the four castes were born from different parts of Brahma, the Supreme Being, and implies Dalits as outcastes. Brahmins, the priestly class, were originated from the mouth. The rulers (Kshatriyas) were born from the arms. Vaishyas, the merchant class, were born from the thighs, and the servant class (Sudras) were originated from the feet. This theory has many implications. The Brahmins used this narrative to maintain their power over the dominated castes and argued that they are the highest caste with a pure origin because they are born straight from the mouth of Brahma.[52]

The claims of the Brahmins, unfortunately, overlooked some specific facts. For instance, *Manusmriti* implies that the four castes are not separate entities. Their ancestor Brahma connects them. A similar rereading of Dalit and non-Dalit narratives that develops mutual partnerships is possible. As we know, the partnership is one of the fundamental dynamics of God's mission. It, too, can promote inter-Dalit and intra-Dalit partnerships. For Christians, Muslims and Jews, the partnership is God's will and purpose for God's people. Similarly, Abraham's crossings can help Dalit theology reimagine the concept of Dalit women along with Dalits' worldview and the epistemology of resistance.

Reimagining the role of Dalit women

The treatment of Dalit women is a highly explosive and delicate issue in India. Dalit women have been subjected to double patriarchy. Dominant caste men and Dalit men oppress Dalit women. Paswan, Jaideva, Radhika Chandiramani and M. Elavarasi designate Dalit women as thrice alienated, noting that the class, caste and gender often compromise the Dalit women's dignity.[53] So too, Muriel Orevillo-Montenegro argues that Dalit women are considered as the most impure of the impure.[54] Bama explains:

> The position of women is both pitiful and humiliating, really. In the fields, they have to escape from upper caste men's molestations. At Church, they must lick the priest's shoes and be his slaves while he threatens them with tales of God, Heaven, and Hell. Even when they go to their own homes, before they have had a chance to cook some kanji or lie down and rest a little, they have to submit themselves to their husband's torment.[55]

Dalit women are confronting significant discrimination, exclusion and violence more than Dalit men. Therefore, Ruth Manorama designates the Dalit woman as the 'Dalit among the Dalits' and 'downtrodden among the downtrodden.'[56] N. G. Prasuna comments that the Dalit men follow Manudharmashastras' principles in oppressing the Dalit women.[57] Dalit men do not share domestic labour and leave the household duties to the absolute responsibility of a wife. Further, 94 per cent of Dalit men expect that providing sexual needs to the husband is an exclusive responsibility of the wife. Similarly, they leave childcare entirely to their wives.[58]

After noting similar situations, Prasuna describes society as 'eating the flesh and drinking the blood of Dalit women'.[59] This quotation echoes the Eucharistic formula of Jesus. The churches in India need to explore Prasuna's words further. This formula suggests that the believers unite with the historical Jesus and participate in his mission through eating and drinking in the Eucharist. Thus, Prasuna invites Dalit women to identify themselves with Jesus' mission. The marginalized, as we know, were the epicentre of Jesus' mission. Participating in Jesus' mission, therefore, demands a change in priorities and a commitment to suffering humanity. Thus, Prasuna asks Dalit women to model their lives as a saving presence of Jesus' mission. They, as participants of Jesus' mission, are expected to bring liberation to the less fortunate in society. The same is true with Sarah, the endangered ancestress. As will be clarified, she was an agent of God's saving presence for Abraham in Egypt and Philistia.

Sarah's trauma and Dalit women

Sarah's trauma is relevant to Dalit women. As seen, she is a powerless victim like Dalit women. Abraham's actions landed her in trouble. Naomi Steinberg is critical of Abraham's actions. She claims that Abraham abandons Sarah to get another wife instead of Sarah, who is barren.[60] While such a reading has some merits, the text does not support her hypothesis entirely. Similarly, Pharaoh and Abimelech abuse her (unknowingly). Sarah, as seen, is highly compromised by the patriarchy and the empire. She endures the sufferings and rejections silently. However, her silence deserves further study. As seen, she did not remain silent before Yahweh. She communicated her deplorable situation with Yahweh, and Yahweh intervenes to help her. She appears to be of particular concern to Yahweh. Yahweh acts as Sarah's covenant partner.[61]

Analysing God's intervention in liberating Sarah and reconciling the couple with foreign monarchs can offer some imperatives to uplift Dalit women. Such a claim does not seek to discredit Dalit theology. Indeed, Dalit theology is ideologically pro-women. Dalit spirituality has matriarchal deities as well. However, caste, class and gender – as seen – have alienated Dalit women. Surekha Nelavala, a Dalit feminist theologian, laments that Dalit theology 'has failed to debate and discuss the issues of Dalit women'. She calls for a Dalit feminist standpoint to examine the issues of Dalit women.[62] Her proposal is vital in Dalits' contexts since Dalit women are repeatedly raped and abused. *The Times of India*, for instance, reports an alleged rape of a Dalit woman by six men on 3 April 2018.[63] Similarly, in December 2017, a thirty-year-old Dalit woman committed suicide after her family was repeatedly threatened by two men who barged into her home in July and gang-raped her.[64]

Sad to say, the list is infinite. A sixteen-year-old Dalit girl, for instance, was sexually assaulted and killed in Odisha in March 2018. Her decomposed body was found in a paddy field.[65] Such events show that Yahweh's initiatives are vital in Dalits' contexts. They will inspire theological discussion on the Dalit women's sufferings. Further, they might help a rereading of the scriptures from a Dalit feminist point of view. Genesis 12.10-20 and Genesis 20 are relevant to Dalit contexts and the question of Dalit women.

Dalit women: Participants in God's mission and mediators of God's liberation

God, as seen in Abraham's crossings, is a liberator. God came down to rescue Sarah, who had been abandoned by her husband and abused by colonial powers, not by mighty hands but peacefully through dialogues. God's actions in Genesis 12.10-20 and Genesis 20 align with the Hebrew scriptures' message. It acknowledges God's preferential option for the oppressed. The Exodus event, for example, depicts God as the one who listens to the cry of the people to set them free. The prophets, similarly, portray God as the one who defends the oppressed. They developed their vision of God's preferential option for the oppressed. They hoped for liberation in the context of the socio-economic oppression of the poor by the wealthy and a small, colonized nation by the great empires of antiquity.[66] God's preferential option for the less fortunate is one of the features of Dalit deities as well. In praise of Ellaiyamman, the goddess of the Dalit communities in Tamil Nadu, we read:[67]

> You are the deity who expels our troubles; come rid us of evil.
> You are present in the neem leaves used for driving out women's afflictions.
> You are present in the fire, the head of our religion.
> You have lived with fame in our village, Malaipallaiyani.
> In Padavethi a buffalo was sacrificed to You, even in Poothukaadu;
> A sacrifice to inspire You, our goddess, to destroy evil.
> You are the goddess who guards our boundaries:
> You protect with your spear;
> You will protect us from 4408 diseases;
> You will protect the Harijans from the torture of the High caste.[68]

This song shows that the concept of God as the liberator is appealing. However, emphasizing God's role in Abraham's crossings should not direct us to discredit Sarah's role in Abraham's encounters. Sarah displays moral and spiritual integrity in these narratives. God is intimately related to her and saved the endangered couple because of her words. God liberates them because of a woman compromised by patriarchy and empire. Accordingly, Abraham amassed wealth because of Sarah. Hence, Sarah seems to be the real hero in these narratives.

Hence, Sarah acts as a participant in God's mission for Abraham and a mediator of liberation. Sarah, as the mediator of God's liberation and His covenant partner, would provide theological orientations to reimagine the role of Dalit women in a society dominated by the oppressive structures of caste and patriarchy. Her model can inspire Dalit women to reinvent their role as participants in God's mission and mediators of God's liberation. However, I do not wish to idealize Sarah since she had her flaws as well. Her indifference to Hagar, an Egyptian slave woman, is questionable. Similarly, Sarah betrayed Hagar as an abusive slave mistress by giving Hagar to Abraham for sex and causing Hagar to lose her household status. Nevertheless, Yahweh comes to her rescue. As Hemchand Gossai observes, unlike Moses, who called out to Yahweh for water, Yahweh provided Hagar water without her calling. Yahweh helps her in her abandonment. It seems that Yahweh is the refuge of the oppressed, be it Sarah, Hagar or anyone else.[69]

Conclusion

Dalit theology is an advocacy theology for the Dalits, which seeks to subvert the influence of the caste system. The counter-discourse which it offers, however, alienated Dalit theology from Dalits' counter-ontology and the epistemology of resistance, pushed Dalit culture into the periphery and overlooked Dalits' liberative vision. This book addresses such imbalances and suggests that a methodological switch and an intertextual reading, respecting the counter-worldview and the epistemology of resistance communicated through Dalits' subversive voices and the counter-colonial worldview narrated through Abraham's crossings, can advance Dalit theology. From such a background, I suggest the counter-assertions of the Second Temple community narrated through Abraham's postcolonial crossings as a paradigm to redress discontinuities in Dalit theology, as hinted by scholars like Ayrookuzhiel.

Abraham's crossings will help Dalit theology revisit its image of God along the lines of Dalits' contexts. Dalits' contexts, for example, demand liberation and reconciliation. The image of God who emerges from Abraham's crossings is in line with this requirement. It will empower Dalit theology to affirm that Dalits' liberator is not dichotomous but an author of reconciliation between the Dalits and non-Dalits. Further, the suffering image of God advanced by Dalit theology, as clarified, has limitations to liberate the Dalits. The image of God in Abraham's crossings is not a suffering God, but a God who is sensitive to the sufferings. God responds to the sufferings dialogically, liberates the oppressed and reconciles the oppressed with the oppressor without compromising the freedom and dignity of the oppressed. Such an image can help Dalit theology overcome its bipolar outlook and develop cross-cultural fertilizations.

Similarly, Abraham's crossings will facilitate inter-Dalit and intra-Dalit relations. As seen, the Dalits remain as an oppressed majority in Indian Christian churches. They are poorly represented, and caste controls church practices significantly. Dalit theology challenges such injustices. However, the hermeneutical examples of Dalit theology, especially the binary opposition inherent in them, disempowers Dalit theology considerably. Abraham's crossings, especially the counter-colonial worldview in Genesis 12.10-20 and Genesis 20, which subvert the prejudices of the Second Temple community, can offer praxis-oriented guidelines to promote a crossing to appreciate the best in outsiders like similar examples at Neve Shalom and Kuron villages. Such initiatives will help Dalit theology concentrate more on the process of categorization in Indian Christian churches, empower the Dalits and non-Dalits to be active listeners and learners, promote dialogue as an opportunity to know outsiders and rescript ancient traditions to develop dialogues and collaborations with other religious traditions and suffering communities. So too, the proposed paradigm can empower the Dalits and the non-Dalits to know each other as 'others with some differences' and join together in living Christian life authentically.

Further, the proposed paradigm would help Dalit theology to rescript the role of Dalit women. As seen, they suffer multiple discriminations. Sarah's trauma and God's reaction to her sufferings suggest that God is intimately related to her and God saved the couple because of Sarah's words. Sarah, therefore, acts like a partaker in God's mission for Abraham and a mediator of liberation. Such a paradigm could inspire Dalit theology to reimagine the role of the Dalit women as mediators and participants in God's mission. Hence, the proposed paradigm would be radical in Dalit contexts. Besides these developments, the proposed paradigm, as will be explained in the next chapter, can reimagine Syrian Christians' social praxis to Dalits.

Chapter 9

AUTHOR'S NOTE: DALIT THEOLOGY, DISSOLVING DALIT–SYRIAN CHRISTIAN BOUNDARIES AND LIBERATION IN INDIA

Introduction

Michelangelo was born on 6 March 1475 in Caprese, Italy.[1] He was a sculptor, painter, architect and poet. He is recognized as one of the greatest artists of all time. He believed that every stone has a statue submerged in it, and his task was to liberate the image sleeping inside the stone. The famous quotation, often attributed to him, 'I saw the angel in the marble and carved until I set him free', reveals his mind. This book is a similar task. It is a discovery. The driving forces behind this research are Dalits' resources and their counter-formulations. I am only a facilitator who helps the liberative vision already submerged in Dalits' contexts to speak. My claim, however, does not include that this book is entirely free from my value judgements. My religious and social location – as a Syrian Christian priest born and brought up in Kerala – has undoubtedly impacted the study. Therefore, I see my book as part of an ongoing conversation that needs further input from Dalit academics.

As clarified, this book proposes an alternate path for Dalit theology through Dalits' assertions and counter-caste worldviews. Though such assertions reflect Dalits' life and their epistemology of resistance authentically, Dalit theology's hermeneutical and conceptual frameworks tended to overlook them, which alienated Dalit theology from Dalits' counter-caste Hindu hegemonic worldview and alternate moral visions substantially. From such backgrounds, this book suggests that a hermeneutics of return to Dalits' resources and constructive dialogues between biblical and Dalits' dissenting voices including the anti-caste philosophers – such as Chokhamela, Karmamela, Ravidas, Kabir, Nandanar and Narayana Guru – can reconnect Dalit theology with Dalits' worldview meaningfully and promote Dalit–Syrian Christian dialogues. Drawing on scriptures and Dalits' religio-cultural resources, this study weaves together an intertextual dialogue between Dalits' counter-caste assertions and counter-colonial assertions of the Second Temple community narrated through Abraham's crossings, suggesting that these dialogue partners can offer an alternate path for Dalit theology through Dalits' resistance and promote Dalit–Syrian Christian dialogues.

Dalit theology, boundary crossings and liberation

Dalits have been the Indian suffering servants for many centuries. The caste system relegated their bodies as untouchable and unholy. Born as untouchable and unapproachable in the casteist society, some Dalits joined Christianity. However, conversion did not change Dalits' social situation considerably, and the Dalits continued to suffer multiple discriminations in various Christian denominations. Secular assertions like the Dalit Panther movement, Dalit Sangharsh Samiti, the Dalit literature movement as well as the churches' failure in facilitating the Dalits and the insensitivity of Indian Christian theologians to Dalits' lived experiences convinced the Dalit Christian academics of the need to offer a theological alternative to complement secular movements to redress Dalits' situation. They found Latin American and African American theologies as their dialogue partners, which further convinced them that the society, Indian churches and the Indian Christian theology failed to appreciate Dalits' pathos, caste's negative impact upon the Dalits and Dalits' longing for liberation. Dalit theology emerged as an Indian form of liberation theology from such contexts.

The proposals of liberation theologians were a strong point of departure for the Dalit academics, who were discontent with their lived experiences. They depended heavily on Latin American and African American conceptual and hermeneutical examples. Such an undertaking created an imbalance in Dalit theology and suggested how biblical paradigms and worldviews, proposed in predominately Christian cultures, could redress Dalits' situation. It reduced Dalits' traditions as objects and alienated Dalit theology from Dalits' counter-assertions against dominant Hindu Vedic worldview expressed through Dalits' liberative voices and constructed the biblical messages developed in alien contexts as the dominant self at the centre and Dalits' subversive voices as the dominated self at the margins of Dalit theology.

This book seeks to redress this unintended outcome through constructive dialogues between the Bible and Dalits' traditions. Nevertheless, this book is not the only solution to the problem. It suggests only one of the avenues to reconnect Dalit theology with Dalits' contexts through constructive dialogues between the Bible and Dalit traditions. As indicated, what this book proposes is not a conquest model but ongoing dialogues between the Bible and Dalits' contexts, requiring willingness from both participants to be modified and updated. From such backgrounds, this book examines the dominant paradigms of Dalit theology against Dalits' cultural and religious traditions and argues that they overlook some essential aspects of Dalits' contexts. Building upon this analysis, this book initiates a process of listening to and learning from the pathos, ethos and vision submerged in Dalits' culture and spirituality.

Such listening and learning, as argued, clarify that Dalits' contexts require a hermeneutical switch and further interrogation in Dalit theology. Dalits' liberative voices and their counter-caste assertions, for example, aim neither at Dalits' isolated existence nor at their dominion over the dominant castes. Instead, they demand the liberation of Dalits and reconciliation between Dalits and non-Dalits. Similarly, the reconciliation in Dalits' contexts is not an event. Instead, it is a process, which continuously renegotiates the space between Dalits and non-Dalits, demanding mutually enriching partnerships across differences. So too, the reconciliation, which Dalit contexts require, is not a compromise but a conscious move towards a liberated-reconciled society connected through partnerships, irrespective of caste orientations. This book proposes that Dalit theology should honour these contextual realities and liberation of the Dalits, and the reconciliation between the Dalits and non-Dalits should be the twin goals of Dalit theology.

From such a background, this book, adding to the existing research, proposes the Second Temple community's counter-colonial assertions expressed through Abraham's crossings as a paradigm to complement Dalits' subversive voices. Indeed, Abraham was not a Dalit and had no association with Dalits or the Indian caste system. However, Abraham has some striking similarities with Dalits' contexts. He is like a Dalit ancestor envisioned in the Deuteronomic creed. Similarly, Abraham was a landless man like the Dalits. He lived as an immigrant on the Promised Land like most Dalit agricultural labourers, who work for wages on land they do not own.[2] Likewise, his role as an ecumenical ancestor of the Jews, Christians and Muslims is crucial since Dalits cut across various religious affiliations. Abraham's proposed association to the Babylonian Golah community, which shares Dalits' ethos, also enhances his appeal to the Dalits. Further, Abraham's non-Jewish background described in Joshua 24 may remind the Dalits of their pre-conversion religious orientations. Hence, the person and work of Abraham, interpreted through a postexilic optic, could appeal to Dalits.

Nevertheless, Abraham's crossings are not an invention of the postexilic period. They existed in some form before the exile. However, the postexilic community reformulated Abrahamic traditions amidst the Persian Empire's ethnocentric policies, which, as seen, divided the class layers sharply and deeply within Yehudites. The Persian policy strengthened hostility and intense opposition to internal minorities such as foreign wives and created internal and external outsiders in Yehud. The anti-imperialists living in Achaemenid Yehud responded to this crisis and rescripted the pre-exilic traditions about Abraham to register their discontent. As the products of postcolonial hybridity, Abraham's crossings counter the colonialist rhetoric and Persian imperial ambitions and their impacts upon the lives and identities of the Second Temple community, who had married Egyptian and Philistine women. They challenge the attempts to demonize the Egyptians and Philistines by narrating Abraham's crossings and Yahweh's initiatives to liberate the endangered couple. They highlight God as an immanent source of liberation and reconciliation, God's association with and revelation to Egyptians and Philistines, Egyptians and Philistines as behavioural models and God's concern for the endangered matriarch. Drawing from these counter-assertions, which seek to reimagine the Second Temple community's colonial worldview and its representation of Egyptians and Philistines, this book proposes that an intertextual reading between the Second Temple community's responses to their traumatic experiences and Dalits' assertions against the dominant Hindu Vedic worldview could help Dalit theology to develop and mature as a source of liberation and reconciliation.

The Indian caste system, for example, compartmentalizes different castes and creates insiders and outsiders. Further, each caste has its prejudices against the other. There are also inter-Dalit and intra-Dalit misreadings, and, as seen, Dalits are not a homogenous category. Such preoccupations are present in Indian Christian churches as well, and they influence inter-church and intra-church relations and practices negatively. Abraham's crossings, which project liberation, reconciliation and cross-border relations, are relevant in such contexts. They will advance liberation in India, helping Dalit theology to develop and mature as a source of liberation and reconciliation for the church and society by

- reimagining God as an immanent source of liberation and reconciliation, who inaugurates the process of liberation and reconciliation;
- revisiting the nature of God's agency in liberating the Dalits and reconciling the Dalits and the non-Dalits;
- redefining God's response to Dalits' suffering, not by participating in Dalits' suffering but peacefully initiating the process of liberation through dialogues and negotiations;
- developing a positive assessment of outsiders by acknowledging God's immanent presence and activities among outsiders and learning from them;
- moving from Christocentrism to theocentrism (with some reservations);
- breaking the barriers of the caste system that generate categories like the Dalits and non-Dalits in Indian Christian churches and society;
- empowering the Dalits and the non-Dalits to be active listeners and learners;
- promoting ongoing inter-Dalit and intra-Dalit dialogues, negotiations and mutually enriching partnerships;
- rescripting ancient traditions to promote peace and harmony in Indian Christian churches and society and
- reinventing the role of Dalit women as God's covenant partners, mediators of God's liberation and participants in God's mission.

Such rereadings will assist Dalit theology in focusing on breaking barriers, crossing boundaries and bridging differences by redefining God's agency in liberating Dalits and reconciling the liberated Dalits with non-Dalits, and empowering Dalits and non-Dalits to continue God's mission by crossing the boundaries of the caste system to appreciate the best in their religious, cultural and gender outsiders, as envisioned in Dalits' subversive voices. They can help Dalit theology mature and develop as a source of liberation and reconciliation for entire Indian Christian churches. Similarly, the present research, as noted, was liberative for me. It informed me about various aspects in Dalits' contexts. It too can empower Syrian Christians in Kerala to develop mutually enriching dialogues with Dalits also.

Dalit theology, boundary crossings and Dalit–Syrian Christian dialogues

As will be further explained, the Dalits' experiences with the Syrian Christians have been contentious and contradictory. Poykayil Yohannan (1879–1939), for example, was a Dalit activist, poet and social reformer.[3] His parents were the serfs of an aristocratic Syrian Christian family. They named him Komaran. Komaran was baptized at the age of five, and they called him Yohannan when his family joined the church, as the landlord had instructed.[4] Yohannan studied the Bible enthusiastically and became an *Upadesi*.[5] Nevertheless, the Syrian Christians' caste hesitations annoyed Yohannan. He believed that the Syrian Christians overlooked Dalit Christians' dilemma. Yohannan's mindset is evident from the following stanza:

> Like orphans, we roamed the back alleys of Hinduism.
> Like orphans, we wandered through the outskirts of Christianity
> The Hindus did not admit us, my friends
> Neither did the Christians, oh, my people![6]

These verses highlight the Syrian Christians' dominant caste profile and Dalit Christians' discriminations and deprivations.[7] The Syrian Christians, with very few exceptions, have been hostile to Dalits. They relegated Dalit converts and segregation, hierarchy and graded ritual purity haunted Dalit Christians within the Syrian Christian parishes. From such contexts, this book evaluates the Syrian Christian bodies' hesitations against the Dalit bodies in a self-reflexive manner. It suggests that Dalits' demand for liberation and their longing for reconciliation can advance some proposals for reconstructing Syrian Christians' approach to Dalits.

Syrian Christians' divided mindset

Syrian Christians' community conscience traces their conversion to St Thomas, who arrived in Kerala in 52 CE and baptized the upper caste Hindus. Scholars like S. N. Sadasivan, however, indicate a potential anachronism in this narrative and question the historicity of the dominant caste claim.[8] Sadasivan notes that the casteism got crystallized in Kerala much later than the first century CE. There was neither caste nor any brand of Brahminism in Kerala in the first century CE. From such contexts, Sadasivan suggests that the dominant caste association myth might have emerged in the eighteenth century when the different Christian denominations were in the making. The Syrian Christians, the early converts of the land, Sadasivan believes, claimed dominant caste origin to affirm the social privileges of the Syrian Christians over the new converts.[9] There are alternate proposals as well. Scholars such as Kochurani Abraham interpret the Syrian Christians' dominant caste claim against the Syrian Christians' aspirations to consolidate the social privileges and land ownership in a caste-ridden society.[10]

Whatever be the case, as George Samuel observes, the dominant caste Hindus viewed Syrian Christians as a separate caste group.[11]

The dominant caste rulers were also benevolent to Syrian Christians. The copper plates from the fourth, eighth, ninth and thirteenth centuries, for example, confirm that the Syrian Christians, as a trading community who brought wealth to the rulers and country, flourished through the trade and patronage of the Hindu rulers.[12] Through such patronage and protection, Syrian Christians advanced their social standing in the casteist Kerala society. They tended to enjoy many social, political and royal privileges, including the right to use public roads, ride the elephants, use the palanquins and sit before kings on the carpet after their conversion.[13] Such advantages and practices helped the Syrian Christians maintain a dominant caste identity and lineage, ranking after the Brahmins, roughly equal to the upper caste Nairs.

Similarly, the Syrian Christians tended to mimic the dominant caste's ceremonial practices in birth, feeding the baby, beginning education, marriage, celebrating festivals, death and remembering the dead.[14] Noting similar instances, Susan Bayly, while surveying various developments in Tamil Nadu and Kerala from 1700 to 1900, suggests that the Syrian Christians tended to share the casteist society's social praxis during this period.[15] The Syrian Christians also celebrated Hindu festivals like Onam and Vishu, and their prelates used to participate in the local Hindu rulers' installation ceremonies.[16] For example, the Syrian Christian dignitaries participated in the installation ceremonies of the dominant caste Hindu rulers in Cochin. Similarly, a Syrian church supplied some essential items of sacred regalia during the Onam celebrations. The processional image of Krishna, a prominent Hindu deity, was expected by custom to stop at the house of a prominent Syrian family well into the nineteenth century.[17] Subscribing to the dominant caste philosophy and customs helped the Syrian Christians to integrate well with the casteist society. Consequently, the casteist Kerala society tended to consider the Syrian Christians as 'persons of clean caste and standing in the Hindu moral order' and 'granted one of the most critical signs of ritual status within the society, the right of access to Hindu temples and sacred precincts, which was denied to low caste Hindus'.[18]

Such incorporation, however, has compromised Syrian Christians' social praxis, and Syrian Christians continue to practice a caste-Hindu body politic in everyday life during this time. Similarly, Syrian Christians, as Elamkulam Kunjan Pillai clarifies, tended to proselytize the dominant caste Hindus only.

> Christians were honoured in the same way as high-class Hindus. Conversion to Christianity at that time was permitted only to people belonging to the higher levels of society who had real faith in the teachings of Jesus Christ. The Christian converts continued to practice the same social systems and practices as before.[19]

Such dominant caste conversions helped the Syrian Christians continue the normativity of their caste baggage in a casteist society. The claim to the Brahminic origin, as noted, might have been deliberately circulated and used by the community for social privileges at this time. Nevertheless, the social outlook of the Western missionaries, the Church Missionary Society's mission to help Syrian Christians, social reformers like Chattampi Swamikal (1854–1924), Sree Narayana Guru (1856–1928) and Sree Ayyankali (1863–1941) challenged the Syrian Christians' social praxis in the nineteenth century.[20] Consequently, some Syrian Christians began to follow the social outlooks of the Western missionaries in the latter half of the nineteenth century, emphasizing universal education, seminary education for the clergy, translating the Bible to vernacular languages, Syrian Christians' vulnerability to the caste system and Syrian Christian mission among the Dalits.[21]

The Jacobite Syrian Orthodox Church, one of the Syrian Christian churches and the one to which I belong, also responded to this social awakening in the nineteenth century. Consequently, Dalits joined the Jacobite Church in many parts of Kerala, like Kallunkathara, Puthuppally, Amayannoor, Pampadi, Kottayam, Veliyanadu, Chenganoor, Kallisseri and Chennithala in Kerala due to the missionary work of Mor Gregorios Chathuruthil, a bishop of our church. An article published in 1897 in *Edavaka Pathrika*, a publication of the church, titled *Pula Sabhakal* (The Dalit Churches), revisits Jacobite Syrian Christians' caste hesitations in a self-reflexive manner. This article challenges the practical inefficacy of the church's social praxis, designates the caste hesitations as Satanic and suggests that overlooking the mission to Dalits a sin. Such a position was revolutionary in the nineteenth century. An encyclical from Patriarch Ignatius Peter III, the then head of the Jacobite Church, reproduced in the *Pula Sabhakal*, also advises the church members to accommodate the Dalit converts.[22]

Unfortunately, the ethos of *Pula Sabhakal* and the patriarch's encyclical failed to significantly reconstruct the Jacobite Syrian Christians' approach to the social margins because a dominant section of the church still considered Dalit Christians polluted. They segregated Dalit converts, discouraged intermarriage with Dalit Christians and constructed separate chapels for the Dalit Christians because of institutional casteism. Most Dalits, therefore, deserted the Jacobite Church and either joined other denominations or returned to their original tradition. The case is also the same with other Syrian Christian churches. Dalit Christians had to remove their headdress and keep their mouths closed with a hand while approaching Syrian Christians. So too, Dalit Christians were not given food inside Syrian Christian homes. Similarly, Syrian Christians forced Dalit Christians to declare in public their willingness to continue the caste body politic even after baptism.[23] Hence, Syrian Christians' attempts to embrace Dalits created further layers of othering for Dalits.

Such layers of othering and subsequent cruelties continue to impair the Syrian Christians' social praxis significantly. Paulose Mor Gregorios, a Syrian Christian bishop, in an article published in 1961, acknowledged the caste issues which continued to plague the Syrian Christians and Dalit Christians' critical standing in the Syrian Christian churches.[24] Geevarghese Mor Coorilos, another Syrian Christian bishop, has recently noted dominant caste tendencies among Syrian Christians. Mor Coorilos laments that the Syrian Christians overlook Dalits' socio-political struggles significantly.[25]

Hence, caste assumptions shape and reshape Syrian Christians' psyches subversively. Similarly, Syrian Christians have been silent about the sin of casteism, and Syrian Christian academics, with very few exceptions like Ayirookuzhiel, Eliaz and Mor Coorilos, do not attend seriously to caste discriminations. This chapter seeks to join such dissenting voices and understand the silences and indifferences as products of institutional sins, which assist the perpetuation of the caste system. Such instances, I believe, demand Syrian Christians' repentance. The Syrian Christians must accept the shortcomings in their social praxis. From such contexts, this chapter seeks to re-embrace the ethos of *Pula Sabhakal* and the Patriarch's encyclical in proposing further dialogues between Syrian Christians and the social margins aimed at reconciliation, forgiveness and structural change.

Such an undertaking needs much clarification. For example, 'What is the moral right of the Syrian Christians?' and 'Who are responsible for keeping the Dalit converts at the margins of the Syrian Christian churches?' Such questions are valid. Perhaps, Deenabandhu Manchala's proposal for 'a movement of churches together for life of all, countering the forces that deny and abuse life' can, I think, redirect Syrian Christians in developing proposals for mutual collaborations with Dalits.[26] My recommendations to redress inter-Dalit and intra-Dalit disconnects based upon Dalits' forgotten voices and Abraham's crossings, it is hoped, can also serve as a point of departure for healing the caste assumptions among Syrian Christians and building bridges between Syrian Christians and Dalit Christians.

Reconstructing Syrian Christians' approach to the social margins

As noted, the Syrian Christians and Dalit Christians are often understood as miles apart. Some sceptics on both sides of the divide, based upon historical experiences, emphasize that Dalits and Syrian Christians can never coalesce. However, there are a few connecting links between them, which might help them move forward with dialogue. First and foremost, Dalits' subversive voices, as demonstrated elsewhere in the study, envision a conversation between dominant castes and Dalits. Likewise, Syrian Christians and Dalit Christians have co-existed, though with some difficulties, for many centuries. So too, they are united through their faith in Christ. Such associations, though often overlooked, call for further research to bridge the gap, empowering Dalit Christians and Syrian Christians to work in dialogical and non-hierarchical collaboration as communities united through their faith. As our engagement with the biblical stories has demonstrated, the careful listening of ancient kings to God's communication and their willingness to listen to Abraham and Sarah explain their version, even after the couple's plots were uncovered, is just one example of how Syrian Christians and Dalit Christians can bridge the gap reimagining the other as a partner in dialogue.

Listening to bridge the gap

As Tracy Davis and Laura M. Harrison rightly observe, listening is essential in crossing the thresholds of differences. There is no substitute for listening in furthering associations through dialogue.²⁷ The listening and subsequent conversations seek not to conquer the other, but as in Abraham's crossings, seek to explain the individual situation, which will promote further exchanges, mutual co-operation and appreciation, suspending prejudices. Edmund Kee-Fook Chia, for example, clarifies how listening can advance dialogue and mutuality:

> If sharing and witnessing to our faith is important in interfaith dialogue, so is receiving and learning. Both parties in dialogue will have to be open to not only hearing what the other has to say but also to listening sincerely and attentively. Interfaith dialogue is premised on the hope that people are willing to open their eyes and minds as well as their hearts and souls to receive what the other has to offer. The process of listening requires that we suspend or bracket our previous understandings of what we think we know of the other is sharing with us. Such courtesy facilitates authentic and respectful listening.²⁸

Similarly, Ralph Underwood clarifies that listening promotes mutuality, helps persons move beyond prejudices and interact constructively with dialogue partners.²⁹ Such radical listening, which opens the eyes, minds, hearts and souls of the dialogue partners, suspending presuppositions, has the potential to liberate Syrian Christians and Dalit Christians. For example, my attempts to listen to Dalits' subversive voices, as indicated, educated me about Dalits' alternate, yet empowering, moral visions. Such a new orientation further reframed me as a dissenting voice, seeking to bridge Syrian Christians with Dalit Christians and join scholars like Eliaz and Mor Coorilos.

What is needed in Syrian Christian and Dalit Christian interactions is not a 'chosen-subaltern' language, affirming the superiority or inferiority of one of the dialogue partners. Instead, constructive listening may enrich both partners to understand the other as 'other' (with some differences) and live Christian life authentically in the subcontinent, overcoming caste barriers. Edmund Emeka Ezegbobelu, in a different but related field of interreligious dialogue between Christians and Muslims, has argued similarly:

> Interreligious dialogue has nothing to do with previous attitudes towards those who are different from us and is not there for us to trounce the opponent or learn about an opponent but is in place so that we may deal more effectively with them.³⁰

Such dialogical and non-hierarchical listening, as David Tracy emphasize, is not an easy task. It demands 'intellectual, moral, and, at the limit, religious ability to struggle to hear another and to respond'.³¹ As John C. Cavadini and Donald Wallenfang note, what David Tracy suggests is a struggling experience. It may even hurt the listener, allowing the listener's convictions to be challenged, rebuked, humiliated and stretched in every act of listening.³² Similarly, there could be some surprises and puzzles for Syrian and Dalit listeners. However, deliberate listening and subsequent dialogues, despite the difference in caste, as will be further clarified, might clear the surprises and puzzles gradually and can open new ground for Syrian and Dalit Christians to celebrate their equality amidst their differences. So too, Yahweh's dialogues with the emperors and the emperors' conversation with the couple, as narrated in Abraham's crossings, can benefit Dalit Christians and Syrian Christians in their unfolding encounters.

Dialogue: An opportunity for reconciliation forgiveness and structural change

As outlined in Chapters 7 and 8, Abraham's crossings highlight God's dialogue with the emperors to inform them about Sarah's status and the kings' engagement with the couple to understand more about them. A similar undertaking, which emphasizes discussion to bridge the gap, can facilitate a constructive dialogue between Syrian Christians and Dalit Christians. What I propose is not a one-way affair from the Syrian Christians to the Dalit Christians or from the Dalit Christians to the Syrian Christians. Neither do I wish to idealize dialogue. As Julia T. Wood rightly cautions, the 'search for (and belief in) common ground may thwart, rather than facilitate, genuine dialogue, because almost inevitably the dominant culture defines what ground is common or legitimate'.[33] She proposes a kind of dialogue that allows differences to exist among the dialogue partners.[34]

Such a dialogue that embraces and learns from conflicts and differences, as Cervenak et al. clarify, can open new avenues for mutuality, and unity may become less critical in such instances.[35] Hence, I am not suggesting any structural unity. Instead, what I propose is a willingness to ensure that Dalits and Syrian Christians have a special right to live in freedom and dignity, recognizing the present gap between the Syrian Christians and the Dalit Christians as a reality, seeking to be bridged as much as possible through reciprocal dialogues. From such contexts, I believe that there should be mutual learning and teaching between these dialogue partners, which will allow learning about each other and entering each other's worldview. It will also provide a basis for a reciprocal recognition of each other, informed by the counter-hegemonic language of the subversive voices in Dalits' contexts, expressed in cultural ways and historical events.[36]

Conclusion

This book is a humble attempt to engage with Dalit theology. As an author, I am aware of my privileged social location in the caste system, which, as acknowledged, might have impaired my social praxis to the margins and my encounter with Dalit theology. Similarly, I am aware of my limitations in proposing a methodology for Dalit theology. For example, Dr M. P. Joseph, one of my lecturers, an established author and a friend of Dr A. P. Nirmal, asked me after reading this chapter: How can Syrian Christians, a community responsible for keeping Dalits at the margins, pontificate to them about their methodology?

9. Author's Note

Dr Joseph's apprehension is valid. Together with Dr Joseph, I understand the Syrian Christians' moral bankruptcy in proposing Dalit theological hermeneutics. However, as noted in Chapter 4, there is an alternate path taken by Syrian Christian scholars such as Abraham Ayrookuzhiel. As noted, Dalit theologians such as Peniel Rajkumar have already accepted the validity of Ayrookuzhiel's contributions. Following such instances, I see this book as part of an ongoing dialogue initiated many decades ago by Syrian Christian theologians such as Ayrookuzhiel.

Similarly, this book, as clarified in the first chapter, collaborates with the dissenting voices in Dalit theology and recognizes Dalits as a protesting category with alternate moral visions. From such contexts, this book attempts to reposition Dalits' counter-ontology and the epistemology of resistance from the periphery of Dalit hermeneutics to the centre as a dominant self. It suggests that ongoing dialogues between the alternate moral visions submerged in Dalits' counter-formulations and that of the Bible would reorient Dalit theology.

From such contexts, this book proposes the counter-colonial assertions of the Second Temple community narrated through Abraham's postcolonial crossings as a paradigm, which agrees with Dalits' epistemology of resistance and counter-caste Hindu hegemonic worldview. Such a proposal, as indicated, helps to build upon Dalits' identity, not as a victimized category resigned to their dehumanized status like Isaiah's suffering servant; but as a community with alternate moral visions. It adds to existing scholarship, opens avenues for ongoing research and will help Dalit theology challenge the caste system, respecting the shared cultural ethic envisioned in Dalits' liberating voices. It will further assist Dalit theology in actualizing a liberated-reconciled church and society, connected through mutually enriching partnerships along the lines of Dalits' counter-worldview and the epistemology of resistance.

Besides offering an alternate path for Dalit theology, the present research advanced my cross-cultural competency and guided me through a process of active learning, unlearning and relearning. So too, this research informed me that Dalit Christians' experiences with the Syrian Christians, as seen in the noted example of Poykayil Yohannan, have been antagonistic and incongruous. Such instances demand Syrian Christians' repentance and reconstructing Syrian Christians' social praxis. As noted, Abraham's crossings and Dalits' assertions can empower Syrian Christians to become active listeners, request forgiveness from Dalits and ensure necessary structural changes to realize reconciliation with Dalits.

NOTES

Chapter 1

1 B. R. Ambedkar on 25 November 1949, *Constituent Assembly Debates* (New Delhi: Lok Sabha Secretariat, 1989), vol. IX, 979.
2 S. Raju, 'Dalit Boy Killed over Prayer at UP Temple', accessed 21 November 2020, https://www.hindustan times.com/india-news/dalit-boy-killed-over-prayer-at-up-temple/story-evS5ludyWjLWkJruO9Dk2J.html.
3 Syrian Christians, called also as St Thomas Christians, traditionally live in Kerala, in southwestern India. Syrian Christians spread across Catholic, Orthodox and Protestant traditions. The Syro-Malabar, Syro-Malankara and Knanaya Syrian churches belong to the Roman Catholic Church. The Jacobite Syrian Church, the Knanaya Jacobite Syrian Church, the Malankara Orthodox Syrian Church, the Malankara Mar Thoma Syrian Church and the St Thomas Evangelical Church profess Orthodox faith.
4 Sunder John Boopalan, *Memory, Grief, and Agency: A Political Theological Account of Wrongs and Rites* (New York: Palgrave Macmillan, 2017), 11; Jai B. P. Sinha, *Psycho-Social Analysis of the Indian Mindset* (New Delhi: Springer, 2014), 203; Nicholas B. Dirks, *Castes of Mind: Colonialism and the Making of Modern India* (Princeton: Princeton University Press, 2001), 3.
5 Azra Khanam, *Muslim Backward Classes: A Sociological Perspective* (New Delhi: Sage Publications, 2013), 22.
6 David Keane, *Caste-Based Discrimination in International Human Rights Law* (London: Routledge, 2016), 37.
7 Axel Michaels, *Hinduism: Past and Present*, trans. Barbara Harshav (Princeton: Princeton University Press, 2004), 161.
8 Susan Bayly, *Caste, Society and Politics in India from the Eighteenth Century to the Modern Age* (Cambridge: Cambridge University Press, 2001), 106.
9 Daniel Nehring and Ken Plummer, *Sociology: An Introductory Textbook and Reader* (London: Routledge, 2013), 393.
10 Laura A. Lewis, 'Between Casta and Raza: The Example of Colonial Mexico', in *Race and Blood in the Iberian World*, eds María Elena Martínez, David Nirenberg and Max-Sebastián Hering Torres (Zurich: Lit Verlag GmbH, 2012), 100.
11 Mey-Yen Moriuchi, 'From *Casta* to *Costumbrismo*: Representations of Racialized Social Spaces', in *Envisioning Others: Race, Color, and the Visual in Iberia and Latin America*, ed. Pamela P. Patton (Leiden: Brill, 2016), 214.
12 Christian Büschges, 'Ethnicity', in *The Routledge Handbook to the History and Society of the Americas*, eds Olaf Kaltmeier, Josef Raab, Mike Foley, Alice Nash, Stefan Rinke and Mario Rufer (Abingdon: Routledge, 2019), 263.
13 Lori L. Tharps, *Same Family, Different Colors: Confronting Colorism in America's Diverse Families* (Boston: Beacon Press, 2017), 68.
14 Ibid.
15 Bayly, *Caste, Society*, 106.

16 Gerald James Larson, 'Hinduism in India and America', in *World Religions in America*, ed. Jacob Neusner (Louisville: Westminster John Knox Press, 2002), 188.
17 Morton Klass, *Caste: The Emergence of the South Asian Social System* (Delhi: Manohar, 1998), 25–6.
18 K. A. Geetha, *Contesting Categories, Remapping Boundaries: Literary Interventions by Tamil Dalits* (Newcastle Upon Tyne: Cambridge Publishing House, 2014), 18.
19 Anderson H. M. Jeremiah, *Community and Worldview among Paraiyars of South India: 'Lived' Religion* (London: Bloomsbury, 2013), 1.
20 Robin Coningham and Ruth Young, *The Archaeology of South Asia: From the Indus to Asoka, c. 6500 BCE–200 CE* (New York: Cambridge University Press, 2015), 57–8.
21 Ibid., 58.
22 Lynne Gibson, *Hinduism* (Oxford: Heinemann Educational Publishers, 2002), 26.
23 Sathianathan Clarke, *Dalits and Christianity: Subaltern Religion and Liberation Theology in India* (New Delhi: Oxford University Press, 1999), 32–3.
24 Y. T. Vinayaraj, *Dalit Theology after Continental Philosophy* (London: Palgrave Macmillan, 2016), 91.
25 Roja Singh, *Spotted Goddesses: Dalit Women's Agency-Narratives on Caste and Gender Violence* (Berlin: LIT Verlag, 2018), 23.
26 *Manusmriti* 10:51–4.
27 Boopalan, *Memory, Grief, and Agency*, 46; Singh, *Spotted Goddesses*, 23.
28 Anand Teltumbde, *Dalits: Past, Present and Future* (London: Routledge, 2017), 1.
29 Y. T. Vinayaraj, 'Dalit Body without God: Challenges for Epistemology and Theology', in *Body, Emotion and Mind*, eds Martin Tamcke and Gladson Jathanna (Zurich: LIT Verlag, 2013), 27, 88.
30 Yashpal Jogdand, 'Humiliated by Caste: Understanding Emotional Consequences of Identity Denial', accessed 5 June 2019. https://www.academia.edu/2369690/Humiliated_by_Caste_Understanding_Emotional_Consequences_of_Identity_Denial.
31 BBC News, 'Caste Hatred in India – What It Looks Like', accessed 6 June 2019, https://www.bbc.com/news/world-asia-india-43972841.
32 Poornima Murali, 'This Dalit Doctor from Tamil Nadu Survived Casteism, and a Suicide Attempt, in Medical College', accessed 30 September 2019, https://www.news18.com/news/india/this-dalit-doctor-from-tamil-nadu-survived-casteism-and-a-suicide-attempt-in-medical-college-2167521.html.
33 Sukanya Shantha, 'Wardha: Caste Hindu Strips Dalit Boy, Forces Him to Sit on Hot Tiles for Entering Temple', accessed 25 June 2008, https://thewire.in/caste/wardha-caste-hindu-dalit-boy-strip-entering-temple.
34 Vineet Khare, 'The Indian Dalit Man Killed for Eating in Front of Upper-Caste Men', accessed 30 September 2019. https://www.bbc.com/news/world-asia-india-48265387
35 Surekha Nelavala, 'Inclusivity and Distinctions: The Future of Dalit Feminist Biblical Studies', in *New Feminist Christianity: Many Voices, Many Views*, eds Mary E. Hunt and Diann L. Neu (Woodstock: Skylight Paths Publishing, 2010), 105.
36 Bama, *Karukku*, trans. Lakshmi Holmstrom (Chennai: Macmillan, 1992), 103–4.
37 Ibid., 26.
38 Cardinal Baselios Cleemis, 'Policy of Dalit Empowerment in the Catholic Church in India: An Ethical Imperative to Build Inclusive Communities', accessed 29 April 2018, www.cbci.in/Policies/Policy922172823534.pdf.
39 Sandip Roy, 'Harassment of Dalit Professor in IIT Kanpur Exemplifies the Subtle Ways of Caste Discrimination in India Today', accessed 24 April 2018, https://www.

firstpost.com/india/harassment-of-dalit-professor-in-iit-kanpur-exemplifies-the-subtle-ways-of-caste-discrimination-in-india-today-4417983.html.
40 P. Antoniraj, *Discrimination against Dalit Christians* (Madurai: IDEAS Centre, 1992), 256.
41 Nirmala Carvalho, 'Indian Church Admits Dalits Face Discrimination', accessed 30 April 2018, https://cruxnow.com/global-church/2017/03/24/indian-church-admits-dalits-face-discrimination/.
42 Staff Reporter, 'Dalit Christians Still Trapped in Caste', accessed 22 April 2018, https://www.thehindu.com/news/cities/chennai/dalit-christians-still-trapped-in-caste/article23485606.ece.
43 G. Prakash Reddy, 'Caste and Christianity: A Study of Shudra Caste Converts in Rural Andhra Pradesh', in *Religion and Society in South India*, eds V. Sudarsan, G. Prakash Reddy and M. Suryanarayana (Delhi: B. R. Publishing, 1987): 119.
44 Walter Fernandes, 'Conversion to Christianity, Caste Tension and Search for an Identity in Tamilnadu', in *The Emerging Dalit Identity: Re-assertion of the Subalterns*, ed. Walter Fernandes (New Delhi: Indian Social Institute, 1996), 144–5.
45 Clarke, *Dalits and Christianity*, 12. The drum is a musical instrument often associated with Dalits.
46 Catholic Bishops Conference of India, 'Statement of the General Body Meeting of the CBCI, Tiruchirapalli, 1982', *Vidyajyoti Journal of Theological Reflection* 46 (1982): 149.
47 Address of John Paul II to the Bishops of India on their 'ad limina' visit, dated 17 November 2003.
48 Monica Jyotsna Melanchthon, 'Liberation Hermeneutics and India's Dalits', in *The Bible and the Hermeneutics of Liberation*, eds Alejandro F. Botta and Pablo R. Andiñach (Atlanta: Society of Biblical Literature, 2009), 200, 210.
49 Special Correspondent, 'Discrimination within the Church', accessed 22 April 2018, www.thehindu.com/news/national/tamil-nadu/Discrimination-within-the-Church/article14388130.ece.
50 Deborah Castellano Lubov, 'First Dalit Cardinal: My mission, help as many poor children as possible', accessed on 23 June 2022, https://www.vaticannews.va/en/church/news/2022-06/dalit-india-consistory-cardinal-anthony-poola-interview.html.
51 Z. Devasagayaraj, 'Archbishop Arulappa Condemns Vatican for Promoting a Dalit Bishop as His Successor in Hyderabad, India', accessed 25 April 2018, http://www.dalitchristians.com/html/arulappa.htm.
52 Pon Vasanth, 'Acknowledgement of Bias Raises Hope for Dalit Christians', accessed 22 April 2018, www.thehindu.com/news/national/tamil-nadu/acknowledgement-of-bias-raises-hope-for-dalit-christians/article16895188.ece1.
53 Cleemis, 'Policy of Dalit Empowerment in the Catholic Church'.
54 Anderson, *Community and Worldview*, 31, 32.
55 A. Mathias Mundadan, *History of Christianity in India: From the Beginning up to the Middle of the Sixteenth Century (Up to 1542)* (Bangalore: Theological Publication of India, 1989), 24–30; Elamkulam P. N. Kunjanpillai, *Chila Kerala Charithra Prasnangal* (Kottayam: National Book Stall, 1970), 187–221; Ninan Koshy, *Caste in the Kerala Churches* (Bangalore: The Christian Institute for the Study of Religion and Society, 1968), 39–42.
56 P. S. Iype, *The Parumala Kochu Thirumeni* (Mavelikkara: St. Paul's Mission Press, 1981), 15–25.
57 Susan Visvanathan, *The Christians of Kerala: History, Belief and Ritual among the Yakoba* (Madras: Oxford University Press, 1993), 2.

58 P. P. Varkey and K. V. Mammen, *Pathros Mor Osthatheos: A Prophet Like Revolutionary*, trans. Punnoose U. Panoor (Kottayam: Kottackal Publishers, 2012), 52.
59 Susan Visvanathan. *The Christians of Kerala: History, Belief and Ritual among the Yakoba* (Madras: Oxford University Press, 1993), 34.
60 Gita Aravamudan, ' "Honour Killing" in Kerala: Kevin-Neenu Case Indicative of a Bigger, More Frightening Trend', accessed 5 June 2018, https://www.firstpost.com/life/honour-killing-in-kerala-kevin-neenu-case-indicative-of-a-bigger-more-frightening-trend-4491953.html.
61 P. T. Thufail, 'Bishop Demolishes the Biggest Conversion "Myth" of Kerala', accessed 30 April 2018, https://www.outlookindia.com/website/story/bishop-demolishes-the-biggest-conversion-myth-of-kerala/310974.
62 A. P. Nirmal, 'Toward a Christian Dalit Theology', in *Frontiers in Asian Christian Theology: Emerging Trends*, ed. R. A. Sugirtharajah (Maryknoll: Orbis, 1994), 30.
63 James Massey, 'Ingredients for a Dalit Theology', in *Indigenous People: Dalits: Dalit Issues in Today's Theological Debate*, ed. James Massey (New Delhi: Indian Society for Promoting Christian Knowledge, 1994), 338–43.
64 A. P. Nirmal, 'Toward a Christian Dalit Theology', 28–31.
65 R. S. Sugirtharajah and Cecil Hargreaves, *Introduction to Readings in Indian Christian Theology* (London: Society for Promoting Christian Knowledge, 1993), 2.
66 Ashok Kumar M. and Sunder J. Boopalan, 'Indian Christians in Conflict: Dalit Christian Movement in Contemporary India', in *Handbook of Global Contemporary Christianity: Themes and Developments in Culture, Politics, and Society*, ed. Stephen Hunt (Leiden: Brill, 2015), 318.
67 James Massey, 'A Review of Dalit Theology', in *Dalit and Minjung Theologies: A Dialogue*, eds Samson Prabhakar and Jinkwan Kwon (Bangalore: SATHRI, 2006), 3.
68 Clarke, *Dalits and Christianity*, 45; Peniel Rajkumar, *Dalit Theology and Dalit Liberation: Problems, Paradigms and Possibilities* (Surrey: Ashgate Publishing, 2010), 39.
69 Kothappalli Wilson, *The Twice Alienated: Culture of Dalit Christians* (Hyderabad: Booklinks Cooperation, 1982).
70 John C. B. Webster, *The Dalit Christians: A History* (New Delhi: Indian Society for Promoting Christian Knowledge, 1994), 234; Dionysius Rasquinha, 'A Brief Historical Analysis of the Emergence of Dalit Christian Theology', *Vidyajyoti Journal of Theological Reflection* 66, no. 5 (2002): 363.
71 Rajkumar, *Dalit Theology and Dalit Liberation*, 39.
72 Anuparthi John Prabhakar, *Preaching Contextually: A Case with Rural Dalits in India* (Chennai: Notion Press, 2016), 30.
73 M. E. Prabhakar (ed.), *Towards a Dalit Theology* (Delhi: Indian Society for Promoting Christian Knowledge, 1998); John Paratt, 'Recent Writing on Dalit Theology: A Bibliographic Essay', in *International Review of Mission* 83 (April 1994): 329.
74 A. P. Nirmal, 'A Dialogue with Dalit Literature', in *Towards a Dalit Theology*, ed. M. E. Prabhakar (Delhi: Indian Society for Promoting Christian Knowledge, 1988), 79.
75 Xavier Irudayaraj (ed.), *Emerging Dalit Theology* (Madras: Jesuit Theological Secretariat, 1990).
76 Arvind P. Nirmal, 'Towards a Dalit Theology', in *Emerging Dalit Theology*, ed. Xavier Irudayaraj (Madras: Jesuit Theological Secretariat, 1990), 123–42.

77 Arvind P. Nirmal (ed.), *A Reader in Dalit Theology* (Madras: Gurukul Lutheran Theological College and Research Institute, 1991), A. P. Nirmal (ed.), *Heuristic Explorations* (Madras: CLS, 191).
78 Paratt, *Recent Writings on Dalit Theology*, 29.
79 Webster, *The Dalit Christians*, 294.
80 James Massey, *Towards Dalit Hermeneutics: Rereading the Text, the History and the Literature* (Delhi: Indian Society for Promoting Christian Knowledge, 1994).
81 James Massey (ed.), *Indigenous People: Dalits, Dalit Issues in Today's Theological Debate* (Delhi: Indian Society for Promoting Christian Knowledge, 1994), V. Devasahayam (ed.), *Frontiers of Dalit Theology* (New Delhi: Indian Society for Promoting Christian Knowledge, 1997).
82 A. P. Nirmal, 'Towards a Christian Dalit Theology', in *Indigenous People: Dalits, Dalit Issues in Today's Theological Debate*, ed. James Massey (Delhi: Indian Society for Promoting Christian Knowledge, 1998).
83 M. E. Prabhakar, 'The Search for a Dalit Theology', in *Indigenous People: Dalits, Dalit Issues in Today's Theological Debate*, ed. James Massey (Delhi: Indian Society for Promoting Christian Knowledge, 1998).
84 Abraham Ayrookuzhiel, 'Dalit Theology: A Movement of Counter-Culture', in *Indigenous People: Dalits, Dalit Issues in Today's Theological Debate*, ed. James Massey (Delhi: Indian Society for Promoting Christian Knowledge, 1994).
85 James Massey, 'Historical Roots', in *Indigenous People: Dalits, Dalit Issues in Today's Theological Debate*, ed. James Massey (Delhi: Indian Society for Promoting Christian Knowledge, 1994).
86 Nirmal, 'Towards a Christian Dalit Theology', 227.
87 Prabhakar, 'The Search for a Dalit Theology', 211.
88 Devasahayam (ed.), *Frontiers of Dalit Theology*.
89 James Massey and Samson Prabhakar (eds), *Frontiers in Dalit Hermeneutics* (Delhi: SATHRI, 2005).
90 James Massey, S. Lourdunathan and I. John Mohan Razu (eds), *Breaking Theoretical Grounds for Dalit Studies* (New Delhi: Centre for Dalit/Subaltern Studies, 2006).
91 James Massey and Shimreingam Shimray (eds), *Dalit–Tribal Theological Interface: Current Trends in Subaltern Theologies* (New Delhi: Tribal Study Centre/ Women Study Centre, 2007).
92 Felix Wilfred, *Dalit Empowerment* (Bangalore: National Biblical, Catechetical and Liturgical Centre, 2007).
93 Y. T. Vinayaraj, *Re-imagining Dalit Theology: Postmodern Readings* (Thiruvalla: Christava Sahitya Samithi, 2010).
94 James Massey, 'Revisiting and Resignifying the Methodology for Dalit Theology', in *Revisiting and Resignifying Methodology for Dalit Theology*, eds James Massey and Indukuri John Mohan Razu (New Delhi: cds, 2008), 55; Charles Singaram, *The Question of Method in Dalit Theology: In Search of a Systematic Approach to the Practice of an Indian Liberation Theology* (Delhi: Indian Society for Promoting Christian Knowledge, 2008), 5–12.
95 Sathianathan Clarke, Deenabandhu Manchala and Philip Vinod Peacock, 'Introduction: Enflamed Words, Engaging Worlds, Embryonic Word-Worlds', in *Dalit Theology in the Twenty-First Century: Discordant Voices, Discerning Pathways*, eds Sathianathan Clarke, Deenabandhu Manchala and Philip Vinod Peacock (Delhi: Oxford University Press, 2010), 6.

96 Anderson, *Community and Worldview*, 75.
97 Samuel, Joshua, 'Practicing Multiple Religious Belonging for Liberation: A Dalit Perspective', *Current Dialogue* 57 (December 2015): 82.
98 Y. T. Vinayaraj, *Re-visiting the Other: Discourses on Postmodern Theology* (Tiruvalla: Christava Sahitya Samithi, 2010), 72; Rajkumar, *Dalit Theology and Dalit Liberation*, 170, Joshua Samuel, *Untouchable Bodies, Resistance, and Liberation: A Comparative Theology of Divine Possessions* (Leiden: Brill, 2020), 48.
99 Samuel, 'Practicing Multiple Religious Belonging for Liberation', 80.
100 Anderson, *Community and Worldview*, 5.
101 Deenabandhu Manchala, 'Expanding the Ambit: Dalit Theological Contribution to Ecumenical Social Thought', in *Dalit Theology in the Twenty-First Century: Discordant Voices, Discerning Pathways*, eds Sathianathan Clarke, Deenabandhu Manchala and Philip Vinod Peacock (Delhi: Oxford University Press, 2010), 41.
102 Rajkumar, *Dalit Theology and Dalit Liberation*, 115.
103 Boopalan, *Memory, Grief, and Agency*.
104 Anderson H. M. Jeremiah, 'Dalit Christians in India: Reflections from the "Broken Middle"', *Studies in World Christianity* 17, no. 3 (2001): 258–74.
105 Anderson H. M. Jeremiah, 'Exploring New Facets of Dalit Christology: Critical Interaction with J. D. Crossan's Portrayal of the Historical Jesus', in *Dalit Theology in the Twenty-First Century: Discordant Voices, Discerning Pathways*, eds Sathianathan Clarke, Deenabandhu Manchala and Philip Vinod Peacock (New Delhi: Oxford University Press, 2010), 153–4.
106 Ibid., 155.
107 Vinayaraj, *Dalit Theology*, 2.
108 Scholars use 'African American theology' and 'Black theology' interchangeably to denote the Black theology developed by African Americans in the United States. However, there are some notable distinctions between these two terminologies. Black theology responds to African descendants' oppression in the Diaspora and in the African continent, while African American theology revisits African lives in the United States alone. I will follow this distinction and use African American theology to denote theological responses from African Americans, even though they use Black theology.
109 V. Devasahayam, 'Conflicting Roles of the Bible and Culture in Shaping Asian Theology', in *Christianity and Cultures: Shaping Christian Thinking in Context*, eds. David Emmanuel Singh and Bernard C. Farr (Cumbria: Regnum Books, 2008), 71.
110 Victor Anderson, 'Critical Reflection on the Problems of History and Narrative in a Recent African-American Research Problem', in *A Dream Unfinished: Theological Reflections on America from the Margins*, eds Eleazar S. Fernandez and Fernando F. Segovia (Eugene: Wipf and Stock, 2006), 38.
111 Devasahayam, 'Conflicting Roles of the Bible', 77.
112 K. Renato Lings, 'Culture Clash in Sodom: Patriarchal Texts of Heroes, Villains and Manipulation', in *Patriarchs, Prophets and Other Villains*, ed. Lisa Isherwood (London: Routledge, 2014), 204.
113 Pablo Richard, 'Biblical Interpretation from the Perspective of Indigenous Cultures of Latin America (Mayas, Kunas, and Queschuas)', in *Ethnicity and the Bible*, ed. Mark G. Brett (Boston: Brill Publishers, 2002), 297.

114 Jawanza Eric Clark, *Indigenous Black Theology: Toward an African-Centred Theology of the African-American Religious Experience* (New York: Palgrave Macmillan, 2012), 101–2.
115 Devasahayam, 'Conflicting Roles of the Bible', 78.

Chapter 2

1 Omprakash Valmiki, *Joothan: An Untouchable's Life*, trans. Arun Prabha Mukherjee (New York: Columbia University Press, 2003) 3.
2 Ibid., 97–8.
3 Uma Majumdar, *Gandhi's Pilgrimage of Faith: From Darkness to Light* (Albany: State University of New York Press, 2005), 205.
4 Devadasi system was an infamous practice in which Dalit girls were ritually married to a Hindu God/Goddess and sexually exploited by the dominant caste individuals.
5 Carey M. Watt, 'Philanthropy and Civilizing Missions in India c. 1820–1960: States, NGOs and Development', in *Civilizing Missions in Colonial and Postcolonial South Asia: From Improvement to Development*, eds Carey Anthony Watt and Michael Mann (London: Anthem Press, 2011), 289.
6 Gopal Guru, 'Understanding the Category Dalit', in *Atrophy in Dalit Politics*, ed. Gopal Guru (Mumbai: Vikas Adhyayan Kendra, 2005), 63–75.
7 Paul Ghuman, *British Untouchables: A Study of Dalit Identity and Education* (Surrey: Ashgate Publishing, 2011), 1.
8 Boopalan, Memory, Grief, 26.
9 H. C. Sadangi, *Emancipation of Dalits and Freedom Struggle* (Delhi: Isha Books, 2008), 130.
10 Vasant Brave and S. R. Medhe, 'Agenda for Emancipation and Empowerment of Dalits in India', in *Dalits and Tribes of India*, ed. J. Cyril Kanmony (New Delhi: Mittal Publications, 2010), 52.
11 Debjani Ganguly, 'Dalit Life Stories', in *The Cambridge Companion to Modern Indian Culture*, eds Vasudha Dalmia and Rashmi Sadhana (Cambridge: Cambridge University Press, 2012), 145.
12 Sathianathan Clarke, 'Viewing the Bible through the Eyes and Ears of Subalterns in India', *Biblical Interpretation: A Journal of Contemporary Approaches* 10 (2002): 246.
13 Bruce V. Malchow, *Social Justice in the Hebrew Bible* (Minnesota: The Liturgical Press, 1996), 13; Naveen Rao, *The Formulation of Scripture: Liberative Hebrew Paradigm for Dalit Scripture* (Delhi: Indian Society for Promoting Christian Knowledge, 2010), 282.
14 Chandran Paul Martin, 'Globalisation and Its Impact on Dalits: A Theological Response', in *Globalisation and Its Impact on Dalits: A Theological Response*, ed. James Massey (New Delhi: Centre for Dalit/Subaltern Studies, 2004), 21–4.
15 Simon Chauchard, *Why Representation Matters: The Meaning of Ethnic Quotas in Rural India* (Cambridge: Cambridge University Press, 2017), 60.
16 Amnesty International, 'INDIA 2017/2018', accessed 27 April 2018, https://www.amnesty.org/en/countries/asia-and-the-pacific/india/report-india/.
17 Bhattacharjee, Manash, 'The Clarity of a Suicide Note', accessed 21 February 2018, https://www.thehindu.com/opinion/op-ed/dalit-scholar-rohith-vemulas-suicide-letter-clarity-of-a-suicide-note/article62112096.ece.

18 BBC News, 'Indian Lowest-Caste Dalit Man Killed "for Owning Horse"', accessed 19 April 2018, http://www.bbc.com/news/world-asia-india-43605550.
19 Priyangi Agarwal, *'Dalit Assaulted, Humiliated in Badaun Village'*, accessed 1 May 2018, https://timesofindia.indiatimes.com/city/bareilly/dalit-assaulted-humiliated-in-badaun-village/articleshow/63964413.cms.
20 Sriparna Ghosh, 'Farmers Force Dalit Man to Drink Urine for Refusing to Harvest Crops', accessed 1 May 2018, https://www.ibtimes.co.in/farmers-force-dalit-man-drink-urine-refusing-harvest-crops-768159.
21 James Massey, *Dalits in India: Religion as a Source of Bondage or Liberation with a Special Reference to Christians* (New Delhi: Manohar Publishers, 1995), 169, 173.
22 V. Devasahayam, 'Pollution, Poverty and Powerlessness: A Dalit Perspective', in *A Reader in Dalit Theology*, ed. A. P. Nirmal (Madras: Gurukul, 1991).
23 Ely Aaronson, *From Slave Abuse to Hate Crime: The Criminalization of Racial Violence in American History* (New York: Cambridge University Press, 2014), 10; Christian Smith, *The Emergence of Liberation Theology: Radical Religion and Social Movement Theory* (Chicago: The University of Chicago Press, 1991), 71; Maha Abdelrahman, *Egypt's Long Revolution: Protest Movements and Uprisings.* (New York: Routledge, 2014), 50; Tore Bjorgo, *Strategies for Preventing Terrorism* (Basingstoke: Macmillan Publishers, 2013), 39.
24 Adrian Bird, 'Caste and Christianity since Gandhi and Ambedkar', in *Forrester on Christian Ethics and Practical Theology: Collected Writings on Christianity, India and the Social Order*, ed. Duncan B. Forrester (Surrey: Ashgate Publishing, 2010), 83; Leonard Fernando and G. Gispert–Sauch, *Two Thousand Years of Faith: Christianity in India* (London: Penguin Books India, 2004), 199–200.
25 Y. T. Vinayaraj, 'Envisioning a Postmodern Method of Doing Dalit Theology', in *Dalit Theology in the Twenty-First Century: Discordant Voices, Discerning Pathways*, eds Sathianathan Clarke, Deenabandhu Manchala and Philip Vinod Peacock (New Delhi: Oxford University Press, 2010), 93; Peniel Rajkumar, 'In Witness to God's "With-ness": Dalit Theology, the God of Life, and the Path Towards Justice and Peace', *Ecumenical Review* 64, no. 4 (2012): 546–58.
26 M. E. Prabhakar, 'Introduction', in *Towards a Dalit Theology*, ed. M. E. Prabhakar (Delhi: Indian Society for Promoting Christian Knowledge, 1989), 1–2.
27 K. Steenbrink, 'Seven Indonesian Perspectives on Theology of Liberation', in *Liberation Theologies on Shifting Grounds*, ed. G. De Schrijver (Leuven: Leuven University Press, 1998), 380.
28 Felix Wilfred, *Margins: Site of Asian Theologies* (Delhi: Indian Society for Promoting Christian Knowledge, 2008), 62.
29 R. K. Kshirsagar, *Dalit Movement in India and Its Leaders, 1857–1956* (New Delhi: MD Publications, 1994), 422–3; Ghanshyam Shah, *Social Movements in India: A Review of Literature* (New Delhi: Sage Publications, 2004), 135.
30 Kumar M. Boopalan, 'Indian Christians in Conflict', 310.
31 Smita Narula, *Broken People: Caste Violence against India's 'Untouchables'* (New York: Human Rights Watch, 1999), 34.
32 Shweta Majumdar, 'Challenging the Master Frame through Dalit Organizing in the United States', in *Living Our Religions: Hindu and Muslim South Asian-American Women Narrate Their Experiences*, eds Anjana Narayan and Bandana Purkayastha (Sterling: Kumarian Press, 2009), 267.
33 Gyanendra Pandey, *A History of Prejudice: Race, Caste, and Difference in India and the United States* (New York: Cambridge University Press, 2013), 6.

34 Keith Hebden, *Dalit Theology and Christian Anarchism* (Surrey: Ashgate, 2011), 113.
35 Surinder S. Jodhka, 'Sikhs Today: Development, Disparity and Difference', in *Religion, Community and Development: Changing Contours of Politics and Policy in India*, eds Gurpreet Mahajan and Surinder S. Jodhka (Abingdon: Routledge, 2010), 179; Rowena Robinson, *Christians of India* (New Delhi: Sage Publications, 2003), 193; Suresh V. 'The Dalit Movement in India', in *Region, Religion, Caste, Gender and Culture in Contemporary India*, ed. T. Sahithyamurthy (Delhi: Oxford University Press, 1996), 355–87; Sarah Beth Hunt, *Hindi Dalit Literature and the Politics of Representation* (London: Routledge, 2014), 4.
36 Andrew Wyatt, 'Dalit Theology and the Politics of Untouchability among Indian Christian Churches', in *From Stigma to Assertion: Untouchability, Identity and Politics in Early and Modern India*, eds. Mikael Aktor and Robert Deliege (Copenhagen: Museum Tusculanum Press and the Authors, 2010), 119.
37 Gail Omvedt, 'The Anti-Caste Movement and the Discourse of Power', in *Region, Religion, Caste, Gender and Culture in Contemporary India*, ed. T. Sahithyamurthy (Delhi: Oxford University Press, 1996), 422.
38 Prahlad Gangaram Jogdand, *Dalit Movement in Maharashtra* (New Delhi: Kanak Publications, 1991), 71; Hugo Gorringe, *Untouchable Citizens: Dalit Movements and Democratisation in Tamil Nadu* (New Delhi: Sage Publications India, 2005), 53.
39 Michael L. Clemons and Charles E. Jones, 'Global Solidarity: The Black Panther Party in the International Arena', in *Liberation, Imagination, and the Black Panther Party: A New Look at the Panthers and their Legacy*, eds Kathleen Cleaver and George N. Katsiaficas (New York: Routledge, 2001), 24.
40 Rattan Singh and Mamta Mehmi, 'Constitutional Protection to the Dalits: A Myth or Reality?' in *Dalit and Minority Empowerment*, ed. Santosh Bhartiya (New Delhi: Raj Kamal Prakashan, 2008), 230.
41 Don Schweitzer, 'Two Theological Movements in India That Complicate Western Reformed Identities', *Toronto Journal of Theology*, 28, no. 2 (2012): 228; Gail Omvedt, *Reinventing Revolution: New Social Movements and the Socialist Tradition in India* (New York: An East Gate Book, 1993), 74.
42 Uma Chakraborty, *Gendering Caste Through a Feminist Lens* (Calcutta: STREE, 2003), 142.
43 M. Azariah, 'Christ and Dalit Liberation', in *A Pastor's Search for Dalit Theology*, ed. M. Azariah (Delhi: Indian Society for Promoting Christian Knowledge, 2000), 137–51.
44 Mangala Subramaniam, *The Power of Women's Organizing: Gender, Caste, and Class in India* (Lanham: Lexington Books, 2006), 57.
45 Mary F. Katzentein, Kothari S. and Mehta U., 'Social Movement Politics in India: Institutions, Interests, and Identities', in *The Success of India's Democracy*, ed. Atul Kohli (New Delhi: Cambridge University, 2001), 260.
46 Subramaniam, *The Power of Women's Organizing*, 57.
47 M. H. Prahalladappa, 'Impact of DSS and Dalit Movement on Emerging Dalit Leadership in Karnataka', *Research Directions* 1, no. 2 (August 2013): 1.
48 Manohar Yadav, 'Career of Dalit Movement in India', *Journal of Social and Economic Development* 1, no. 1 (1998): 107–27.
49 Gail Omvedt, *Dalits and the Democratic Revolution: Dr Ambedkar and the Dalit Movement in Colonial India* (New Delhi: Sage Publications, 1994), 337.
50 Mumtaz Ali Khan, 'Legal Enactments and the Status of Dalits', in *Policing India in the New Millennium*, ed. P. J. Alexander (Mumbai: Allied Publishers, 2002), 506.

51 Manohar Yadav, 'Dalit Movement: A Critical Analysis of Its Current Realities in Karnataka', in *Contextualising Dalit Movement in South India: Selfhood, Culture and Economy* (Vikalp Alternatives, 2005), 114, accessed 13 May 2022, http://docplayer.net/51915031-August-contextualising-dalit-movement-in-south-india-selfhood-culture-and-economy.html.
52 Eva-Maria Hardtmann, 'In Touch with Politics: Three Individuals in the Midst of the Dalit Movement', in *Contesting 'Good' Governance: Crosscultural Perspectives on Representation, Accountability and Public Space*, eds Eva Poluha and Mona Rosendahl (London: Routledge, 2012), 139.
53 Darshana Trivedi, 'Literature of Their Own: Dalit Literary Theory in Indian Context', in *Dalit Literature: A Critical Exploration*, eds Amar Nath Prasad and M. B. Gaijan (New Delhi: Sarup, 2007), 3–5.
54 Partha Chatterjee, *The Politics of the Governed: Reflections on Popular Politics in Most of the World* (New York: Columbia University Press, 2004), 8.
55 Arundhathi Roy, 'Arundhathi Roy's Preface to BR Ambedkar's Annihilation of Caste', accessed 24 July 2018, https://www.theaustralian.com.au/arts/review/arundhati-roys-preface-to-br-ambedkars-annihilation-of-caste/news-story/8f7eb291a6e916ee686e098466cf16e7?sv=eced52f1527dbf0abe7cf98765b5bf3c.
56 TkhalliGopalKrishna, *Dalit Worship English Goddess* (Bangalore: Lulu.com, 2012), 40.
57 S. K. Paul, 'Dalit Literature and Dalit Poetry', in *Dalit Literature: A Critical Exploration*, eds Amar Nath Prasad and M. B. Gaijan (New Delhi: Sarup, 2007), 60.
58 Trivedi, 'Literature of Their Own', 3.
59 Omprakash Valmiki, *Dalit Sahithya Ka Saundaryashashtra* (The Aesthetic of Dalit Literature) (Delhi: Radhakrishnan, 2001), 15.
60 Kanwal Bharti, 'The Concept of Dalit Literature'. Quoted from Hunt, *Hindi Dalit Literature*, 218.
61 Debjani Ganguly, *Caste, Colonialism and Counter-Modernity: Notes on a Postcolonial Hermeneutics of Caste* (New York: Routledge, 2005), 179.
62 Rohinton Mistry, *A Fine Balance* (New Delhi: Rupa, 1996), 146.
63 M. N. Wankhade, 'Friends, the Day of Irresponsible Writing Is Over', in *Poisoned Bread: Translations from Modern Marathi Dalit Literature*, ed. Arjun Dangle, trans. Maxine Berntsen (Bombay: Orient Longman, 1992), 316; Valmiki, *Dalit Sahitya*, 34.
64 Vijay Tendulkar, *Kanyadan*, trans. Gowri Ramnarayan (New Delhi: Oxford India Paper Backs, 1996).
65 Ania Loomba, 'Marriage and the Liberal Imagination: Vijay Tendulkar's Kanyadaan', *Economic and Political Weekly* 47, no. 43 (October 26, 2013).
66 Sharan Kumar Limbale, *Towards an Aesthetic of Dalit Literature* (New Delhi: Orient Longman, 2004), 92.
67 Trivedi, 'Literature of Their Own', 6.
68 Quoted from Julius Lipner, *Hindus: Their Religious Beliefs and Practices* (London: Routledge, 1994), 96; John Maliekal, *Caste in Indian Society* (Bangalore: CSA Publications, 1980), 100.
69 Daya Pawar, 'The City'. Quoted in Razi Abedi, 'Dalit Literature: The Voice of the Downtrodden', in *The Best of Gowanus: New Writing from Africa, Asia, and the Caribbean*, ed. Thomas J. Hubschman (Brooklyn: Gonanus Books, 2001), 89.
70 K. Purushotham, 'Resisting Assimilation: A Reading of Daniel Fuchs' *Summer in Williamsburg*', *Kakatiya Journal of English Studies* 21 (2001).
71 Aravindra Kumar Varma, *Political Science* (New Delhi: Rahul Jain, 2011), 137.

72 L. S. Deshpande, *Makers of Indian Literature: Narhar Kurundkar* (New Delhi: Akademi, 2005), 34ff.
73 Arvind Nirmal, 'A Dialogue with Dalit Literature', in *Towards a Dalit Theology*, ed. M. E. Prabhakar (Delhi: Indian Society for Promoting Christian Knowledge, 1989), 73.
74 Ibid., 66.
75 K. S. Subramanian, *Political Violence and the Police in India* (New Delhi: Sage Publications, 2007), 116.
76 A. Satyanarayana, *Dalits and Upper Castes: Essays in Social History* (New Delhi: Kanishka Publishers, 2005), 210.
77 Kusuma Krishna Murthy, 'Ineffective Control of Violence Against Harijans', in *Untouchable! Voices of the Dalit Liberation Movement*, ed. Barbara Joshi (London: Zed Books, 1986), 118–21.
78 John Parratt, 'Recent Writing on Dalit Theology: A Bibliographical Essay', *International Review of Mission* 83, no. 329 (1994): 329–37.
79 James Massey, 'An Analysis of the Dalit Situation with Special Reference to Dalit Christians and Dalit Theology', in *Religion and Society* 5, nos 3–4 (2007): 74.
80 S. M. Michael, 'Dalit Encounter with Christianity: Change and Continuity', in *Margins of Faith: Dalit and Tribal Christianity in India*, eds Rowena Robinson and Joseph Marianus Kujur (New Delhi: Sage Publications, 2010), 71.
81 Sebastian Kappen, *Jesus and Freedom* (New York: Orbis Books, 1977); Sebastian Kappen, *Jesus and the Cultural Revolution: An Asian Perspective* (Bombay: Build Publications, 1983); Sebastian Kappen, *Liberation Theology and Marxism* (Puntamba: Asha Kendra, 1986).
82 Geevarghese Mar Osthathios, *Theology of a Classless Society* (Maryknoll: Orbis Press, 1980).
83 Nirmal, 'Towards a Christian Dalit Theology', 539.
84 Leo G. Perdue, *Reconstructing Old Testament Theology: After the Collapse of History* (Minneapolis: Augsburg Fortress, 2005), 333; Xavier Irudayaraj, *Emerging Dalit Theology* (Madras: Tamil Nadu Theological Seminary, 1990), 126.
85 Hans Ucko, *The People and the People of God: Minjung and Dalit Theology in Interaction with Jewish-Christian Dialogue* (Hamburg: LIT Verlag Münster, 2002), 104.
86 Rasquinha, 'A Brief Historical Analysis of the Emergence of Christian Theology', 354.
87 Raj Sekhar Basu, *Nandanar's Children: The Paraiyans' Tryst with Destiny, Tamil Nadu 1850–1956* (New Delhi: Sage Publications, 2011), 96.
88 Prakash Louis, 'Caste-Based Discrimination of Dalit Christians and the Demand for Reservation', in *Dalit and Minority Empowerment*, ed. Santosh Bhartiya (New Delhi: Rajkamal Prakashan, 2008), 367–8.
89 John C. B. Webster, 'From Indian Church to Indian Theology: An Attempt at Theological Construction', in *A Reader in Dalit Theology*, ed. Arvind P. Nirmal (Chennai: Gurukul Lutheran Theological College & Research Institute, 2007), 97; Yoginder Sikand, *Muslims in India since 1947: Islamic Perspectives on Inter-faith Relations* (London: Routledge, 2004), 122; Chad M. Bauman, *Christian Identity and Dalit Religion in Hindu India, 1868–1947* (Michigan: Wm B. Eerdmans, 2008), 4.
90 Paulson Pulikottil, 'Ramankutty Paul: A Dalit Contribution to Pentecostalism', in *Asian and Pentecostal: The Charismatic Face of Christianity in Asia*, eds Allan Anderson and Edmond Tang (Oxford: Regnum Books International, 2005), 250.
91 Ucko, *The People and the People of God*, 105.

92 Joanne Punzo Waghorne, 'Chariots of the God/s: Riding the Line between Hindu and Christian', in *Popular Christianity in India: Reading between the Lines*, eds Selva J. Raj and Corinne G. Dempsey (Albany: State University of New York, 2002), 17.
93 L. Stanislaus, *The Liberative Mission of the Church among Dalit Christians* (Delhi: Indian Society for Promoting Christian Knowledge, 1999), 127–8.
94 Rupa Viswanath, *The Pariah Problem: Caste, Religion, and the Social in Modern India* (Chichester: Columbia University Press, 2014), 49.
95 Webster, *The Dalit Christians*, 35.
96 Stanislaus, *The Liberation Mission*, 127, 128.
97 Akepogu Jammanna and Pasala Sudhakar, *Dalits' Struggle for Social Justice, in Andhra Pradesh (1956–2008): From Relays to Vacuum Tubes* (Newcastle upon Tyne: Cambridge Scholars Publishing, 2016), 121.
98 Jayachitra Lalitha, 'Postcolonial Feminism, The Bible and the Native Indian Women', in *Evangelical Postcolonial Conversations: Global Awakening in Theology and Praxis*, eds Kay Higuera Smith, Jayachitra Lalitha and L. Daniel Hawk (Downers Grove, Intervarsity Press, 2014), 78; Michael Barnes, *Theology and the Dialogue of Religions* (Cambridge: University of Cambridge, 2002), 168; George M. Soares-Prabhu, 'Exodus 20:1-17: An Asian Perspective', in *Return to Babel: Global Perspectives on the Bible*, eds John R. Levison and Priscilla Pope Levison (Louisville: Westminster John Knox Press, 1999), 49ff; George Oommen, 'Majoritarian Nationalism and the Identity Politics of Dalits in Post-Independent India', in *The God of All Grace: Essays in Honour of Orgien Vasantha Jathanma*, ed. Joseph George (Bangalore: Asian Trading Corporation and the United Theological College, 2005), 339–40; Lancy Lobo, 'Visions and Illusions of Dalit Christians in India', in *Dalit Identity and Politics*, ed. Ghanshyam Shah (Delhi; Sage Publications, 2001), 252.
99 Quoted from Sherinian, *Transforming Dalit Identity: Ancient Drum Beat, New Song*, accessed 13 May 2022, https://core.ac.uk/download/pdf/41335719.pdf.

Chapter 3

1 Badri Narayan, *Women Heroes and Dalit Assertion in North India: Culture, Identity and Politics* (New Delhi: Sage Publications, 2006), 67.
2 The Pandavas are the five sons of Pandu, by his wives Kunti and Madri. The Kauravas are the 100 sons of Dhritarashtra and his wife Gandhari. Pandavas and Kauravas had a significant role in the Mahabharata.
3 *Gurudakshina* is a teacher's tribute. The Indian tradition allows a teacher to demand *gurudakshina* from his student.
4 Shashikant Hingnekar, 'Ekalavya'. Quoted by Shashikant Hingnekar, 'Ekalavya'. Quoted by Gail Omvedt, *Dalit Visions: The Anti-caste Movement and the Construction of an Indian Identity* (Hyderabad: Orient BlackSwan, 2006), 98.
5 Arun Prabha Mukherjee, 'Introduction', in *Joothan: An Untouchable's Life*, Omprakash Valmiki, trans. Arun Prabha Mukherjee (New York: Columbia University Press, 2003), XLII; Roy Moxham, *Outlaw: India's Bandit Queen and Me* (London: Rider, 2010), 90.
6 Chakraborty, Gendering Caste, 19-20; Thummapudi Bharathi, *A History of Telugu Dalit Literature* (Delhi: Kalpaz Publications, 2008), 35–6.
7 Faiz Siddiqui, 'Dalit Farmer Beaten to Death, Wife and Daughter Critically Injured in UP's Kannauj', accessed 3 May 2018, https://timesofindia.indiatimes.com/city/kanpur/

dalit-farmer-beaten-to-death-wife-and-daughter-critically-injured-in-ups-kannauj/articleshow/63683409.cms.
8. United Nations Human Rights, Office of the High Commissioner, 'High Commissioner's Global Update of Human Rights Concerns', accessed 3 May 2018, https://www.ohchr.org/EN/NewsEvents/Pages/DisplayNews.aspx?NewsID=22772.
9. PTI, 'Atrocities against Minorities, Dalits Increasing: Former PM Manmohan Singh', accessed 12 October 2018, https://www.hindustantimes.com/india-news/atrocities-against-minorities-dalits-increasing-former-pm-manmohan-singh/story-9lMgjqKzmqrqLhmwiGFY8L.html.
10. Thanzauva and R. L. Hnuni, 'Ethnicity, Identity and Hermeneutics: An Indian Tribal Perspective', in *Ethnicity and the Bible*, ed. Mark G. Brett (New York: E. J. Brill, 1996), 350.
11. Felix Wilfred, *Beyond Settled Foundations: The Journey of Indian Theology* (Madras: University of Madras, 1995), viii; Franklyn J. Balasundaram, 'Dalit Theology and Other Theologies', in *Frontiers of Dalit Theology*, ed. V. Devasahayam (Chennai: Gurukul Lutheran Theological College & Research Institute, 1996), 252.
12. Duncan B. Forrester, *Truthful Action: Explorations in Practical Theology* (Edinburgh: T&T Clark, 2000), 23.
13. Keshab Chandra Sen, *India Asks, Who Is Christ?* (Calcutta: The Indian Mirror Press, 1879), 3.
14. Sebastian Kappen, 'Jesus and Transculturation', in *Asian Faces of Jesus*, ed. R. S. Sugirtharaja (Maryknoll: Orbis Books, 1993), 173; Wilson, *The Twice Alienated*, 59; Aloysius Pieris, *An Asian Theology of Liberation* (Edinburgh: T&T Clark, 1988), 112.
15. John Mansford Prior, 'Unfinished Encounter: A Note on the Voice and Tone of Ecclesia in Asia', *East Asian Pastoral Review* 37 (2000): 261.
16. The validity of Sen's proposal is hotly debated. Samartha, however, clarifies that the statements that 'Brahman is *sat-cit-ananda*' and 'God is triune' could be regarded as two responses to the same mystery in two cultural settings, and one cannot be used as a norm to judge the other. S. J. Samartha, *One Christ – Many Religions: Toward a Revised Christology* (Eugene: Wipf and Stock, 2015), 83.
17. Anne Dondapati Allen, 'No Garlic, Please, We Are Indian: Reconstructing the De-eroticized Indian Woman', in *Off the Menu: Asian and Asian North American Women's Religion & Theology*, eds Rita Nakashima Brock, Jung Ha Kim, Kwok Pui-lan and Seung Ai Yung (Louisville: Westminster John Knox Press, 2007), 191.
18. Ananta Kumar Giri, 'The Multiverse of Hindu Engagement with Christianity: Plural Streams of Creative Co-walking, Contradictions, and Confrontations', in *The Oxford Handbook of Christianity in Asia*, ed. Felix Wilfred (Oxford: Oxford University Press, 2014), 396.
19. Quoted in Julius J. Lipner, *Brahmabandhab Upadhyaya: The Life and Thought of a Revolutionary* (Oxford: Oxford University Press, 1999), xv.
20. Mario I. Aguilar, *Christian Ashrams, Hindu Caves and Sacred Rivers: Christian-Hindu Monastic Dialogue in India 1950–1993* (London: Jessica Kingsley Publishers, 2006), 37.
21. B. Upadhyay, 'An Exposition of Catholic Belief as Compared with the Vedanta', *Sophia* 5, no. 1 (January 1898): 10; K. P. Aleaz, 'The Theological Writings of Brahmabandhav Upadhyaya Re-examined', *Indian Journal of Theology* 28, no. 2 (April–June 1979): 55–77.

22. Lancy Lobo, 'Dalit Religious Movements and Dalit Identity', in *The Emerging Dalit Identity: The Re-assertion of the Subalterns*, ed. Walter Fernandes (New Delhi: Indian Social Institute, 1996), 170.
23. Bendangjungshi, *Confessing Christ in the Naga Context: Towards a Liberating Ecclesiology* (Zurich: LIT Verlag, 2011), 4.
24. *Advaita* is a Sanskrit term. *Advaita* means 'not duality'. *Advaita* implies there are not two things. It suggests that Brahman (the Supreme Being) is the only reality. The world is not real. The individual self and Brahman are the same.
25. Ramanuja suggests that Brahman is not distinct from the world. However, Ramanuja did not agree with the teachings of *Advaita*. He believed that the Brahman and the world (matter, souls etc.) exist. Brahman is not identical to the world. However, Brahman is not ontologically separate from the world either. Brahman is the Creator of the world and stands above and beyond the world. Ramanuja compares the relationship between God and humans to that between the body and soul. He claims that just as the body and soul act on one another and cannot exist without one another, so too God, souls, and matter are all one in creation, and no one component can exist without the other.
26. A. J. Appasamy, *The Gospel and India's Heritage* (London: Indian Society for Promoting Christian Knowledge, 1942), 36.
27. Massey, *Towards Dalit Hermeneutics*, 58.
28. Teresa A Meade, *History of Modern Latin America: 1800 to the Present* (Chichester: John Wiley, 2016), 291.
29. Jon Sobrino, *Jesus the Liberator: A Historical Theological Reading of Jesus of Nazareth*, trans. Paul Burns and Francis McDonagh (Maryknoll: Orbis Books, 1993), 40–1.
30. Roberto Oliveros, 'History of the Theology of Liberation', in *Mysterium Liberationis: Fundamental Concepts of Liberation Theology*, eds Ignacio Ellacuria and Jon Sobrino (Maryknoll: Orbis Books, 1989), 18.
31. Craig L. Nessan, *The Vitality of Liberation Theology* (Eugene: Pickwick Publications, 2012), 54.
32. Anthony C. Thiselton, *The Thiselton Companion to Christian Theology* (Michigan: William B. Eerdmans, 2015), 356.
33. Gustavo Gutiérrez, *A Theology of Liberation* (Maryknoll: Orbis Books, 1988), xxi.
34. David G. Timberman, *A Changeless Land: Continuity and Change in Philippine Politics, Continuity and Change in Philippine Politics* (London: Routledge, 2015), 132.
35. Gustavo Gutiérrez, 'Liberation Praxis and Christian Faith', in *Frontiers of Theology in Latin America*, ed. Rosino Gibellini, trans. John Drury (Maryknoll: Orbis Books, 1979), 17.
36. Hendrik J. C. Pieterse, 'South African Liberation Theology', in *Desmond Tutu's Message: A Qualitative Analysis*, ed. H. J. C. Pieterse (Leiden: Brill, 2001.
37. Camilo Pérez Bustillo and Karla Hernández Mares, *Human Rights, Hegemony, and Utopia in Latin America: Poverty, Forced Migration and Resistance in Mexico and Colombia* (Brill: Leiden, 2016), 36.
38. Mario I. Aguilar, *Church, Liberation and World Religions* (London: Bloomsbury T&T Clark, 2012), 36.
39. Robert McAfee Brown, *Liberation Theology: An Introductory Guide* (Louisville: Westminster John Knox Press, 1993), 74.
40. Joshua Prokopy and Christian Smith, 'Introduction', in *Latin American Religion in Motion*, eds Christian Smith, Christian Stephen Smith and Joshua Prokopy (New York: Routledge, 1999), 13.

41 Ana Maria Diaz-Stevens, 'Liberation Theology', in *Latinas in the United States: A Historical Encyclopaedia*, eds Vicki L. Ruiz and Virginia Sánchez Korrol (Bloomington: Indiana University Press, 2006), 390.
42 Alfred T. Hennelly, *Liberation Theology: A Documentary History* (Maryknoll: Orbis Books 1990), xvii.
43 Orlando Coastas, 'Evangelism and the Gospel of Salvation', *International Review of Mission* 63, no. 249 (1974): 25, xiii.
44 Mukti Barton, 'Race, Gender, Class and the Theology of Empowerment: An Indian Perspective', in *Gender, Religion and Diversity: Cross-Cultural Perspectives*, eds Ursula King and Tina Beattie (London: Continuum, 2005), 226.
45 Rebecca S. Chopp, *The Praxis of Suffering: An Interpretation of Liberation and Liberation Theologies* (Eugene: Wipf and Stock, 2007), 26; John R. Pottenger, *The Political Theory of Liberation Theology: Toward a Reconvergence of Social Values and Social Sciences* (Albany: State University of New York Press, 1989), 92.
46 Charles Davis James, *Indian Liberation Theology: A Critique* (Norderstedt: Books on Demand, 2009), 10–11.
47 Eileen Flynn and Gloria Thomas, *Living Faith: An Introduction to Theology* (Oxford: Sheed & Ward, 1995), 260.
48 Wilder Robles, 'Liberation Theology, Christian Base Communities, and Solidarity Movements: A Historical Reflection', in *Capital, Power, and Inequality in Latin America and the Caribbean*, eds Richard L. Harris and Jorge Nef (Lanham: Rowman & Littlefield, 2008), 225.
49 Philip Kennedy, *A Modern Introduction to Theology: New Questions for Old Beliefs* (London: I.B. Tauris, 2006), 193.
50 R. Douglas Geivett, *Evil and the Evidence for God: The Challenge of John Hick's Theodicy* (Philadelphia: Temple University Press, 1993), 113.
51 D. Brockman, *No Longer the Same: Religious Others and the Liberation of Christian Theology* (New York: Palgrave Macmillan, 2011), 11.
52 Stephen T. Davis, *Christian Philosophical Theology* (Oxford: Oxford University Press, 2006), 37–8; Susan Brooks Thistlethwaite, *Sex, Race, and God: Christian Feminism in Black and White* (Eugene: Wipf and Stock, 2009), 62.
53 Justo L. González and Ondina E. González, *Christianity in Latin America: A History* (Cambridge: Cambridge University Press, 2008), 256; Gustavo Gutierrez, 'Theology and the Social Sciences', in *The Truth Shall Make You Free: Confrontations*, trans. Matthew O'Connell (Maryknoll: Orbis Books, 1991), 56; Judith Ann Brady, *A Place at the Table: Justice for the Poor in a Land of Plenty* (New London: Twenty-Third Publications, 2008), 160; Manfred K. Bahamann, 'Liberation Theology: Latin American Style', *Lutheran Quarterly* 27, no. 2 (1 May 1975): 147.
54 Brantley W. Gasaway, *Progressive Evangelicals and the Pursuit of Social Justice* (Chapel Hill: The University of North Carolina Press, 2014), 204.
55 Gustavo Gutiérrez, *A Theology of Liberation: History, Politics, and Salvation*, trans. Caridad Inda and John Eagleson (London: SCM Press, 1974), 116.
56 James Massey, Downtrodden: The Struggle of India's Dalits for Identity, Solidarity and Liberation (Geneva: WCC Publications, 1997), 76.
57 M. Stephen, *Christian Ethics: Issues and Insights* (New Delhi: Concept Publishing, 2007), 35.
58 Rosemary Radford Reuther, 'Is Christ White? Racism and Christology', in *Christology and Whiteness: What Would Jesus Do?* ed. George Yancy (London: Routledge, 2012), 109.

59 Sobrino, *Jesus the Liberator*, 11.
60 Daniel L. Migliore, *Faith Seeking Understanding: An Introduction to Christian Theology* (Grand Rapids: William B. Eerdmans, 2014), 208.
61 Jon Sobrino, *Christology at the Crossroads: A Latin America Approach*, trans. John Drury (Maryknoll: Orbis Books, 1978), 3–5.
62 Thomas Bohache, *Christology from the Margins* (London: SCM Press, 2008), 88.
63 Lisa Isherwood, *Liberating Christ* (Ohio: Pilgrims Press, 1999), 49.
64 Michael Prior, *Jesus the Liberator: Nazareth Liberation Theology (Luke 4:16–30)* (Sheffield: Sheffield Academic Press, 1995).
65 Sobrino, *Jesus the Liberator*, 12.
66 K. P. Kuruvila, *The Word Became Flesh: A Christological Paradigm for Doing Theology in India* (Delhi: Indian Society for Promoting Christian Knowledge, 2002), 178.
67 Martien E. Brinkman, 'The Reciprocal Relation between Anthropology and Christology', in *Strangers and Pilgrims on Earth: Essays in Honour of Abraham van de Beek*, eds Paul van Geest and Eduardus van der Borght (Leiden: Brill, 2012), 212.
68 Denis Carrol, *What Is Liberation Theology?* (Dublin: The Mercier Press, 1987), 26; John R. Potteenger, *The Political Theory of the Liberation Theology: Toward a Reconvergence of Social Values and Social Science* (Albany: University of New York Press, 1989), 59.
69 G. Michael Zbaraschuk, *The Purposes of God: Providence as Process-Historical Liberation* (Eugene: Pickwick Publications, 2015), 140.
70 Alister E. McGrath, *Historical Theology: An Introduction to the History of Christian Thought* (Chichester: John Wiley, 2013), 205.
71 Hugo Magallanes, 'Preferential Option for the Poor', in *Dictionary of Scripture and Ethics*, ed. Joel B. Green (Grand Rapids: Baker Academic, 2011), 619.
72 Ethna Regan, *Theology and the Boundary Discourse of Human Rights* (Washington: Georgetown University Press, 2010), 151; Virgilio Elizondo, 'Editorial: Theology from the Viewpoint of the Poor', in *Option for the Poor: Challenge to the Rich Countries*, eds Leonardo Boff and Virgilo Elizondo (Edinburgh: T&T Clark, 1986), ix.
73 Gustavo Gutierrez, 'Liberation Theology for the Twenty-First Century', in *Romero's Legacy: The Call to Peace and Justice*, eds Pilar Hogan Closkey and John P. Hogan (Lanham: Rowman & Littlefield, 2007), 51.
74 T. Victor, 'Christian Commitment and Subaltern Perspectives', *Religion and Society* 49, nos 2 and 3 (June and September, 2004): 103; Felix Wilfred, On the Banks of Ganges: *Doing Contextual Theology* (Delhi: Indian Society for Promoting Christian Knowledge, 2005), 133; M. Gnanavaram, 'Dalit Theology and the Parable of the Good Samaritan', *Journal for the Study of the New Testament* 50 (1993): 59.
75 Dwight N. Hopkins, 'General Introduction', in *The Cambridge Companion to Black Theology*, eds Dwight N. Hopkins and Edward P. Antonio (Cambridge: Cambridge University Press, 2012), 13; Anthony G. Reddie, *Black Theology in Transatlantic Dialogue* (New York: Palgrave Macmillan, 2006), 84.
76 James Cone, *Black Theology and Black Power* (New York: Orbis Books, 1984), 73; Harry H. Singleton, *Black Theology and Ideology: Deideological Dimensions in the Theology of James H. Cone* (Minnesota: Liturgical Press, 2002), 115.
77 Anthony G. Reddie, *Black Theology* (London: SCM Press, 2012), 12.
78 Josef Sorett, 'African American Theology and the American Hemisphere', in *The Oxford Handbook of African American Theology*, eds Katie G. Cannon and Anthony B. Pinn (Oxford: Oxford University Press, 2014), 419.

79 Francis C. L. Rakotsoane, 'Major Themes in Black Theology', in *Biblical Studies, Theology, Religion and Philosophy: An Introduction for African Universities*, eds J. N. Amenze, F. Nkomazana and O. N. Kealotswe (Eldoref: Zapf Chancery Research Consultants and Publishers, 2010), 201–2.
80 Andrew F. Pearson, *Distant Freedom: St Helena and the Abolition of the Slave Trade, 1840–1872* (Liverpool: Liverpool University Press, 2016), 177.
81 Terri L. Snyder, *The Power to Die: Slavery and Suicide in British North America* (Chicago: University of Chicago Press, 2015), 33.
82 C. Eric Lincoln, *Race, Religion, and the Continuing American Dilemma* (New York: Hill & Wang, 1984), 42.
83 Ibrahim Sundiata, ' "The Stolen Garment": Historical Reflections on Blacks and Jews in the Time of Obama', in *Race, Color, Identity: Rethinking Discourses about Jews in the Twenty-First Century*, ed. Efraim Sicher (New York: Berghahn Books, 2013), 57.
84 James H. Cone, *For My People: Black Theology and the Black Church Where Have We Been and Where Are We Going* (Maryknoll: Orbis Books, 1984), 5.
85 Dwight N. Hopkins, 'More Than Ever: The Preferential Option for the Poor', in *Opting for the Margins: Postmodernity and Liberation in Christian Theology*, ed. Jeorg Rieger (Oxford: Oxford University Press, 2003), 132.
86 Allison Calhoun-Brown, 'What a Fellowship: Civil Society, African American Churches, and Public Life', in *New Day Begun: African American Churches and Civic Culture in Post-Civil Rights America*, ed. R. Drew Smith (Durham: Duke University Press, 2003), 49.
87 Gayraud Wilmore, 'A Revolution Unfulfilled, But Not Invalidated', in *A Black Theology of Liberation: Twentieth Anniversary Edition*, ed. James H. Cone (Maryknoll: Orbis Books, 1990), 147.
88 Rufus Burrow, James H. Cone and Black Liberation Theology (North Carolina: McFarland, 1994), 146.
89 K. P. Singh, 'Liberation Movements in Comparative Perspective: Dalit Indians and Black Americans', in *Dalits in Modern India: Vision and Values*, ed. S. M. Michael (New Delhi: Sage Publications, 2007), 162–3.
90 Y. Rajshekhar Shetty, *Dalit: The Black Untouchables of India* (Atlanta: Clarity Press, 1987); Runoko Rashidi, 'Dalits: The Black Untouchables of India', in *Encyclopedia of the African Diaspora: Origins, Experiences, and Culture*, ed. Carole Boyce Davies (California: ABC-Clio, 2008), 354–5.
91 Jan Peter Schouten, Jesus as Guru: The Image of Christ among Hindus and Christians in India (Amsterdam: Rodopi, 2008), 241; James H. Cone, 'The Vocation of a Theologian', in *Living Stones in the Household of God: The Legacy and Future of Black Theology*, ed. Linda E. Thomas (Minneapolis: Fortress Press, 2004), 210.
92 George Katsificas, 'Introduction', in *Liberation, Imagination and the Black Panther Party: A New Look at the Panthers and Their Legacy*, eds Kathleen Cleaver and George Katsificas (New York: Routledge, 2001), vii.
93 Joshua Bloom and Waldo E. Martin Jr., *The History and the Politics of the Black Panther Party: Black Against the Empire* (London: University of California Press, 2013), 2.
94 Chakraborty, *Gendering Caste*, 142; Deepa S. Reddy, *Religious Identity and Political Destiny: Hindutva in the Culture of Ethnicism* (Oxford: Altamira Press, 2006), 87.
95 Lata Maurugkar, *Dalit Panther Movement in Maharashtra: A Sociological Approach* (London: Sangam Books, 1991), 237.

96 James H. Cone, 'Jesus Christ in Black Theology', in *Liberation Theology: An Introductory Reader*, eds Curt Cadorette, Marie Giblin, Marilyn J. Legge and Mary Hembrow Snyder (Eugene: Wipf and Stock, 2004), 143.
97 Anthony B. Pinn, 'Black Theology', in *Liberation Theologies in the United States: An Introduction*, eds Stacey M. Floyd-Thomas and Anthony B. Pinn (New York: New York University Press, 2010), 21.
98 Albert B. Cleage, *The Black Messiah* (New York: Sheed and Ward, 1968), 3.
99 Kelly Brown Douglas, *The Black Christ* (Maryknoll: Orbis Books, 1994), 106–7.
100 James Cone, *God of the Oppressed* (Maryknoll: Orbis Books, 1975), 125–6.
101 Cone, *Black Theology and Black Power*, 68–9.
102 Antony Kalliyath, 'Re-cognizing Christ in Asia', in *Sharing Diversity in Missiological Research and Education*, ed. L. Stanislaus, John F. Gorski (Delhi: Indian Society for Promoting Christian Knowledge, 2006), 139.
103 M. R. Arulraja, *Jesus, the Dalit: Liberation Theology by Victims of Untouchability, an Indian Version of Apartheid* (Secunderabad: Author, 1996), 66–117.
104 Kuruvila, *The Word Became Flesh*, 193.
105 James H. Cone, 'A Black Theology of Liberation', in *Readings in Christian Ethics: A Historical Sourcebook*, eds J. Philip Woaman and Douglas M. Strong (Kentucky: Westminster John Knox Press, 1996), 359.
106 James H. Cone, *A Black Theology of Liberation: Twentieth Anniversary Edition* (Maryknoll: Orbis Books, 1990), 1.
107 Cone, *Black Theology and Black Power*, 13.
108 Cone, *God of the Oppressed*, 52.
109 Cone, *For My People*, 13–14.
110 James H. Cone, *A Theology of Black Liberation, Twentieth Anniversary Edition* (Maryknoll: Orbis Books, 1990), 23.
111 Hans Schwarz, *Theology in a Global Context: The Last Two Hundred Years* (Grand Rapids: William B. Eerdmans, 2005), 529.
112 Felix Wilfred, *Margins: Site of Asian Theologies* (Delhi: Indian Society for Promoting Christian Knowledge, 2008), 61; K. V. Kuruvila, 'Dalit Theology: An Indian Christian Attempt to Give Voice to the Voiceless', in *World Christianity in the Twentieth Century: A Reader*, eds Noel Davies and Martin Conway (London: SCM Press, 2008), 132; Kuruvila, The Word Became Flesh, 168; Nirmal, 'Towards a Christian Dalit Theology', 219.

Chapter 4

1 Bede Griffiths, *Retorno ao Centro: O Conhecimento da verdade – o ponto de reconciliação de todas as religiões* (Return to the Center: The Knowledge of Truth – The Point of Reconciliation for All the Religions) (Ibrasa: São Paulo, 1992), 9.
2 Jonathan Fox, *A World Survey of Religion and the State* (Cambridge: Cambridge University Press, 2008), 290.
3 José C. Moy, Adriana Brodsky and Raanan Rein, 'The Jewish Experience in Argentina in a Diaspora Comparative Perspective', in *The New Jewish Argentina: Facets of Jewish Experiences in the Southern Cone*, eds Adriana Brodsky and Raanan Rein (Leiden: Brill, 2013), 114.

4. Peter C. Phan, 'A Common Journey, Different Paths, the Same Destination: Method in Liberation Theologies', in *A Dream Unfinished: Theological Reflections on America from the Margins*, eds Eleazar S. Fernandez and Fernando F. Segovia (Eugene: Wipf and Stock, 2005), 135.
5. Michelle A. Gonzalez, *A Critical Introduction to Religion in the Americas: Bridging the Liberation Theology and Religious Studies Divide* (New York: New York University Press, 2014), 105.
6. Ibid., 59; Frederick L. Ware, *Methodologies of Black Theology* (Eugene: Wipf and Stock, 2007), 15.
7. Delroy A. Reid-Salmon, *Home Away from Home: The Caribbean Diasporan Church in the Black Atlantic Tradition* (London: Routledge, 2014), 34.
8. Tonghou Ngong, 'Theological Significance of Africa and Africans in the Bible', in *A New History of African Christian Thought: From Cape to Cairo*, ed. David Tonghou Ngong (New York: Routledge, 2017), 36.
9. Nirmal, 'A Dialogue with Dalit Literature', 201.
10. Nirmal, 'Toward a Christian Dalit Theology', 33.
11. F. J. Balasundaram, 'Dalit Struggle and Its Implications for Theological Education', *Bangalore Theological Forum* 29, nos 3 and 4 (September and December 1997), 89–90.
12. Boopalan, *Memory, Grief, and Agency*, 35.
13. Clarke, *Dalits and Christianity*, 45; Samuel, *Untouchable Bodies, Resistance and Liberation*, 48.
14. Viji Varghese Eapen, 'Christ in "Theyyam": Performative Word – Further an Exploration into the Subaltern Cultural Christology', in *The Yobel Spring: Festschrift to Dr Chilkuri Vasantha Rao*, eds Praveen P. S. Perumalla, Royce M. Victor and Naveen Rao (Hyderabad: Indian Society for Promoting Christian Knowledge and Andhra Christian Theological College, 2014), 626.
15. Anderson, 'Dalit Christians in India', 258–274.
16. Ibid.; Rajkumar, *Dalit Theology and Dalit Liberation*, 62.
17. Anderson, *Community and Worldview*, 75.
18. Victor Anderson, *Beyond Ontological Blackness: An Essay on African American Religious and Cultural Criticism* (London: Bloomsbury Academic, 2016), 91–3; Victor Anderson, 'Theorizing African American Religion', in *African American Studies*, ed. Jeanette R. Davidson (Edinburgh: Edinburgh University Press, 2010), 270.
19. Abraham Ayrookuzhiel, *Essays on Dalits, Religion and Liberation* (Bangalore: Christian Institute for the Study of Religion and Society, 2006), 127ff.
20. Luke Mbefo, 'Theology and Inculturation: Problems and Prospects – The Nigerian Experience', *The Nigerian Journal of Theology* 1, no. 1 (December 1985): 55.
21. Samuel, *Practicing Multiple Religious Belonging*, 80.
22. Gerhard von Rad, *The Problem of the Hexateuch and Other Essays*, trans. E. W. Trueman Dicken (London: SCM Press, 1966), 3ff.
23. John Van Seters, *Prologue to History: The Yahwist as Historian in Genesis* (Kentucky: Westminster John Knox Press, 1992), 216.
24. Ernest Nicholson, *The Pentateuch in the Twentieth Century: The Legacy of Julius Wellhausen* (Oxford: Oxford University Press, 1998), 89; Norbert Lohfink, *Theology of the Pentateuch: Themes of the Priestly Narrative and Deuteronomy*, trans. L. Maloney (Minneapolis: Fortress Press, 1994), 265–89.
25. Wilfred, *On the Banks of Ganges*, 132.
26. Nirmal, 'A Dialogue with Dalit Literature', 80.
27. Ibid.

28 Nirmal, 'Towards a Christian Dalit Theology', 221–2.
29 Ibid.
30 Keith Hebden, *Dalit Theology and Christian Anarchism* (Surrey: Ashgate, 2011), 16; Antony Thumma, *Springs from the Subalterns: Patterns and Perspectives in People's Theology* (Delhi: Indian Society for Promoting Christian Knowledge, 1997).
31 Clarke, *Dalits and Christianity*, 47.
32 Sathianathan Clarke, 'Dalits Overcoming Violation and Violence: A Contest between Overpowering and Empowering Identities in Changing India', *The Ecumenical Review* 54, no. 3 (July 2002): 285–6.
33 Rajkumar, *Dalit Theology and Dalit Liberation*, 63.
34 Eveline Masilamani-Meyer, *Guardians of Tamil Nadu: Folk Deities, Folk Religion, Hindu Themes* (Halle: Frackesche Stiftungen zu Halle, 2004), 97.
35 Kancha Iliah, 'Hindu Gods and Us: Our Goddesses and the Hindus', in *Perspectives on Modern South Asia: A Reader in Culture, History, and Representation*, ed. Kamala Visweswaran (Chichester: Wiley-Blackwell, 2011), 42.
36 Leela Prasad, 'Hinduism in South India', in *Hinduism in the Modern World*, ed. Brian A. Hatcher (New York: Routledge, 2016), 23.
37 Iliah, 'Hindu Gods and Us', 43.
38 Ibid.
39 Kancha Iliah, *Why I Am Not a Hindu: A Sudra Critique of Hindutva Philosophy, Culture and Political Economy* (Calcutta: Samya, 2005), 91.
40 Ibid.
41 Seth Daniel Kunin, *We Think What We Eat: Structuralist Analysis of Israelite Food Rules and Other Mythological and Cultural Domains* (London: T&T Clark, 2004), 147.
42 Rajkumar, *Dalit Theology and Dalit Liberation*, 16, 64; Samuel, *Untouchable Bodies, Resistance, and Liberation*, 43.
43 The Sangam was a college of Tamil poets that composed 2,279 poems. The rest are considered to be the works of 473 poets. The Sangam Age was a period of great literary glory. The Sangam Age can be dated between 500 BCE and 500 CE.
44 Charles E. Grover (trans.), *The Folk-Songs of Southern India* (London: Forgotten Books, 2013), 168–9.
45 Ibid., 159.
46 Rajkumar, *Dalit Theology and Dalit Liberation*, 172.
47 Robert Allen Warrior, 'Canaanites, Cowboys and Indians', in *Native and Christian Indigenous Voices on Religious Identity in the United States and Canada*, ed. James Treat (London: Routledge, 1996), 95; Rajkumar, *Dalit Theology and Dalit Liberation*, 64.
48 Rajkumar, *Dalit Theology and Dalit Liberation*, 64.
49 A. D. H. Mayes, *Deuteronomy* (Grand Rapids: William B. Eerdmans, 1979), 334–5.
50 Lawrence A. Hoffman, *Beyond the Text: A Holistic Approach to Liturgy* (Bloomington: Indiana University Press, 1989), 97.
51 F. V. Greifenhagen, *Egypt on the Pentateuch's Ideological Map* (London: Sheffield Academic Press, 2002), 201.
52 Alison Salveson, 'Keeping It in the Family? Jacob and His Aramean Heritage according to Jewish and Christian Sources', in *The Exegetical Encounter between Jews and Christians in Late Antiquity*, eds E. Grypeou and H. Spurling (Boston: Brill, 2009), 213.
53 Lieve M. Teugels, *Bible and Midrash: The Story of 'The Wooing of Rebekah' (Gen. 24)* (Leuven: Peeters, 2004), 116.

54 Shlomo Riskin, *The Passover Haggadah with a Traditional and Contemporary Commentary by Rabbi Shlomo Riskin* (New York: Ktav Publishing, 1983), 73; S. T. Lachs, 'Two Related Arameans: A Difficult Reading in the Passover Haggadah', *Journal for the Study of Judaism* 17 (1986): 65–9.
55 Greifenhagen, *Egypt on the Pentateuch's Ideological Map*, 201.
56 David Instone Brewer, 'Balaam-Laban as the Key to the Old Testament Quotations in Matthew 2', in *Built Upon the Rock: Studies in the Gospel of Mathew*, eds Daniel M. Gurtner and John Nolland (Grand Rapids: William B. Eerdmans, 2008), 215.
57 Salveson, 'Keeping It in the Family?', 214.
58 Menahem Kasher, *Haggadah Shelemah* (Jerusalem: Torah Shelemah Institute, 1967), 125.
59 Calum Carmichael, 'The Passover Haggadah', in *The Historical Jesus in Context*, eds Amy-Jill Levine, Dale C. Allison Jr. and John Dominic Crossan (Princeton: Princeton University Press, 2006), 345.
60 Hoffman, *Beyond the Text*, 99–100.
61 Nirmal, 'Toward a Christian Dalit Theology', 34.
62 M. E. Prabhakar, 'Christology in Dalit Perspective', in *Frontiers of Dalit Theology*, ed. V. Devasahayam (Delhi: Indian Society for Promoting Christian Knowledge, 1997), 402.
63 Thomas D. Hanks, *God So Loved the World: The Biblical Vocabulary of Oppression*, trans. James C. Dekker (Eugene: Wipf and Stock, 2000), 73.
64 Cone, *God of the Oppressed*, 160.
65 Rajkumar, *Dalit Theology and Dalit Liberation*, 51.
66 Wilfred, *Dalit Empowerment*, 160; Nirmal, 'Towards a Christian Dalit Theology', 66–7.
67 Nirmal, 'Towards a Christian Dalit Theology', 31.
68 Wyatt, "Dalit Theology and the Politics of Untouchability," 135.
69 Nirmal, 'Towards a Christian Dalit Theology', 224.
70 Samuel Rayan, 'The Challenge of the Dalit Issue', in *Dalits and Women: Quest for Humanity*, ed. V. Devasahayam (Madras: Gurukul Lutheran Theological College and Research Institute, 1992), 117–37.
71 Ibid., 121.
72 Ibid., 123.
73 Sathianathan Clarke, 'Dalit Theology: An Introductory and Interpretive Theological Exposition', in *Dalit Theology in the Twenty-First Century: Discordant Voices, Discerning Pathways*, eds Sathianathan Clarke, Deenabandhu Manchala and Philip Vinod Peacock (Oxford: Oxford University Press, 2010), 30.
74 Joseph A. Fitzmyer, *The One Who Is to Come* (Grand Rapids: William B. Eerdmans, 2007), 40.
75 Leo Trepp, *A History of the Jewish Experience* (New Jersey: Behrman House, 2001), 42.
76 David A. deSilva, *The Jewish Teachers of Jesus, James and Jude: What Earliest Christianity Learned from the Apocrypa and Pseudepigrapha* (Oxford: Oxford University Press, 2012), 171.
77 George A. F. Knight, *Servant Theology: A Commentary on the Book of Isaiah 40–55* (Grand Rapids: William B. Eerdmans, 1984), 171.
78 Mordecai Schreiber, *The Man Who Knew God: Decoding Jeremiah* (Lanham: Lexington Books, 2010), 1.
79 Christopher R. North, *The Suffering Servant in Deutero-Isaiah: An Historical and Critical Study* (Eugene: Wipf and Stock, 2005), 61.
80 James L. Crenshaw, *Defending God: Biblical Responses to the Problem of Evil* (Oxford: Oxford University Press, 2005), 144.

81 Gerhard Von Rad, *Old Testament Theology*, trans. D. M. G. Stalker (London: SCM Press, 1975), 259–62.
82 C. Begg, 'Zedekiah and the Servant', *Ephemarides Theologie Lovaniences* 62 (1986): 393–8.
83 Ulrich Berges, 'The Literary Construction of the Servant in Isaiah 40–55: A Discussion about Individual and Collective Identities', *Scandinavian Journal of the Old Testament* 24, no. 1 (2010): 37.
84 F. M. Shinde, 'Habit', in *No Entry for the New Sun: Translations from Modern Marathi Dalit Poetry*, ed. Arjun Dangle, trans. Priya Adarkar (Bombay: Orient Longman, 1992), 69.
85 Mary Daly, *Beyond God the Father* (Boston: Beacon Press, 1973), 77.
86 Elisabeth Schüssler Fiorenza, *Jesus, Miriam's Child, Sophia's Prophet* (New York: Continuum, 1994), 106.
87 Rajkumar, *Dalit Theology and Dalit Liberation*, 67.
88 Peniel Rajkumar, 'How Does the Bible Mean? The Bible and Dalit Liberation in India', *Political Theology* 11, no. 3 (2010): 417.
89 Balasundaram, 'Dalit Struggle', 90.
90 'Mantra' is a word, sound, slogan or a motivating chant repeated in meditation, often practised in Hinduism.
91 B. Jayashree and Gokhale-Turner, 'Bhakti or Virodha: Continuity and Change in Dalit Sahitya', in *Tradition and Modernity in Bhakti Movements*, ed. Jayant Lele (Leiden: Brill, 1981), 29.
92 Narendra Jadhav, *Untouchables: My Family's Triumphant Escape from India's Caste System* (Berkeley: University of California Press, 2005), 5.
93 George Oommen, *The Emerging Dalit Theology: A Historical Appraisal*, accessed 25 July 2018, https://www.religion-online.org/article/the-emerging-dalit-theology-a-historical-appraisal; Rajkumar, *Dalit Theology and Dalit Liberation*, 33.
94 Joseph Mundananikkal Thomas, 'Subalternity, Language and Projects of Emancipation: An Analysis of Dalit Literature', in *Language, Identity and Symbolic Culture*, ed. David Evans (London: Bloomsbury Academic, 2018), 172.
95 Sharmila Rege, *Writing Caste/Writing Gender: Narrating Dalit Women's Testimonies* (New Delhi: Subaan, 2013), 183.
96 Irina Glushkova, 'Norms and Values in the Varkari Tradition', in *Intersections: Socio-cultural Trends in Maharashtra*, ed. Meera Kosambi (Hyderabad: Orient Longman, 2000), 48.
97 Eleanor Zelliot, 'The Early Voices of Untouchables: The Bhakti Saints', in *From Stigma to Assertion: Untouchability, Identity and Politics in Early and Modern India*, eds Mikael Aktor and Robert Deliège (Copenhagen: Museum Tusculanum Press, 2010), 77.
98 Ibid.
99 B. S. Nimavat, 'Chokhamela: The Pioneer of Untouchable Movement in Maharashtra', in *Dalit Literature: A Critical Exploration*, eds Amar Nath Prasad and M. B. Gaijan (New Delhi: Sarup, 2007), 11.
100 Zelliot, 'Chokhamela: Piety and Protest', 215.
101 Ibid., 213.
102 Massey, *Towards Dalit Hermeneutics*, 69.
103 Zelliot, 'The Early Voices of Untouchables', 77–8.
104 Ibid.

105 Wendy Doniger, *Textual Sources for the Study of Hinduism* (Manchester: Oxford University Press, 1988), 91.
106 Ashok S. Chousalkar, *Revisiting the Political Thought of Ancient India: Pre-Kautilyan Arthashastra Tradition* (New Delhi: Sage Publications, 2018), 47.
107 Rajendra Chandra Hazra, *Studies in the Puranic Records on Hindu Rites and Customs* (Delhi: Motilal Banarsidass Publishers, 1987), xiiii.
108 Michael R. Leming and George E. Dickinson, *Understanding Dying, Death, and Bereavement* (Belmont: Wadsworth, 2011), 129.
109 Hiro G. Badlani, *Hinduism: Path of the Ancient Wisdom* (New York: iUniverse, 2008), 88.
110 Quoted from Vijay Mishra, *Devotional Poetics and the Indian Sublime* (Albany: State University of New York Press, 1998), 40.
111 James G. Lochtefeld, *The Illustrated Encyclopaedia of Hinduism: N-Z* (New York: Rosen Publishing, 2002), 569.
112 Peter Friedlander, 'The Struggle for Salvation in the Hagiographies of Ravidas', in *Myth and Mythmaking: Continuous Evolution in Indian Tradition*, ed. Julia Leslie (Surrey: Curzon Press, 1996), 111.
113 Sheela Devi, 'Ravidas', in *Poet Saints of India*, eds M. Sivaramkrishna and Sumita Roy (New Delhi: Sterling Paperbacks, 1998), 85.
114 S. C. Bhatt and Gopal K. Bhargava (eds), *Land and People of Indian States and Union Territories*, vol. 25 (Delhi: Kalpaz Publications, 2006), 464.
115 James Theophilus Appavoo, *Forklore for Change* (Madurai: T. T. S. Publications, 1986), 66.
116 Abraham Ayrookuzhiel, 'Chinna Pulayan: The Dalit Teacher of Sankaracharya', in *Doing Theology with the Poetic Traditions of India: Focus on Dalit and Tribal Poems*, ed. Joseph Patmury (Bangalore: South Asia Theological Research Institute, 1996), 63. Chovar was a taskmaster of Dalits during ancient times. Please note that there is a Brahmanized version of this Theyyam where the argument is between Lord Siva, disguised as Pulayan and Sankaracharya. The Pulayas do not recognize the Brahmanized version.
117 When the upper caste nobles came out on public roads, one of their attendants preceded them shouting 'get away, get away' so that they would not be polluted by a lower caste member even by a chance of encounter within the suggested distance. This idea of pollution led to many behavioural patterns. When a lower caste man happens to interact with an upper caste person, they had to observe certain rules like keeping aloof at the prescribed distance in order not to pollute the superior person, removing the clothes covering shoulders or head, using special expressions and assuming bodily postures.
118 Ayrookuzhiel, 'Chinna Pulayan', 68.
119 Appavoo, *Forklore for Change*, 78. I did a few changes to make it more appealing. The original translation of Appavoo reads Pennathi for Brahmin women and Parachchi for outcaste women.
120 Ayrookuzhiel, 'Chinna Pulayan', 69.
121 A. Ayyappan, *Social Revolution in a Kerala Village: A Study in Culture Change* (New Delhi: Asia Publication House, 1965), 85.
122 Ayrookuzhiel, 'Chinna Pulayan', 68.
123 Ibid., 71.
124 Sreedhara Menon, *A Survey of Kerala History* (Chennai: S. Viswanathan Printers and Publishers, 2005), 396.

125 P. K. K. Menon, *The History of Freedom Movement in Kerala (1885–1938)* (Thiruvananthapuram: Department of Cultural Publications, 2001), 13.
126 Ibid., 17–19.
127 Mohanty, *Dalits Development and Change*, 8.
128 Nataraja Guru, *Life and Teachings of Narayana Guru* (Sreenivasapuram: East-West University Publication, 1990), 273.
129 Ibid.
130 Ibid.
131 Ibid.
132 Ibid.
133 G. Priyadarsan (ed.), *S. N. D. P. Yogam Platinum Jubilee Souvenir* (Quilon: Jubilee Celebration Committee, 1978), 15.
134 Balachandran Nair (ed.), *In Quest of Kerala* (Trivandrum: Access Publications, 1974), 129.
135 M. K. Sanoo, *Narayana Guru* (Bombay: Bhartiya Vidya Bhavan, 1978), 83.
136 Ibid., 85.
137 Ibid., 113.
138 Ibid.
139 Felix Wilfred, *The Sling of Utopia* (Delhi: Indian Society for Promoting Christian Knowledge, 2005), 147.

Chapter 5

1 Walt Harrington, *Crossings: A White Man's Journey into Black America* (New York: HarperCollins, 1993).
2 Madurai Veeran is a Tamil folk deity popular in southern Tamil Nadu, India.
3 A. Maria Arul Raja, 'Breaking Hegemonic Boundaries: An Intertextual Reading of the Madurai Veeran Legend and Mark's Story of Jesus', in *Voices from the Margin: Interpreting the Bible in the World*, ed. R. S. Sugirtharajah (Maryknoll: Orbis Books, 2006), 108.
4 Peniel Rajkumar, 'A Dalithos Reading of a Markan Exorcism: Mark 5:1-20', *The Expository Times* 118, no. 9 (2007): 428–35.
5 Ayrookuzhiel, 'Chinna Pulayan', 66.
6 Lasara Firefox Allen, *Jailbreaking the Goddess, A Radical Revisioning of Feminist Spirituality* (Woodbury: Llewellyn Publications, 2016), 152.
7 Quoted from Sanjay Paswan and Paramanshi Jaideva (eds), Encyclopaedia of Dalits in India Struggle for Self Liberation (Delhi: Kalpaz Publications, 2004), 16.
8 Quoted from Gail Omvedt, *Buddhism in India: Challenging Brahmanism and Caste* (New Delhi: Sage Publications, 2003), 193–4.
9 A pandit is a Hindu scholar learned in Sanskrit, Hindu philosophy and religion.
10 Linda Hess, 'Kabir's Rough Rhetoric', in *The Sants: Studies in a Devotional Tradition of India*, eds Karine Schomer and W. H. McLeod (Delhi: Motilal Banarsidass, 1987), 156–7.
11 David C. Scott, 'The Rough Rhetoric of Kabir', in *Doing Theology with the Poetic Traditions of India*, ed. Joseph Patmury (Bangalore: PTCA/SATHRI, 1996), 49.
12 Quoted from Zelliot, 'The Early Voices of Untouchables', 92.

13 Quoted from W. S. Annie, 'Nandanar: The Dalit Martyr', in *Doing Theology with the Poetic Traditions of India: Focus on Dalit and Tribal Poems*, ed. Joseph Patmury (Bangalore: PTCA/SATHRI, 1996), 173.
14 Ibid., 172–5.
15 Dwight N. Hopkins, *Black Theology USA and South Africa: Politics, Culture, and Liberation* (Eugene: Wipf and Stock, 2005), 48.
16 Dwight N. Hopkins, 'A Dialogue in Black Theology: Black Theology of Liberation', in *Mormonism in Dialogue with Contemporary Christian Theologies*, eds Donald W. Musser and David Lamont Paulsen (Macon: Mercer University Press, 2007), 354.
17 Ayrookuzhiel, 'Chinna Pulayan', 69.
18 Ibid., 67.
19 James H. Olthuis, 'Face to Face: Ethical Asymmetry or the Symmetry of Mutuality?' in *Knowing Otherwise: Philosophy at the Threshold of Spirituality*, ed. James H. Olthuis (New York: Fordham University Press, 1997), 147.
20 Ibid.
21 Vasuki Nesiah, 'Federalism and Diversity in India', in *Autonomy and Ethnicity: Negotiating Competing Claims in Multi-Ethnic States*, ed. Yash Ghai (Cambridge: Cambridge University Press, 2000), 53; Amartya Sen, *Development as Freedom* (Oxford: Oxford University Press, 2001), 157; Pradeep Sharma, *Human Geography: The Land* (New Delhi: Discovery Publishing House, 2007), 12–13.

Chapter 6

1 Pablo Richard, '1492: The Violence of God and the Future of Christianity', in *1492–1992: The Voice of the Victims*, eds Leonardo Boff and Virgilio Elizondo (London: SCM Press, 1990), 66.
2 Sarah Travis, *Decolonizing Preaching: Decolonizing Preaching the Pulpit as Postcolonial Space* (Eugene: Cascade Books, 2014), 109; Willard M. Swartley, 'The Bible in Society', in *The New Cambridge History of the Bible: Volume 4, From 1750 to the Present*, ed. John Riches (New York: Cambridge University Press, 2015), 636.
3 Chris Shannahan, *Voices from the Borderland: Re-imagining Cross-Cultural Urban Theology in the Twenty-First Century* (London: Routledge, 2016), 37; Zuzana Klimova, 'The Social Function of Postcolonial Theories', in *Cultural Difference and Social Solidarity: Solidarities and Social Function*, eds Scott H. Boyd and Mary Ann Walter (Newcastle upon Tyne: Cambridge Scholars Publishing, 2014), 80; Bill Ashcroft, Gareth Griffiths and Helen Tiffin, *The Empire Writes Back: Theory and Practice in Post-colonial Literatures* (London: Routledge, 2002), 2.
4 Stephen D. Moore, 'What Is Postcolonial Studies? Paul after Empire', in *The Colonized Apostle: Paul through Postcolonial Eyes*, ed. Stephen D. Moore (Minneapolis: Fortress Press, 2011), 4.
5 Edward Said, *Orientalism: Western Conceptions of the Orient* (London: Penguin Books, 1978).
6 Bill Aschcroft, 'Post-colonial Horizons', in *(In)fusion Approach: Theory, Contestation, Limits: (In)fusionising a Few Indian English Novels*, ed. Ranjan Ghosh (Lanham: University Press of America, 2006), 73–6.

7   R. S. Sugirtharajah, 'Biblical Studies in India: From Imperialistic Scholarship to Postcolonial Interpretation', in *Teaching the Bible: The Discourses and Politics of Biblical Pedagogy*, eds F. F. Segovia and M. A. Tolbert (Maryknoll: Orbis Books, 1998), 283.
8   Stephen D. Moore and Fernando F. Segovia, 'Postcolonial Biblical Criticism: Beginnings, Trajectories, Intersections', in *Postcolonial Biblical Criticism: Interdisciplinary Intersections*, ed. Stephen D. Moore and Fernando F. Segovia (London: T&T Clark International, 2005), 1–22; R. S. Sugirtharajah, *Exploring Postcolonial Biblical Criticism: History, Method, Practice* (Chichester: Blackwell Publishing, 2012).
9   R. S. Sugirtharajah, 'Postcolonial Biblical Interpretation', in *The Oxford Encyclopedia of Biblical Interpretation*, ed. Steven L. McKenzie (Oxford: Oxford University Press, 2013), 123.
10 Matthew Liebmann and Uzma Z. Rizvi, *Archaeology and the Postcolonial Critique* (Lanham: Altamira Press, 2008), 9; Kwok Pui-lan, *Postcolonial Imagination and Feminist Theology* (Louisville: Westminster John Knox Press, 2005), 2.
11 Stephen Selmon, 'The Scramble for Post-Colonialism', in *The Post-Colonial Studies Reader*, ed. Bill Ashcroft, Gareth Griffiths and Helen Tiffin (London: Routledge, 2004), 51.
12 Susan VanZanten Gallagher, 'Mapping the Hybrid World: Three Postcolonial Motifs', *Semeia* 75 (1996): 230.
13 John W. Marshall discusses the relevance of studying ancient empires using the tools developed by postcolonial studies. See John W. Marshall, 'Postcolonialism and the Practice of History', in *Her Master's Tools? Feminist and Postcolonial Engagements of Historical-Critical Discourse*, eds Caroline Vander Stichele and Todd Penner (Atlanta: Society of Biblical Literature, 2005), 98.
14 Timothy Brennan, 'From Development to Globalisation: Postcolonial Studies and Globalisation Theory' in *The Cambridge Companion to Postcolonial Literary Studies*, ed. Neil Lazarus (Cambridge: Cambridge University Press, 2004), 135.
15 Musa W. Dube, *Postcolonial Feminist Interpretation of the Bible* (St Louis: Chalice Press, 2000), 48.
16 Warren Carler, 'Postcolonial Biblical Criticism', in *Recent Approaches to Biblical Criticism and Their Applications*, eds Steven L. McKenzie and John Kaltner (Louisville: Westminster John Knox Press, 2013), 101; Fernando F. Segovia, 'Mapping the Postcolonial Optic in Biblical Criticism: Meaning and Scope', in *Postcolonial Biblical Criticism: Interdisciplinary Intersections*, eds Stephen D. Moore and Fernando F. Segovia (London: T&T Clark, 2005), 23–78; R. S. Sugirtharajah, *The Bible and Empire: Postcolonial Explorations* (Cambridge: Cambridge University Press, 2005).
17 Jeremy Punt, 'Discerning Empire in Biblical Studies: Tools of the Trade', in *The New Testament in the Graeco-Roman World: Articles in Honour of Abe Malherbe*, eds Marius Nel, Jan G. van der Watt and Fika J. van Rensburg (Zurich: LIT Verlag), 213; Barbara Bush, *Imperialism and Postcolonialism* (London: Routledge, 2014), 6; Jean-Pierre Ruiz, 'An Exile's Baggage: Toward a Postcolonial Reading of Ezekiel', in *Approaching Yehud: New Approaches to the Study of the Persian Period*, ed. Jon L. Berquist (Atlanta: Society of Biblical Literature, 2007), 124.
18 Marshall, 'Postcolonialism and the Practice of History', 98.
19 Dube, *Postcolonial Feminist Interpretation*, 48.
20 R. S. Sugirtharajah, *Asian Biblical Hermeneutics and Post Colonialism: Contesting Interpretations* (Maryknoll: Orbis Books, 1998), 19.
21 R. S. Sugirtharajah, 'A Brief Memorandum on Postcolonialism and Biblical Studies', *Journal for the Study of the New Testament* 73 (1999), 5.

22 Jeremy Punt, *Postcolonial Biblical Interpretation: Reframing Paul* (Boston: Brill, 2015), 1; Ingeborg Mongstad-Kvammen, *Toward a Postcolonial Reading of the Epistle of James: James 2:1-13 in its Roman Imperial Context* (Leiden: Brill, 2013), 5; Uriah Y. Kim, 'Postcolonial Criticism: Who Is the Other in the Book of Judges?' in *Judges and Methods: New Approaches in Biblical Studies*, ed. Gale H. Yee (Minneapolis: Fortress Press, 1995), 165; Kwok Pui-Ian, 'Making the Connections: Postcolonial Studies and Feminist Biblical Interpretation', in *The Postcolonial Biblical Reader*, ed. R. S. Sugirtharajah (London: Blackwell, 2006), 46.
23 R. S. Sugirtharajah, *Exploring Postcolonial Biblical Criticism: History, Method, Practice* (Oxford: Wiley-Blackwell, 2012), 171; Eryl W. Davies, *Biblical Criticism: A Guide for the Perplexed* (London: Bloomsbury, 2013), 82.
24 Louis C. Jonker, *Defining All-Israel in Chronicles* (Tübingen: Mohr Siebeck, 2016), 36.
25 Christopher D. Stanley, 'Introduction', in *The Colonized Apostle: Paul through Postcolonial Eyes*, ed. Christopher D. Stanley (Minneapolis: Augsburg Fortress, 2011), 4.
26 Musa W. Dube, 'Toward a Post-Colonial Feminist Interpretation', *Semeia* 78 (1997): 11–25:15; Pui-lan, *Postcolonial Imagination*, 61; Janet Wooten, 'Who's Been Reading MY Bible? Post-Structuralist Hermeneutics and Sacred Text', in *Post-Christian Feminisms: A Critical Approach*, ed. Kathleen McPhillips (Aldershot: Ashgate Publishing, 2008), 80–1; Travis, Decolonizing Preaching, 109; Uriah Y. Kim, 'Is There an 'Anticonquest' Ideology in the Book of Judges', in *Postcolonialism and the Hebrew Bible: The Next Step*, ed. Roland Boer (Atlanta: Society of Biblical Literature, 2013), 112–13.
27 Carolyn J. Sharp, *Wrestling the Word: The Hebrew Scriptures and the Christian Believer* (Louisville: Westminster John Knox Press, 2010), 126–7; Dube, *Postcolonial Feminist Interpretation*, 48.
28 Yvonne Sherwood, 'The Hagaramic and the Abrahamic; or Abraham the Non-European', in *Reading the Abrahamic Faiths: Rethinking Religion and Literature*, ed. Emma Mason (London: Bloomsbury Academic, 2016), 30.
29 Israel Kamudzandu, *Abraham as Spiritual Ancestor: A Postcolonial Zimbabwean Reading of Romans 4* (Boston: Brill, 2010) 146.
30 Obvious Vengeyi, *Aluta Continua Biblical Hermeneutics for Liberation: Interpreting Biblical Texts on Slavery for Liberation of Zimbabwean Underclasses* (Bamberg: University of Bamberg Press, 2013), 23.
31 Jobymon Skaria, 'Reading the Promises to Abraham in Genesis 12:1-3 through the Post-Exilic Deuteronomic Eyes', *Vidyajyoti Journal of Theological Reflection* 81, no. 9 (September 2017): 25–40: Jobymon Skaria, 'Reimagining Moab and Ammon: Genesis 19:30-38 through Persian Imperialism', *Hekamtho: Syrian Orthodox Theological Journal* 3 (November 2017): 23–44.
32 Julius Wellhausen, *Prolegomena to the History of Israel*, trans. J. Sutherland Black and Allan Menzies (Edinburgh: A&C Black, 1885), 331.
33 Ibid.
34 Hermann Gunkel, *The Legends of Genesis*, trans. W. H. Caruth (New York: Schocken, 1964), 1–19.
35 William F. Albright, *The Archeology and the Religions of Israel* (Baltimore: John Hopkins Press, 1956), 176; John Bright, *A History of Israel* (London: SCM Press, 1972), 94–5.

36 John H. Sailhamer, *The Meaning of the Pentateuch: Revelation, Composition and Interpretation* (Illinois: IVP Academic, 2009), 71; G. E. Wright, *Biblical Archaeology* (Philadelphia: Westminster Press, 1962), 40.
37 Joseph Blenkinsopp, *The Pentateuch* (London: SCM Press, 1992), 120–1; Rainer Albertz, 'Religion in Israel During and After the Exile', in *The Biblical World*, vol. II, ed. John Barton (London: Routledge, 2002), 110–2; Philip R. Davies, *In Search of 'Ancient Israel* (New York: Continuum, 2006), 84; Bright, *A History of Israel*, 94–5.
38 Thomas L. Thompson, *The Historicity of the Patriarchal Narratives* (Berlin: Walter de Gruyter, 1974), 328.
39 J. Van Seters, *Abraham in History and Tradition* (New Haven: Yale University Press, 1975), 309.
40 Philip R. Davies, *The Origins of Biblical Israel* (London: T&T Clark, 2007), 4.
41 William H. Stiebing Jr., *Ancient Near Eastern History and Culture* (London: Routledge, 2009), 255ff.
42 Mario Liverani, *Israel's History and the History of Israel*, trans. Chiara Peri and Philip R. Davies (London: Equinox, 2005).
43 Ibid., xv–xvi.
44 James M. Trotter, *Reading Hosea in Achaemenid Yehud* (London: Sheffield Academic Press, 2001), 10.
45 Mark G. Brett, 'Reading the Bible in the Context of Methodological Pluralism: The Undermining of Ethnic Exclusivism in Genesis', in *Rethinking Contexts, Reading Texts: Contributions from the Social Sciences to Biblical Interpretation*, ed. M. Daniel Carroll R. (Sheffield: Sheffield Academic Press, 2000), 51; R. C. Heard, *The Dynamics of Diselection: Ambiguity in Genesis 12–26 and Ethnic Boundaries in Post-Exilic Judah* (Atlanta: SBL Press, 2001), 8–16 and 171–84; Naveen Rao, 'Decolonizing the Formulation of Scripture: A Postcolonial Reading of Genesis 12, 20, and 26,' in *Decolonizing the Body of Christ: Theology and Theory after Empire?* eds D. Joy and J. Duggan (New York: Palgrave Macmillan, 2012), 59.
46 Gosta W. Ahlstrom, *The History of the Ancient Palestine from the Palaeolithic Period to Alexander's Conquest*, ed. Diana V. Edelman (Sheffield: Sheffield Academic Press, 1993), 182.
47 R. Norman Whybray, *Introduction to the Pentateuch* (Grand Rapids: William B. Eerdmans, 1995), 49ff.
48 S. David Sperling, *The Original Torah: The Political Intent of the Bible's Writers* (New York: New York University Press, 1998), 44.
49 Rainer Albertz, *Israel in Exile: The History and Literature of the Sixth Century BCE*, trans. David Green (Atlanta: Society of Biblical Literature, 2003), 249.
50 Israel Finkelstein, 'Patriarchs, Exodus, Conquest: Fact or Fiction,' in *The Quest for the Historical Israel*, ed. Brian B Schmidt (Atlanta: Society of Biblical Literature, 2007), 51.
51 Jean-Louis Ska, *The Exegesis of the Pentateuch: Exegetical Studies and Basic Questions* (Tübingen: Mohr Siebeck, 2009), 38.
52 Norman C. Habel, *The Land Is Mine: Six Biblical Land Ideologies* (Augsburg: Fortress Press, 1995), 117–18.
53 Gard Graerod, *Abraham and Melchizedek Scribal Activity of Second Temple Times in Genesis 14 and Psalm 110* (Berlin: Walter de Gruyter, 2010); John Ha, *Genesis 15* (Berlin: Walter de Gruyter, 1989); Gershom Hepner, *Legal Friction, Law, Narrative, and Identity in Biblical Israel* (New York: Peter Lang Publishing, 2010); Francesca Stavrakopoulou, *The Land of Our Fathers: The Role of the Ancestor Veneration in Biblical Land Claims* (London: T&T Clark International, 2010).

54 Stavrakopoulou, *Land of Our Fathers*, 29.
55 Thomas Römer, 'Conflicting Models of Identity and the Publication of the Torah in the Persian Period', in *Between Cooperation and Hostility: Multiple Identities in Ancient Judaism and the Interaction with Foreign Powers*, eds Rainer Albertz and Jakob Wöhrle (Gottingen: Vandenhoeck & Ruprecht, 2013), 45.
56 Joseph Blenkinsopp, *Judaism, the First Phase: The Place of Ezra and Nehemiah in the Origins of Judaism* (Grand Rapids: William B. Eerdmans, 2009), 38; Joseph Blenkinsopp, 'Continuity–Discontinuity in Isaiah 40–66: Issue of Location', in *Continuity and Discontinuity: Chronological and Thematic Development in Isaiah 40–66*, eds Hans M. Barstad and Lena-Sofia Tiemeyer (Gottingen: Vandenhoeck & Ruprecht, 2014), 87; Meindert Dijkstra, 'The Valley of Dry Bones: Coping with the Reality of the Exile in the Book of Ezekiel', in *The Crisis of Israelite Religion: Transformation of Religious Tradition in Exilic and Post-exilic Times*, eds Bob Becking, Marjo Christina Annette Korpel (Leiden: Brill, 1999), 124; Matthew Michael, *Yahweh's Elegant Speeches of the Abrahamic Narratives: A Study of the Stylistics; Characterizations; and Functions of the Divine Speeches in Abrahamic Narratives* (Carlisle: Langham Monographs, 2014), 74–5.
57 Frederick V. Winnett, 'Re-examining the Foundations', *Journal of Biblical Literature* 84, no. 1 (March 1965): 4, 11.
58 Ska, *Introduction to Reading the Pentateuch*, 203.
59 Claus Westermann, *Genesis 12–36*, trans. David E. Green (London: T&T Clarke, 2004), 189–93; Hermann Gunkel, *Genesis*, trans. Mark E. Biddle (Macon: Mercer University Press, 1997) 189–90, 283–85; Mark W. Bartusch, *Understanding Dan: An Exegetical Study of a Biblical City, Tribe and Ancestor* (Sheffield: Sheffield Academic Press, 2003), 25.
60 Seters, *Abraham in History and Tradition*, 292.
61 Heerak Christian Kim, *Nuzi, Women's Rights and Hurrian Ethnicity and Other Academic Essays* (Cheltenham: Hermit Kingdom Press, 2006) 1; Marvin A. Sweeney, 'Form Criticism', in *To Each Its Own Meaning: An Introduction to Biblical Criticisms and Their Application*, eds Stephen R. Haynes, Steven L. McKenzie (Louisville: Westminster John Knox Press, 1999), 82, Matthew Thiessen, *Contesting Conversion: Genealogy, Circumcision, and Identity in Ancient Judaism and Christianity* (Oxford: Oxford University Press, 2011), 40.
62 Paul R. Williamson, *Abraham, Israel and the Nations: The Patriarchal Promise and Its Covenantal Development in Genesis* (Sheffield: Sheffield Academic Press, 2000), 59.
63 Hepner, *Legal Friction*, 5.
64 Tracy Maria Lemos, *Marriage Gifts and Social Change in Ancient Palestine: 1200 BCE to 200 CE* (Cambridge: Cambridge University Press, 2010), 60.
65 Ibid., 49.
66 Thomas Römer, 'Deuteronomy in Search of Origins', in *Reconsidering Israel and Judah: Recent Studies on the Deuteronomistic History*, eds Gary N. Knoppers and J. Gordon McConville (Winona Lake: Eisenbrauns, 2000), 135.
67 Römer, 'Deuteronomy in Search of Origins', 135; Gard Granerod, *Abraham and Melchizedek Scribal Activity of Second Temple Times in Genesis 14 and Psalm 110* (Berlin: Walter de Gruyter, 2010), 49–50.
68 Konrad Schmid, *Genesis and the Moses Story: Israel's Dual Origins in the Hebrew Bible*, trans. James Nogalski (Winona Lake: Eisenbrauns, 2010) for more details.
69 Linda M. Stargel, *The Construction of Exodus Identity in Ancient Israel: A Social Identity Approach* (Eugene: Wipf and Stock, 2018), 39.

70 J. Van Seters, 'Joshua 24 and the Problem of Tradition in the Old Testament', in *In the Shelter of Elyon: Essays on Ancient Palestinian Life and Literature in Honor of G. W. Ahlström*, eds W. B. Barrick and J. R. Spencer (Sheffield: JSOT Press, 1984), 139–58; A. D. H. Mayes, *The Story of Israel between Settlement and Exile: A Redactional Study of the Deuteronomistic History* (London: SCM Press, 1983), 51; Malden Popovic, 'Conquest of the Land, Loss of the Land', in *The Land of Israel in Bible, History, and Theology: Studies in Honor of Ed Noort*, eds Jacques Van Ruiten and J. Cornelis de Vos (Leiden: Brill, 2009), 97; Thomas Römer and Jean Daniel Macchi, 'Luke, Disciple of the Deuteronomistic School', in *Luke's Literary Achievement*, ed. C. M. Tuckett (Sheffield: Sheffield Academic Press, 1995), 185.

71 Rodney A. Werline, *Pray Like This: Understanding Prayer in the Bible* (New York: T&T Clark International, 2007), 14; Jesse C. Long, *The College Press New Commentary: 1 & 2 Kings* (Joplin: College Press, 2002), 17.

72 Roger Tomes, '1 and 2 Kings', in *Eerdmans Commentary on the Bible*, eds James D. G. Dunn and John W. Rogerson (Michigan: William B. Eerdmans, 2003), 262.

73 Jyrki Keinänen, *Traditions in Collision: A Literary and Redaction-Critical Study on the Elijah Narratives: 1 Kings 17–19* (Helsinki: The Finnish Exegetical Society, 2001), 85.

74 R. N. Whybray, 'Genesis', in *The Oxford Bible Commentary: The Pentateuch*, eds John Muddiman and John Barton (Oxford: Oxford University Press, 2001), 57.

75 Richard J. Bautch, *Glory and Power, Ritual and Relationship: The Sinai Covenant in the Postexilic Period* (New York: A&C Black, 2009), 44.

76 Mark A. Throntveit, 'Chronicles', in *Theological Interpretation of the Old Testament: A Book-by-Book Survey*, ed. Kevin J. Vanhoozer (Grand Rapids: Baker Academic, 2008), 126–7; John Mark Hicks, *The College Press NIV Commentary: 1 & 2 Chronicles* (Joplin: College Press, 2001), 20–1; Werline, *Pray Like This*, 14; James McKeown, *Genesis* (Michigan: William B. Eerdmans, 2008), 364.

77 Paul S. Evans, 'Worship That Fulfils the Law: The Book of Chronicles and Its Implications for a Contemporary Theology of Worship', in *Rediscovering Worship: Past, Present, and Future*, ed. Wendy J. Porter (Eugene: Pickwick Publications, 2015), 33.

78 Brevard S. Childs, *Biblical Theology of the Old and New Testaments: Theological Reflection on the Christian Bible* (Minneapolis: Fortress Press, 1992), 127.

79 Walter Brueggemann, *An Introduction to the Old Testament: The Canon and the Christian Imagination* (Louisville: Westminster John Knox Press, 2003), 47.

80 Hepner, *Legal Friction*, 104; Terence E. Fretheim, *Abraham: Trials of Family and Faith* (South Carolina: University of South Carolina Press, 2007), 149.

81 Whybray, *Introduction to the Pentateuch*, 49ff.

82 David M. Carr, *An Introduction to the Old Testament: Sacred Texts and Imperial Contexts of the Hebrew Bible* (Chichester: Blackwell Publishing, 2010), 191.

83 Ibid.

84 Whybray, *Introduction to the Pentateuch*, 49ff; Philip F. Esler, *Sex, Wives and Warriors: Reading Old Testament Narrative with Its Ancient Audience* (Cambridge: James Clarke, 2011), 23; Danna Nolan Fewell and R. Christopher Heard, 'The Genesis of Identity in the Biblical World', in *The Oxford Handbook of Biblical Narrative* (Oxford: Oxford University Press, 2016), 110.

85 Thomas Römer, 'Conflicting Models of Identity and the Publication of the Torah in the Persian Period', in *Between Cooperation and Hostility: Multiple Identities in Ancient Judaism and the Isnteraction with Foreign Powers*, eds Rainer Albertz and Jakob Wohrle (Gottingen: V & R, 2013), 42; H. G. M. Williamson, 'Abraham in Exile', in

Perspectives on Our Father Abraham: Essays in Honor of Marvin R. Wilson, ed. Steven A. Hunt (Grand Rapids: William B. Eerdmans Publishing Company, 2010), 78.
86 Römer, 'Conflicting Models of Identity', 42.
87 R. Norman Whybray, *The Making of the Pentateuch: A Methodological Study* (Sheffield: JSOT Press, 1994), 104.
88 Michael Prior, *The Bible and Colonialism: A Moral Critique* (Sheffield: Sheffield Academic Press, 1999), 222; Martien A. Halvorson-Taylor, 'Displacement and Diaspora in Biblical Narrative', in *The Oxford Handbook of Biblical Narrative*, ed. Danna Nolan Fewell (Oxford: Oxford University Press, 2016), 498.
89 McKeown, *Genesis*, 10.
90 Mark Brett, *Genesis: Procreation and the Politics of Identity* (New York: Routledge, 2000); R. W. L. Moberly, 'Abraham and Aeneas: Genesis as Israel's Foundation Story', in *Genesis and Christian Theology*, eds Nathan MacDonald, Mark W. Elliot, Grant Macaskill (Michigan: William B. Eerdmans Publishing Company, 2012), 303.
91 Roland Boer, 'Marx, Postcolonialism and the Bible', in *Postcolonial Biblical Criticism: Interdisciplinary Intersections*, eds Stephen D. Moore and Fernando F. Segovia (London: T&T Clark, 2005), 176.
92 Gale A. Yee, 'Postcolonial Biblical Criticism', in *Methods in Biblical Interpretation: Methods for Exodus*, ed. Thomas B. Dozeman (Cambridge: Cambridge University Press, 2010), 213; Mark G. Brett, 'Reading the Bible in the Context of Methodological Pluralism: The Undermining of Ethnic Exclusivism in Genesis', in *Rethinking Contexts, Reading Texts: Contributions from the Social Sciences to Biblical Interpretation*, ed. M. Daniel Carroll R. (Sheffield: Sheffield Academic Press, 2000), 70.
93 Yee, 'Postcolonial Biblical Criticism', 213.
94 Thalia Gur-Klein, *Sexual Hospitality in the Hebrew Bible: Patronymic, Metronymic, Legitimate and Illegitimate Relations* (London: Routledge, 2014), 91.
95 Borgman, Genesis, 121.
96 Musa W. Dube, 'Religion, Race, Gender and Identity', in *Biblical Studies, Theology, Religion and Philosophy: An Introduction for African Universities*, eds Fidelis Nkomazana and Obed N. Kealotswe (Eldoret: Zapf Chancery Research Consultants and Publishers, 2010), 113.
97 J. A. Loader, *A Tale of Two Cities: Sodom and Gomorrah in the Old Testament, Early Jewish and Early Christian Traditions* (Kampen: Peters Publishers, 1990), 15.
98 Casey W. Davis, *Oral Biblical Criticism: The Influence of the Principles of Orality on the Literary Structure of Paul's Epistle to the Philip* (Sheffield: Sheffield Academic Press, 1999), 100.
99 Loader, *A Tale of Two Cities*, 44.
100 Susan Ackerman, 'The Blind, the Lame, and the Barren Shall Not Come into the House', in *Disability Studies and Biblical Literature*, eds Candida R. Moss and Jeremy Schipper (New York: Palgrave Macmillan, 2011), 36; Kenneth A. Mathews, *Genesis 11:27-50:26* (Nashville: Broadman & Holman, 2005), 208; Robert Ignatius Letellier, *Day in Mamre, Night in Sodom: Abraham and Lot in Genesis 18 and 19* (Brill: Leiden, 1995), 33; George W. Coats, *Genesis, with an Introduction to Narrative Literature* (Grand Rapids: William B. Eerdmans, 1983), 127; Jerome T. Walsh, *Style and Structure in Biblical Hebrew Narrative* (Collegeville: Liturgical Press, 2001), 65.
101 Benno Jacob, *Das erste Buch der Thora: Genesis* (Berlin: Schocken, 1934), 464. Quoted in Johanna Stiebert, Fathers and Daughters in the Hebrew Bible, 134.
102 André Lacocque, *Ruth: A Continental Commentary*, trans., K. C. Hanson (Minneapolis: Fortress Press, 2004), 119.

103 Esther Marie Menn, *Judah and Tamar (Genesis 38) in Ancient Jewish Exegesis: Studies in Literary Form and Hermeneutics* (Leiden: Brill, 1997), 100.
104 Walter Brueggemann, *Genesis: Interpretation: A Bible Commentary for Teaching and Preaching* (Louisville: Westminster John Knox Press, 1982), 176, 177.

Chapter 7

1 Mahabali was a wise and generous king. The gods became jealous of Mahabali's just rule. So, Lord Vishnu disguised as a poor Brahmin boy called Vamana and came to Mahabali. Vamana asked for three footlongs of land. The king obliged. Soon after Mahabali agreed, Vamana began to grow. Vamana covered the whole earth with his first step. He covered the whole skies with his second step. Vamana then asked the king for space for his third foot. Mahabali bowed before Vamana and asked him to place the third step on his head. Vamana placed his foot on Mahabali's head, which pushed him to the netherworld. Mahabali was granted a return to his land once a year. The people of Kerala celebrate Onam to welcome Mahabali on his homecoming.
2 According to this Malayalam folk song, 'when Mahabali ruled the land, all the people were equal. People were joyful and merry. They were all free from harm. There was neither anxiety nor sickness, and no one heard of children's deaths. No wicked person was in sight anywhere. All the people on the land were right. There was neither theft nor deceit and no false words or promises. Measures and weights were right. There were no lies. No one cheated or wronged his neighbour. When Mahabali ruled the land, all the people formed one casteless race'.
3 Moshé Machover, *Israelis and Palestinians: Conflict and Resolution* (Chicago: Haymarket Books, 2012), 50; Raymond Allen Morrow and Carlos Alberto Torres, *Reading Freire and Habermas: Critical Pedagogy and Transformative Social Change* (New York: Teachers College Press, 2002), 135.
4 Victor P. Hamilton, *The Book of Genesis, Chapters 18–50* (Michigan: William B. Eerdmans, 1995), 190–1; Diana Lipton, *Revisions of the Night: Politics and Promises in the Patriarchal Dreams of Genesis* (Sheffield: Sheffield Academic Press, 1999), 35.
5 John H. Sailhamer, 'Genesis', in *The Expositor's Bible Commentary: Genesis-Leviticus*, eds Tremper Longman III and David E. Garland (Michigan: Zondervan, 2009), 37.
6 Niels Peter Lemche, *The Old Testament between Theology and History: A Critical Survey* (Louisville: Westminster John Knox Press, 2008), 66; Susan Niditch, *A Prelude to Biblical Folklore: Underdogs and Tricksters* (Chicago: University of Illinois Press, 2000), 23.
7 Sailhamer, 'Genesis', 37; Hamilton, *The Book of Genesis, Chapters 18–50*, 190–1; T. D. Alexander. 'Are the Wife/Sister Incidents of Genesis Literary Compositional Variants?' *Vetus Testamentum* 42, no. 2 (1992): 145–53; David W. Baker and Bill T. Arnold, *The Face of Old Testament Studies* (Michigan: Baker Academic, 1999), 123; Ska, *Introduction to Reading the Pentateuch*, 57; Mathews, *Genesis 11:27-50:26*, 124; Mark E. Biddle, 'The "Endangered Ancestress" and Blessing for the Nations'. *Journal of Biblical Literature* 109, no. 4 (1990), 611.
8 Martin Noth, *A History of Pentateuchal Traditions* (Englewood Cliffs, Prentice Hall, 1972), 102–9.

9   Roy B. Zuck, *Basic Bible Interpretation: A Practical Guide to Discovering Biblical Truth* (Colorado Springs: David C. Cook, 1991), 61.
10 Meir Sternberg, *The Poetics of Biblical Narrative: Ideological Literature and the Drama of Reading* (Bloomington: Indiana University Press, 1987), 1; Adele Berlin, *Poetics and Interpretation of Biblical Narrative* (Eisenbrauns, Winona Lake: 2005), 21; Jeannine K. Brown, *Scripture as Communication: Introducing Biblical Hermeneutics* (Grand Rapids: Baker Academics, 2007), 14.
11 Janet W. Dyk and Percy S. F. van Keulen, *Language System, Translation Technique, and Textual Tradition in the Peshitta of Kings* (Leiden: Brill, 2013), 402; Paul S. Evans, *The Invasion of Sennacherib in the Book of Kings: A Source-Critical and Rhetorical Study of 2 Kings 18–19* (Leiden: Brill, 2009), 89.
12 Sailhamer, 'Genesis', 158.
13 Gordon J. Wenham, *Genesis 1–15* (Waco: Word Books, 1987), 285–7.
14 Jon D. Levenson, 'The Conversion of Abraham', in *The Idea of Biblical Interpretation: Essays in Honour of James L. Kugel*, eds James L. Kugel, Judith H. Newman and Judith Hood Newman (Leiden: Brill, 2004), 126; W. Lee Humphreys, *The Character of God in the Book of Genesis: A Narrative Appraisal* (London: Westminster John Knox Press, 2001), 86; Ska, *Introduction to Reading the Pentateuch*, 56.
15 Susan Niditch, 'Genesis', in *The Women's Bible Commentary*, eds Carol A. Newsom and Sharon H. Ringe (Louisville: John Knox Press, 1992), 18; Steven L. McKenzie, *All God's Children: A Biblical Critique of Racism* (Kentucky: Westminster John Knox Press, 1997) 15.
16 Michael Harvey, *Creating a Culture of Invitation in Your Church* (Oxford: Monarch Books, 2015), 54.
17 Theodore Hiebert, 'Genesis', in *Theological Bible Commentary*, eds Gail R. O'Day and David L. Petersen (Louisville: Westminster John Knox Press, 2009), 24.
18 Victor P. Hamilton, *The Book of Genesis: Chapters 1–17* (Grand Rapids: Eerdmans, 1990), 294.
19 David M. Carr, *Reading the Fractures of Genesis: Historical and Literary Approaches* (Louisville: Westminster John Knox Press, 1996), 194.
20 Dianne Bergant, *Genesis: In the Beginning* (Minnesota: Collegeville Press, 2013), 66.
21 Phyllis Trible, 'Ominous Beginning for a Promise of Blessing', in *Hagar, Sarah, and Their Children: Jewish, Christian, and Muslim Perspectives*, eds Phyllis Trible and Letty M. Russel (Louisville: Westminster John Knox Press, 2006), 37.
22 Herbert Lockyer, *All the Miracles of the Bible* (Michigan: Zondervan, 1961), 36; Jack W. Vancil 'Sarah – Her Life and Legacy', in *Essays on Women in Earliest Christianity*, ed. Carroll D. Osburn (Eugene: Wipf and Stock, 1993), 49.
23 Clare Amos, *The Book of Genesis* (Peterborough: Epworth, 2004), 79.
24 J. Cheryl Exum, 'Who's Afraid of "The Endangered Ancestors"', in *Women in the Hebrew Bible: A Reader*, ed. Alice Bach (New York: Routledge, 1999), 144; Shula Keshet, *Say I Pray Thee, Thou Art My Sister: Intertextual Narrative in Jewish Culture* (Tel Aviv: Hakibbutz Hameuhad, 2003), 47–60.
25 Exum, 'Who's Afraid of 'The Endangered Ancestors', 146ff; Keshet, *Say I Pray Thee*, 47–60.
26 McKenzie, *All God's Children*, 13.
27 Charles E. Carter, *The Emergence of Yehud in the Persian Period: A Social and Demographic Study* (Sheffield: Sheffield Academic Press, 1999), 39; Megan Bishop Moore and Brad E. Kelle, *Biblical History and Israel's Past: The Changing Study of the*

Bible and History (Michigan: William B. Eerdmans, 2011), 407; H. G. M. Williamson, *Ezra and Nehemiah* (Sheffield: Sheffield Academic Press, 1996), 48.
28 Matt Waters, *Ancient Persia: A Concise History of the Achaemenid Empire, 550–330 BCE* (New York: Cambridge University Press, 2014), 162; Albertz, *Israel in Exile*, 124.
29 Yee, 'Postcolonial Biblical Criticism', 27.
30 Michael David Coogan, *The Oxford History of the Biblical World* (Oxford: Oxford University Press, 2001), 8.
31 Othniel Margalit, 'The Political Background of Zerubbabel's Mission and the Samaritan Schism', *VT* 41, no. 3 (1991): 312; Robert J. Littman, 'Athens, Persia and the Book of Ezra', *Transactions of the American Philological Association (1974–2014)* 125 (1995): 251.
32 Littman, 'Athens, Persia and the Book of Ezra', 223; Greifenhagen, *Egypt on the Pentateuch's Ideological Map*, 223; Coogan, *The Oxford History*, 8; Samuel Eugene Balentine, *The Torah's Vision of Worship* (Minneapolis: Fortress Press, 1999), 46.
33 Gerrie F. Snyman, 'A Possible World of Text Production for the Genealogy in 1 Chronicles 2.3-4.23,' in *The Chronicler as Theologian*, eds M. Patrick Graham, Gary N. Knoppers and Steven L. McKenzie (New York: T&T Clark, 2003), 52.
34 Donald P. Moffat, *Ezra's Social Drama: Identity Formation, Marriage and Social Conflict in Ezra 9 and 10* (New York: Bloomsbury, 2013), 76.
35 Moffat, *Ezra's Social Drama*, 76; Eve Levavi Feinstein, *Sexual Pollution in the Hebrew Bible* (Oxford: Oxford University Press, 2014), 148.
36 Robert R. Duke, *The Social Location of the Visions of Amram (4Q543-547)* (New York: Peter Lang, 2010), 52–3.
37 Joseph Blenkinsopp, *Ezra-Nehemiah* (Pennsylvania: Westminster Press, 1988), 59.
38 Feinstein, *Sexual Pollution in the Hebrew Bible*, 148.
39 Kvammen, *Toward a Postcolonial Reading of the Epistle of James*, 216.
40 Wietske de Jong-Kumru, *Postcolonial Feminist Theology* (Berlin: LIT Verlag Dr W. Hopf, 2013), 83; Shaun L. Gabbidon, *Criminological Perspectives on Race and Crime* (New York: Routledge, 2015), 179; Jane M. Jacobs, *Edge of Empire: Postcolonialism and the City* (London: Routledge, 1996), 2.
41 Igor Maver, 'Post-Colonial Literatures in English ab origine ad futurum', in *Critics and Writers Speak: Revisioning Post-colonial Studies*, ed. Igor Maver (Lanham: Rowman & Littlefield, 2006), 11; Marek Tesar, *Te Whāriki in Aotearoa New Zealand: Witnessing and Resisting Neo-liberal and Neo-colonial Discourses in Early Childhood Education*, ed. Veronica Pacini-Ketchabaw and Africa Taylor (Abingdon: Routledge, 2015), 100; Tezenlo Thong, *Progress and Its Impact on the Nagas: A Clash of Worldviews* (London: Routledge, 2016), 156; Tan Chung, *Across the Himalayan Gap: An Indian Quest for Understanding China* (New Delhi: Indira Gandhi National Centre for the Arts, 1998), 85.
42 Abidin Kusno, *Behind the Postcolonial: Architecture, Urban Space and Political Cultures in Indonesia* (London: Routledge, 2014), 165.
43 Ibid.
44 Coogan, *The Oxford History*, 8.
45 Yoon Kyung Lee, 'Postexilic Jewish Experience and Korean Multiculturalism', in *Migration and Diaspora* (Atlanta: SBL Press, 2014), 12.
46 Mary Douglas, 'Responding to Ezra: The Priests and the Foreign Wives', *Biblical Interpretation* 10, no. 1 (2002): 1–23.
47 Wes Howard-Brook, *'Come Out My People!': God's Call Out of Empire in the Bible and Beyond* (New York: Orbis Books, 2010), 264; Caroline N. Mbonu and Ngozi N.

Iheanacho, 'Women & Intercultural Communication', in *Intercultural Communication and Public Policy*, ed. Ngozi Iheanacho (Port Harcourt: M & J Grand Orbit Communications, 2016) 177.

48 Gordon J. Wenham, *Story as Torah: Reading the Old Testament Ethically* (Edinburgh: T&T Clark, 2000), 94.
49 There are biblical passages that depict Pharaoh as a cruel and wicked monarch. This book, without challenging such representations, analyses the Second Temple community's assertions skilfully embedded in Abraham's crossings. This book emphasizes not on Pharaoh but on the Second Temple community and their anti-Persian assertions.
50 Harry M. Orlinsky, *Notes on the New Translation of the Torah* (Philadelphia: Jewish Publication Society, 1969), 85.
51 Daniel Gordis, 'Lies, Wives and Sisters: The Wife–Sister Motif Revisited,' *Judaism: A Quarterly Journal of Jewish Life and Thought* 34, no. 3 (1985): 352.
52 Irmtraud Fischer, *Women Who Wrestled with God: Biblical Stories of Israel's Beginnings*, trans. Linda M. Maloney (Minnesota: Liturgical Press, 2005), 10.
53 L. Robert Arthur, *The Sex Texts: Sexuality, Gender, and Relationships in the Bible* (Pittsburgh: Dorrance Publishing, 2013), 90.
54 Terry Puett, *The Book of Genesis* (Pueblo: P & L Publications, 2013), 192.
55 Arthur, *The Sex Texts*, 90.
56 Francis D. Ritter, *Sex, Lies and the Bible: The Controlling of Human Sexual Behavior Through the Corruption of the Bible* (Oceanside: Diverse Publications, 2006), 29–30.
57 Margaret Nutting Ralph, *And, God Said What? An Introduction to Biblical Literary Forms* (New York: Paulist Press, 1986), 60.
58 It might seem that Pharaoh's act of taking Sarah justifies Abraham's fear. However, Pharaoh rebuking Abraham clarifies that he would not have married Sarah if he knew that she was Abraham's wife.
59 Iain Provan, *Discovering Genesis: Content, Interpretation, Reception* (Grand Rapids: William B. Eerdmans, 2015), 136; Alan Segal, *Sinning in the Hebrew Bible: How the Worst Stories Speak for Its Truth* (New York: Columbia University Press, 2012), 33–4; Eugene March, *The Wide, Wide Circle of Divine Love: A Biblical Case for Religious Diversity* (Louisville: Westminster John Knox Press, 2005), 49; James A. Sanders, *God Has a Story Too: Sermons in Context* (Eugene: Wipf and Stock, 2000), 35.
60 Marvin A. Sweeney, 'Formation and Form in Prophetic Literature', in *Old Testament Interpretation: The Past, Present, and Future, Essays in Honour of Gene M. Tucker*, eds J. L. Mays, D. L. Petersen and K. H. Richards (Nashville: Abingdon, 1995), 116; Simon Bar-Efrat, 'Some Observations on the Analysis of Structure in Biblical Narrative,' *Vetus Testamentum* 30 (1980): 172. The central part in a concentric structure would be of fundamental importance. Please see, Davis, *Oral Biblical Criticism*, 154.
61 The structural lines surround the centre in regular layers in a concentric structure. It arranges concentrically around a centre, reversing the order of the elements after the central element. Please see Wucius Wong, *Principles of Form and Design* (New York: John Wiley, 1993), 51; Robert L. Cohn, David W. Cotter, Jerome T. Walsh and Chris Franke, *2 Kings* (Minnesota: The Liturgical Press, 2000), 10.
62 Wenham, *Genesis 1–15*, 286.
63 Richard N. Longenecker, *Introducing Romans: Critical Issues in Paul's Most Famous Letter* (Grand Rapids: William B. Eerdmans, 2011), 188.
64 The Egyptians and the Princes of Pharaoh saw Sarah. But they did not approach her (12.14-15).

65 W. L. Moran, 'A Note on the Treaty Terminology of the Sefire Stelas', *Journal of Near Eastern Studies* 22 (1963): 174–6.
66 James K. Hoffmeier, 'The Wives' Tales of Genesis 12, 20 & 26 and the Covenants at Beer-Sheba', *Tyndale Bulletin* 43, no. 1 (1992): 93; R. Hillers, 'A Note on Some Treaty Terminology in the Old Testament,' *Bulletin of the American Schools of Oriental Research* 176 (1964): 46–7; A. Malamat, 'Organs of Statecraft in the Israelite Monarchy', *Biblical Archaeologist* 28, no. 2 (1965): 34–64; T. N. D. Mettinger, 'King and Messiah: The Civil and Sacral Legitimation of the Israelite Kings' in *Coniectanea Biblica*, Old Testament Series, no. 8 (Lund, 1976), 147; D. J. McCarthy, *Treaty and Covenant: A Study in Form in the Ancient Oriental Documents and in the Old Testament* (Rome: Biblical Institute Press), 1978, 21.
67 Gerard Gertoux, *Abraham and Chedorlaomer: Chronological, Historical and Archaeological Evidence* (California: Lulu.com, 2015), 45; J. Rosalie Hooge, *Providential Beginnings* (Longwood: Xulon Press, 2003), 167.
68 Ralph, *And, God Said What*, 60.
69 Munster L. Schwienhorst, 'נגע Nega Touch Afflict Reach,' in *Theological Dictionary of the Old Testament, vol. 9*, eds G. Johannes Botterweck, Helmer Ringgren and Heinz-Josef Fabry, trans. David E. Green (Grand Rapids: William B. Eerdmans, 1998), 204.
70 Ibid.
71 Gregory Glazov, *The Bridling of the Tongue and the Opening of the Mouth in Biblical Prophecy* (Sheffield: Sheffield Academic Press, 2001), 328–9; Avrāhām Malāmāṭ, *Mari and the Bible* (Leiden: Brill, 1998), 148–9; Michael A. Fishbane, *The JPS Bible Commentary: Haftarot* (Philadelphia: The Jewish Publication Society, 2002), 77; Victor H. Matthews, *Judges and Ruth* (Cambridge: Cambridge University Press, 2004), 84.
72 Jonathan Macy, *In the Shadow of His Wings: The Pastoral Ministry of Angels: Yesterday, Today, and for Heaven* (Cambridge: Lutterworth Press, 2015), 118.
73 Joseph Blenkinsopp, *Abraham: The Story of a Life* (Grand Rapids: William B. Eerdmans, 2015), 48.
74 Gunkel, *Genesis*, 173.
75 Westermann, *Genesis 12–36*, 163.
76 J. Skinner, *A Critical and Exegetical Commentary on Genesis* (Edinburgh: T&T Clark, 1912), 240; Hamilton, *The Book of Genesis, Chapters 1–17*, 382; Wenham, *Genesis 1–15*, 288.
77 S. P. Jeansonne, *The Women of Genesis: From Sarah to Potiphar's Wife* (Minneapolis: Fortress, 1990), 17.
78 Jon L. Berquist, *Reclaiming Her Story: The Witness of Women in the Old Testament* (Eugene: Wipf and Stock, 2006), 48.
79 Naomi Steinberg, *Kinship and Marriage in Genesis: A Household Economics Perspective* (Minneapolis: Fortress Press, 1993), 53.
80 Ibid., 54.
81 Trible, 'Ominous Beginning for a Promise of Blessing,' 36; William E. Phipps, *Assertive Biblical Women* (London: Greenwood Press, 1992), 10.
82 Trible, 'Ominous Beginning for a Promise of Blessing,' 36.
83 Please see *New Revised Standard Version, New American Bible, Revised English Bible* and *New Jerusalem Bible*.
84 Roger Ferlo, *Opening the Bible* (Lanham: A Cowley Publications Book, 1997), 51.
85 Robert Letellier, *Creation, Sin and Reconciliation: Reading Primordial and Patriarchal Narrative in the Book of Genesis* (Newcastle upon Tyne: Cambridge Scholars Publishing, 2015), 201.

86 Trible, 'Ominous Beginning for a Promise of Blessing', 37.
87 Fischer, *Women Who Wrestled with God*, 11.
88 Westermann, *Genesis 12–36*, 161–62, 318–21.
89 Barnabe Assohoto and Samuel Ngewa, 'Genesis', in *Africa Bible Commentary: A One-Volume Commentary Written by 70 African Scholars*, ed. Tokunboh Kdeyemo (Nairobi: WordAlive Publishers, 2006), 40.
90 Robert Alter, *The Art of Biblical Narrative* (New York: Basic Books, 1983), 49ff; D. J. A. Clines, 'The Ancestor in Danger: But Not the Same Danger', in *What Does Eve Do to Help? and Other Readerly Questions to the Old Testament* (Sheffield: JSOT Press, 1990), 67–84; Bradford A. Anderson, *An Introduction to the Study of the Pentateuch*, 2nd Edition (London: Bloomsbury T&T Clark, 2017), 101.
91 Joel S. Baden, *J, E, and the Redaction of the Pentateuch* (Tubingen: Mohr Siebeck, 2009), 214; Marc Zvi Brettler, *How to Read the Bible* (Philadelphia: The Jewish Publication Society, 2005), 54.
92 Baden, *J, E, and the Redaction of the Pentateuch*, 214; Mathews, *Genesis 11:27–50:26*, 247; D. L. Petersen, 'A Thrice-Told Tale: Genre, Theme and Motif', *Bible Review* 18 (1973): 30–43.
93 Yehoshua Gitay, *Methodology, Speech, Society: The Hebrew Bible* (Sellenbosch: Sun Media, 2011), 30.
94 Clines, 'The Ancestor in Danger', 67–84.
95 David L. Petersen, *Method Matters: Essays on the Interpretation of the Hebrew Bible in Honour of David L. Petersen* (Atlanta: Society of Biblical Literature, 2009), 29.
96 Mathews, *Genesis 11:27–50:26*, 251.
97 Steven L. McKenzie and John Kaltner, *The Old Testament: Its Background, Growth, & Content* (Nashville: Abingdon Press, 2007), 88.
98 R. W. L. Moberly, *The Bible, Theology, and Faith: A Study of Abraham and Jesus* (Cambridge: Cambridge University Press, 2000), 93.
99 John H. Salihamer, 'Genesis', in *Genesis–Leviticus*, vol. 1, eds. Tremper Longman III and David E. Garland (Michigan: Zondervan, 2009), 203.
100 Peter Machinist, 'Biblical Traditions: The Philistines and Israelite History', in *The Sea Peoples and Their World: A Reassessment*, ed. Eliezer D. Oren (Philadelphia: The University Museum, 2000), 56.
101 Denzil Chetty, *Divorce Discourses: A Biblical Dilemma* (Delhi: Concept Publishing, 2007), 69.
102 Joseph Blenkinsopp, *Ezra-Nehemiah: A Commentary* (Philadelphia: Westminster Press, 1988), 247.
103 Niels Peter Lemche, *Ancient Israel: A New History of Israel* (London: Bloomsbury T&T Clark, 2015), 183; Robert H. Kennett, *The Composition of the Book of Isaiah in the Light of History and Archaeology: The Schweich Lectures 1909* (Eugene: Wipf and Stock, 2004), 19; Benedikt Otzen, 'Israel under the Assyrians. Reflections on Imperial Policy in Palestine', in *Annual of the Swedish Theological Institute*, vol. XI (Leiden: Brill, 1978), 106.
104 Feinstein, *Sexual Pollution in the Hebrew Bible*, 148.
105 Benedikt Otzen, 'Israel under the Assyrians', 106.
106 Kermit Zarley, *Palestine Is Coming: The Revival of Ancient Philistia* (Hannibal: Hannibal Books, 1990), 38.
107 Andrew Knowles, *The Bible Guide: An All-in-One Introduction to the Book of Books* (Oxford: Lion Publishing, 2001), 209; Paul Heger, *The Three Biblical Altar*

Laws: Developments in the Sacrificial Cult in Practice and Theology, Political and Economic Background (Berlin: Walter de Gruyter, 1999), 341.
108 Jacob Milgrom, 'Religious Conversion and the Revolt Model for the Formation of Israel,' *Journal of Biblical Literature* 101 (1982): 173.
109 Rainer Albertz, 'Purity Strategies and Political Interests in the Policy of Nehemiah', in *Confronting the Past: Archaeological and Historical Essays on Ancient Israel in Honour of William G. Dever*, eds S. Gittin, J. E. Wright and J. P. Dessel (Winona Lake: Eisenbraus, 2006), 199–206.
110 Fredrick Carlson Holmgren, *Israel Alive Again: A Commentary on the Books of Ezra and Nehemiah* (Michigan: William B. Eerdmans, 1987), 107.
111 Knute Larson, Max Anders and Kathy Dahlen, *Holman Old Testament Commentary – Ezra, Nehemiah, Esther* (Nashville: B & H Publishing, 2005), 172.
112 Ibid.
113 Ibid., K. L. Noll, *Canaan and Israel in Antiquity: An Introduction* (London: Sheffield Academic Press, 2001), 296.
114 Blenkinsopp, *Judaism, the First Phase*, 70–1.
115 Gale A. Yee, *Poor Banished Children of Eve: Woman as Evil in the Hebrew Bible* (Minneapolis: Fortress Press, 2003), 146.
116 Chetty, *Divorce Discourses*, 71.
117 Yee, *Poor Banished Children of Eve*, 146.
118 Peter H. W. Lau, *Identity and Ethics in the Book of Ruth: A Social Identity Approach* (Berlin: Walter de Gruyter, 2011), 182.
119 Aryeh Kasher, *Jews and Hellenistic Cities in Eretz-Israel: Relations of the Jews in Eretz-Israel with the Hellenistic Cities During the Second Temple Period (332 BCE–70 CE)* (Tübingen: Mohr Siebeck, 1990), 27.
120 Jeremiah W. Cataldo, *Biblical Terror: Why Law and Restoration in the Bible Depend upon Fear* (London: Bloomsbury T&T Clark, 2017), 85–6.
121 Kristin Moen Saxegaard, *Character Complexity in the Book of Ruth* (Tübingen: Mohr Siebeck, 2010), 46.
122 Nehemiah, unlike Ezra, did not ask the Jews to divorce their Ashdodite women.
123 J. G. Vos, *Genesis* (Pittsburgh: Crown & Covenant, 2006), 295.
124 David VanDrunen, *Divine Covenants and Moral Order: A Biblical Theology of Natural Law* (Grand Rapids: Eerdmans, 2014), 157.
125 Fretheim, *Abraham: Trials of Family and Faith*, 53.
126 Brett, *Genesis: Procreation*, 52.
127 Ibid.
128 Hamilton, *The Book of Genesis, Chapters 18–50*, 50.
129 Robert R. Gonzales, *Where Sin Abounds: The Spread of Sin and the Curse in Genesis with Special Focus on the Patriarchal Narratives* (Eugene: Wipf and Stock, 2010), 136; Ska, *Introduction to Reading the Pentateuch*, 58.
130 VanDrunen, *Divine Covenants and Moral Order*, 157.
131 Hamilton, *The Book of Genesis: Chapters 18–50*, 67.
132 James E. Smith, *The Pentateuch* (Joplin: College Press Publishing, 2006), 155; Vos, *Genesis*, 297.
133 Lockyer, *All the Miracles*, 42.
134 Laurence A. Turner, *Genesis* (Sheffield: Sheffield Academic Press, 2000), 90.
135 Hamilton, *The Book of Genesis: Chapters 18–50*, 94.
136 Ibid.
137 Kermit Zarley, *Palestine Is Coming*, 226.

138 Hamilton, *The Book of Genesis: Chapters 18–50*, 94.
139 Bruce K. Waltke, *Genesis: A Commentary* (Grand Rapids: Zondervan, 2016), 280.
140 Tremper Longman III and Peter Enns (eds), *Dictionary of the Old Testament: Wisdom, Poetry & Writings: A Compendium of Contemporary Biblical Scholarship* (Nottingham: Inter-Varsity Press, 2008), 930.
141 Steven Lawson, *Holman Old Testament Commentary – Psalms* (Nashville: B & H Publishing, 2003), 130.
142 Ibid, Michelle Pesando, *Why God Doesn't Hate You* (Bloomington: Balboa Press, 2014), 10.
143 Joel N. Lohr, *Chosen and Unchosen: Conceptions of Election in the Pentateuch and Jewish-Christian Interpretation* (Winona Lake: Eisenbrauns, 2009), 99.
144 Ibid., Shaul Bar, *Daily Life of the Patriarchs* (Oxford: Peter Lang, 2014), 79.
145 Lohr, *Chosen and Unchosen*, 99.
146 Ibid.
147 Ibid. See also Brett, *Genesis: Procreation*, 52.
148 Brett, *Genesis: Procreation*, 52.
149 Aaron Koller, *Esther in Ancient Jewish Thought* (Cambridge: Cambridge University Press, 2014), 25.
150 Ibid.
151 Dalit experience is the starting point for Dalit theology. It is the experience of oppression, discrimination, suffering and pain. Jangkholam Haokip, *Can God Save My Village? A Theological Study of Identity among the Tribal People of North-East India with a Special Reference to the Kukis of Manipur* (Cumbria: Langham Monographs, 2014), 257 (please see introduction and chs 1, 2 and 3 for more details).
152 Ibid.
153 Eric J. Sharpe, 'The Goals of Inter-Religious Dialogue', in *Truth and Dialogue in World Religions: Conflicting Truth Claims*, ed. John Hick (Philadelphia: Westminster Press, 1974), 83. Let me clarify that this book does not intend to identify Abraham or the outsiders in Indian contexts. On the other hand, we will propose how the attempts to reimagine the Egyptians and Philistines might help Dalit theology.
154 This does not mean sex is the only means of abusing a woman. Taking a married woman to a harem is an abuse.
155 Humphreys, *The Character of God in the Book of Genesis*, 87.
156 Surekha Nelavala, *Liberation Beyond Borders: Dalit Feminist Hermeneutics and Four Gospel Women* (New Jersey: Drew University, 2008), 23.
157 Ibid.

Chapter 8

1 Anita Ghosh, 'Dalit Feminism: A Psycho-social Analysis of Indian English Literature', in *Dalit Literature: A Critical Exploration*, eds. Amar Nath Prasad and M. B. Gaijan (New Delhi: Sarup, 2007), 50.
2 Usha Devi Shukla, *Rāmacaritamānasa in South Africa* (Delhi: Motilal Banarsidass Publishers, 2002), 10.
3 Manish Verma, *Fasts and Festivals of India* (Delhi: Diamond Books, 2007), 51.

4 T. Nanjundaiya Sreekantaiya, *Indian Poetics*, trans. N. Balasubrahmanya (New Delhi: Sahitya Academy, 2001), 37.
5 Nilanshu Kumar Agarwal, 'An Assessment of Northeastern Sensibility in Kiran Desai's *The Inheritance of Loss* and Mamang Dai's *River Poems*', in *Emerging Literatures from Northeast India: The Dynamics of Culture, Society and Identity*, ed. Margaret Ch. Zama (New Delhi: Sage Publications India, 2013), 126.
6 Ramesh Menon, *The Ramayana: A Modern Retelling of the Great Indian Epic* (New York: North Point Press, 2001), 6.
7 Shambuka's episode starts when a Brahmin arrives at Rama's court carrying the body of his dead son. The father declares that an undeserved death never occurs in a kingdom where a just ruler ensures that each citizen performs the duty according to one's social rank and stage of life. When Rama consults his ministers about the state of the kingdom, they pinpoint that Shambuka, the Shudra, has been performing *Tapas*. Since *Tapas* is a form of ascetic self-discipline reserved exclusively for the dominant caste men, Rama's ministers urge him to kill Shambuka. Rama finds Shambuka, and after confirming that he is indeed a Shudra by birth, Rama cuts off Shambuka's head. See Paula Richman, *Ramayana Stories in Modern South India: An Anthology* (Bloomington: Indiana University Press, 2008), 111.
8 Eleanor Zelliot, *From Untouchable to Dalit* (New Delhi: Manohar Publishers, 1998), 320–1.
9 S. K. Chatterji, 'Why Dalit Theology', in *Indigenous People: Dalits-Dalit Issues in Today's Theological Debate*, ed. James Massey (Delhi: Indian Society for Promoting Christian Knowledge, 2006), 28.
10 Simon C. Kim, *An Immigration of Theology: Theology of Context as the Theological Method of Virgilio Elizondo and Gustavo Gutierrez* (Eugene: Wipf and Stock, 2012), 24.
11 Samuel Cueva, *Mission Partnership in Creative Tension: An Analysis of Relationships within the Evangelical Missions Movement with Special Reference to Peru and Britain from 1987–2006* (Cumbria: Langham Monographs, 2015), 55.
12 Richard J. Payne and Jamal Nassar, *Politics and Culture in the Developing World* (London: Routledge, 2016), 53.
13 Sharon Welch, 'Dangerous Memory and Alternate Knowledges', in *On Violence: A Reader*, eds. Bruce B. Lawrence and Aisha Karim (Durham: Duke University Press, 2007), 366.
14 James H. Cone, *A Black Theology of Liberation* (New York: Orbis Books, 2010), 23–35; Dwight N. Hopkins, *Black Theology USA and South Africa: Politics, Culture, and Liberation* (Eugene: Wipf and Stock, 1989), 89; Anthony B. Pinn, *Embodiment and the New Shape of Black Theological Thought* (New York: New York University Press, 2010), 44.
15 Bama, *Sangati: Events*, trans. Lakshmi Holmstrom (Oxford: Oxford University Press, 2009), 14.
16 Sathianathan Clarke, 'Subalterns, Identity Politics and Christian Theology in India', in *Christian Theology in Asia*, ed. Sebastian C. H. Kim (Cambridge: Cambridge University Press, 2008), 284.
17 Praveen Gadhvi, *The Voice of the Last* (Delhi: Yash Publication, 2008), 17.
18 Chandrabahen Shrimali, 'Paradise, at a Stone's Throw Distance', in *Valonum* (Gandhinagar, 2007), 3, Chapter 5: Aesthetics of Dalit Poetry, accessed on 17 May 2022, https://kipdf.com/chapter-aesthetics-of-dalit-poetry_5ae66fcf7f8b9ad4718b458f.html.

19 Kim Knott, *Hinduism: A Very Short Introduction* (Oxford: Oxford University Press, 2016), 83.
20 Amos Yong, *Discerning the Spirit(s): A Pentecostal-Charismatic Contribution to Christian Theology of Religions* (Sheffield: Sheffield Academic Press, 2000), 44ff.
21 K. C. Abraham, 'Paradigm Shift in Contemporary Theological Thinking', in *Prejudice: Issues in Third World Theologies*, ed. Andreas Nehring (Chennai: Gurukul Theological College and Research Institute, 1996), 40, 47; Stanley J. Samartha, 'The Cross and the Rainbow', in *The Myth of Christian Uniqueness: Toward a Pluralistic Theology of Religions*, eds John Hick and Paul F. Knitter (Eugene: Wipf and Stock, 1987), 75; I. John Mohan Razu, *Globalization and Dalitho-ethics: Interrelationships between Homoeconomics and Homo-hierarchicus* (New Delhi: Centre for Dalit/Subaltern Studies, 2004), 33–6.
22 Felix Wilfred, *Sunset in the East? Asian Challenges and Christian Involvement* (Madras: University of Madras, 1991), 149.
23 John Hick, *God and the Universe of Faiths: Essays in the Philosophy of Religion* (London: Macmillan, 1973), 69ff.
24 Ibid., 121.
25 J. Peter Schneller, 'Christ and Church: A Spectrum of Views', *Theological Studies* 37 (1976): 552–3.
26 Kumar and Boopalan, 'Indian Christians in Conflict', 316.
27 S. P. Srivastava, 'Unravelling the Dynamics of Dalit Oppression', in *Social Exclusion: Essays in Honour of Dr. Bindeshwar Pathak*, ed. A. K. Lal (New Delhi: Concept Publishing, 2003), 228; Jagdish Kumar Pundir, 'Dalits in India: Past Identities and Present Scenario', in *Emerging Social Science Concerns: Festschrift in Honour of Professor Yogesh Atal*, ed. Surendra K. Gupta (New Delhi: Concept Publishing, 2007), 367; S. M. Michael, *Dalits in Modern India: Vision and Values* (New Delhi: Sage Publications, 2007), 174; Tamsin Bradley, *Religion and Gender in the Developing World: Faith-Based Organizations and Feminism in India* (London: I.B. Tauris, 2011), xi.
28 K. Divya, 'Domestic Violence Induced Social Exclusion of Dalit Women: Evidence from Puducherry', *International Journal of Innovative Research and Development* 4, no. 12 (November 2015): 221.
29 Ramesh P. Mohanty, *Dalits Development and Change: An Empirical Study* (New Delhi: Discovery Publishing, 2003), 49.
30 N. Sudhakar Rao, 'A Reconsideration of the Structural Replication in the Tamil Untouchable Castes in South India', *Religion and Society* 45, no. 3 (1998): 12.
31 V. Mohini Giri, *Deprived Devils: Women's Unequal Status in Society* (New Delhi: Gyan Publishing House, 2006), 27; V. K. Agnihotri and S. V. Subramanian, 'Andhra Pradesh', in *Socio Economic Profile of Rural India: South India*, ed. V. K. Agnihotri (New Delhi: Concept Publishing, 2002), 8.
32 Paulo Freire, *Pedagogy of the Oppressed* (New York: Seabury, 1968), 61.
33 Ibid., 29–30.
34 Victor I. Ezigbo, *Re-imagining African Christologies: Conversing with the Interpretations and Appropriations of Jesus in Contemporary African Christianity* (Eugene: Wipf and Stock, 2010), 86.
35 Tariq Thachil, *Elite Parties, Poor Voters: How Social Services Win Votes in India* (New York: Cambridge University Press, 2014), 44.
36 Nelavala, *Liberation Beyond Borders*, 23; Rajkumar, *Dalit Theology and Dalit Liberation*, 182; Monica Jyotsna Melanchthon, 'Towards Mapping Feminist

Biblical Interpretations in Asia', in *Feminist Biblical Studies in the Twentieth Century: Scholarship and Movement*, ed. Elisabeth Schussler Fiorenza (Atlanta: Society of Biblical Literature, 2014), 113.
37 Grace Feuerverger, *Oasis of Dreams: Teaching and Learning Peace in a Jewish-Palestinian Village in Israel* (London: Routledge, 2013), xv.
38 H. Svi Shapiro, 'All We Are Saying: Identity, Communal Strife, and the Possibility of Peace', in *Examining Social Theory: Crossing Borders/Reflecting Back*, ed. Daniel Ethan Chapman (New York: Peter Lang, 2010), 104.
39 Ronald J. Fisher, *Interactive Conflict Resolution* (New York: Syracuse University Press, 1997), 125.
40 Quoted from Feuerverger, *Oasis of Dreams: Teaching and Learning*, 115.
41 Laura C. Wunder and Kennedy Mkutu, 'Policing Where the State Is Distant Community Policing in Kuron, South Sudan', in *Security Governance in East Africa: Pictures of Policing from the Ground*, ed. Kennedy Agade Mkutu (Lanham: Lexington Books, 2018), 3.
42 John Ashworth, 'The Attempts of Dialogue in Sudan', in *Dialogue and Conflict Resolution: Potential and Limits*, eds Pernille Rieker and Henrik Thune (London: Routledge, 2015), 178.
43 Marc Gopin, *Holy War, Holy Peace: How Religion Can Bring Peace to the Middle East* (New York: Oxford University Press, 2002), 109; John Valk, Halis Albayrak and Mualla Selçuk, *An Islamic Worldview from Turkey: Religion in a Modern, Secular and Democratic State* (Cham: Springer, 2017), 84.
44 John Hick, *An Interpretation of Religion* (New Haven: Yale University Press, 1989), 240.
45 Thomas J. Fararo and Kenji Kosaka, *Generating Images of Stratification: A Formal Theory* (Dordrecht: Springer Science + Business Media, 2003), 108.
46 Yael Petretti, 'Listening out Way to Peace', in *Making Peace with Faith: The Challenges of Religion and Peacebuilding*, eds Michelle Garred, Mohammed Abu-Nimer (Lanham: Rowman & Littlefield, 2018), 82.
47 Parichart Suvanbubha, 'Dialogue in Buddhism: A Case Study in Addressing Violence in Southern Thailand', in *Religions and Dialogue: International Approaches*, eds Wolfram Weiße, Katajun Amirpur, Anna Körs and Dörthe Vieregge (Munster: Waxmann, 2014), 308.
48 Diemut Bubeck, 'Feminism in Political Philosophy: Women's Difference', in *The Cambridge Companion to Feminism in Philosophy*, eds Miranda Fricker and Jennifer Hornsby (Cambridge: Cambridge University Press, 2000), 193; A. Poruthur, 'A Decade of Dialoguing: A Non-elitist Approach', *Mission Today* 2 (2000): 490.
49 Wilfred, *On the Banks of Ganges*, 95.
50 Laurel B. Kennedy and Mary Rose Williams, 'The Past without the Pain: The Manufacture of Nostalgia in Vietnam's Tourism Industry', in *The Country of Memory: Remaking the Past in Late Socialist Vietnam*, ed. Hue-Tam Ho Tai (Berkeley: University of California Press, 2001), 136.
51 Ibid., 136–9.
52 Douglas A. Phillips and Charles F. Gritzner, *India* (Philadelphia: Chelsea House Publications, 2003), 68; Candrakīrti, *Four Illusions: Candrakīrti's Advice for Travelers on the Bodhisattva Path*, trans. Karen C. Lang (Oxford: Oxford University Press, 2003), 69; Paul Kuritz, *The Making of Theatre History* (Englewood Cliffs: Prentice Hall, 1988), 70.
53 Paswan and Jaideva (eds), *Encyclopaedia of Dalits*, 261; Radhika Chandiramani, 'Mapping the Contours: Reproductive Health and Rights and Sexual Health and Rights in India', in *Where Human Rights Begin: Health, Sexuality, and Women in the*

New Millennium, eds Wendy Chavkin and Ellen Chesler (New Brunswick: Rutgers Press, 2005), 131; M. Elavarasi, 'Dignity of Dalit Women', in *Human Rights: Challenges of 21st Century*, ed. V. N. Viswanathan (Delhi: Kalpaz Publications, 2008), 289.
54 Muriel Orevillo-Montenegro, *The Jesus of Asian Women* (New Delhi: Logos Press, 2010), 63.
55 Faustina, *Sangati: Events*, 122.
56 Ruth Manorama, 'Dalit Women in Struggle: Transforming Pain into Power', in *Life as a Dalit: Views from the Bottom on Caste in India*, eds Subhadra Mitra Channa and Joan P Mencher (New Delhi: Sage Publications, 2013), 258.
57 N. G. Prasuna, 'The Dalit Woman', in *Frontiers of Dalit Theology*, ed. V. Devasahayam (Delhi: Indian Society for Promoting Christian Knowledge, 1996), 103.
58 S. Anandhi and J. Jeyaranjan, 'The Abusers', in *Men of the Global South: A Reader*, ed. Adam Jones (London: Zed Books, 2006), 66.
59 N. G. Prasuna, 'The Dalit Woman', 111.
60 Steinberg, *Kinship and Marriage in Genesis*, 53.54.
61 F. van Dijk-Hemmes, 'Sarai's Exile: A Gender-Motivated Reading of Genesis 12: 10-13:2', in *A Feminist Companion to Genesis*, ed. A. Brenner (Sheffield: Sheffield Academic Press, 1993), 232.
62 Nelavala, *Liberation Beyond Borders*, 23.
63 The Times of India. '6 Booked for Dalit Woman's Gang-Rape', accessed on 4 April 2018 https://timesofindia.indiatimes.com/city/chandigarh/6-booked-for-dalit-womans-gang-rape/articleshow/63587285.cms.
64 The Times of India, 'Witness in Gang-Rape, Suicide of Dalit Woman Attacked', accessed 4 April 2018 https://timesofindia.indiatimes.com/city/jaipur/witness-in-gang-rape-suicide-of-dalit-woman-attacked/articleshow/63372363.cms
65 Debabrata Mohanty, 'Three Arrested for Rape and Murder of Minor Dalit Girl in Odisha', accessed 4 April 2018 https://www.hindustantimes.com/india-news/three-arrested-for-rape-and-murder-of-minor-dalit-girl-in-odisha/story-FBeWWrLELzj5yzNnYmzyMM.html.
66 Rosemary Radford Ruether, 'Women and Interfaith Relations: Toward a Transitional Feminism', in *Women and Interreligious Dialogue*, eds Catherine Cornille and Jillian Maxey (Eugene: Cascade Books, 2013), 13.
67 Pupul Jayakar, *Earth Mother: Legends, Ritual Arts, and Goddesses of India* (San Francisco: Harper and Row, 1990), 43ff.
68 Sathianathan Clarke, 'Paraiyars Ellaiyamman as an Iconic Symbol of Collective Resistance and Emancipatory Mythography' in *Religions of the Marginalised: Towards a Phenomenology and the Methodology of Study*, ed. Robinson Gnana (Delhi: Indian Society for Promoting Christian Knowledge, 1998), 43.
69 Hemchand Gossai, *Power and Marginality in the Abraham Narrative – Second Edition* (Eugene: Pickwick Publications, 2010), 14.

Chapter 9

1 Shelley Swanson Sateren, *Michelangelo* (Mankato: Bridgestone Books, 2002), 7.
2 Harry Stevens, 'Seven Decades after Independence, Most Dalit Farmers Still Landless', accessed 19 July 2018, https://www.hindustantimes.com/interactives/dalit-farmers-landless-agricultural-labourers-minimum-support-price.

3 Michael Bergunder, *The South Indian Pentecostal Movement in the Twentieth Century* (Grand Rapids: William B. Eerdmans, 2008), 30.
4 P. Sanal Mohan, 'Religion, Social Space, and Identity: The Prathyaksha Raksha Daiva Sabha and the Making of Cultural Boundaries in Twentieth Century Kerala', in *Life as a Dalit: Views from the Bottom on Caste in India*, eds Subhadra Mitra Channa and Joan P. Mencher (New Delhi: Sage Publications, 2013), 231.
5 An *Upadesi* is a layperson who functions as a catechist among the believers, offering spiritual guidance.
6 V. V. Swamy, 'Prathyaksha Raksha Daiva Sabha: Historical Absences and the Other Text', in *No Alphabet in Sight: New Dalit Writing from South India*, eds K. Satyanarayana and Susie Tharu (New Delhi: Penguin Books, 2011), 606.
7 Mundadan, *History of Christianity in India*; Placid Podipara, 'Hindu in Culture, Christian in Religion, Oriental in Worship', in *The St. Thomas Christian Encyclopaedia of India*, ed. George Menachery (Trichur: The St Thomas Christian Encyclopaedia of India, 1973), 5; John C. B. Webster, 'Who Is a Dalit?' in *Dalits in Modern India: Vision and Values*, ed. S. M. Michael (New Delhi: Vistaar Publications, 1999); E. M. Philip, *The Indian Church of St. Thomas* (Puthencruz: Mor Adai Study Centre, 2014).
8 S. N. Sadasivan, *A Social History of India* (New Delhi: A. P. H. Publishing, 2000), 414.
9 Ibid, 414–17.
10 Kochurani Abraham, *Persisting Patriarchy: Intersectionalities, Negotiations, Subversions* (Gewerbestrasse: Palgrave Macmillan, 2019), 48.
11 George Samuel, 'Conversion and Caste in Kerala', *Transformation* 2, no. 2 (1985); 19–22.
12 A. Mathias Mundadan, *History of Christianity in India*, 166.
13 A. Mathias Mundadan, *Traditions of St. Thomas Christians* (Bangalore: Dharmaram, 1970), 30–1; Placid J. Podipara, *The Thomas Christians* (London: Longman & Todd, 1970), 84.
14 Jacob Kollaparambil, *The St. Thomas' Christian Revolution of 1653* (Kottayam: The Catholic Bishop's House, 1981), 4.
15 Susan Bayly, *Saints, Goddesses and Kings: Muslims and Christians in South Indian Society, 1700–1900* (Cambridge: Cambridge University Press, 2004), 252.
16 L. W. Brown, *The Indian Christians of St. Thomas: An Account of the Ancient Syrian Church of Malabar* (Madras: B. I. Publications, 1980).
17 Bayly, *Saints, Goddesses and Kings*, 275.
18 Ibid., 244–7, 249–53. It is to be noted, however, that the Brahminic Hindu temples and sacred precincts were outside the reach of the community while they have access to the sacred spaces of the dominant caste Nairs.
19 Elamkulam Kunjan Pillai, *Studies in Kerala History* (Kottayam: National Book Stall, 1970), 376.
20 Alex Thomas, *A History of the First Cross-Cultural Mission of the Mar Thoma Church 1910–2000* (New Delhi: Indian Society for Promoting Christian Knowledge, 2007), 40.
21 Susan Visvanathan, *The Christians of Kerala: History, Belief and Ritual among the Yakoba* (Madras: Oxford University Press, 1993), 16–20.
22 *Pula Sabhakal*, accessed 16 May 2021, https://ia801001.us.archive.org/1/items/1897_Malankara_Edavaka_Pathrika_Volume_06_Issue_07/1897_Malankara_Edavaka_Pathrika_Volume_06_Issue_07_bw.pdf.
23 Palakunnel Mathai Mariyam Kathanar, *Palakunnel Valyachante Nallagam* (Changanacherry: Palakunnel Mathai Mariyam Kathanar Death Centenary Committee, 2000), 10–12.

24 T. Paul Varghese, 'The Ancient Syrian Church of India: A Contemporary Picture', *The Ecumenical Review* 13, no. 3 (1961): 286.
25 P. T. Thufail, *Bishop Demolishes the Biggest Conversion 'Myth' of Kerala*, accessed 30 April 2018, https://www.outlookindia.com/website/story/bishop-demolishes-the-biggest-conversion-myth-of-kerala/310974; Geevarghese Mor Coorilos, 'God of Life, Lead Us to Justice and Peace: Some Missiological Perspectives', *International Review of Mission* 102, no. 1 (2013): 14
26 Deenabandhu Manchala, 'Migration: An Opportunity for Broader and Deeper Ecumenism', in *Theology of Migration in the Abrahamic Religions*, eds Elaine Padilla and Peter C. Phan (New York: Palgrave Macmillan, 2014), 156.
27 Tracy Davis and Laura M. Harrison, *Advancing Social Justice: Tools, Pedagogies, and Strategies to Transform Your Campus* (San Francisco: John Wiley, 2013), 96.
28 Edmund Kee-Fook Chia, *World Christianity Encounters World Religions: A Summa of Interfaith Dialogue* (Minnesota: Liturgical Press, 2018), 51.
29 Ralph Underwood, *Empathy and Confrontation in Pastoral Care* (Eugene: Wipf and Stock, 2002), 57.
30 Edmund Emeka Ezegbobelu, *Challenges of Interreligious Dialogue: Between the Christian and the Muslim Communities in Nigeria* (Frankfurt: Peter Lang, 2009), 93.
31 David Tracy, *Dialogue with the Other: The Inter-religious Dialogue* (Louvain: Peeters Press, 1990), 4.
32 John C. Cavadini and Donald Wallenfang, 'Introduction', in *Evangelization as Interreligious Dialogue*, eds John C. Cavadini and Donald Wallenfang (Eugene: Pickwick Publications, 2019), xxvii.
33 Julia T. Wood, 'Forward: Entering into Dialogue', in *Dialogue: Theorizing Difference in Communication Studies*, eds Rob Anderson, Leslie A. Baxter and Kenneth N. Cissna (London: Sage Publications, 2004), xvii.
34 Ibid.
35 Sarah J. Cervenak, Karina L. Cespedes, Caridad Souza and Andrea Straub, *This Bridge We Call Home: Radical Visions for Transformation*, eds Gloria Anzaldúa and AnaLouise Keating (New York: Routledge, 2002), 352.
36 Barbara C. Wallace, Robert T. Carter, Jose E. Nanin, Richard Keller and Vanessa Alleye, 'Identity Development for "Diverse and Different Others": Integrating Stages of Change, Motivational Interviewing, and Identity Theories for Race, People of Coloraturas, Sexual Orientation, and Disability', in *Understanding and Dealing With Violence: A Multicultural Approach*, eds Barbara C. Wallace and Robert T. Carter (Thousand Oaks: Sage Publications, 2003), 85; William B. Gudykunst, *Bridging Differences: Effective Intergroup Communication* (London: Sage Publications, 2004), 347.

BIBLIOGRAPHY

Aaronson, Ely. *From Slave Abuse to Hate Crime: The Criminalization of Racial Violence in American History* (New York: Cambridge University Press, 2014).

Abdelrahman, Maha. *Egypt's Long Revolution: Protest Movements and Uprisings* (New York: Routledge, 2014).

Abedi, Razi. 'Dalit Literature: The Voice of the Downtrodden', in *The Best of Gowanus: New Writing from Africa, Asia, and the Caribbean*, ed. Thomas J. Hubschman (Brooklyn: Gonanus Books, 2001).

Abraham, K. C. 'Paradigm Shift in Contemporary Theological Thinking', in *Prejudice: Issues in Third World Theologies*, ed. Andreas Nehring (Chennai: Gurukul Theological College and Research Institute, 1996).

Ackerman, Susan. 'The Blind, the Lame, and the Barren Shall Not Come into the House', in *Disability Studies and Biblical Literature*, eds Candida R. Moss and Jeremy Schipper (New York: Palgrave Macmillan, 2011).

Agarwal, Nilanshu Kumar. 'An Assessment of Northeastern Sensibility in Kiran Desai's *The Inheritance of Loss* and Mamang Dai's *River Poems*', in *Emerging Literatures from Northeast India: The Dynamics of Culture, Society and Identity*, ed. Margaret Ch. Zama (New Delhi: Sage Publications India, 2013).

Agnihotri, V. K. and S. V. Subramanian. 'Andhra Pradesh', in *Socio Economic Profile of Rural India: South India*, ed. V. K. Agnihotri (New Delhi: Concept Publishing, 2002).

Aguilar, Mario I. *Christian Ashrams, Hindu Caves and Sacred Rivers: Christian–Hindu Monastic Dialogue in India 1950–1993* (London: Jessica Kingsley Publishers, 2006).

Aguilar, Mario I. *Church, Liberation and World Religions* (London: Bloomsbury T&T Clark, 2012).

Ahlstrom, Gosta W. *The History of the Ancient Palestine from the Palaeolithic Period to Alexander's Conquest*, ed. Diana V. Edelman (Sheffield: Sheffield Academic Press, 1993).

Albertz, Rainer. *Israel in Exile: The History and Literature of the Sixth Century* BCE, trans. David Green (Atlanta: Society of Biblical Literature, 2003).

Albertz, Rainer. 'Purity Strategies and Political Interests in the Policy of Nehemiah', in *Confronting the Past: Archaeological and Historical Essays on Ancient Israel in Honour of William G. Dever*, eds S. Gittin, J. E. Wright and J. P. Dessel (Winona Lake: Eisenbrauns, 2006).

Albertz, Rainer. 'Religion in Israel During and after the Exile', in *The Biblical World*, vol. II, ed. John Barton (London: Routledge, 2002).

Albright, William F. *The Archeology and the Religions of Israel* (Baltimore: John Hopkins Press, 1956).

Aleaz, K. P. 'The Theological Writings of Brahmabandhav Upadhyaya Re-examined', *Indian Journal of Theology* 28, no. 2 (April–June 1979).

Alexander, T. D. 'Are the Wife/Sister Incidents of Genesis Literary Compositional Variants?', *Vetus Testamentum* 42, no. 2 (1992).

Allen, Anne Dondapati. 'No Garlic, Please, We Are Indian: Reconstructing the De-eroticized Indian Woman', in *Off the Menu: Asian and Asian North American Women's Religion & Theology*, eds Rita Nakashima Brock, Jung Ha Kim, Kwok Pui-lan and Seung Ai Yung (Louisville: Westminster John Knox Press, 2007).
Allen, Lasara Firefox. *Jailbreaking the Goddess, A Radical Revisioning of Feminist Spirituality* (Woodbury: Llewellyn Publications, 2016).
Ambedkar, B. R. *Constituent Assembly Debates* (New Delhi: Lok Sabha Secretariat, 1989), vol. IX.
Amos, Clare. *The Book of Genesis* (Peterborough: Epworth, 2004).
Anandhi, S. and J. Jeyaranjan. 'The Abusers', in *Men of the Global South: A Reader*, ed. Adam Jones (London: Zed Books, 2006).
Anderson, Bradford A. *An Introduction to the Study of the Pentateuch*, 2nd Edition (London: Bloomsbury T&T Clark, 2017).
Anderson, Victor. *Beyond Ontological Blackness: An Essay on African American Religious and Cultural Criticism* (London: Bloomsbury Academic, 2016).
Anderson, Victor. 'Critical Reflection on the Problems of History and Narrative in a Recent African-American Research Problem', in *A Dream Unfinished: Theological Reflections on America from the Margins*, eds Eleazar S. Fernandez and Fernando F. Segovia (Eugene: Wipf and Stock, 2006).
Anderson, Victor. 'Theorizing African American Religion', in *African American Studies*, ed. Jeanette R. Davidson (Edinburgh: Edinburgh University Press, 2010).
Annie, W. S. 'Nandanar: The Dalit Martyr', in *Doing Theology with the Poetic Traditions of India: Focus on Dalit and Tribal Poems*, ed. Joseph Patmury (Bangalore: PTCA/SATHRI, 1996).
Antoniraj, P. *Discrimination against Dalit Christians* (Madurai: IDEAS Centre, 1992).
Appasamy, A. J. *The Gospel and India's Heritage* (London: Indian Society for Promoting Christian Knowledge, 1942).
Appavoo, James Theophilus. *Folklore for Change* (Madurai: T. T. S. Publications, 1986).
Arthur, L. Robert. *The Sex Texts: Sexuality, Gender, and Relationships in the Bible* (Pittsburgh: Dorrance Publishing, 2013).
Arulraja, M. R. *Jesus, the Dalit: Liberation Theology by Victims of Untouchability, an Indian Version of Apartheid* (Secunderabad: Author, 1996).
Aschcroft, Bill. 'Post-colonial Horizons', in *(In)fusion Approach: Theory, Contestation, Limits: (In)fusionising a Few Indian English Novels*, ed. Ranjan Ghosh (Lanham: University Press of America, 2006).
Aschcroft, Bill, Gareth Griffiths and Helen Tiffin. *The Empire Writes Back: Theory and Practice in Post-colonial Literatures* (London: Routledge, 2002).
Ashworth, John. 'The Attempts of Dialogue in Sudan', in *Dialogue and Conflict Resolution: Potential and Limits*, eds Pernille Rieker and Henrik Thune (London: Routledge, 2015).
Assohoto, Barnabe and Samuel Ngewa. 'Genesis', in *Africa Bible Commentary: A One-Volume Commentary Written by 70 African Scholars*, ed. Tokunboh Kdeyemo (Nairobi: WordAlive Publishers, 2006).
Ayrookuzhiel, Abraham. 'Chinna Pulayan: The Dalit Teacher of Sankaracharya', in *Doing Theology with the Poetic Traditions of India: Focus on Dalit and Tribal Poems*, ed. Joseph Patmury (Bangalore: South Asia Theological Research Institute, 1996).
Ayrookuzhiel, Abraham. 'Dalit Theology: A Movement of Counter-Culture', in *Indigenous People: Dalits, Dalit Issues in Today's Theological Debate*, ed. James Massey (Delhi: Indian Society for Promoting Christian Knowledge, 1994).

Ayrookuzhiel, Abraham. *Essays on Dalits, Religion and Liberation* (Bangalore: Christian Institute for the Study of Religion and Society, 2006).
Ayyappan, A. *Social Revolution in a Kerala Village: A Study in Culture Change* (New Delhi: Asia Publication House, 1965).
Azariah, M. 'Christ and Dalit Liberation', in *A Pastor's Search for Dalit Theology*, ed. M. Azariah (Delhi: Indian Society for Promoting Christian Knowledge, 2000).
Baden, Joel S. *J, E, and the Redaction of the Pentateuch* (Tubingen: Mohr Siebeck, 2009).
Badlani, Hiro G. *Hinduism: Path of the Ancient Wisdom* (New York: iUniverse, 2008).
Bahamann, Manfred K. 'Liberation Theology: Latin American Style', *Lutheran Quarterly* 27, no. 2 (1 May 1975).
Baker, David W. and Bill T. Arnold. *The Face of Old Testament* Studies (Michigan: Baker Academic, 1999).
Balasundaram, F. J. 'Dalit Struggle and Its Implications for Theological Education', in *Bangalore Theological Forum* 29, nos 3 and 4 (September and December 1997).
Balasundaram, F. J. 'Dalit Theology and Other Theologies', in *Frontiers of Dalit Theology*, ed. V. Devasahayam (Chennai: Gurukul Lutheran Theological College and Research Institute, 1996).
Balentine, Samuel Eugene. *The Torah's Vision of Worship* (Minneapolis: Fortress Press, 1999).
Bama. *Karukku*, trans. Lakshmi Holmstrom (Chennai: Macmillan, 1992).
Bama. *Sangati: Events*, trans. Lakshmi Holmstrom (Oxford: Oxford University Press, 2009).
Bar-Efrat, Simon. 'Some Observations on the Analysis of Structure in Biblical Narrative', *Vetus Testamentum* 30 (1980).
Bar, Shaul. *Daily Life of the Patriarchs* (Oxford: Peter Lang, 2014).
Barnes, Michael. *Theology and the Dialogue of Religions* (Cambridge: University of Cambridge, 2002).
Barton, Mukti. 'Race, Gender, Class and the Theology of Empowerment: An Indian Perspective', in *Gender, Religion and Diversity: Cross-Cultural Perspectives*, eds Ursula King and Tina Beattie (London: Continuum, 2005).
Bartusch, Mark W. *Understanding Dan: An Exegetical Study of a Biblical City, Tribe and Ancestor* (Sheffield: Sheffield Academic Press, 2003).
Basu, Raj Sekhar. *Nandanar's Children: The Paraiyans' Tryst with Destiny, Tamil Nadu 1850–1956* (New Delhi: Sage Publications, 2011).
Bauman, Chad M. *Christian Identity and Dalit Religion in Hindu India, 1868–1947* (Michigan: William B. Eerdmans, 2008).
Bautch, Richard J. *Glory and Power, Ritual and Relationship: The Sinai Covenant in the Postexilic Period* (New York: A&C Black, 2009).
Bayly, Susan. *Caste, Society and Politics in India from the Eighteenth Century to the Modern Age* (Cambridge: Cambridge University Press, 2001).
Bayly, Susan. *Saints, Goddesses and Kings: Muslims and Christians in South Indian Society, 1700–1900* (Cambridge: Cambridge University Press, 2004).
Begg, C. 'Zedekiah and the Servant', *Ephemarides Theologie Lovaniences* 62 (1986).
Bendangjungshi. *Confessing Christ in the Naga Context: Towards a Liberating Ecclesiology* (Zurich: LIT Verlag, 2011).
Bergant, Dianne. *Genesis: In the Beginning* (Minnesota: Collegeville Press, 2013).
Berges, Ulrich. 'The Literary Construction of the Servant in Isaiah 40–55: A Discussion about Individual and Collective Identities', in *Scandinavian Journal of the Old Testament* 24, no. 1 (2010).

Bergunder, Michael. *The South Indian Pentecostal Movement in the Twentieth Century* (Grand Rapids: William B. Eerdmans, 2008).
Berlin, Adele. *Poetics and Interpretation of Biblical Narrative* (Winona Lake: Eisenbrauns, 2005).
Berquist, Jon L. *Reclaiming Her Story: The Witness of Women in the Old Testament* (Eugene: Wipf and Stock, 2006).
Bharathi, Thummapudi. *A History of Telugu Dalit Literature* (Delhi: Kalpaz Publications, 2008).
Bhatt, S. C. and Gopal K. Bhargava. (eds) *Land and People of Indian States and Union Territories*, vol. 25 (Delhi: Kalpaz Publications, 2006).
Biddle, Mark E. 'The "Endangered Ancestress" and Blessing for the Nations', *Journal of Biblical Literature* 109, no. 4 (1990).
Bird, Adrian. 'Caste and Christianity since Gandhi and Ambedkar', in *Forrester on Christian Ethics and Practical Theology: Collected Writings on Christianity, India and the Social Order*, ed. Duncan B. Forrester (Surrey: Ashgate Publishing, 2010).
Bjorgo, Tore. *Strategies for Preventing Terrorism* (Basingstoke: Macmillan Publishers, 2013).
Blenkinsopp, Joseph. *Abraham: The Story of a Life* (Grand Rapids: William B. Eerdmans, 2015).
Blenkinsopp, Joseph. 'Continuity–Discontinuity in Isaiah 40–66: Issue of Location', in *Continuity and Discontinuity: Chronological and Thematic Development in Isaiah 40–66*, eds Hans M. Barstad and Lena-Sofia Tiemeyer (Gottingen: Vandenhoeck & Ruprecht, 2014).
Blenkinsopp, Joseph. *Ezra-Nehemiah: A Commentary* (Philadelphia: Westminster Press, 1988).
Blenkinsopp, Joseph. *Judaism, the First Phase: The Place of Ezra and Nehemiah in the Origins of Judaism* (Grand Rapids: William B. Eerdmans, 2009).
Blenkinsopp, Joseph. *The Pentateuch* (London: SCM Press, 1992).
Bloom, Joshua and Waldo E. Martin. *The History and the Politics of the Black Panther Party: Black against the Empire* (London: University of California Press, 2013).
Boer, Roland. 'Marx, Postcolonialism and the Bible', in *Postcolonial Biblical Criticism: Interdisciplinary Intersections*, eds Stephen D. Moore and Fernando F. Segovia (London: T&T Clark, 2005).
Bohache, Thomas. *Christology from the Margins* (London: SCM Press, 2008).
Boopalan, Sunder John. *Memory, Grief, and Agency: A Political Theological Account of Wrongs and Rites* (New York: Palgrave Macmillan, 2017).
Bradley, Tamsin. *Religion and Gender in the Developing World: Faith-Based Organizations and Feminism in India* (London: I.B. Tauris, 2011).
Brady, Judith Ann. *A Place at the Table: Justice for the Poor in a Land of Plenty* (New London: Twenty-Third Publications, 2008).
Brave, Vasant and S. R. Medhe. 'Agenda for Emancipation and Empowerment of Dalits in India', in *Dalits and Tribes of India*, ed. J. Cyril Kanmony (New Delhi: Mittal Publications, 2010).
Brennan, Timothy. 'From Development to Globalisation: Postcolonial Studies and Globalisation Theory', in *The Cambridge Companion to Postcolonial Literary Studies*, ed. Neil Lazarus (Cambridge: Cambridge University Press, 2004).
Brett, Mark G. *Genesis: Procreation and the Politics of Identity* (New York: Routledge, 2000).

Brett, Mark G. 'Reading the Bible in the Context of Methodological Pluralism: The Undermining of Ethnic Exclusivism in Genesis', in *Rethinking Contexts, Reading Texts: Contributions from the Social Sciences to Biblical Interpretation*, ed. Mark Daniel Carroll R. (Sheffield: Sheffield Academic Press, 2000).

Brettler, Marc Zvi. *How to Read the Bible* (Philadelphia: The Jewish Publication Society, 2005).

Brewer, David Instone. 'Balaam-Laban as the Key to the Old Testament Quotations in Matthew 2', *Built Upon the Rock: Studies in the Gospel of Mathew*, eds Daniel M. Gurtner and John Nolland (Grand Rapids: William B. Eerdmans, 2008).

Bright, John. *A History of Israel* (London: SCM Press, 1972).

Brinkman, Martien E. 'The Reciprocal Relation between Anthropology and Christology', in *Strangers and Pilgrims on Earth: Essays in Honour of Abraham van de Beek*, eds Paul van Geest and Eduardus van der Borght (Leiden: Brill, 2012).

Brockman, D. *No Longer the Same: Religious Others and the Liberation of Christian Theology* (New York: Palgrave Macmillan, 2011).

Brown, Jeannine K. *Scripture as Communication: Introducing Biblical Hermeneutics* (Grand Rapids: Baker Academics, 2007).

Brown, L. W. *The Indian Christians of St. Thomas: An Account of the Ancient Syrian Church of Malabar* (Madras: B. I. Publications, 1980).

Brown, Robert McAfee. *Liberation Theology: An Introductory Guide* (Louisville: Westminster John Knox Press, 1993).

Brueggemann, Walter. *Genesis: Interpretation: A Bible Commentary for Teaching and Preaching* (Louisville: Westminster John Knox Press, 1982).

Brueggemann, Walter. *An Introduction to the Old Testament: The Canon and the Christian Imagination* (Louisville: Westminster John Knox Press, 2003).

Bubeck, Diemut. 'Feminism in Political Philosophy: Women's Difference', in *The Cambridge Companion to Feminism in Philosophy*, eds Miranda Fricker and Jennifer Hornsby (Cambridge: Cambridge University Press, 2000).

Büschges, Christian. 'Ethnicity', in *The Routledge Handbook to the History and Society of the Americas*, eds Olaf Kaltmeier, Josef Raab, Mike Foley, Alice Nash, Stefan Rinke and Mario Rufer (Abingdon: Routledge, 2019).

Bush, Barbara. *Imperialism and Postcolonialism* (London: Routledge, 2014).

Bustillo, Camilo Pérez and Karla Hernández Mares. *Human Rights, Hegemony, and Utopia in Latin America: Poverty, Forced Migration and Resistance in Mexico and Colombia* (Brill: Leiden, 2016).

Calhoun-Brown, Allison. 'What a Fellowship: Civil Society, African American Churches, and Public Life', in *New Day Begun: African American Churches and Civic Culture in Post-Civil Rights America*, ed. R. Drew Smith (Durham: Duke University Press, 2003).

Candrakīrti, *Four Illusions: Candrakīrti's Advice for Travelers on the Bodhisattva Path*, trans. Karen C. Lang (Oxford: Oxford University Press, 2003).

Carler, Warren. 'Postcolonial Biblical Criticism', in *Recent Approaches to Biblical Criticism and Their Applications*, eds Steven L. McKenzie and John Kaltner (Louisville: Westminster John Knox Press, 2013).

Carmichael, Calum. 'The Passover Haggadah', in *The Historical Jesus in Context*, eds Amy-Jill Levine, Dale C. Allison Jr. and John Dominic Crossan (Princeton: Princeton University Press, 2006).

Carr, David M. *An Introduction to the Old Testament: Sacred Texts and Imperial Contexts of the Hebrew Bible* (Chichester: Blackwell Publishing, 2010).

Carr, David M. *Reading the Fractures of Genesis: Historical and Literary Approaches* (Louisville: Westminster John Knox Press, 1996).
Carrol, Denis. *What Is Liberation Theology?* (Dublin: Mercier Press, 1987).
Carter, Charles E. *The Emergence of Yehud in the Persian Period: A Social and Demographic Study* (Sheffield: Sheffield Academic Press, 1999).
Cataldo, Jeremiah W. *Biblical Terror: Why Law and Restoration in the Bible Depend upon Fear* (London: Bloomsbury T&T Clark, 2017).
Cavadini, John C. and Donald Wallenfang. 'Introduction', in *Evangelization as Interreligious Dialogue*, eds John C. Cavadini and Donald Wallenfang (Eugene: Pickwick Publications, 2019).
Cervenak, Sarah J., Karina L. Cespedes, Caridad Souza and Andrea Straub. 'Imagining Differently: The Politics of Listening in a Feminist Classroom', in *This Bridge We Call Home: Radical Visions for Transformation*, eds Gloria E. Anzaldúa and Analouise Keating (New York: Routledge, 2002).
Chakraborty, Uma. *Gendering Caste through a Feminist Lens* (Calcutta: STREE, 2003).
Chandiramani, Radhika. 'Mapping the Contours: Reproductive Health and Rights and Sexual Health and Rights in India', in *Where Human Rights Begin: Health, Sexuality, and Women in the New Millennium*, eds Wendy Chavkin and Ellen Chesler (New Brunswick: Rutgers Press, 2005).
Chatterjee, Partha. *The Politics of the Governed: Reflections on Popular Politics in Most of the World* (New York: Columbia University Press, 2004).
Chauchard, Simon. *Why Representation Matters: The Meaning of Ethnic Quotas in Rural India* (Cambridge: Cambridge University Press, 2017).
Chetty, Denzil. *Divorce Discourses: A Biblical Dilemma* (Delhi: Concept Publishing, 2007).
Chia, Edmund Kee-Fook. *World Christianity Encounters World Religions: A Summa of Interfaith Dialogue* (Minnesota: Liturgical Press, 2018).
Childs, Brevard S. *Biblical Theology of the Old and New Testaments: Theological Reflection on the Christian Bible* (Minneapolis: Fortress Press, 1992).
Chopp, Rebecca S. *The Praxis of Suffering: An Interpretation of Liberation and Liberation Theologies* (Eugene: Wipf and Stock, 2007).
Chousalkar, Ashok S. *Revisiting the Political Thought of Ancient India: Pre-Kautilyan Arthashastra Tradition* (New Delhi: Sage Publications, 2018).
Chung, Tan. *Across the Himalayan Gap: An Indian Quest for Understanding China* (New Delhi: Indira Gandhi National Centre for the Arts, 1998).
Clark, Jawanza Eric. *Indigenous Black Theology: Toward an African-Centred Theology of the African-American Religious Experience* (New York: Palgrave Macmillan, 2012).
Clarke, Sathianathan. *Dalits and Christianity: Subaltern Religion and Liberation Theology in India* (New Delhi: Oxford University Press, 1999).
Clarke, Sathianathan. 'Dalits Overcoming Violation and Violence: A Contest between Overpowering and Empowering Identities in Changing India', *The Ecumenical Review* 54, no. 3 (July 2002).
Clarke, Sathianathan. 'Dalit Theology: An Introductory and Interpretive Theological Exposition', in *Dalit Theology in the Twenty-First Century: Discordant Voices, Discerning Pathways*, eds Sathianathan Clarke, Deenabandhu Manchala and Philip Vinod Peacock (Oxford: Oxford University Press, 2010).
Clarke, Sathianathan. 'Paraiyars Ellaiyamman as an Iconic Symbol of Collective Resistance and Emancipatory Mythography', in *Religions of the Marginalised: Towards a Phenomenology and the Methodology of Study*, ed. Robinson Gnana (Delhi: Indian Society for Promoting Christian Knowledge, 1998).

Clarke, Sathianathan. 'Subalterns, Identity Politics and Christian Theology in India', in *Christian Theology in Asia*, ed. Sebastian C. H. Kim (Cambridge: Cambridge University Press, 2008).

Clarke, Sathianathan. 'Viewing the Bible through the Eyes and Ears of Subalterns in India', *Biblical Interpretation: A Journal of Contemporary Approaches* 10 (2002).

Clarke, Sathianathan, Deenabandhu Manchala and Philip Vinod Peacock. 'Introduction: Enflamed Words, Engaging Worlds, Embryonic Word-Worlds', in *Dalit Theology in the Twenty-First Century: Discordant Voices, Discerning Pathways*, eds Sathianathan Clarke, Deenabandhu Manchala, and Philip Vinod Peacock (Delhi: Oxford University Press, 2010).

Cleage, Albert B. *The Black Messiah* (New York: Sheed and Ward, 1968).

Clemons Michael L. and Charles E. Jones. 'Global Solidarity: The Black Panther Party in the International Arena', in *Liberation, Imagination, and the Black Panther Party: A New Look at the Panthers and Their Legacy*, eds Kathleen Cleaver and George N. Katsiaficas (New York: Routledge, 2001).

Clines, D. J. A. 'The Ancestor in Danger: But Not the Same Danger', in *What Does Eve Do to Help? and Other Readerly Questions to the Old Testament* (Sheffield: JSOT Press, 1990).

Coastas, Orlando. 'Evangelism and the Gospel of Salvation', *International Review of Mission* 63, no. 249 (1974).

Coats, George W. *Genesis, with an Introduction to Narrative Literature* (Grand Rapids: William B. Eerdmans, 1983).

Cohn, Robert L., David W. Cotter, Jerome T. Walsh and Chris Franke. *2 Kings* (Minnesota: The Liturgical Press, 2000).

Cone, James H. *Black Theology and Black Power* (New York: Orbis Books, 1984).

Cone, James H. 'A Black Theology of Liberation', in *Readings in Christian Ethics: A Historical Sourcebook*, eds J. Philip Woaman and Douglas M. Strong (Kentucky: Westminster John Knox Press, 1996).

Cone, James H. *A Black Theology of Liberation* (New York: Orbis Books, 2010).

Cone, James H. *A Black Theology of Liberation: Twentieth Anniversary Edition* (Maryknoll, New York: Orbis Books, 1990).

Cone, James H. *For My People: Black Theology and the Black Church: Where Have We Been and Where Are We Going* (Maryknoll: Orbis Books, 1984).

Cone, James H. *God of the Oppressed* (Maryknoll: Orbis Books, 1975).

Cone, James H. 'Jesus Christ in Black Theology', in *Liberation Theology: An Introductory Reader*, eds Curt Cadorette, Marie Giblin, Marilyn J. Legge and Mary Hembrow Snyder (Eugene: Wipf and Stock, 2004).

Cone, James H. 'The Vocation of a Theologian', in *Living Stones in the Household of God: The Legacy and Future of Black Theology*, ed. Linda E. Thomas (Minneapolis: Fortress Press, 2004).

Coningham, Robin and Ruth Young. *The Archaeology of South Asia: From the Indus to Asoka, c. 6500 BCE–200 CE* (New York: Cambridge University Press, 2015).

Coogan, Michael David. *The Oxford History of the Biblical World* (Oxford: Oxford University Press, 2001).

Crenshaw, James L. *Defending God: Biblical Responses to the Problem of Evil* (Oxford: Oxford University Press, 2005).

Cueva, Samuel. *Mission Partnership in Creative Tension: An Analysis of Relationships within the Evangelical Missions Movement with Special Reference to Peru and Britain from 1987–2006* (Cumbria: Langham Monographs, 2015).

Daly, Mary. *Beyond God the Father* (Boston: Beacon Press, 1973).
Davies, Eryl W. *Biblical Criticism: A Guide for the Perplexed* (London: Bloomsbury, 2013).
Davies, Philip R. *In Search of 'Ancient Israel'* (New York: Continuum, 2006).
Davies, Philip R. *The Origins of Biblical Israel* (London: T&T Clark, 2007).
Davis, Casey W. *Oral Biblical Criticism: The Influence of the Principles of Orality on the Literary Structure of Paul's Epistle to the Philip* (Sheffield: Sheffield Academic Press, 1999).
Davis, Stephen T. *Christian Philosophical Theology* (Oxford: Oxford University Press, 2006).
Davis, Tracy and Laura M. Harrison. *Advancing Social Justice: Tools, Pedagogies, and Strategies to Transform Your Campus* (San Francisco: John Wiley, 2013).
Deshpande, L. S. *Makers of Indian Literature: Narhar Kurundkar* (New Delhi: Akademi, 2005).
DeSilva, David A. *The Jewish Teachers of Jesus, James and Jude: What Earliest Christianity Learned from the Apocrypa and Pseudepigrapha* (Oxford: Oxford University Press, 2012).
Devasahayam, V. 'Pollution, Poverty and Powerlessness: A Dalit Perspective', in *A Reader in Dalit Theology*, ed. A. P. Nirmal (Madras: Gurukul, 1991).
Devasahayam, V. (ed.) *Frontiers of Dalit Theology* (New Delhi: Indian Society for Promoting Christian Knowledge, 1997).
Devi, Sheela. 'Ravidas', in *Poet Saints of India*, eds M. Sivaramkrishna and Sumita Roy (New Delhi: Sterling Paperbacks, 1998).
Diaz-Stevens, Ana Maria. 'Liberation Theology', in *Latinas in the United States: A Historical Encyclopaedia*, eds Vicki L. Ruiz and Virginia Sánchez Korrol (Bloomington: Indiana University Press, 2006).
Dijkstra, Meindert. 'The Valley of Dry Bones: Coping with the Reality of the Exile in the Book of Ezekiel', in *The Crisis of Israelite Religion: Transformation of Religious Tradition in Exilic and Post-exilic Times*, eds Bob Becking, Marjo Christina and Annette Korpel (Leiden: Brill, 1999).
Dirks, Nicholas B. *Castes of Mind: Colonialism and the Making of Modern India* (Princeton: Princeton University Press, 2001).
Divya, K. 'Domestic Violence Induced Social Exclusion of Dalit Women: Evidence from Puducherry', *International Journal of Innovative Research & Development* 4, no. 12 (November 2015).
Doniger, Wendy. *Textual Sources for the Study of Hinduism* (Manchester: Oxford University Press, 1988).
Douglas, Kelly Brown. *The Black Christ* (Maryknoll: Orbis Books, 1994).
Douglas, Mary. 'Responding to Ezra: The Priests and the Foreign Wives', *Biblical Interpretation* 10, no. 1 (2002).
Dube, Musa W. *Postcolonial Feminist Interpretation of the Bible* (St. Louis: Chalice Press, 2000).
Dube, Musa W. 'Religion, Race, Gender and Identity', in *Biblical Studies, Theology, Religion and Philosophy: An Introduction for African Universities*, eds Fidelis Nkomazana and Obed N. Kealotswe (Eldoret: Zapf Chancery Research Consultants and Publishers, 2010).
Dube, Musa W. 'Toward a Post-colonial Feminist Interpretation', in *Semeia* 78 (1997).
Duke, Robert R. *The Social Location of the Visions of Amram (4Q543–547)* (New York: Peter Lang, 2010).

Dyk, Janet W. and Percy S. F. van Keulen. *Language System, Translation Technique, and Textual Tradition in the Peshitta of Kings* (Leiden: Brill, 2013).
Eapen, Viji Varghese. 'Christ in "Theyyam": Performative Word – Further an Exploration into the Subaltern Cultural Christology', in *The Yobel Spring: Festschrift to Dr Chilkuri Vasantha Rao*, eds Praveen P. S. Perumalla, Royce M. Victor and Naveen Rao (Hyderabad: Indian Society for Promoting Christian Knowledge, 2014).
Elavarasi, M. 'Dignity of Dalit Women', in *Human Rights: Challenges of 21st Century*, ed. V. N. Viswanathan (Delhi: Kalpaz Publications, 2008).
Elizondo, Virgilio. 'Editorial: Theology from the Viewpoint of the Poor', in *Option for the Poor: Challenge to the Rich Countries*, eds Leonardo Boff and Virgilo Elizondo (Edinburgh: T&T Clark, 1986).
Esler, Philip F. *Sex, Wives and Warriors: Reading Old Testament Narrative with Its Ancient Audience* (Cambridge: James Clarke, 2011).
Evans, Paul S. *The Invasion of Sennacherib in the Book of Kings: A Source-Critical and Rhetorical Study of 2 Kings 18–19* (Leiden: Brill, 2009).
Evans, Paul S. 'Worship That Fulfils the Law: The Book of Chronicles and Its Implications for a Contemporary Theology of Worship', in *Rediscovering Worship: Past, Present, and Future*, ed. Wendy J. Porter (Eugene: Pickwick Publications, 2015).
Exum, J. Cheryl. 'Who's Afraid of "The Endangered Ancestors"', in *Women in the Hebrew Bible: A Reader*, ed. Alice Bach (New York: Routledge, 1999).
Ezegbobelu, Edmund Emeka. *Challenges of Interreligious Dialogue: Between the Christian and the Muslim Communities in Nigeria* (Frankfurt: Peter Lang, 2009).
Ezigbo, Victor I. *Re-imagining African Christologies: Conversing with the Interpretations and Appropriations of Jesus in Contemporary African Christianity* (Eugene: Wipf and Stock, 2010).
Fararo, Thomas J. and Kenji Kosaka. *Generating Images of Stratification: A Formal Theory* (Dordrecht: Springer Science + Business Media, 2003).
Feinstein, Eve Levavi. *Sexual Pollution in the Hebrew Bible* (Oxford: Oxford University Press, 2014).
Ferlo, Roger. *Opening the Bible* (Lanham: Cowley Publications, 1997).
Fernandes, Walter. 'Conversion to Christianity, Caste Tension and Search for an Identity in Tamil Nadu', in *The Emerging Dalit Identity: Re-assertion of the Subalterns*, ed. Walter Fernandes (New Delhi: Indian Social Institute, 1996).
Fernando, Leonard and G. Gispert-Sauch. *Two Thousand Years of Faith: Christianity in India* (London: Penguin Books India, 2004).
Feuerverger, Grace. *Oasis of Dreams: Teaching and Learning Peace in a Jewish-Palestinian Village in Israel* (London: Routledge, 2013).
Fewell, Danna Nolan and R. Christopher Heard. 'The Genesis of Identity in the Biblical World', in *The Oxford Handbook of Biblical Narrative* (Oxford: Oxford University Press, 2016).
Finkelstein, Israel. 'Patriarchs, Exodus, Conquest: Fact or Fiction', in *The Quest for the Historical Israel*, ed. Brian B. Schmidt (Atlanta: Society of Biblical Literature, 2007).
Fiorenza, Elisabeth Schüssler. *Jesus, Miriam's Child, Sophia's Prophet* (New York: Continuum, 1994).
Fischer, Irmtraud. *Women Who Wrestled with God: Biblical Stories of Israel's Beginnings*, trans. Linda M. Maloney (Minnesota: Liturgical Press, 2005).
Fishbane, Michael A. *The JPS Bible Commentary: Haftarot* (Philadelphia: The Jewish Publication Society, 2002).

Fisher, Ronald J. *Interactive Conflict Resolution* (New York: Syracuse University Press, 1997).
Fitzmyer, Joseph A. *The One Who Is to Come* (Grand Rapids: William B. Eerdmans, 2007).
Flynn, Eileen and Gloria Thomas. *Living Faith: An Introduction to Theology* (Oxford: Sheed & Ward, 1995).
Forrester, Duncan B. *Truthful Action: Explorations in Practical Theology* (Edinburgh: T&T Clark, 2000).
Fox, Jonathan. *A World Survey of Religion and the State* (Cambridge: Cambridge University Press, 2008).
Freire, Paulo. *Pedagogy of the Oppressed* (New York: Seabury, 1968).
Fretheim, Terence E. *Abraham: Trials of Family and Faith* (South Carolina: University of South Carolina Press, 2007).
Friedlander, Peter. 'The Struggle for Salvation in the Hagiographies of Ravidas', in *Myth and Mythmaking: Continuous Evolution in Indian Tradition*, ed. Julia Leslie (Surrey: Curzon Press, 1996).
Gabbidon, Shaun L. *Criminological Perspectives on Race and Crime* (New York: Routledge, 2015).
Gadhvi, Praveen. *The Voice of the Last* (Delhi: Yash Publication, 2008).
Gallagher, Susan VanZanten. 'Mapping the Hybrid World: Three Postcolonial Motifs', *Semeia* 75 (1996).
Ganguly, Debjani. *Caste, Colonialism and Counter-Modernity: Notes on a Postcolonial Hermeneutics of Caste* (New York: Routledge, 2005).
Ganguly, Debjani. 'Dalit Life Stories', in *The Cambridge Companion to Modern Indian Culture*, eds Vasudha Dalmia and Rashmi Sadhana (Cambridge: Cambridge University Press, 2012).
Gasaway, Brantley W. *Progressive Evangelicals and the Pursuit of Social Justice* (Chapel Hill: The University of North Carolina Press, 2014).
Geetha, K. A. *Contesting Categories, Remapping Boundaries: Literary Interventions by Tamil Dalits* (Newcastle Upon Tyne: Cambridge Publishing House, 2014).
Geivett, R. Douglas. *Evil and the Evidence for God: The Challenge of John Hick's Theodicy* (Philadelphia: Temple University Press, 1993).
George, Samuel. 'Conversion and Caste in Kerala', *Transformation* 2, no. 2 (1985).
Gertoux, Gerard. *Abraham and Chedorlaomer: Chronological, Historical and Archaeological Evidence* (California: Lulu.com, 2015).
Ghosh, Anita. 'Dalit Feminism: A Psycho-social Analysis of Indian English Literature', in *Dalit Literature: A Critical Exploration*, eds Amar Nath Prasad and M. B. Gaijan (New Delhi: Sarup & Sons, 2007).
Ghuman, Paul. *British Untouchables: A Study of Dalit Identity and Education* (Surrey: Ashgate Publishing, 2011).
Gibson, Lynne. *Hinduism* (Oxford: Heinemann Educational Publishers, 2002).
Giri, Ananta Kumar. 'The Multiverse of Hindu Engagement with Christianity: Plural Streams of Creative Co-Walking, Contradictions, and Confrontations', in *The Oxford Handbook of Christianity in Asia*, ed. Felix Wilfred (Oxford: Oxford University Press, 2014).
Gitay, Yehoshua. *Methodology, Speech, Society: The Hebrew Bible* (Stellenbosch: Sun Media, 2011).
Glazov, Gregory. *The Bridling of the Tongue and the Opening of the Mouth in Biblical Prophecy* (Sheffield: Sheffield Academic Press, 2001).

Glushkova, Irina. 'Norms and Values in the Varkari Tradition', in *Intersections: Socio-cultural Trends in Maharashtra*, ed. Meera Kosambi (Hyderabad: Orient Longman, 2000).
Gnanavaram, M. '"Dalit Theology" and the Parable of the Good Samaritan', *Journal for the Study of New Testament* 50 (1993).
Gokhale-Turner, Jayashree B. 'Bhakti or Virodha: Continuity and Change in Dalit Sahitya', in *Tradition and Modernity in Bhakti Movements*, ed. Jayant Lele (Leiden: Brill, 1981).
González, Justo L. and Ondina E. González. *Christianity in Latin America: A History* (Cambridge: Cambridge University Press, 2008).
Gonzalez, Michelle A. *A Critical Introduction to Religion in the Americas: Bridging the Liberation Theology and Religious Studies Divide* (New York: New York University Press, 2014).
Gopin, Marc. *Holy War, Holy Peace: How Religion Can Bring Peace to the Middle East* (New York: Oxford University Press, 2002).
Gordis, Daniel. 'Lies, Wives and Sisters: The Wife-Sister Motif Revisited', in *Judaism: A Quarterly Journal of Jewish Life and Thought* 34, no. 3 (Summer Issue, 1985).
Gorringe, Hugo. *Untouchable Citizens: Dalit Movements and Democratisation in Tamil Nadu* (New Delhi: Sage Publications, 2005).
Graerod, Gard. *Abraham and Melchizedek Scribal Activity of Second Temple Times in Genesis 14 and Psalm 110* (Berlin: Walter de Gruyter, 2010).
Griffiths, Bede. *Retorno ao Centro: O Conhecimento da verdade – o ponto de reconciliação de todas as religiões* (Return to the Center: The Knowledge of Truth – The Point of Reconciliation for All the Religions) (São Paulo: Ibrasa, 1992).
Grover, Charles E. (trans.) *The Folk-Songs of Southern India* (London: Forgotten Books, 2013).
Gudykunst, William B. *Bridging Differences: Effective Intergroup Communication* (London: Sage Publications, 2004).
Gunkel, Hermann. *Genesis*, trans. Mark E. Biddle (Macon: Mercer University Press, 1997).
Gunkel, Hermann. *The Legends of Genesis*, trans. W. H. Caruth (New York: Schocken, 1964).
Gur-Klein, Thalia. *Sexual Hospitality in the Hebrew Bible: Patronymic, Metronymic, Legitimate and Illegitimate Relations* (London: Routledge, 2014).
Guru, Gopal. 'Understanding the Category Dalit', in *Atrophy in Dalit Politics*, ed. Gopal Guru (Mumbai: Vikas Adhyayan Kendra, 2005).
Guru, Nataraja. *Life and Teachings of Narayana Guru* (Sreenivasapuram: East-West University Publication, 1990).
Gutierrez, Gustavo. 'Liberation Praxis and Christian Faith', in *Frontiers of Theology in Latin America*, ed. Rosino Gibellini, trans. John Drury (Maryknoll: Orbis Books, 1979).
Gutierrez, Gustavo. 'Theology and the Social Sciences', in *The Truth Shall Make You Free: Confrontations*, trans. Matthew O'Connell (Maryknoll: Orbis Books, 1991).
Gutierrez, Gustavo. *A Theology of Liberation* (Maryknoll: Orbis Books, 1988).
Gutierrez, Gustavo. *A Theology of Liberation: History, Politics, and Salvation*, trans. Caridad Inda and John Eagleson (London: SCM Press, 1974).
Ha, John. *Genesis 15* (Berlin: Walter de Gruyter, 1989).
Habel, Norman C. *The Land Is Mine: Six Biblical Land Ideologies* (Augsburg: Fortress Press, 1995).

Halvorson-Taylor, Martien A. 'Displacement and Diaspora in Biblical Narrative', in *The Oxford Handbook of Biblical Narrative*, ed. Danna Nolan Fewell (Oxford: Oxford University Press, 2016).

Hamilton, Victor P. *The Book of Genesis: Chapters 1–17* (Grand Rapids: Eerdmans, 1990).

Hamilton, Victor P. *The Book of Genesis: Chapters 18–50* (Michigan: William B. Eerdmans, 1995).

Hanks, Thomas D. *God So Loved the World: The Biblical Vocabulary of Oppression*, trans. James C. Dekker (Eugene: Wipf and Stock, 2000).

Hardtmann, Eva-Maria. 'In Touch with Politics: Three Individuals in the Midst of the Dalit Movement', in *Contesting 'Good' Governance: Crosscultural Perspectives on Representation, Accountability and Public Space*, eds Eva Poluha and Mona Rosendahl (London: Routledge, 2012).

Harrington, Walt. *Crossings: A White Man's Journey into Black America* (New York: HarperCollins, 1993).

Harvey, Michael. *Creating a Culture of Invitation in Your Church* (Oxford: Monarch Books, 2015).

Hazra, Rajendra Chandra. *Studies in the Puranic Records on Hindu Rites and Customs* (Delhi: Motilal Banarsidass Publishers, 1987).

Heard, R. C. *The Dynamics of Diselection: Ambiguity in Genesis 12-26 and Ethnic Boundaries in Post-exilic Judah* (Atlanta: Society of Biblical Literature, 2001).

Heger, Paul. *The Three Biblical Altar Laws: Developments in the Sacrificial Cult in Practice and Theology, Political and Economic Background* (Berlin: Walter de Gruyter, 1999).

Hennelly, Alfred T. *Liberation Theology: A Documentary History* (Maryknoll: Orbis Books, 1990).

Hepner, Gershom. *Legal Friction, Law, Narrative, and Identity in Biblical Israel* (New York: Peter Lang, 2010).

Hess, Linda. 'Kabir's Rough Rhetoric', in *The Sants: Studies in a Devotional Tradition of India*, eds Karine Schomer and W. H. McLeod (Delhi: Motilal Banarsidass Publishers, 1987).

Hick, John. *An Interpretation of Religion* (New Haven: Yale University Press, 1989).

Hicks, John Mark. *The College Press NIV Commentary: 1 & 2 Chronicles* (Joplin: College Press, 2001).

Hiebert, Theodore. 'Genesis', in *Theological Bible Commentary*, eds Gail R. O'Day and David L. Petersen (Louisville: Westminster John Knox Press, 2009).

Hillers, R. 'A Note on Some Treaty Terminology in the Old Testament', *Bulletin of the American Schools of Oriental Research* 176 (1964).

Hoffman, Lawrence A. *Beyond the Text: A Holistic Approach to Liturgy* (Bloomington: Indiana University Press, 1989).

Hoffmeier, James K. 'The Wives' Tales of Genesis 12, 20 & 26 and the Covenants at Beer-Sheba', *Tyndale Bulletin* 43, no. 1 (1992).

Holmgren, Fredrick Carlson. *Israel Alive Again: A Commentary on the Books of Ezra and Nehemiah* (Michigan: William B. Eerdmans, 1987).

Hooge, J. Rosalie. *Providential Beginnings* (Longwood: Xulon Press, 2003).

Hopkins, Dwight N. *Black Theology USA and South Africa: Politics, Culture, and Liberation* (Eugene: Wipf and Stock, 2005).

Hopkins, Dwight N. 'A Dialogue in Black Theology: Black Theology of Liberation', in *Mormonism in Dialogue with Contemporary Christian Theologies*, eds David Lamont Paulsen and Donald W. (Macon: Mercer University Press, 2007).

Hopkins, Dwight N. 'General Introduction', in *The Cambridge Companion to Black Theology*, eds Dwight N. Hopkins and Edward P. Antonio (Cambridge: Cambridge University Press, 2012).

Hopkins, Dwight N. 'More Than Ever: The Preferential Option for the Poor', in *Opting for the Margins: Postmodernity and Liberation in Christian Theology*, ed. Jeorg Rieger (Oxford: Oxford University Press, 2003).

Howard-Brook, Wes. *'Come Out My People!': God's Call Out of Empire in the Bible and Beyond* (New York: Orbis Books, 2010).

Humphreys, W. Lee. *The Character of God in the Book of Genesis: A Narrative Appraisal* (London: Westminster John Knox Press, 2001).

Hunt, Sarah Beth. *Hindi Dalit Literature and the Politics of Representation* (London: Routledge, 2014).

Iliah, Kancha. 'Hindu Gods and Us: Our Goddesses and the Hindus', in *Perspectives on Modern South Asia: A Reader in Culture, History, and Representation*, ed. Kamala Visweswaran (Chichester: Wiley-Blackwell, 2011).

Iliah, Kancha. *Why I Am Not a Hindu: A Sudra Critique of Hindutva Philosophy, Culture and Political Economy* (Calcutta: Samya, 2005).

Irudayaraj, Xavier. (ed.) *Emerging Dalit Theology* (Madras: Jesuit Theological Secretariat, 1990).

Isherwood, Lisa. *Liberating Christ* (Ohio: Pilgrims Press, 1999).

Iype, P. S. *The Parumala Kochu Thirumeni* (Mavelikkara: St Paul's Mission Press, 1981).

Jacob, Benno. *Das erste Buch der Thora: Genesis* (Berlin: Schocken, 1934).

Jacobs, Jane M. *Edge of Empire: Postcolonialism and the City* (London: Routledge, 1996).

Jadhav, Narendra. *Untouchables: My Family's Triumphant Escape from India's Caste System* (Berkeley: University of California Press, 2005).

James, Charles Davis. *Indian Liberation Theology: A Critique* (Norderstedt: Books on Demand, 2009).

Jayakar, Pupul. *Earth Mother: Legends, Ritual Arts, and Goddesses of India* (San Francisco: Harper and Row, 1990).

Jeansonne, S. P. *The Women of Genesis: From Sarah to Potiphar's Wife* (Minneapolis: Fortress, 1990).

Jeremiah, Anderson H. M. *Community and Worldview among Paraiyars of South India: 'Lived' Religion* (London: Bloomsbury, 2013).

Jeremiah, Anderson H. M. 'Dalit Christians in India: Reflections from the 'Broken Middle', *Studies in World Christianity* 17, no. 3 (2001).

Jeremiah, Anderson H. M. 'Exploring New Facets of Dalit Christology: Critical Interaction with J. D. Crossan's Portrayal of the Historical Jesus', in *Dalit Theology in the Twenty-First Century: Discordant Voices, Discerning Pathways*, eds Sathianathan Clarke, Deenabandhu Manchala and Philip Vinod Peacock (New Delhi: Oxford University Press, 2010).

Jodhka, Surinder S. 'Sikhs Today: Development, Disparity and Difference', in *Religion, Community and Development: Changing Contours of Politics and Policy in India*, eds Gurpreet Mahajan and Surinder S. Jodhka (Abingdon: Routledge, 2010).

Jogdand, Prahlad Gangaram. *Dalit Movement in Maharashtra* (New Delhi: Kanak Publications, 1991).

Jong-Kumru, Wietske de. *Postcolonial Feminist Theology* (Berlin: LIT Verlag Dr W. Hopf, 2013).

Jonker, Louis C. *Defining All-Israel in Chronicles* (Tübingen: Mohr Siebeck, 2016).

Joseph, George Gheverghese. *George Joseph: The Life and Times of a Kerala Christian Nationalist* (Hyderabad: Orient Longman, 2003).
Kalliyath, Antony. 'Re-cognizing Christ in Asia', in *Sharing Diversity in Missiological Research and Education*, eds L. Stanislaus and John F. Gorski (Delhi: Indian Society for Promoting Christian Knowledge, 2006).
Kamudzandu, Israel. *Abraham as Spiritual Ancestor: A Postcolonial Zimbabwean Reading of Romans 4* (Boston: Brill, 2010).
Kappen, Sebastian. *Jesus and the Cultural Revolution: An Asian Perspective* (Bombay: Build Publications, 1983).
Kappen, Sebastian. *Jesus and Freedom* (New York: Orbis Books, 1977).
Kappen, Sebastian. 'Jesus and Transculturation', in *Asian Faces of Jesus*, ed. R. S. Sugirtharaja (Maryknoll: Orbis Books, 1993).
Kappen, Sebastian. *Liberation Theology and Marxism* (Puntamba: Asha Kendra, 1986).
Kasher, Aryeh. *Jews and Hellenistic Cities in Eretz-Israel: Relations of the Jews in Eretz-Israel with the Hellenistic Cities during the Second Temple Period (332 BCE–70 CE)* (Tübingen: Mohr Siebeck, 1990).
Kasher, Menahem. *Haggadah Shelemah* (Jerusalem: Torah Shelemah Institute, 1967).
Kathanar, Palakunnel Mathai Mariyam. *Palakunnel Valyachante Nallagam* (The Diary of Fr Palakunnel) (Changanacherry: Palakunnel Mathai Mariyam Kathanar Death Centenary Committee, 2000).
Katsificas, George. 'Introduction', in *Liberation, Imagination and the Black Panther Party: A New Look at the Panthers and Their Legacy*, eds Kathleen Cleaver and George Katsificas (New York: Routledge, 2001).
Katzentein, Mary, Smitu Kothari and Uday Mehta. 'Social Movement Politics in India: Institutions, Interests, and Identities', in *The Success of India's Democracy*, ed. Atul Kohli (New Delhi: Cambridge University, 2001).
Keane, David. *Caste-Based Discrimination in International Human Rights Law* (London: Routledge, 2016).
Keinänen, Jyrki. *Traditions in Collision: A Literary and Redaction-Critical Study on the Elijah Narratives: 1 Kings 17–19* (Helsinki: The Finnish Exegetical Society, 2001).
Kennedy, Laurel B. and Mary Rose Williams. 'The Past without the Pain: The Manufacture of Nostalgia in Vietnam's Tourism Industry', in *The Country of Memory: Remaking the Past in Late Socialist Vietnam*, ed. Hue-Tam Ho Tai (Berkeley: University of California Press, 2001).
Kennedy, Philip. *A Modern Introduction to Theology: New Questions for Old Beliefs* (London: I.B. Tauris, 2006).
Kennett, Robert H. *The Composition of the Book of Isaiah in the Light of History and Archaeology: The Schweich Lectures 1909* (Eugene: Wipf and Stock, 2004).
Keshet, Shula. *Say I Pray Thee, Thou Art My Sister: Intertextual Narrative in Jewish Culture* (Tel Aviv: Hakibbutz Hameuhad, 2003).
Khan, Mumtaz Ali. 'Legal Enactments and the Status of Dalits', in *Policing India in the New Millennium*, ed. P. J. Alexander (Mumbai: Allied Publishers, 2002).
Khanam, Azra. *Muslim Backward Classes: A Sociological Perspective* (New Delhi: Sage Publications, 2013).
Kim, Heerak Christian. *Nuzi, Women's Rights and Hurrian Ethnicity and Other Academic Essays* (Cheltenham: Hermit Kingdom Press, 2006).
Kim, Simon C. *An Immigration of Theology: Theology of Context as the Theological Method of Virgilio Elizondo and Gustavo Gutierrez* (Eugene: Wipf and Stock, 2012).

Kim, Uriah Y. 'Is There an "Anticonquest" Ideology in the Book of Judges', in *Postcolonialism and the Hebrew Bible: The Next Step*, ed. Roland Boer (Atlanta: Society of Biblical Literature, 2013).

Kim, Uriah Y. 'Postcolonial Criticism: Who Is the Other in the Book of Judges?', in *Judges and Methods: New Approaches in Biblical Studies*, ed. Gale H. Yee (Minneapolis: Fortress Press, 1995).

Klass, Morton. *Caste: The Emergence of the South Asian Social System* (Delhi: Manohar, 1998).

Klimova, Zuzana. 'The Social Function of Postcolonial Theories', in *Cultural Difference and Social Solidarity: Solidarities and Social Function*, eds Scott H. Boyd and Mary Ann Walter (Newcastle Upon Tyne: Cambridge Scholars Publishing, 2014).

Knight, George A. F. *Servant Theology: A Commentary on the Book of Isaiah 40–55* (Grand Rapids: Williams B. Eerdmans, 1984).

Knott, Kim. *Hinduism: A Very Short Introduction* (Oxford: Oxford University Press, 2016).

Knowles, Andrew. *The Bible Guide: An All-in-One Introduction to the Book of Books* (Oxford: Lion Publishing, 2001).

Kollaparambil, Jacob. *The St. Thomas' Christian Revolution of 1653* (Kottayam: The Catholic Bishop's House, 1981).

Koller, Aaron. *Esther in Ancient Jewish Thought* (Cambridge: Cambridge University Press, 2014).

Koshy, Ninan. *Caste in the Kerala Churches* (Bangalore: The Christian Institute for the Study of Religion and Society, 1968).

Kshirsagar, R. K. *Dalit Movement in India and Its Leaders, 1857–1956* (New Delhi: MD Publications, 1994).

Kumar, M. Ashok and Sunder J. Boopalan. 'Indian Christians in Conflict: Dalit Christian Movement in Contemporary India', in *Handbook of Global Contemporary Christianity: Themes and Developments in Culture, Politics, and Society*, ed. Stephen Hunt (Leiden: Brill, 2015).

Kunin, Seth Daniel. *We Think What We Eat: Structuralist Analysis of Israelite Food Rules and Other Mythological and Cultural Domains* (London: T&T Clark, 2004).

Kunjanpillai, Elamkulam P. N. *Chila Kerala Charithra Prasnangal* (Kottayam: National Book Stall, 1970).

Kuritz, Paul. *The Making of Theatre History* (Englewood Cliffs: Prentice Hall, 1988).

Kusno, Abidin. *Behind the Postcolonial: Architecture, Urban Space and Political Cultures in Indonesia* (London: Routledge, 2014).

Lachs, S. T. 'Two Related Arameans: A Difficult Reading in the Passover Haggadah', *Journal for the Study of Judaism*, 17 (1986).

Lacocque, André. *Ruth: A Continental Commentary*, trans. K. C. Hanson (Minneapolis: Fortress Press, 2004).

Lalitha, Jayachitra. 'Postcolonial Feminism, the Bible and the Native Indian Women', in *Evangelical Postcolonial Conversations: Global Awakening in Theology and Praxis*, eds Kay Higuera Smith, Jayachitra Lalitha and L. Daniel Hawk (Downers Grove: InterVarsity Press, 2014).

Larson, Gerald James. 'Hinduism in India and America', in *World Religions in America*, ed. Jacob Neusner (Louisville: Westminster John Knox Press, 2002).

Larson, Knute, Max Anders and Kathy Dahlen. *Holman Old Testament Commentary – Ezra, Nehemiah, Esther* (Nashville: B & H Publishing, 2005).

Lau, Peter H. W. *Identity and Ethics in the Book of Ruth: A Social Identity Approach* (Berlin: Walter de Gruyter, 2011).

Lawson, Steven. *Holman Old Testament Commentary – Psalms* (Nashville: B & H Publishing, 2003).
Lee, Yoon Kyung. 'Postexilic Jewish Experience and Korean Multiculturalism', in *Migration and Diaspora*, ed. Hisako Kinukawa (Atlanta: Society of Biblical Literature, 2014).
Lemche, Niels Peter. *Ancient Israel: A New History of Israel* (London: Bloomsbury T&T Clark, 2015).
Lemche, Niels Peter. *The Old Testament between Theology and History: A Critical Survey* (Louisville: Westminster John Knox Press, 2008).
Leming, Michael R. and George E. Dickinson. *Understanding Dying, Death, and Bereavement* (Belmont: Wadsworth, 2011).
Lemos, Tracy Maria. *Marriage Gifts and Social Change in Ancient Palestine: 1200 BCE to 200 CE* (Cambridge: Cambridge University Press, 2010).
Letellier, Robert Ignatius. *Creation, Sin and Reconciliation: Reading Primordial and Patriarchal Narrative in the Book of Genesis* (Newcastle upon Tyne: Cambridge Scholars Publishing, 2015).
Letellier, Robert Ignatius. *Day in Mamre, Night in Sodom: Abraham and Lot in Genesis 18 and 19* (Brill: Leiden, 1995).
Levenson, Jon D. 'The Conversion of Abraham', in *The Idea of Biblical Interpretation: Essays in Honour of James L. Kugel*, eds James L. Kugel, Judith H. Newman and Judith Hood Newman (Leiden: Brill, 2004).
Lewis, Laura A. 'Between Casta and Raza: The Example of Colonial Mexico', in *Race and Blood in the Iberian World*, eds María Elena Martínez, David Nirenberg and Max-Sebastián Hering Torres (Zurich: LIT Verlag, 2012).
Liebmann, Matthew and Uzma Z. Rizvi. *Archaeology and the Postcolonial Critique* (Lanham: Altamira Press, 2008).
Limbale, Sharan Kumar. *Towards an Aesthetic of Dalit Literature* (New Delhi: Orient Longman, 2004).
Lincoln, C. Eric. *Race, Religion, and the Continuing American Dilemma* (New York: Hill & Wang, 1984).
Lings, K. Renalo. 'Culture Clash in Sodom: Patriarchal Texts of Heroes, Villains and Manipulation', in *Patriarchs, Prophets and Other Villains*, ed. Lisa Isherwood (London: Routledge, 2014).
Lipner, Julius J. *Brahmabandhab Upadhyaya: The Life and Thought of a Revolutionary* (Oxford: Oxford University Press, 1999).
Lipner, Julius J. *Hindus: Their Religious Beliefs and Practices* (London: Routledge, 1994).
Lipton, Diana. *Revisions of the Night: Politics and Promises in the Patriarchal Dreams of Genesis* (Sheffield: Sheffield Academic Press, 1999).
Littman, Robert J. 'Athens, Persia and the Book of Ezra', *Transactions of the American Philological Association (1974–2014)* 125 (1995).
Liverani, Mario. *Israel's History and the History of Israel*, trans. Chiara Peri and Philip R. Davies (London: Equinox, 2005).
Loader, J. A. *A Tale of Two Cities: Sodom and Gomorrah in the Old Testament, Early Jewish and Early Christian Traditions* (Kampen: Peters Publishers, 1990).
Lobo, Lancy. 'Dalit Religious Movements and Dalit Identity', in *The Emerging Dalit Identity: The Re-assertion of the Subalterns*, ed. Walter Fernandes (New Delhi: Indian Social Institute, 1996).
Lobo, Lancy. 'Visions and Illusions of Dalit Christians in India', in *Dalit Identity and Politics*, ed. Ghanshyam Shah (Delhi: Sage Publications, 2001).

Lochtefeld, James G. *The Illustrated Encyclopaedia of Hinduism: N–Z* (New York: Rosen Publishing, 2002).
Lockyer, Herbert. *All the Miracles of the Bible* (Michigan: Zondervan, 1961).
Lohfink, Norbert. *Theology of the Pentateuch: Themes of the Priestly Narrative and Deuteronomy*, trans. L. Maloney (Minneapolis: Fortress Press, 1994).
Lohr, Joel N. *Chosen and Unchosen: Conceptions of Election in the Pentateuch and Jewish-Christian Interpretation* (Winona Lake: Eisenbrauns, 2009).
Long, Jesse C. *The College Press New Commentary: 1 & 2 Kings* (Joplin: College Press, 2002).
Longenecker, Richard N. *Introducing Romans: Critical Issues in Paul's Most Famous Letter* (Grand Rapids: William B. Eerdmans, 2011).
Longman, Tremper, III and Peter Enns. (eds) *Dictionary of the Old Testament: Wisdom, Poetry & Writings: A Compendium of Contemporary Biblical Scholarship* (Nottingham: InterVarsity Press, 2008).
Loomba, Ania. 'Marriage and the Liberal Imagination: Vijay Tendulkar's *Kanyadaan*', *Economic and Political Weekly* 47, no. 43 (October 26, 2013).
Louis, Prakash. 'Caste-Based Discrimination of Dalit Christians and the Demand for Reservation', in *Dalit and Minority Empowerment*, ed. Santosh Bhartiya (New Delhi: Rajkamal Prakashan, 2008).
Machinist, Peter. 'Biblical Traditions: The Philistines and Israelite History', in *The Sea Peoples and Their World: A Reassessment*, ed. Eliezer D. Oren (Philadelphia: The University Museum, 2000).
Machover, Moshé. *Israelis and Palestinians: Conflict and Resolution* (Chicago: Haymarket Books, 2012).
Macy, Jonathan. *In the Shadow of His Wings: The Pastoral Ministry of Angels: Yesterday, Today, and for Heaven* (Cambridge: Lutterworth Press, 2015).
Magallanes, Hugo. 'Preferential Option for the Poor', in *Dictionary of Scripture and Ethics*, ed. Joel B. Green (Grand Rapids: Baker Academic, 2011).
Majumdar, Shweta. 'Challenging the Master Frame through Dalit Organizing in the United States', in *Living Our Religions: Hindu and Muslim South Asian-American Women Narrate Their Experiences*, eds Anjana Narayan and Bandana Purkayastha (Sterling: Kumarian Press, 2009).
Majumdar, Uma. *Gandhi's Pilgrimage of Faith: From Darkness to Light* (Albany: State University of New York Press, 2005).
Malamat, A. 'Organs of Statecraft in the Israelite Monarchy', *Biblical Archaeologist* 28, no. 2 (1965).
Malāmāṭ, Avrāhām. *Mari and the Bible* (Leiden: Brill, 1998).
Malchow, Bruce V. *Social Justice in the Hebrew Bible* (Minnesota: The Liturgical Press, 1996).
Maliekal, John. *Caste in Indian Society* (Bangalore: CSA Publications, 1980).
Manchala, Deenabandhu. 'Expanding the Ambit: Dalit Theological Contribution to Ecumenical Social Thought', in *Dalit Theology in the Twenty-First Century: Discordant Voices, Discerning Pathways*, eds Sathianathan Clarke, Deenabandhu Manchala and Philip Vinod Peacock (Delhi: Oxford University Press, 2010).
Manchala, Deenabandhu. 'Migration: An Opportunity for Broader and Deeper Ecumenism', in *Theology of Migration in the Abrahamic Religions*, eds Elaine Padilla and Peter C. Phan (New York: Palgrave Macmillan, 2014).
Manorama, Ruth. 'Dalit Women in Struggle: Transforming Pain into Power', in *Life as a Dalit: Views from the Bottom on Caste in India*, eds Subhadra Mitra Channa and Joan P. Mencher (New Delhi: Sage Publications, 2013).

March, Eugene. *The Wide, Wide Circle of Divine Love: A Biblical Case for Religious Diversity* (Louisville: Westminster John Knox Press, 2005).
Margalit, Othniel. 'The Political Background of Zerubbabel's Mission and the Samaritan Schism', *Vetus Testamentum* 41, no. 3 (1991).
Marshall, John W. 'Postcolonialism and the Practice of History', in *Her Masters Tools? Feminist and Postcolonial Engagements of Historical-Critical Discourse*, eds Caroline Vander Stichele and Todd Penner (Atlanta: Society of Biblical Literature, 2005).
Martin, Chandran Paul. 'Globalisation and Its Impact on Dalits: A Theological Response', in *Globalisation and Its Impact on Dalits: A Theological Response*, ed. James Massey (New Delhi: Centre for Dalit/Subaltern Studies, 2004).
Masilamani-Meyer, Eveline. *Guardians of Tamil Nadu: Folk Deities, Folk Religion, Hindu Themes* (Halle: Frackesche Stiftungen zu Halle, 2004).
Massey, James. 'An Analysis of the Dalit Situation with Special Reference to Dalit Christians and Dalit Theology', *Religion and Society* 5, nos 3–4, 2007.
Massey, James. *Dalits in India: Religion as a Source of Bondage or Liberation with a Special Reference to Christians* (New Delhi: Manohar Publishers, 1995).
Massey, James. 'Historical Roots', in *Indigenous People: Dalits, Dalit Issues in Today's Theological Debate*, ed. James Massey (Delhi: Indian Society for Promoting Christian Knowledge, 1994).
Massey, James. (ed.) *Indigenous People: Dalits, Dalit Issues in Today's Theological Debate* (Delhi: Indian Society for Promoting Christian Knowledge, 1994).
Massey, James. 'Ingredients for a Dalit Theology', in *Indigenous People: Dalits: Dalit Issues in Today's Theological Debate*, ed. James Massey (New Delhi: Indian Society for Promoting Christian Knowledge, 1994).
Massey, James. 'A Review of Dalit Theology', in *Dalit and Minjung Theologies: A Dialogue*, eds Samson Prabhakar and Jinkwan Kwon (Bangalore: South Asia Theological Research Institute, 2006).
Massey, James. 'Revisiting and Resignifying the Methodology for Dalit Theology', in *Revisiting and Resignifying Methodology for Dalit Theology*, eds James Massey and Indukuri John Mohan Razu (New Delhi: Centre for Dalit/Subaltern Studies, 2008).
Massey, James. *Towards Dalit Hermeneutics: Re-reading the Text, the History and the Literature* (Delhi: Indian Society for Promoting Christian Knowledge, 1994).
Massey, James and Samson Prabhakar. (eds), *Frontiers in Dalit Hermeneutics* (Delhi: South Asia Theological Research Institute, 2005).
Massey, James and Shimreingam Shimray. (eds). *Dalit–Tribal Theological Interface: Current Trends in Subaltern Theologies* (New Delhi: Tribal Study Centre/Women Study Centre, 2007).
Massey, James, S. Razu Lourdunathan and I. John Mohan. (eds). *Breaking Theoretical Grounds for Dalit Studies* (New Delhi: Centre for Dalit/Subaltern Studies, 2006).
Mathews, Kenneth A. *Genesis 11:27–50:26* (Nashville: Boardman & Holman Publishers, 2005).
Matthews, Victor H. *Judges and Ruth* (Cambridge: Cambridge University Press, 2004).
Maurugkar, Lata. *Dalit Panther Movement in Maharashtra: A Sociological Approach* (London: Sangam Books, 1991).
Maver, Igor. 'Post-colonial Literatures in English ab origine ad futurum', in *Critics and Writers Speak: Revisioning Post-colonial Studies*, ed. Igor Maver (Lanham: Rowman & Littlefield, 2006).
Mayes, A. D. H. *Deuteronomy* (Grand Rapids: William B. Eerdmans, 1979).

Mayes, A. D. H. *The Story of Israel between Settlement and Exile: A Redactional Study of the Deuteronomistic History* (London: SCM Press, 1983).
Mbefo, Luke. 'Theology and Inculturation: Problems and Prospects – The Nigerian Experience', *The Nigerian Journal of Theology* 1, no. 1 (December 1985).
Mbonu, Caroline N. and Ngozi N. Iheanacho. 'Women & Intercultural Communication', in *Intercultural Communication and Public Policy*, ed. Ngozi Iheanacho(Port Harcourt: M & J Grand Orbit Communications, 2016).
McCarthy, D. J. *Treaty and Covenant: A Study in Form in the Ancient Oriental Documents and in the Old Testament* (Rome: Biblical Institute Press, 1981).
McGrath, Alister E. *Historical Theology: An Introduction to the History of Christian Thought* (Chichester: John Wiley, 2013).
McKenzie, Steven L. *All God's Children: A Biblical Critique of Racism* (Kentucky: Westminster John Knox Press, 1997).
McKenzie, Steven L. and John Kaltner. *The Old Testament: Its Background, Growth, & Content* (Nashville: Abingdon Press, 2007).
McKeown, James. *Genesis* (Michigan: William B. Eerdmans, 2008).
Meade, Teresa A. *History of Modern Latin America: 1800 to the Present* (Chichester: John Wiley, 2016).
Melanchthon, Monica Jyotsna. 'Liberation Hermeneutics and India's Dalits', in *The Bible and the Hermeneutics of Liberation*, eds Alejandro F. Botta and Pablo R. Andiñach (Atlanta: Society of Biblical Literature, 2009).
Melanchthon, Monica Jyotsna. 'Towards Mapping Feminist Biblical Interpretations in Asia', in *Feminist Biblical Studies in the Twentieth Century: Scholarship and Movement*, ed. Elisabeth Schussler Fiorenza (Atlanta: Society of Biblical Literature, 2014).
Menn, Esther Marie. *Judah and Tamar (Genesis 38) in Ancient Jewish Exegesis: Studies in Literary Form and Hermeneutics* (Leiden: Brill, 1997).
Menon, P. K. K. *The History of Freedom Movement in Kerala (1885–1938)* (Thiruvananthapuram: Department of Cultural Publications, 2001).
Menon, Ramesh. *The Ramayana: A Modern Retelling of the Great Indian Epic* (New York: North Point Press, 2001).
Menon, Sreedhara. *A Survey of Kerala History* (Chennai: S. Viswanathan Printers and Publishers, 2005).
Mettinger, T. N. D. 'King and Messiah: The Civil and Sacral Legitimation of the Israelite Kings', *Coniectanea Biblica*, Old Testament Series, no. 8 (Lund: Lund University, 1976).
Michael, Matthew. *Yahweh's Elegant Speeches of the Abrahamic Narratives: A Study of the Stylistics; Characterizations; and Functions of the Divine Speeches in Abrahamic Narratives* (Carlisle: Langham Monographs, 2014).
Michael, S. M. 'Dalit Encounter with Christianity: Change and Continuity', in *Margins of Faith: Dalit and Tribal Christianity in India*, eds Rowena Robinson and Joseph Marianus Kujur (New Delhi: Sage Publications, 2010).
Michael, S. M. *Dalits in Modern India: Vision and Values* (New Delhi: Sage Publications, 2007).
Michaels, Axel. *Hinduism: Past and Present*, trans. Barbara Harshav (Princeton: Princeton University Press, 2004).
Migliore, Daniel L. *Faith Seeking Understanding: An Introduction to Christian Theology* (Grand Rapids: William B. Eerdmans, 2014).
Milgrom, Jacob. 'Religious Conversion and the Revolt Model for the Formation of Israel', *Journal of Biblical Literature* 101 (1982).

Mishra, Vijay. *Devotional Poetics and the Indian Sublime* (Albany: State University of New York Press, 1998).

Mistry, Rohinton. *A Fine Balance* (New Delhi: Rupa, 1996).

Moberly, R. W. L. 'Abraham and Aeneas: Genesis as Israel's Foundation Story', in *Genesis and Christian Theology*, eds Nathan MacDonald, Mark W. Elliot and Grant Macaskill (Michigan: William B. Eerdmans, 2012).

Moberly, R. W. L. *The Bible, Theology, and Faith: A Study of Abraham and Jesus* (Cambridge: Cambridge University Press, 2000).

Moffat, Donald P. *Ezra's Social Drama: Identity Formation, Marriage and Social Conflict in Ezra 9 and 10* (New York: Bloomsbury, 2013).

Mohan, P. Sanal. 'Religion, Social Space, and Identity: The Prathyaksha Raksha Daiva Sabha and the Making of Cultural Boundaries in Twentieth Century Kerala', in *Life as a Dalit: Views from the Bottom on Caste in India*, eds Subhadra Mitra Channa and Joan P. Mencher (New Delhi: Sage Publications, 2013).

Mohanty, Ramesh P. *Dalits Development and Change: An Empirical Study* (New Delhi: Discovery Publishing House, 2003).

Mohini Giri, V. *Deprived Devils: Women's Unequal Status in Society* (New Delhi: Gyan Publishing House, 2006).

Mongstad-Kvammen, Ingeborg. *Toward a Postcolonial Reading of the Epistle of James: James 2:1–13 in Its Roman Imperial Context* (Leiden: Brill, 2013).

Moore, Megan Bishop and Brad E. Kelle. *Biblical History and Israel's Past: The Changing Study of the Bible and History* (Michigan: William B. Eerdmans, 2011).

Moore, Stephen D. 'What Is Postcolonial Studies? Paul after Empire', in *The Colonized Apostle: Paul through Postcolonial Eyes*, ed. Stephen D. Moore (Minneapolis: Fortress Press, 2011).

Moore, Stephen D. and Fernando F. Segovia. 'Postcolonial Biblical Criticism: Beginnings, Trajectories, Intersections', in *Postcolonial Biblical Criticism: Interdisciplinary Intersections*, eds Stephen D. Moore and Fernando F. Segovia (London: T&T Clark International, 2005).

Mor Coorilos, Geevarghese. 'God of life, Lead Us to Justice and Peace: Some Missiological Perspectives', *International Review of Mission*, no.1 (2013).

Moran, W. L. 'A Note on the Treaty Terminology of the Sefire Stelas', *Journal of Near Eastern Studies* 22 (1963).

Moriuchi, Mey-Yen. 'From *Casta* to *Costumbrismo*: Representations of Racialized Social Spaces', in *Envisioning Others: Race, Color, and the Visual in Iberia and Latin America*, ed. Pamela P. Patton (Leiden: Brill, 2016).

Morrow, Raymond Allen and Carlos Alberto Torres. *Reading Freire and Habermas: Critical Pedagogy and Transformative Social Change* (New York: Teachers College Press, 2002).

Moxham, Roy. *Outlaw: India's Bandit Queen and Me* (London: Rider, 2010).

Moy, José C., Adriana Brodsky and Raanan Rein. 'The Jewish Experience in Argentina in a Diaspora Comparative Perspective', in *The New Jewish Argentina: Facets of Jewish Experiences in the Southern Cone*, eds Adriana Brodsky and Raanan Rein (Leiden: Brill, 2013).

Mukherjee, Arun Prabha. 'Introduction', in *Joothan: An Untouchable's Life*, ed. Omprakash Valmiki, trans. Arun Prabha Mukherjee (New York: Columbia University Press, 2003).

Mundadan, A. Mathias. *History of Christianity in India: From the Beginning up to the Middle of the Sixteenth Century (Up to 1542)* (Bangalore: Theological Publication of India, 1989).

Mundadan, A. Mathias. *Traditions of St. Thomas Christians* (Bangalore: Dharmaram, 1970).
Murthy, Kusuma Krishna. 'Ineffective Control of Violence against Harijans', in *Untouchable! Voices of the Dalit Liberation Movement*, ed. Barbara Joshi (London: Zed Books, 1986).
Nair, Balachandran. (ed.) *In Quest of Kerala* (Trivandrum: Access Publications, 1974).
Narayan, Badri. *Women Heroes and Dalit Assertion in North India: Culture, Identity and Politics* (New Delhi: Sage Publications, 2006).
Narula, Smita. *Broken People: Caste Violence against India's 'Untouchables'* (New York: Human Rights Watch, 1999).
Nehring, Daniel and Ken Plummer. *Sociology: An Introductory Textbook and Reader* (London: Routledge, 2013).
Nelavala, Surekha. 'Inclusivity and Distinctions: The Future of Dalit Feminist Biblical Studies', in *New Feminist Christianity: Many Voices, Many Views*, eds Mary E. Hunt and Diann L. Neu (Woodstock: Skylight Paths Publishing, 2010).
Nelavala, Surekha. *Liberation beyond Borders: Dalit Feminist Hermeneutics and Four Gospel Women* (New Jersey: Drew University, 2008).
Nesiah, Vasuki. 'Federalism and Diversity in India', in *Autonomy and Ethnicity: Negotiating Competing Claims in Multi-ethnic States*, ed. Yash Ghai (Cambridge: Cambridge University Press, 2000).
Nessan, Craig L. *The Vitality of Liberation Theology* (Eugene: Pickwick Publications, 2012).
Ngong, Tonghou. 'Theological Significance of Africa and Africans in the Bible', in *A New History of African Christian Thought: From Cape to Cairo*, ed. David Tonghou Ngong (New York: Routledge, 2017).
Nicholson, Ernest. *The Pentateuch in the Twentieth Century: The Legacy of Julius Wellhausen* (Oxford: Oxford University Press, 1998).
Niditch, Susan. 'Genesis', in *The Women's Bible Commentary*, eds Carol A. Newsom and Sharon H. Ringe (Louisville: Westminster John Knox Press, 1992).
Niditch, Susan. *A Prelude to Biblical Folklore: Underdogs and Tricksters* (Chicago: University of Illinois Press, 2000).
Nimavat, B. S. 'Chokhamela: The Pioneer of Untouchable Movement in Maharashtra', in *Dalit Literature: A Critical Exploration*, eds Amar Nath Prasad and M. B. Gaijan (New Delhi: Sarup, 2007).
Nirmal, A. P. 'A Dialogue with Dalit Literature', in *Towards a Dalit Theology*, ed. M. E. Prabhakar (Delhi: Indian Society for Promoting Christian Knowledge, 1988).
Nirmal, A. P. (ed.) *Heuristic Explorations* (Madras: Christian Literature Society, 1990).
Nirmal, A. P. *A Reader in Dalit Theology* (Madras: Gurukul Lutheran Theological College and Research Institute, 1991).
Nirmal, A. P. 'Towards a Christian Dalit Theology', in *Frontiers in Asian Christian Theology: Emerging Trends*, ed. R. S. Sugirtharajah (Maryknoll: Orbis Books, 1994).
Nirmal, A. P. 'Towards a Christian Dalit Theology', in *Indigenous People: Dalits, Dalit Issues in Today's Theological Debate*, ed. James Massey (Delhi: Indian Society for Promoting Christian Knowledge, 1998).
Nirmal, A. P. 'Towards a Dalit Theology', in *Emerging Dalit Theology*, ed. Xavier Irudayaraj (Madras: Jesuit Theological Secretariat, 1990).
Noll, K. L. *Canaan and Israel in Antiquity: An Introduction* (London: Sheffield Academic Press, 2001).

North, Christopher R. *The Suffering Servant in Deutero-Isaiah: An Historical and Critical Study* (Eugene: Wipf and Stock, 2005).
Noth, Martin. *A History of Pentateuchal Traditions* (Englewood Cliffs: Prentice-Hall 1972).
Oliveros, Roberto. 'History of the Theology of Liberation', in *Mysterium Liberationis: Fundamental Concepts of Liberation Theology*, eds Ignacio Ellacuria and Jon Sobrino (Maryknoll: Orbis Books, 1989).
Olthuis, James H. 'Face to Face: Ethical Asymmetry or the Symmetry of Mutuality?', in *Knowing Otherwise: Philosophy at the Threshold of Spirituality*, ed. James H. Olthuis (New York: Fordham University Press, 1997).
Omvedt, Gail. 'The Anti-caste Movement and the Discourse of Power', in *Region, Religion, Caste, Gender and Culture in Contemporary India*, ed. T. Sahithyamurthy (Delhi: Oxford University Press, 1996).
Omvedt, Gail. *Buddhism in India: Challenging Brahmanism and Caste* (New Delhi: Sage Publications, 2003).
Omvedt, Gail. *Dalits and the Democratic Revolution: Dr Ambedkar and the Dalit Movement in Colonial India* (New Delhi: Sage Publications, 1994).
Omvedt, Gail. *Reinventing Revolution: New Social Movements and the Socialist Tradition in India* (New York: An East Gate Book, 1993).
Oommen, George. 'Majoritarian Nationalism and the Identity Politics of Dalits in Post-independent India', in *The God of All Grace: Essays in Honour of Orgien Vasantha Jathanna*, ed. Joseph George (Bangalore: Asian Trading Corporation and the United Theological College, 2005).
Orlinsky, Harry M. *Notes on the New Translation of the Torah* (Philadelphia: Jewish Publication Society, 1969).
Osthathios, Geevarghese Mar. *Theology of a Classless Society* (Maryknoll: Orbis Press, 1980).
Otzen, Benedikt. 'Israel under the Assyrians. Reflections on Imperial Policy in Palestine', in *Annual of the Swedish Theological Institute*, vol. 11, ed. Gerhard Larsson (Leiden: Brill, 1978).
Pandey, Gyanendra. *A History of Prejudice: Race, Caste, and Difference in India and the United States* (New York: Cambridge University Press, 2013).
Paratt, John. 'Recent Writing on Dalit Theology: A Bibliographical Essay', *International Review of Mission* 83, no. 329 (1994).
Paul, S. K. 'Dalit Literature and Dalit Poetry', in *Dalit Literature: A Critical Exploration*, eds Amar Nath Prasad and M. B. Gaijan (New Delhi: Sarup, 2007).
Payne, Richard J. and Jamal Nassar. *Politics and Culture in the Developing World* (London: Routledge, 2016).
Pearson, Andrew F. *Distant Freedom: St Helena and the Abolition of the Slave Trade, 1840–1872* (Liverpool: Liverpool University Press, 2016).
Perdue, Leo G. *Reconstructing Old Testament Theology: After the Collapse of History* (Minneapolis: Augsburg Fortress, 2005).
Pesando, Michelle. *Why God Doesn't Hate You* (Bloomington: Balboa Press, 2014).
Petersen, D. L. 'A Thrice-Told Tale: Genre, Theme and Motif', *Bible Review* 18 (1973).
Petersen, D. L. *Method Matters: Essays on the Interpretation of the Hebrew Bible in Honour of David L. Petersen* (Atlanta: Society of Biblical Literature, 2009).
Petretti, Yael. 'Listening out Way to Peace', in *Making Peace with Faith: The Challenges of Religion and Peacebuilding*, eds Michelle Garred and Mohammed Abu-Nimer (Lanham: Rowman & Littlefield, 2018).

Phan, Peter C. 'A Common Journey, Different Paths, the Same Destination: Method in Liberation Theologies', in *A Dream Unfinished: Theological Reflections on America from the Margins*, eds Eleazar S. Fernandez and Fernando F. Segovia (Eugene: Wipf and Stock, 2005).

Philip, E. M. *The Indian Church of St. Thomas* (Puthencruz: Mor Adai Study Centre, 2014).

Phillips, Douglas A. and Charles F. Gritzner. *India* (Philadelphia: Chelsea House Publications, 2003).

Phipps, William E. *Assertive Biblical Women* (London: Greenwood Press, 1992).

Pieris, Aloysius. *An Asian Theology of Liberation* (Edinburgh: T&T Clark, 1988).

Pieterse, Hendrik J. C. 'South African Liberation Theology', in *Desmond Tutu's Message: A Qualitative Analysis*, ed. H. J. C. Pieterse (Leiden: Brill, 2001).

Pillai, Elamkulam Kunjan. *Studies in Kerala History* (Kottayam: National Book Stall, 1970).

Pinn, Anthony B. 'Black Theology', in *Liberation Theologies in the United States: An Introduction*, eds Stacey M. Floyd-Thomas and Anthony B. Pinn (New York: New York University Press, 2010).

Pinn, Anthony B. *Embodiment and the New Shape of Black Theological Thought* (New York: New York University Press, 2010).

Podipara, Placid J. 'Hindu in Culture, Christian in Religion, Oriental in Worship', in *The St. Thomas Christian Encyclopaedia of India*, ed. George Menachery (Trichur: The St Thomas Christian Encyclopaedia of India, 1973).

Podipara, Placid J. *The Thomas Christians* (London: Longman & Todd, 1970).

Popovic, Malden. 'Conquest of the Land, Loss of the Land', in *The Land of Israel in Bible, History, and Theology: Studies in Honor of Ed Noort*, eds Jacques Van Ruiten and J. Cornelis de Vos (Leiden: Brill, 2009).

Poruthur, A. 'A Decade of Dialoguing: A Non-Elitist Approach', *Mission Today* 2 (2000).

Pottenger, John R. *The Political Theory of the Liberation Theology: Toward a Reconvergence of Social Values and Social Science* (Albany: University of New York Press, 1989).

Prabhakar, Anuparthi John. *Preaching Contextually: A Case with Rural Dalits in India* (Chennai: Notion Press, 2016).

Prabhakar, M. E. 'Introduction', in *Towards a Dalit Theology*, ed. M. E. Prabhakar (Delhi: The Indian Society for Promoting Christian Knowledge, 1989).

Prabhakar, M. E. 'The Search for a Dalit Theology', in *Indigenous People: Dalits, Dalit Issues in Today's Theological Debate*, ed. James Massey (Delhi: Indian Society for Promoting Christian Knowledge, 1998).

Prabhakar, M. E. (ed.) *Towards a Dalit Theology* (Delhi: Indian Society for Promoting Christian Knowledge, 1998).

Prahalladappa, M. H. 'Impact of DSS and Dalit Movement on Emerging Dalit Leadership in Karnataka', *Research Directions* 1, no. 2 (August 2013).

Prasad, Leela. 'Hinduism in South India', in *Hinduism in the Modern World*, ed. Brian A. Hatcher (New York: Routledge, 2016).

Prasuna, N. G. 'The Dalit Woman', in *Frontiers of Dalit Theology*, ed. V. Devasahayam (Delhi: Indian Society for Promoting Christian Knowledge, 1996).

Prior, John Mansford. 'Unfinished Encounter: A Note on the Voice and Tone of Ecclesia in Asia', *East Asian Pastoral Review* 37 (2000).

Prior, Michael. *The Bible and Colonialism: A Moral Critique* (Sheffield: Sheffield Academic Press, 1999).

Prior, Michael. *Jesus the Liberator: Nazareth Liberation Theology (Luke 4:16–30)* (Sheffield: Sheffield Academic Press, 1995).

Priyadarsan, G. (ed.) *S. N. D. P. Yogam Platinum Jubilee Souvenir* (Quilon: Jubilee Celebration Committee, 1978).

Prokopy, Joshua and Christian Smith. 'Introduction', in *Latin American Religion in Motion*, eds Christian Smith, Christian Stephen Smith and Joshua Prokopy (New York: Routledge, 1999).

Provan, Iain. *Discovering Genesis: Content, Interpretation, Reception* (Grand Rapids: William B. Eerdmans, 2015).

Puett, Terry. *The Book of Genesis* (Pueblo: P & L Publications, 2013).

Pui-lan, Kwok. 'Making the Connections: Postcolonial Studies and Feminist Biblical Interpretation', in *The Postcolonial Biblical Reader*, ed. R. S. Sugirtharajah (London: Blackwell Publishing, 2006).

Pui-lan, Kwok. *Postcolonial Imagination and Feminist Theology* (Louisville: Westminster John Knox Press, 2005).

Pulikottil, Paulson. 'Ramankutty Paul: A Dalit Contribution to Pentecostalism', in *Asian and Pentecostal: The Charismatic Face of Christianity in Asia*, eds Allan Anderson and Edmond Tang (Oxford: Regnum Books International, 2005).

Pundir, Jagdish Kumar. 'Dalits in India: Past Identities and Present Scenario', in *Emerging Social Science Concerns: Festschrift in Honour of Professor Yogesh Atal*, ed. Surendra K. Gupta (New Delhi: Concept Publishing, 2007).

Punt, Jeremy. 'Discerning Empire in Biblical Studies: Tools of the Trade', *The New Testament in the Graeco-Roman World: Articles in Honour of Abe Malherbe*, eds Marius Nel, Jan G. van der Watt and Fika J. van Rensburg (Zurich: LIT Verlag).

Punt, Jeremy. *Postcolonial Biblical Interpretation: Reframing Paul* (Boston: Brill, 2015).

Purushotham, K. 'Resisting Assimilation: A Reading of Daniel Fuchs' *Summer in Williamsburg*', *Kakatiya Journal of English Studies* 21 (2001).

Raja, A. Maria Arul. 'Breaking Hegemonic Boundaries: An Intertextual Reading of the Madurai Veeran Legend and Mark's Story of Jesus', in *Voices from the Margin: Interpreting the Bible in the World*, ed. R. S. Sugirtharajah (Maryknoll: Orbis Books, 2006).

Rajkumar, Peniel. *Dalit Theology and Dalit Liberation: Problems, Paradigms and Possibilities* (Surrey: Ashgate Publishing, 2010).

Rajkumar, Peniel. 'A Dalithos Reading of a Markan Exorcism: Mark 5:1–20', *The Expository Times* 118, no. 9 (2007).

Rajkumar, Peniel. 'How Does the Bible Mean? The Bible and Dalit Liberation in India', *Political Theology* 11, no. 3 (2010).

Rajkumar, Peniel. 'In Witness to God's "With-ness": Dalit Theology, the God of Life, and the Path Towards Justice and Peace', *The Ecumenical Review* 64, no. 4 (2012).

Rakotsoane, Francis C. L. 'Major Themes in Black Theology', in *Biblical Studies, Theology, Religion and Philosophy: An Introduction for African Universities*, eds J. N. Amenze, F. Nkomazana and O. N. Kealotswe (Eldoref: Zapf Chancery Research Consultants and Publishers, 2010).

Ralph, Margaret Nutting. *And, God Said What? An Introduction to Biblical Literary Forms* (New York: Paulist Press, 1986).

Rao, Naveen. *The Formulation of Scripture: Liberative Hebrew Paradigm for Dalit Scripture* (Delhi: Indian Society for Promoting Christian Knowledge, 2010).

Rao, N. Sudhakar. 'A Reconsideration of the Structural Replication in the Tamil Untouchable Castes in South India', *Religion and Society* 45, no. 3 (1998).

Rashidi, Runoko. 'Dalits: The Black Untouchables of India', in *Encyclopedia of the African Diaspora: Origins, Experiences, and Culture*, ed. Carole Boyce Davies (Santa Barabara: ABC-Clio, 2008).
Rasquinha, Dionysius. 'A Brief Historical Analysis of the Emergence of Dalit Christian Theology', *Vidyajyoti Journal of Theological Reflection* 66 (May 2002).
Rayan, Samuel. 'The Challenge of the Dalit Issue', in *Dalits and Women: Quest for Humanity*, ed. V. Devasahayam (Madras: Gurukul Lutheran Theological College and Research Institute, 1992).
Razu, I. John Mohan. *Globalization and Dalitho-Ethics: Interrelationships between Homoeconomics and Homo-hierarchicus* (New Delhi: Centre for Dalit/Subaltern Studies, 2004).
Reddie, Anthony G. *Black Theology* (London: SCM Press, 2012).
Reddie, Anthony G. *Black Theology in Transatlantic Dialogue* (New York: Palgrave Macmillan, 2006).
Reddy, Deepa S. *Religious Identity and Political Destiny: Hindutva in the Culture of Ethnicism* (Oxford: Altamira Press, 2006).
Reddy, G. Prakash. 'Caste and Christianity: A Study of Shudra Caste Converts in Rural Andhra Pradesh', in *Religion and Society in South India*, eds V. Sudarsan, G. Prakash Reddy and M. Suryanarayana (Delhi: B. R. Publishing, 1987).
Regan, Ethna. *Theology and the Boundary Discourse of Human Rights* (Washington: Georgetown University Press, 2010).
Rege, Sharmila. *Writing Caste/Writing Gender: Narrating Dalit Women's Testimonies* (New Delhi: Subaan, 2013).
Reid-Salmon, Delroy A. *Home Away from Home: The Caribbean Diasporan Church in the Black Atlantic Tradition* (London: Routledge, 2014).
Reuther, Rosemary Radford. 'Is Christ White? Racism and Christology', in *Christology and Whiteness: What Would Jesus Do?* ed. George Yancy (London: Routledge, 2012).
Richard, Pablo. '1492: The Violence of God and the Future of Christianity', in *1492–1992: The Voice of the Victims*, eds Leonardo Boff and Virgilio Elizondo (London: SCM Press, 1990).
Richard, Pablo. 'Biblical Interpretation from the Perspective of Indigenous Cultures of Latin America (Mayas, Kunas, and Queschuas)', in *Ethnicity and the Bible*, eds Mark G. Brett (Boston: Brill Publishers, 2002).
Richman, Paula. *Ramayana Stories in Modern South India: An Anthology* (Bloomington: Indiana University Press, 2008).
Riskin, Shlomo. *The Passover Haggadah with a Traditional and Contemporary Commentary by Rabbi Shlomo Riskin* (New York: Ktav Publishing, 1983).
Ritter, Francis D. *Sex, Lies and the Bible: The Controlling of Human Sexual Behavior Through the Corruption of the Bible* (Oceanside: Diverse Publications, 2006).
Robinson, Rowena. *Christians of India* (New Delhi: Sage Publications, 2003).
Robles, Wilder. 'Liberation Theology, Christian Base Communities, and Solidarity Movements: A Historical Reflection', in *Capital, Power, and Inequality in Latin America and the Caribbean*, eds Richard L. Harris and Jorge Nef (Lanham: Rowman & Littlefield, 2008).
Römer, Thomas. 'Conflicting Models of Identity and the Publication of the Torah in the Persian Period', in *Between Cooperation and Hostility: Multiple Identities in Ancient Judaism and the Interaction with Foreign Powers*, eds Rainer Albertz and Jakob Wöhrle (Gottingen: Vandenhoeck & Ruprecht, 2013).

Römer, Thomas. 'Deuteronomy in Search of Origins', in *Reconsidering Israel and Judah: Recent Studies on the Deuteronomistic History*, eds Gary N. Knoppers and J. Gordon McConville (Winona Lake: Eisenbrauns, 2000).
Römer, Thomas and Jean Daniel-Macchi. 'Luke, Disciple of the Deuteronomistic School', in *Luke's Literary Achievement*, ed. C. M. Tuckett (Sheffield: Sheffield Academic Press, 1995).
Ruether, Rosemary Radford. 'Women and Interfaith Relations: Toward a Transitional Feminism', in *Women and Interreligious Dialogue*, eds Catherine Cornille and Jillian Maxey (Eugene: Cascade Books, 2013).
Ruiz, Jean-Pierre. 'An Exile's Baggage: Toward a Postcolonial Reading of Ezekiel', in *Approaching Yehud: New Approaches to the Study of the Persian Period*, ed. Jon L. Berquist (Atlanta: Society of Biblical Literature, 2007).
Sadangi, H. C. *Emancipation of Dalits and Freedom Struggle* (Delhi: Isha Books, 2008).
Said, Edward. *Orientalism: Western Conceptions of the Orient* (London: Penguin Books, 1978).
Sailhamer, John H. 'Genesis', in *The Expositor's Bible Commentary: Genesis-Leviticus*, eds Tremper Longman III and David E Garland (Michigan: Zondervan, 2009).
Sailhamer, John H. *The Meaning of the Pentateuch: Revelation, Composition and Interpretation* (Illinois: IVP Academic, 2009).
Salveson, Alison. 'Keeping It in the Family? Jacob and His Aramean Heritage according to Jewish and Christian Sources', in *The Exegetical Encounter Between Jews and Christians in Late Antiquity*, eds E. Grypeou and H. Spurling (Boston: Brill, 2009).
Samartha, S. J. 'The Cross and the Rainbow', in *The Myth of Christian Uniqueness: Toward a Pluralistic Theology of Religions*, eds John Hick and Paul F. Knitter (Eugene: Wipf and Stock, 1987).
Samartha, S. J. *One Christ – Many Religions: Toward a Revised Christology* (Eugene: Wipf and Stock, 2015).
Samuel, Joshua. 'Practicing Multiple Religious Belonging for Liberation: A Dalit Perspective', *Current Dialogue* 57 (December 2015).
Samuel, Joshua. *Untouchable Bodies, Resistance, and Liberation: A Comparative Theology of Divine Possessions* (Leiden: Brill, 2020).
Sanders, James A. *God Has a Story Too: Sermons in Context* (Eugene: Wipf and Stock, 2000).
Sanoo, M. K. *Narayana Guru* (Bombay: Bhartiya Vidya Bhavan, 1978).
Sateren, Shelley Swanson. *Michelangelo* (Mankato: Bridgestone Books, 2002).
Satyanarayana, A. *Dalits and Upper Castes: Essays in Social History* (New Delhi: Kanishka Publishers, 2005).
Saxegaard, Kristin Moen. *Character Complexity in the Book of Ruth* (Tübingen: Mohr Siebeck, 2010).
Schmid, Konrad. *Genesis and the Moses Story: Israel's Dual Origins in the Hebrew Bible*, trans. James Nogalski (Winona Lake: Eisenbrauns, 2010).
Schneller, J. Peter 'Christ and Church: A Spectrum of Views', *Theological Studies* 37 (1976).
Schreiber, Mordecai. *The Man Who Knew God: Decoding Jeremiah* (Lanham: Lexington Books, 2010).
Schwarz, Hans. *Theology in a Global Context: The Last Two Hundred Years* (Grand Rapids: William B. Eerdmans, 2005).
Schweitzer, Don. 'Two Theological Movements in India That Complicate Western Reformed Identities', *Toronto Journal of Theology* 28, no. 2 (2012).

Schwienhorst, Munster L. 'נגע Nega Touch Afflict Reach', in *Theological Dictionary of the Old Testament*, vol. 9, eds G. Johannes Botterweck, Helmer Ringgren and Heinz-Josef Fabry, trans. David E. Green (Grand Rapids: William B. Eerdmans, 1998).
Scott, David C. 'The Rough Rhetoric of Kabir', in *Doing Theology with the Poetic Traditions of India*, ed. Joseph Patmury (Bangalore: PTCA/SATHRI, 1996).
Segal, Alan. *Sinning in the Hebrew Bible: How the Worst Stories Speak for Its Truth* (New York: Columbia University Press, 2012).
Segovia, Fernando F. 'Mapping the Postcolonial Optic in Biblical Criticism: Meaning and Scope', in *Postcolonial Biblical Criticism: Interdisciplinary Intersections*, eds Stephen D. Moore and Fernando F. Segovia (London: T&T Clark, 2005).
Selmon, Stephen. 'The Scramble for Post-colonialism', in *The Post-colonial Studies Reader*, eds Bill Ashcroft, Gareth Griffiths and Helen Tiffin (London: Routledge, 2004).
Sen, Amartya. *Development as Freedom* (Oxford: Oxford University Press, 2001).
Sen, Keshab Chandra. *India Asks, Who Is Christ?* (Calcutta: The Indian Mirror Press, 1879).
Seters, J. Van. *Abraham in History and Tradition* (New Haven: Yale University Press, 1975).
Seters, J. Van. 'Joshua 24 and the Problem of Tradition in the Old Testament', in *In the Shelter of Elyon: Essays on Ancient Palestinian Life and Literature in Honor of G.W. Ahlström*, eds W. B. Barrick and J. R. Spencer (Sheffield: JSOT Press, 1984).
Seters, J. Van. *Prologue to History: The Yahwist as Historian in Genesis* (Kentucky: Westminster John Knox Press, 1992).
Shah, Ghanshyam. *Social Movements in India: A Review of Literature* (New Delhi: Sage Publications, 2004).
Shannahan, Chris. *Voices from the Borderland: Re-imagining Cross-Cultural Urban Theology in the Twenty-First Century* (London: Routledge, 2016).
Shapiro, H. Svi. 'All We Are Saying: Identity, Communal Strife, and the Possibility of Peace', in *Examining Social Theory: Crossing Borders/Reflecting Back*, ed. Daniel Ethan Chapman (New York: Peter Lang, 2010).
Sharma, Pradeep. *Human Geography: The Land* (New Delhi: Discovery Publishing House, 2007).
Sharp, Carolyn J. *Wrestling the Word: The Hebrew Scriptures and the Christian Believer* (Louisville: Westminster John Knox Press, 2010).
Sharpe, Eric J. 'The Goals of Inter-Religious Dialogue', in *Truth and Dialogue in World Religions: Conflicting Truth Claims*, ed. John Hick (Philadelphia: Westminster Press, 1974).
Sherwood, Yvonne. 'The Hagaramic and the Abrahamic; or Abraham the Non-European', in *Reading the Abrahamic Faiths: Rethinking Religion and Literature*, ed. Emma Mason (London: Bloomsbury Academic, 2016).
Shetty, Y. Rajshekhar. *Dalit: The Black Untouchables of India* (Atlanta: Clarity Press, 1987).
Shinde, F. M. 'Habit', in *No Entry for the New Sun: Translations from Modern Marathi Dalit Poetry*, ed. Arjun Dangle, trans. Priya Adarkar (Bombay: Orient Longman, 1992).
Shrimali, Chandrabahen.'Paradise, at a Stone's Throw Distance', in *Valonum* (Gandhinagar, 2007), Chapter 5: Aesthetics of Dalit Poetry, accessed on 17 May 2022, https://kipdf.com/chapter-aesthetics-of-dalit-poetry_5ae66fcf7f8b9ad4718b458f.html.
Shukla, Usha Devi. *Rāmacaritamānasa in South Africa* (Delhi: Motilal Banarsidass Publishers, 2002).
Sikand, Yoginder. *Muslims in India since 1947: Islamic Perspectives on Inter-Faith Relations* (London: Routledge, 2004).

Singaram, Charles. *The Question of Method in Dalit Theology: In Search of a Systematic Approach to the Practice of an Indian Liberation Theology* (Delhi: Indian Society for Promoting Christian Knowledge, 2008).

Singh, K. P. 'Liberation Movements in Comparative Perspective: Dalit Indians and Black Americans', in *Dalits in Modern India: Vision and Values*, ed. S. M. Michael (New Delhi: Sage Publications, 2007).

Singh, Rattan and Mamta Mehmi. 'Constitutional Protection to the Dalits: A Myth or Reality?', in *Dalit and Minority Empowerment*, ed. Santosh Bhartiya (New Delhi: Raj Kamal Prakashan, 2008).

Singh, Roja. *Spotted Goddesses: Dalit Women's Agency – Narratives on Caste and Gender Violence* (Berlin: LIT Verlag, 2018).

Singleton, Harry H. *Black Theology and Ideology: Deideological Dimensions in the Theology of James H. Cone* (Minnesota: Liturgical Press, 2002).

Sinha, Jai B. P. *Psycho-social Analysis of the Indian Mindset* (New Delhi: Springer, 2014).

Ska, Jean Louis. *The Exegesis of the Pentateuch: Exegetical Studies and Basic Questions* (Tübingen: Mohr Siebeck, 2009).

Ska, Jean Louis. *Introduction to Reading the Pentateuch*, trans. Sr. Pascale Dominique (Winona Lake: Eisenbrauns, 2006).

Skaria, Jobymon. 'Reading the Promises to Abraham in Genesis 12:1-3 through the Post-exilic Deuteronomic Eyes', *Vidyajyoti Journal of Theological Reflection*, 81, no. 9 (September 2017).

Skaria, Jobymon. 'Reimagining Moab and Ammon: Genesis 19:30-38 through Persian Imperialism', *Hekamtho: Syrian Orthodox Theological Journal* 3 (November 2017).

Skinner, J. *A Critical and Exegetical Commentary on Genesis* (Edinburgh: T&T Clark, 1912).

Smith, Christian. *The Emergence of Liberation Theology: Radical Religion and Social Movement Theory* (Chicago: University of Chicago Press, 1991).

Smith, James E. *The Pentateuch* (Joplin: College Press, 2006).

Snyder, Terri L. *The Power to Die: Slavery and Suicide in British North America* (Chicago: University of Chicago Press, 2015).

Snyman, Gerrie F. 'A Possible World of Text Production for the Genealogy in 1 Chronicles 2.3-4.23', in *The Chronicler as Theologian*, eds M. Patrick Graham, Gary N. Knoppers and Steven L. McKenzie (New York: T&T Clark, 2003).

Soares-Prabhu, George M. 'Exodus 20:1-17: An Asian Perspective', in *Return to Babel: Global Perspectives on the Bible*, eds John R. Levison and Priscilla Pope Levison (Louisville: Westminster John Knox Press, 1999).

Sobrino, Jon. *Christology at the Crossroads: A Latin America Approach*, trans. John Drury (Maryknoll: Orbis Books, 1978).

Sobrino, Jon. *Jesus the Liberator: A Historical Theological Reading of Jesus of Nazareth*, trans. Paul Burns and Francis McDonagh (Maryknoll: Orbis Books, 1993).

Sorett, Josef. 'African American Theology and the American Hemisphere', in *The Oxford Handbook of African American Theology*, eds Katie G. Cannon and Anthony B. Pinn (Oxford: Oxford University Press, 2014).

Sperling, S. David. *The Original Torah: The Political Intent of the Bible's Writers* (New York: New York University Press, 1998).

Sreekantaiya, T. Nanjundaiya. *Indian Poetics*, trans. N. Balasubrahmanya (New Delhi: Sahitya Academy, 2001).

Srivastava, S. P. 'Unravelling the Dynamics of Dalit Oppression', in *Social Exclusion: Essays in Honour of Dr. Bindeshwar Pathak*, ed. A. K. Lal (New Delhi: Concept Publishing, 2003).
Stanislaus, L. *The Liberative Mission of the Church among Dalit Christians* (Delhi: Indian Society for Promoting Christian Knowledge, 1999).
Stanley, Christopher D. 'Introduction', in *The Colonized Apostle: Paul through Postcolonial Eyes*, ed. Christopher D. Stanley (Minneapolis: Augsburg Fortress, 2011).
Stargel, Linda M. *The Construction of Exodus Identity in Ancient Israel: A Social Identity Approach* (Eugene: Wipf and Stock, 2018).
Stavrakopoulou, Francesca. *The Land of Our Fathers: The Role of the Ancestor Veneration in Biblical Land Claims* (London: T&T Clark International, 2010).
Steenbrink, K. 'Seven Indonesian Perspectives on Theology of Liberation', in *Liberation Theologies on Shifting Grounds*, ed. G. De Schrijver (Leuven: Leuven University Press, 1998).
Steinberg, Naomi. *Kinship and Marriage in Genesis: A Household Economics Perspective* (Minneapolis: Fortress Press, 1993).
Stephen, M. *Christian Ethics: Issues and Insights* (New Delhi: Concept Publishing, 2007).
Sternberg, Meir. *The Poetics of Biblical Narrative: Ideological Literature and the Drama of Reading* (Bloomington: Indiana University Press, 1987).
Stiebing, William H., Jr. *Ancient Near Eastern History and Culture* (London: Routledge, 2009).
Subramaniam, Mangala. *The Power of Women's Organizing: Gender, Caste, and Class in India* (Lanham: Lexington Books, 2006).
Subramanian, K. S. *Political Violence and the Police in India* (New Delhi: Sage Publications, 2007).
Sugirtharajah, R. S. *Asian Biblical Hermeneutics and Post Colonialism: Contesting Interpretations* (Mary Knoll: Orbis Books, 1998).
Sugirtharajah, R. S. *The Bible and Empire: Postcolonial Explorations* (Cambridge: Cambridge University Press, 2005).
Sugirtharajah, R. S. 'Biblical Studies in India: From Imperialistic Scholarship to Postcolonial Interpretation', in *Teaching the Bible: The Discourses and Politics of Biblical Pedagogy*, eds F. F. Segovia and M. A. Tolbert (Maryknoll: Orbis Books, 1998).
Sugirtharajah, R. S. 'A Brief Memorandum on Postcolonialism and Biblical Studies', *Journal for the Study of the New Testament* 73 (1999).
Sugirtharajah, R. S. *Exploring Postcolonial Biblical Criticism: History, Method, Practice* (Chichester: Blackwell Publishing, 2012).
Sugirtharajah, R. S. 'Postcolonial Biblical Interpretation', in *The Oxford Encyclopedia of Biblical Interpretation*, ed. Steven L. McKenzie (Oxford: Oxford University Press, 2013).
Sugirtharajah, R. S. and Cecil Hargreaves, *Introduction to Readings in Indian Christian Theology* (London: Society for Promoting Christian Knowledge, 1993).
Sundiata, Ibrahim. ' "The Stolen Garment": Historical Reflections on Blacks and Jews in the Time of Obama', in *Race, Color, Identity: Rethinking Discourses about Jews in the Twenty-First Century*, ed. Efraim Sicher (New York: Berghahn Books, 2013).
Suresh, V. 'The Dalit Movement in India', in *Region, Religion, Caste, Gender and Culture in Contemporary India*, ed. T. Sahithyamurthy (Delhi: Oxford University Press, 1996).
Suvanbubha, Parichart. 'Dialogue in Buddhism: A Case Study in Addressing Violence in Southern Thailand', in *Religions and Dialogue: International Approaches*, eds Wolfram Weiße, Katajun Amirpur, Anna Körs and Dörthe Vieregge (Munster: Waxmann, 2014).

Swamy, V. V. 'Prathyaksha Raksha Daiva Sabha: Historical Absences and the Other Text', in *No Alphabet in Sight: New Dalit Writing from South India*, eds K. Satyanarayana and Susie Tharu (New Delhi: Penguin Books, 2011).

Swartley, Willard M. 'The Bible in Society', in *The New Cambridge History of the Bible: Volume 4, From 1750 to the Present*, ed. John Riches (New York: Cambridge University Press, 2015).

Sweeney, Marvin A. 'Form Criticism', in *To Each Its Own Meaning: An Introduction to Biblical Criticisms and Their Application*, eds Stephen R. Haynes and Steven L. McKenzie (Louisville: Westminster John Knox Press, 1999).

Sweeney, Marvin A. 'Formation and Form in Prophetic Literature', in *Old Testament Interpretation: The Past, Present, and Future, Essays in Honour of Gene M. Tucker*, eds J. L. Mays, D. L. Petersen and K. H. Richards (Nashville: Abingdon, 1995).

Teltumbde, Anand. *Dalits: Past, Present and Future* (London: Routledge, 2017).

Tendulkar, Vijay. *Kanyadan*, trans. Gowri Ramnarayan (New Delhi: Oxford India Paper Backs, 1996).

Tesar, Marek. *Te Whāriki in Aotearoa New Zealand: Witnessing and Resisting Neo-liberal and Neo-colonial Discourses in Early Childhood Education*, eds Veronica Pacini-Ketchabaw and Africa Taylor (Abingdon: Routledge, 2015).

Teugels, Lieve M. *Bible and Midrash: The Story of 'The Wooing of Rebekah' (Gen. 24)* (Leuven: Peeters, 2004).

Thachil, Tariq. *Elite Parties, Poor Voters: How Social Services Win Votes in India* (New York: Cambridge University Press, 2014).

Thanzauva. Hnuni, R. L. 'Ethnicity, Identity and Hermeneutics: An Indian Tribal Perspective', in *Ethnicity and the Bible*, ed. Mark G. Brett (New York: E. J. Brill, 1996).

Tharps, Lori L. *Same Family, Different Colors: Confronting Colorism in America's Diverse Families* (Boston: Beacon Press, 2017).

Thiessen, Matthew. *Contesting Conversion: Genealogy, Circumcision, and Identity in Ancient Judaism and Christianity* (Oxford: Oxford University Press, 2011).

Thiselton, Anthony C. *The Thiselton Companion to Christian Theology* (Michigan: William B. Eerdmans, 2015).

Thistlethwaite, Susan Brooks. *Sex, Race, and God: Christian Feminism in Black and White* (Eugene: Wipf and Stock, 2009).

Thomas, Alex. *A History of the First Cross-cultural Mission of the Mar Thoma Church 1910–2000* (New Delhi: Indian Society for Promoting Christian Knowledge, 2007).

Thomas, Joseph Mundananikkal. 'Subalternity, Language and Projects of Emancipation: An Analysis of Dalit Literature', in *Language, Identity and Symbolic Culture*, ed. David Evans (London: Bloomsbury Academic, 2018).

Thompson, Thomas L. *The Historicity of the Patriarchal Narratives* (Berlin: Walter de Gruyter, 1974).

Thong, Tezenlo. *Progress and Its Impact on the Nagas: A Clash of Worldviews* (London: Routledge, 2016).

Throntveit, Mark A. 'Chronicles', in *Theological Interpretation of the Old Testament: A Book-by-Book Survey*, ed. Kevin J. Vanhoozer (Grand Rapids: Baker Academic, 2008).

Thumma, Antony. *Springs from the Subalterns: Patterns and Perspectives in People's Theology* (Delhi: Indian Society for Promoting Christian Knowledge, 1997).

Timberman, David G. *A Changeless Land: Continuity and Change in Philippine Politics, Continuity and Change in Philippine Politics* (London: Routledge, 2015).

TkhalliGopalKrishna. *Dalit Worship English Goddess* (Bangalore: Lulu.com, 2012).

Tomes, Roger. '1 and 2 Kings', in *Eerdmans Commentary on the Bible*, eds James D. G. Dunn and John W. Rogerson (Michigan: William B. Eerdmans, 2003).

Tracy, David. *Dialogue with the Other: The Inter-religious Dialogue* (Louvain: Peeters Press, 1990).

Travis, Sarah. *Decolonizing Preaching: Decolonizing Preaching the Pulpit as Postcolonial Space* (Eugene: Cascade Books, 2014).

Trepp, Leo. *A History of the Jewish Experience* (New Jersey: Behrman House, 2001).

Trible, Phyllis. 'Ominous Beginning for a Promise of Blessing', in *Hagar, Sarah, and Their Children: Jewish, Christian, and Muslim Perspectives*, eds Phyllis Trible and Letty M. Russel (Louisville: Westminster John Knox Press, 2006).

Trivedi, Darshana. 'Literature of Their Own: Dalit Literary Theory in Indian Context', in *Dalit Literature: A Critical Exploration*, eds Amar Nath Prasad and M. B. Gaijan (New Delhi: Sarup, 2007).

Trotter, James M. *Reading Hosea in Achaemenid Yehud* (London: Sheffield Academic Press, 2001).

Turner, Laurence A. *Genesis* (Sheffield: Sheffield Academic Press, 2000).

Ucko, Hans. *The People and the People of God: Minjung and Dalit Theology in Interaction with Jewish-Christian Dialogue* (Hamburg: Lit Verlag Münster, 2002).

Underwood, Ralph. *Empathy and Confrontation in Pastoral Care* (Eugene: Wipf and Stock, 2002).

Upadhyaya, B. 'An Exposition of Catholic Belief as Compared with the Vedanta', *Sophia* 5, no. 1 (January 1898).

Valk, John, Halis Albayrak and Mualla Selçuk, *An Islamic Worldview from Turkey: Religion in a Modern, Secular and Democratic State* (Cham: Springer, 2017).

Valmiki, Omprakash. *Dalit Sahithya Ka Saundaryashashtra* (The Aesthetic of Dalit Literature) (Delhi: Radhakrishnan, 2001).

Valmiki, Omprakash. *Joothan: An Untouchable's Life*, trans. Arun Prabha Mukherjee (New York: Columbia University Press, 2003).

Vancil, Jack W. 'Sarah – Her Life and Legacy', in *Essays on Women in Earliest Christianity*, ed. Carroll D. Osburn (Eugene: Wipf and Stock, 1993).

VanDrunen, David. *Divine Covenants and Moral Order: A Biblical Theology of Natural Law* (Grand Rapids: William B. Eerdmans, 2014).

Varghese, T. Paul. 'The Ancient Syrian Church of India: A Contemporary Picture', *The Ecumenical Review* 13, no. 3 (1961).

Varkey, P. P. and K. V. Mammen. *Pathros Mor Osthatheos: A Prophet Like Revolutionary*, trans. Punnoose U. Panoor (Kottayam: Kottackal Publishers, 2012).

Varma, Aravindra Kumar. *Political Science* (New Delhi: Rahul Jain, 2011).

Vengeyi, Obvious. *Aluta Continua Biblical Hermeneutics for Liberation: Interpreting Biblical Texts on Slavery for Liberation of Zimbabwean Underclasses* (Bamberg: University of Bamberg Press, 2013).

Verma, Manish. *Fasts and Festivals of India* (Delhi: Diamond Books, 2007).

Victor, T. 'Christian Commitment and Subaltern Perspectives', *Religion and Society* 49, nos. 2 and 3 (June and September 2004).

Vinayaraj, Y. T. 'Dalit Body without God: Challenges for Epistemology and Theology', in *Body, Emotion and Mind*, eds Martin Tamcke and Gladson Jathanna (Zurich: Lit Verlag, 2013).

Vinayaraj, Y. T. *Dalit Theology after Continental Philosophy* (London: Palgrave Macmillan, 2016).

Vinayaraj, Y. T. 'Envisioning a Postmodern Method of Doing Dalit Theology', in *Dalit Theology in the Twenty-First Century: Discordant Voices, Discerning Pathways*, eds Sathianathan Clarke, Deenabandhu Manchala and Philip Vinod Peacock (New Delhi: Oxford University Press, 2010).

Vinayaraj, Y. T. *Re-visiting the Other: Discourses on Postmodern Theology* (Tiruvalla: Christava Sahitya Samithi, 2010).

Visvanathan, Susan. *The Christians of Kerala: History, Belief and Ritual among the Yakoba* (Madras: Oxford University Press, 1993).

Von Rad, Gerhard. *Old Testament Theology*, trans. D. M. G. Stalker (London: SCM Press, 1975).

Von Rad, Gerhard. *The Problem of the Hexateuch and Other Essays*, trans. E. W. Trueman Dicken (London: SCM Press, 1966).

Vos, J. G. *Genesis* (Pittsburgh: Crown & Covenant, 2006).

Waghorne, Joanne Punzo. 'Chariots of the God/s: Riding the Line between Hindu and Christian', in *Popular Christianity in India: Reading between the Lines*, eds Selva J. Raj and Corinne G. Dempsey (Albany: State University of New York, 2002).

Wallace, Barbara C., Robert T. Carter, Jose E. Nanin, Richard Keller and Vanessa Alleye. Identity Development for 'Diverse and Different Others': Integrating Stages of Change, Motivational Interviewing, and Identity Theories for Race, People of Coloraturas, Sexual Orientation, and Disability', in *Understanding and Dealing with Violence: A Multicultural Approach*, eds Barbara C. Wallace, Robert T. Carter (Thousand Oaks: Sage Publications, 2003).

Walsh, Jerome T. *Style and Structure in Biblical Hebrew Narrative* (Collegeville: Liturgical Press, 2001).

Waltke, Bruce K. *Genesis: A Commentary* (Grand Rapids: Zondervan, 2016).

Wankhade, M. N. 'Friends, the Day of Irresponsible Writing Is Over', in *Poisoned Bread: Translations from Modern Marathi Dalit Literature*, ed. Arjun Dangle, trans. Maxine Berntsen (Bombay: Orient Longman, 1992).

Ware, Frederick L. *Methodologies of Black Theology* (Eugene: Wipf and Stock, 2007).

Warrior, Robert Allen. 'Canaanites, Cowboys and Indians', in *Native and Christian Indigenous Voices on Religious Identity in the United States and Canada*, ed. James Treat (London: Routledge, 1996).

Waters, Matt. *Ancient Persia: A Concise History of the Achaemenid Empire, 550–330 BCE* (New York: Cambridge University Press, 2014).

Watt, Carey M. 'Philanthropy and Civilizing Missions in India c. 1820–1960: States, NGOs and Development', in *Civilizing Missions in Colonial and Postcolonial South Asia: From Improvement to Development*, eds Carey Anthony Watt and Michael Mann (London: Anthem Press, 2011).

Webster, John C. B. *The Dalit Christians: A History* (New Delhi: Indian Society for Promoting Christian Knowledge, 1994).

Webster, John C. B. 'From Indian Church to Indian Theology: An Attempt at Theological Construction', in *A Reader in Dalit Theology*, ed. Arvind P. Nirmal (Chennai: Gurukul Lutheran Theological College and Research Institute, 2007).

Webster, John C. B. 'Who Is a Dalit?', in *Dalits in Modern India: Vision and Values*, ed. S. M. Michael (New Delhi: Vistaar Publications, 1999).

Welch, Sharon. 'Dangerous Memory and Alternate Knowledges', in *On Violence: A Reader*, eds Bruce B. Lawrence and Aisha Karim (Durham: Duke University Press, 2007).

Wellhausen, Julius. *Prolegomena to the History of Israel*, trans. J Sutherland Black and Allan Menzies (Edinburgh: A&C Black, 1885).

Wenham, Gordon J. *Genesis 1–15* (Waco: Word Books, 1987).
Wenham, Gordon J. *Story as Torah: Reading the Old Testament Ethically* (Edinburgh: T&T Clark, 2000).
Werline, Rodney A. *Pray Like This: Understanding Prayer in the Bible* (New York: T&T Clark International, 2007).
Westermann, Claus. *Genesis 12–36*, trans. David E. Green (London: T&T Clark, 2004).
Whybray, R. N. 'Genesis', in *The Oxford Bible Commentary: The Pentateuch*, eds John Muddiman and John Barton (Oxford: Oxford University Press, 2001).
Whybray, R. N. *Introduction to the Pentateuch* (Grand Rapids: William B. Eerdmans, 1995).
Whybray, R. Norman. *The Making of the Pentateuch: A Methodological Study* (Sheffield: JSOT Press, 1994).
Wilfred, Felix. *Beyond Settled Foundations: The Journey of Indian Theology* (Madras: University of Madras, 1995).
Wilfred, Felix. *Dalit Empowerment* (Bangalore: National Biblical Catechetical and Liturgical Centre, 2007).
Wilfred, Felix. *Margins: Site of Asian Theologies* (Delhi: Indian Society for Promoting Christian Knowledge, 2008).
Wilfred, Felix. *The Sling of Utopia* (Delhi: Indian Society for Promoting Christian Knowledge, 2005).
Wilfred, Felix. *Sunset in the East? Asian Challenges and Christian Involvement* (Madras: University of Madras, 1991).
Williamson, H. G. M. 'Abraham in Exile', in *Perspectives on Our Father Abraham: Essays in Honor of Marvin R. Wilson*, ed. Steven A. Hunt (Grand Rapids: William B. Eerdmans, 2010).
Williamson, H. G. M. *Ezra and Nehemiah* (Sheffield: Sheffield Academic Press, 1996).
Williamson, Paul R. *Abraham, Israel and the Nations: The Patriarchal Promise and Its Covenantal Development in Genesis* (Sheffield: Sheffield Academic Press, 2000).
Wilmore, Gayraud. 'A Revolution Unfulfilled, But Not Invalidated', in *A Black Theology of Liberation: Twentieth Anniversary Edition*, ed. James H. Cone, (Maryknoll: Orbis Books, 1990).
Wilson, Kothappalli. *The Twice Alienated: Culture of Dalit Christians* (Hyderabad: Booklinks, 1982).
Winnett, Frederick V. 'Re-examining the Foundations', *Journal of Biblical Literature* 84, no. 1 (March 1965).
Wong, Wucius. *Principles of Form and Design* (New York: John Wiley, 1993).
Wood, Julia T. 'Forward: Entering into Dialogue', in *Dialogue: Theorizing Difference in Communication Studies*, eds Rob Anderson, Leslie A. Baxter and Kenneth N. Cissna (London: Sage Publications, 2004).
Wooten, Janet. 'Who's Been Reading MY Bible? Post-structuralist Hermeneutics and Sacred Text', in *Post-Christian Feminisms: A Critical Approach*, eds Dr Kathleen McPhillips and Professor Lisa Isherwood (Aldershot: Ashgate Publishing, 2008).
Wright, G. E. *Biblical Archaeology* (Philadelphia: Westminster Press, 1962).
Wunder, Laura C. and Kennedy Mkutu. 'Policing Where the State Is Distant: Community Policing in Kuron, South Sudan', in *Security Governance in East Africa: Pictures of Policing from the Ground*, ed. Kennedy Agade Mkutu (Lanham: Lexington Books, 2018).
Yadav, Manohar. 'Career of Dalit Movement in India', *Journal of Social and Economic Development* 1, no. 1 (January–June 1998).

Yadav, Manohar. 'Dalit Movement: A Critical Analysis of Its Current Realities in Karnataka', *Contextualising Dalit Movement in South India: Selfhood, Culture and Economy* (Vikalp Alternatives, 2005), accessed 13 May 2022, http://docplayer.net/51915031-August-contextualising-dalit-movement-in-south-india-selfhood-culture-and-economy.html.

Yee, Gale A. *Poor Banished Children of Eve: Woman as Evil in the Hebrew Bible* (Minneapolis: Fortress Press, 2003).

Yee, Gale A. 'Postcolonial Biblical Criticism', in *Methods in Biblical Interpretation: Methods for Exodus*, ed. Thomas B. Dozeman (Cambridge: Cambridge University Press, 2010).

Yong, Amos. *Discerning the Spirit(s): A Pentecostal-Charismatic Contribution to Christian Theology of Religions* (Sheffield: Sheffield Academic Press, 2000).

Zarley, Kermit. *Palestine Is Coming: The Revival of Ancient Philistia* (Hannibal: Hannibal Books, 1990).

Zbaraschuk, G. Michael. *The Purposes of God: Providence as Process-Historical Liberation* (Eugene: Pickwick Publications, 2015).

Zelliot, Eleanor. 'Chokhamela: Piety and Protest', in *Bhakti Religion in North India: Community Identity and Political Action*, ed. David N. Lorenzen (Albany: State University of New York, 1995).

Zelliot, Eleanor. 'The Early Voices of Untouchables: The Bhakti Saints', in *From Stigma to Assertion: Untouchability, Identity and Politics in Early and Modern India*, eds. Mikael Aktor and Robert Deliege (Copenhagen: Museum Tusculanum Press and the Authors, 2010).

Zelliot, Eleanor. *From Untouchable to Dalit* (New Delhi: Manohar Publishers, 1998).

Zuck, Roy B. *Basic Bible Interpretation: A Practical Guide to Discovering Biblical Truth* (Colorado Springs: David C. Cook, 1991).

INDEX

Abraham's crossings 15, 16, 66, 73–5, 80, 86–7, 90, 92, 93, 95, 98, 101, 106, 107, 114–18, 121–9, 131–2, 136–9
Advaita 7, 33, 153
African Americans 38–41
   theology 38–42, 44–6, 110–12
agency 9, 10, 11, 16, 23, 53, 56, 63, 71, 116, 117, 132
Ambedkar, B. R. 1, 4, 18, 19, 21–2
anti-caste 19, 56, 89
   philosophers 15, 46, 63, 129
Appasamy, A. J. 33–34
Appavoo, James Theophilus 10, 29, 59
assertions, Second Temple community 16, 106, 127, 129, 139
Ayrookuzhiel, Abraham 10, 12–13, 45, 111, 127, 139
Azariah, Masilamani 7, 8, 21

Bagul, Baburao 23
Balasundaram, Franklyn J. 7, 44, 56
Bama 5, 124
Belchi 27
Bhakti movement/ tradition 55–9
Bhusa (cattle fodder) event 21–2
Bible 8, 14, 18, 32–6, 43, 45, 66, 67, 77, 79, 80, 93, 130, 133, 135, 139
   Biblical hermeneutics 14, 79, 80
binary opposition 49–50, 54, 63, 119–20, 127
body politic 134, 135
Boopalan, Sunder John 10, 11, 44
Brahmans 2, 3, 49
   Brahminic 26, 55, 58, 74, 134

caste system 1, 2, 3, 4, 5, 6, 23, 25, 28, 31, 32, 42, 55, 58, 59, 61, 63, 65, 69, 70, 75, 77, 88, 98, 105, 109, 112, 113, 114, 116, 116, 119, 126, 130, 131, 132, 135, 136, 138, 139
   -based 6, 8
   contradictions 1, 7
   discourse/s 5, 45–6
   enclosure 117
   hesitations 1, 5, 7, 133, 135
   questions 2, 122
casteism 1, 7, 42, 133, 135

casteless society 57, 67, 73, 89, 90, 114
Chamar 28
Chathuruthil, Mor Gregorios 7, 135
Chokhamela 56, 57, 58, 63, 67, 74, 129
Christology, Dalit 11–12, 52
Christological paradigms/formulations 11, 12, 36, 115, 117
church 1, 5–7, 9, 13, 15, 20, 27–9, 32, 34, 37, 41–2, 44, 73, 77, 87–8, 98, 106, 110, 114–15, 118–21, 123–4, 127, 130, 132–6
Clarke, Sathianathan 8, 10, 19, 48, 53
colonialism 35, 77–81, 93
   colonial discourse 78, 102, 115
Cone, James 39–41, 52, 112
conflict/s 48–9, 81–2, 94, 96, 99, 104, 122–3
consciousness 8–9, 13, 47, 123
constructive dialogue 14, 122, 129, 130, 138
contextual theologies 13, 34, 38, 111
continuity and negotiation 10, 12
counter-colonial assertions 15, 129, 131, 139

Dalitness 37, 40, 52, 53, 55
Dalit/s/Dalits' 1, 3–41, 46–63, 66–8, 70–5, 85–9, 98, 99, 106, 107, 109–23, 126–8, 130–3, 135, 136, 138, 139
   alternate moral visions 63, 67, 129, 139
   assertions 9, 15, 72, 74, 90, 112, 129, 132, 139
   autobiographies 4, 5
   body/bodies 3, 4, 133
   Christians 7, 8, 12, 20, 21, 27, 29, 42, 45, 47, 52, 88, 115, 117, 118, 119, 120, 121, 122, 133, 135, 136, 137, 138, 139
   contexts 4, 8, 10, 12, 13, 14, 15, 16, 19, 20, 42, 44, 45, 46, 48, 49, 54, 63, 65, 66, 71, 72, 73, 74, 75, 86, 87, 90, 94, 98, 105, 106, 107, 111, 112, 114, 115, 116, 120, 125, 127, 129, 130, 131, 132, 138
   consciousness 21, 44, 47
   conversions 27, 28, 29, 86, 118, 130, 131, 133, 134
   counter-caste worldview 12, 14, 15, 16, 63, 66, 74, 129, 130
   counter-discourse 23, 27, 29, 56, 126
   counter-formulations 15, 16, 45, 67, 70, 78, 114, 139

counter-ontology 14, 45, 65, 120, 127, 139
culture 11, 13, 14, 45, 46, 65, 73, 106, 130
epistemology of resistance 14, 45, 47, 57, 63, 65, 66, 67, 70, 71, 72, 73, 90, 112, 113, 114, 120, 124, 127, 129, 139
forgotten voices 12, 13, 14, 15, 16, 42, 46, 49, 54, 63, 66, 67, 72, 73, 78, 136
hermeneutics 14, 15, 45, 63, 139
immanent experiences 8, 13, 33, 34, 41, 63
liberation movement 8, 11, 20, 47, 119
liberative voices 13, 14, 74, 130
literature movement 22–6, 29, 42, 130
lived experiences 12, 27, 29, 45, 110, 130
Panther Movement 20, 21, 22, 26, 29, 39, 130
pathos 8, 11, 15, 42, 44, 47, 48, 52, 53, 54, 55, 65, 68, 70, 71, 74, 78, 130
religion 48, 50, 58, 61–3, 69, 77, 107
resistance 1, 10, 11, 62, 63, 65, 66, 70, 71, 73, 74, 90, 112, 129
Sangharsh Samiti 20, 21, 22, 26, 29, 130
situation 1, 4, 10, 18, 28, 29, 41, 111, 130
spirituality 49, 59, 62, 63, 66, 73, 74, 90, 106, 107, 125, 130
subversive voices 45, 65, 66, 67, 72, 73, 74, 90, 98, 106, 111, 127, 130, 131, 132, 136, 137
sufferings 5, 6, 7, 23, 25, 27, 55, 66, 116, 119
traditions 13, 111, 130
Dalit theology 7–139
decentring 13, 15
deuteronomic creed 44, 45, 46, 47, 48, 49, 50, 51, 52, 54, 63, 131
emergence of 7–9
exodus narrative 44, 47, 48, 49, 50, 80, 84, 97, 125
founders of 7
hermeneutic of return to 13, 14, 111
reconstructing 111, 115, 133
Sanskritic captivity/obsession 7, 34, 42, 78
suffering servant 44, 46, 48, 51, 52, 53, 55, 63, 130, 139
violence against Dalits 20, 26, 32, 42
wandering Aramean 44, 46, 47, 50, 51
de Nobili, Robert 28
Devasahayam, V. 7, 10, 13, 14
Dharma, Dharma Shastras 52, 57, 124
dialectic 65–6
dialogue, ongoing 36, 67, 130, 139
partner/s 15, 29, 34, 66, 73, 129–30, 137–8
discrimination 5, 6, 18, 19, 27, 29, 32, 38, 50, 119, 124, 127, 130, 133, 136
dissenting voices 12, 63, 75, 85, 106, 129, 136, 139

dominant castes 18, 21, 26, 48, 50, 55, 60, 61, 67, 69, 70, 71, 72, 73, 86, 89, 106, 113, 115, 123, 130, 136
hegemony 22, 26, 29, 58, 63, 89
dominated castes 28, 56, 67–72, 106, 109–10, 113, 123

Eliaz K. P. 137
Ellaiyamman 126
endogamy 2

folk dance 59
folk literature 112
folk tradition 112
folklore 10, 45, 59
forgiveness 136, 138, 139
Forrester, Duncan B. 107
Freire, Paulo 120

Gandhiji 19
Goddess 48, 67, 112, 126

Harijan 18, 26, 126
hegemonic 20, 65, 66, 70, 90, 98, 101, 111, 112, 114–16, 129
heterogeneous/heterogeneity 73, 120
Hinduism 14, 33, 47, 50, 57, 67, 70, 133
Hindu Vedic worldview 65, 89, 90, 98, 106, 112, 130, 132, 14, 18
Hindu/s 113, 118, 134

ideology 2, 18, 26, 35, 80, 110, 114
immanent/immanence 13, 18, 19, 21, 33, 34, 40, 41, 63, 95–8, 104, 110, 114, 116, 118, 131, 132
India's/Indian pluralistic contexts 15, 43, 50, 75, 115, 117, 119
Indian Christian Theology 7, 8, 9, 13, 15, 19, 20, 26, 27, 29, 32, 33, 34, 35, 41, 42, 77, 78, 110, 130
Indigenous 9, 14, 16, 77, 82, 88
injustice 36, 40, 55, 61, 79, 95, 112, 114, 119, 120, 127
intertextual dialogue/reading 15, 16, 66, 73, 74, 75, 78, 90, 106, 112, 114, 127, 129, 132
Isaiah 46, 48, 53, 55, 58–9, 63, 83, 96, 117, 139

Jati 3
Jeremiah, Anderson H. M. 10, 11, 12, 45
Jesus Christ 10, 38–9, 52, 134
Black Christ 39
Jesus as a Dalit 8, 40
Joothan 17, 29
justice 11, 27, 36, 51, 54, 71, 77, 92, 123

Index

Kabir 15, 46, 63, 67, 68, 69, 70, 129
Kappen, Sebastian 27, 32
Kharatt, Shankarrao 23
Kshatriyas 2, 3, 123
Kummi song 55, 59, 74

Latin American liberation theology 15, 34, 35, 36, 37, 38, 42
liberated-reconciled society 72, 73, 74, 78, 89, 97, 98, 107, 112, 116, 117, 131
liberation and reconciliation 16, 48, 71–4, 78, 98, 105, 107, 112, 113, 116, 117, 118, 120–122, 127, 131, 132
liberation theology 34, 48, 110–12, 130
Lot's daughters 86, 87
lower caste 28, 56, 61

Madhav, Bandhu 23
Mahabali 1, 89
Mahars 28, 56, 57, 58
Malas and Madigas 28
Manchala, Deenabandhu 11, 136
Manu Dharma Sastra 52
Manusmriti 3, 67, 123, 124
Massey, James 7, 8, 9, 10, 27, 36, 56
Melanchthon, Monica Jyotsna 6, 120, 143
memory 11, 13, 31
missionaries 3, 28–9, 32, 36, 134–5
Mor Coorilos, Geevarghese 7, 45, 135, 136, 137
myth/s 1, 3, 36, 66, 133

Nandanar 15, 46, 63, 67, 69, 70, 129
Nelavala, Surekha 5, 107, 108, 125
Nirmal, Arvind P. 7, 8, 9, 10, 21, 26, 27, 41, 44, 46, 47, 48, 50, 52, 86, 138
non-Dalits 9, 41, 49, 66, 70, 71, 72, 88, 99, 107, 113, 114, 117, 118, 121, 122, 123, 127, 131, 132

Panchama/s 18
Paraiyars 10, 28, 70
Pochamma Devi 48, 49, 74, 116
postcolonialism 79
    criticism 78, 79, 80
Pottan Theyyam 55, 59, 67, 70, 72, 74
Prabhakar, M. E. 7, 9, 10, 20
praxis 88
    -oriented 32, 68, 88, 110, 114, 127
    social 6, 9, 12–13, 15, 35, 67, 128, 134–6, 138–9
purity and pollution 2, 18, 56, 57, 62, 74, 119

race 2–3
Raja, Maria Arul 66

Rajkumar, Peniel 8, 10, 11, 48, 49, 50, 52, 55, 56, 66, 120, 139
Ravidas 56, 63, 67, 69, 70, 74, 129
Rayan, Samuel 52–3
reconciliation in Dalits' contexts 69, 70, 71, 72, 73, 74, 78, 98, 106, 130, 131
reimagine/reimagining 46, 53, 88, 93, 102, 103, 105, 107, 111, 116, 118, 120, 122, 124, 126, 131, 132, 136
Römer, Thomas 82–85

Samuel, Joshua 10–11, 46, 49
Sarah 91, 94–7, 99, 102–5, 107, 116, 117, 121, 122, 125–7, 138
scheduled caste 4, 18, 20, 61
Shudra/s 2, 21, 26, 52, 68–9
solidarity 6, 16, 36, 54, 67
Sree Narayana Guru 61, 62, 63, 67, 74, 129, 135
stigma/strimatized 4, 87
Sudras 3, 52, 123
Sugirtharajah, R. S. 79
Syrian Christian 6, 7, 12, 13, 15, 16, 28, 45, 63, 66, 72, 73, 88, 90, 112, 115, 128, 129, 132, 133, 134, 135, 136, 137, 138, 139
    approach to the social margins 136, 139
    Dalit–Syrian Christians' Dialogue 45, 66, 90, 129, 136–9

touch/touched/touching 35, 40, 68–9, 95–6, 99, 114
trauma 4, 5, 85, 93, 107, 125, 127, 132

untouchability 5, 15, 17, 24, 60, 68, 69, 120
untouchable/s 3–6, 10, 17–18, 21, 29, 39, 46, 56, 58, 60–1, 68–9, 130
upper-caste/upper caste 16, 24, 25, 31, 119, 124, 113–34

Vaisyas 3
Valmiki, Omprakash 15, 17, 18, 23
Varna 2, 3, 18, 47, 52
Vedas 57, 70
victims 4, 5, 23, 32, 34, 38, 53, 70
Vinayaraj, Y. T. 11, 12
vulnerability 102, 112, 135

Wankhade, M. N. 23
Webster, John C. B. 10
White supremacy 39
Wilfred, Felix 20, 41, 62, 115, 123
Wilson, Kothappalli 7, 8, 32

www.ingramcontent.com/pod-product-compliance
Lightning Source LLC
Chambersburg PA
CBHW062220300426
44115CB00012BA/2145